THE LAW
OF THE
HARVEST

PRACTICAL PRINCIPLES OF
EFFECTIVE MISSIONARY WORK

David G. Stewart, Jr., MD

CONTENTS

Section III

Introduction

THE RESPONSIBILITY TO SHARE the gospel is a defining obligation of Latter-day Saint (LDS) membership. President Ezra Taft Benson taught, "As members of the Lord's Church, we must take missionary work more seriously. The Lord's commission to 'preach the gospel to every creature' (Mark 16:15) will never change in our dispensation. We have been greatly blessed with the material means, the technology, and an inspired message to bring the gospel to all men. More is expected of us than any previous generation. Where 'much is given much is required' (D&C 82:3)."* Elder Bruce R. McConkie stated, "If you will ponder it in your mind, you will come up, in my judgment, with the conclusion that we could bring immeasurably more people into the Church than we are now doing. We could fellowship more than we are now fellowshipping; in practice this could be five or ten or twenty times as many as we are now baptizing. Perhaps in due course it should be 24 times or 100 times as many as at present."† The productivity of LDS missionary efforts has declined in recent years in spite of increasing but underutilized opportunities. The discrepancy between potential and actual church growth largely reflects the discrepancy between the Lord's commandments and our actual performance. Sincere, dedicated missionaries and members often experience limited success because of a lack of understanding of essential principles.

---

*   Benson, Ezra Taft, *Ensign*, May 1985.

†   McConkie, Bruce R., *Mission Presidents' Seminar*, June 21, 1975.

My interest in missionary work is lifelong. During high school, I worked summers at fast-food restaurants to finance my mission in its entirety. By the time I entered the Missionary Training Center (MTC), I had read the entire Book of Mormon in Russian and had largely memorized the missionary discussions without ever taking a formal language course. My mission in Russia in the early 1990s presented great opportunities for growth. My companions and I worked hard, but it took months of prayer, study, sweat, and tears to come to an understanding of basic growth principles that turned frustration and suboptimal results into remarkable success. I am indebted to the insight of exceptional companions, whose wisdom has had a lasting impact on my life.

When I returned home, I felt that my mission was not complete. I felt an obligation to continue to utilize these missionary principles personally and to make them available to others. Over the past decade, I have spent many thousands of hours of personal time making a diligent study of missionary work. I have traveled to over twenty countries and have interviewed hundreds of missionaries and members and numerous mission leaders, taking meticulous notes and recording hundreds of case studies. I found that growth and retention in most areas barely scratched the surface of the potential and sought the insight of exceptional missionaries and leaders. I made a careful study of effective missionaries and member-missionaries to distill common principles of success, while also analyzing challenges in less-productive areas. Thousands of quotes relevant to missionary work from general authorities and scripture were prayerfully contemplated and used both as a source of insight and as a standard to assess the validity of the many competing mission philosophies. I read dozens of books and thousands of articles on missionary work from both LDS and non-LDS sources for any additional bits of information or insight. Finally, I carefully investigated the successful programs of other denominations that had achieved faster growth and higher retention. My understanding of the principles of missionary work today is dramatically different than when I entered the MTC and continues to be refined by ongoing experience and research.

The publication of the *Preach My Gospel* manual in September 2004 represented a major step forward for the LDS missionary program. For the first time in the history of the standardized missionary program, all LDS missionaries were educated about their own essential role in ensuring convert activity through quality prebaptismal preparation. The *Preach My Gospel* program offers a greater focus on tailoring the gospel message to local culture and to individual needs. The manual provides an excellent foundation and merits careful study. However, overall missionary productivity has demonstrated only modest improvement, and convert retention rates remain very low in much of the world. In some cases, challenges remain, because the guidelines of *Preach My Gospel* are not consistently followed; while in other cases, essential principles of missionary work are still not being fully conveyed.

This book is written for an LDS audience. The inclusion of some references from other faiths does not endorse their activities or teachings. Other denominations lack the full gospel, modern revelation, and the divine authority that are necessary to build Christ's Kingdom on Earth. LDS and non-LDS missionary efforts are not equivalent. Nonetheless, it would be a mistake to categorically dismiss positive lessons from other groups without careful investigation and analysis. Selected items are presented in the same spirit that Joseph Smith proclaimed: "Have the Presbyterians any truth? Yes. Have the Baptists, Methodists, etc., any truth? Yes. They all have a little truth mixed with error. We should gather all the good and true principles in the world

and treasure them up, or we shall not come out true 'Mormons.'"* Cita-
tions from successful evangelists of other faiths are used to corroborate
many of my longstanding observations in an LDS setting. Statistical
comparisons with other faiths are also employed, as claims of "rapid
growth" are meaningless without contextualizing benchmarks. To
make comparisons as appropriate as possible, high-commitment
groups such as Jehovah's Witnesses and Seventh-Day Adventists are
most frequently used in comparisons rather than low-commitment
Protestant and evangelical groups.

Many members and missionaries believe that since church growth
is the Lord's work, good results will be achieved regardless of their
own effort or understanding. Poor growth rates and low convert retention even in areas of great opportunity demonstrate the fallacy of such
beliefs. The Lord's promises are conditional. The Savior taught: "By
hearkening to observe all the words which I, the Lord their God, shall
speak unto them, they shall never cease to prevail.... But inasmuch as
they keep not my commandments, and hearken not to observe all my
words, the kingdoms of the world shall prevail against them" (D&C
103:7–8). Fragmentary or incomplete obedience to divine mandates
has not and will not bring forth the Lord's full blessings.

There are many factors that we cannot control completely which
affect the way that people respond to the gospel. However, much can
be done to increase our effectiveness. While the application of righteous principles can bring a greater degree of success, missionaries
should not compare their success or attribute success to their own
abilities. The Lord alone shall be glorified at the last day, and we are
all His servants. The Apostle Paul stated, "So then neither is he that
planteth anything, neither he that watereth, but God that giveth the

---

*   Smith, Joseph Fielding, ed., *Teachings of the Prophet Joseph Smith*, Salt Lake City,
UT: Deseret Book, 1976, p. 316.

increase" (1 Corinthians 3:7).

The purpose of this book is to help missionaries and members to bring full-time and member-missionary efforts up to their full potential. The principles presented here are distilled from scriptures, teachings of modern prophets, extensive research, application, and experience. The principles described in this book work. They are not speculations or ideas, but principles of growth that I have repeatedly seen validated both in their presence and absence in cultural settings around the world. Jim Rohn stated, "Success is the natural consequence of consistently applying basic fundamentals." If these principles are misunderstood or neglected, missionary efforts become frustrating, inefficient, and poorly productive, even under circumstances of great opportunity. The application of these principles consistently results in dramatic and sustained improvement in finding, teaching, and retaining converts for member-missionaries, missionary companionships, wards and branches, and entire missions. The principles in this book can dramatically improve the productivity of any full-time missionary, member-missionary, or mission leader.

This book includes many findings and recommendations that can be implemented by individual members and missionaries and others that can be implemented only by leaders. The latter findings are included for a general LDS audience, because there is no definitive line between membership and leadership in a lay church. Today's missionaries are tomorrow's ward mission leaders and mission and area presidents. A member who teaches primary today may tomorrow find himself as a counselor in a mission presidency or as an expatriate witness in a nation with no established congregations. When members do not have a correct understanding of the principles of missionary work before they receive a leadership calling, such understanding is rarely achieved thereafter. Many excellent official instructions on missionary work have been widely ignored by church membership, demonstrating the need not only to instruct, but also to inform and educate, and to do so not only from the top down, but also in a grass-roots fashion. The LDS missionary program will approach its potential only when there is widespread understanding of the correct principles of missionary work at all level of church membership.

Space does not allow a comprehensive presentation of the vast number of case studies compiled in distilling the principles found in this book. When examples are used, I have usually tried to avoid designation of specific mission names and years which could allow identification of individual leaders and missionaries. With rare exceptions, I have felt that their right to anonymity outweighs any need of mine to provide full documentation of every principle cited. Additional documentation on specific topics is available upon request. I continue to collect data from all sources and welcome feedback.

Although some have disagreed with specific points without attempting to implement them, no one who has implemented the principles here has ever reported to me results that are less than excellent. I hope that those who may disagree with my conclusions on some points will not overlook the abundant material presented that they can benefit from in other areas. Individuals must assess the relevance and applicability of the material presented to their own circumstances.

My motivation is the burning conviction that every soul is precious and deserves the best missionary effort possible in the interest of their eternal welfare and the knowledge that our current performance has barely scratched the surface of the potential. We learn from the story of Gideon (Judges 7) that small numbers of people who do the right things can accomplish far more than much larger numbers who do not. Even a small number of missionaries and members who prayerfully study and implement the principles found in this book can have a major impact on worldwide church growth. I pray that those who read and study this book will gain an understanding of what must be done to improve our personal and collective effectiveness as missionaries and member-missionaries, an understanding of how to do it, and the desire and commitment to get it done.

The material in this book is given "not ... by way of commandment, but by wisdom" (D&C 28:5). I am solely responsible for the content, and any views expressed are mine and not those of the Church of Jesus Christ of Latter-day Saints.

David G. Stewart, Jr., MD

SECTION I

TRENDS IN LDS CHURCH GROWTH

The rapid growth of the Church of Jesus Christ of Latter-day Saints has been a frequent and recurring theme in the secular media. The claim that the Church of Jesus Christ is the "world's fastest growing church" has been repeated in the *Los Angeles Times*,[*] *Salt Lake Tribune*, [†] *Guardian*, [‡] and other media outlets, [§] while sources claiming that the LDS Church is the "fastest growing in the United States" are too numerous to chronicle. Sociologist Rodney Stark's 1984 projection has been widely cited: "A 50 percent per decade growth rate, which is actually lower than the rate each decade since World War II, will result in over 265 million members of the Church by 2080."[¶] In *Mormons in America*, Claudia and Richard Bushman claimed, "Mormonism, one of the world's fastest-growing Christian religions, doubles its membership every 15 years."[**]

Latter-day Saint media have also lauded rapid church growth. The *LDS Church News* has described international LDS growth with a litany

---

[*]   Lobdell, William, "New Mormon Aim: Reach Out to Blacks," *Los Angeles Times*, September 21, 2003.

[†]   Smith, Christopher, "Saints in Las Vegas: LDS Church Thriving in the Glow of Sin City," *Salt Lake Tribune*, April 6, 2002.

[‡]   "Utah's Wheel Greasing History," *Guardian* (UK), January 25, 1999.

[§]   "Atlanta Suburb Flourishes with Church Membership," *The Church in the News*, citing the *Atlanta Constitution Journal*, April 11, 2002, http://lds.org/news/archiv eday/0,5287,10275,00.html.

[¶]   Stark, Rodney, as cited in *BYU Studies*, 29/2 (Spring 1989): 61.

[**]   Bushman, Claudia Lauper and Richard Lyman Bushman. *Mormons in America*, Religion in American Life series, New York: Oxford University Press, 1999, 11.

of superlatives, including "astronomic," "dynamic," "miraculous," and "spectacular." The claim that the LDS Church is the "fastest growing church in the United States" has been repeated in the *Ensign* and *LDS Church News*. In a recent General Conference, the Church of Jesus Christ was described not only as being prolific, but also as retaining and keeping active "a higher percentage of our members" than any other major church of which the speaker was aware.[*]

A closer examination of growth and retention data demonstrates that LDS growth trends have been widely overstated. Annual LDS growth has progressively declined from over 5 percent in the late 1980s to less than 3 percent from 2000 to 2005.[†] Since 1990, LDS missionaries have been challenged to double the number of baptisms, but instead the number of baptisms per missionary has halved. During this same period, other international missionary-oriented faiths have reported accelerating growth, including the Seventh-Day Adventists, Southern Baptists, Assemblies of God, and Evangelical (5.6 percent annual growth)[‡] and Pentecostal churches (7.3 percent annual growth). For 2004, 241,239 LDS convert baptisms were reported, the lowest number of converts since 1987. The number of convert baptisms increased to 272,845 in 2006, but both missionary productivity and the total number of baptisms remained well below the levels of the early 1990s. Even more cause for concern is the fact that little of the growth that occurs is real: while nearly 80 percent of LDS convert baptisms occur outside of the United States, barely one in four international converts becomes an active or participating member of the Church. Natural LDS growth has also fallen as the LDS birth rate

---

[*]   "The Church Grows Stronger," *Ensign*, May 2004, 4.

[†]   *Ensign*, May 1973–May 2005, http://library.lds.org.

[‡]   *Mission Frontiers*, U.S. Center for World Mission, as quoted in *Mennonite Brethren Herald*, June 23, 2000.

has progressively declined. LDS church membership has continued to increase, but the rate of growth has slowed considerably.

A correct understanding of actual church growth, member activity, and convert retention is essential to effective missionary work. Statistics can provide benchmarks showing where we are now and where we have been. Most importantly, good data can help to identify areas where improvement is needed. While recognition alone does not guarantee progress, it is impossible to achieve meaningful improvement without awareness of present reality. Inflated claims that the LDS Church is the "fastest growing" or "highest retaining" church only stunt progress and fuel complacency. In recent years, both missionary productivity and member-missionary participation have declined even as claims of rapid LDS growth have received greater publicity. Most Latter-day Saints believe that the Church is growing very rapidly but have not initiated a gospel discussion with a single nonmember over the past year.

Declining LDS growth rates and continued low convert retention give us cause to reevaluate our programs and approaches to learn what has gone wrong with the harvest. Rationalizations for slow growth belie the fact that church growth has fallen far short of the potential in an age of unprecedented opportunities and receptivity. While there are significant external challenges, much of the key to improved church growth lies in the need for better planning, improved methodologies, wider outreach, more meaningful prebaptismal preparation, and better research and education.

Those whose faith is grounded in a true testimony of our Savior Jesus Christ and His restored Gospel will welcome data and objective analysis related to church growth. We must be able to distinguish between the perfect teachings of Christ and His prophets and the actual behaviors exhibited by members who are sometimes not so perfect. The restored gospel of Jesus Christ is true, and sociologic membership and growth data are a reflection of our faithfulness in implementing gospel principles. The doctrines of the gospel are not on trial. We are on trial for how we respond to the gospel directives given by ancient and modern prophets. My intent is similar to that of George Barna when he wrote, "You cannot enjoy things unless you have a benchmark that shows how you've succeeded, and you cannot improve things unless you know how far and in what direction you need to go. I try to give people an accurate understanding of where things are and what the opportunities for growth are. I'm not asking people to like what the research shows, only to understand it and deal with it intelligently."*

U.S. Growth

The Church of Jesus Christ of Latter-day Saints is growing faster than many large Christian faiths in the United States. The 1990–2000 Glenmary study reported that the LDS Church ranks twenty-third among the 149 participating denominations in overall U.S. growth rate, but first among denominations reporting over one million adherents.[†] This study was widely misreported in both the popular press and the LDS media as finding that the LDS church was the "fastest growing church in the United States."[‡] Over the entire decade of 1990–2000, the Glenmary study reported 19 percent growth in LDS membership (1.76 percent per year, compounded): a solid figure for an increasingly secular Western nation, but hardly a dynamic one. The 2005

---

*   "Barna Responds to Christianity Today Article," *Barna Research Update,* September 17, 2002, http://www.barna.org.

†   "Religious Congregations & Membership: 2000," Glenmary Research Center, September 20, 2002, http://www.glenmary.org.

‡   Zoll, Rachel, "Mormon, Evangelical Christian Churches Growing Fastest, Study Says," *Anchorage Daily News,* September 17, 2002. This same Associated Press article appeared under different titles in numerous U.S. newspapers.

Yearbook of American and Canadian Churches reported that the LDS Church is now the fourth-largest denomination in the United States, up from fifth largest the year before, with a 2003 membership increase of 1.71 percent.* The 2007 *Yearbook* reported further deceleration of LDS growth to 1.63% in 2005.† The Glenmary study cautioned that the main findings are based solely upon the raw number of adherents "claimed by religious bodies," and no data on member activity or convert retention were examined by either the Glenmary or Yearbook authors.

The United States is home to less than 5 percent of the world's population, but nearly 50 percent of all LDS members. While the LDS Church is still one of the faster growing churches in the United States, unique contributors to North American LDS growth include family sizes slightly above the national average and the concentration of nearly one-third of all LDS missions in the United States.

INTERNATIONAL GROWTH

The LDS Church has fared comparatively less well outside of the United States. In 1996, Bennion and Young wrote: "Only on the Christianized or Westernized edges of the eastern hemisphere has the church established significant beachheads."‡ This is still largely true today. LDS sociologist Armand Mauss stated, "We like to think we are a worldwide church, but we're not. We are a hemisphere church.... Eighty-five percent of the LDS Church's membership lives in the western hemisphere.... We ought to be, I think, a little bit more

---

* Herlinger, Chris, "U.S. Catholic, Episcopal, Mormon, Orthodox, *Pentecostal, Churches Grow*," Episcopal News Service, April 5, 2005.

† Lindner, Eileen W., ed., *Yearbook of American and Canadian Churches 2007*, Nashville, TN: Abingdon Press, 2007.

‡ Bennion, Lowell C. and Lawrence Young, "The Uncertain Dynamics of LDS Expansion, 1950–2020," *Dialogue*, Spring 1996: 16.

humble about how we describe our present score geographically."[*]
Another 10 percent of Latter-day Saints live in island nations such as
the Philippines, the United Kingdom, Australia, New Zealand, and
Japan. Only 5 percent of all LDS members live in the contiguous
continental landmass of Europe, Asia, and Africa that is home to 80
percent of the world's population.

While the LDS Church has grown internationally, it has experienced difficulty in leveraging its affluent, high-missionary sending
U.S. population into committed international members on a level
comparable with other outreach-oriented faiths. In 1960, there
were approximately 60 million evangelicals in Western nations
and 25 million in non-Western nations.[†] By 2000, there were 110
million evangelicals in Western nations and over 310 million in
non-Western nations. Pentecostal Christianity, which originated in
Topeka, Kansas, in 1901, now claims approximately 450 million
adherents worldwide.[‡] Latter-day Saints claim over 180 thousand
members in Africa, while Pentecostal groups claim over 150 million
adherents on the continent. The Assemblies of God Church, started
with a revival movement in Topeka, Kansas, in 1914, reports over
35 million members worldwide, adding over 10,000 members each
day, or approximately 3.6 million new members per year.[§] Lawrence
Young noted: "The Mormon church, which was established nearly
eighty-five years before the Assemblies of God, has only one-fifth as

---

[*]   Babbit, Christi C., "Growth of LDS Church Has Upside, Downside," *Deseret News*, November 25, 2000.

[†]   Johnstone, Patrick and Jason Mandryk, *Operation World*. Harrisonburg, VA: Paternoster, 2005, 3.

[‡]   "Pentecostal," Adherents.com, http://www.adherents.com/Na_495.html.

[§]   "Assemblies of God: 10,000 Converts a Day," *Religion Today*, August 11, 2000, http://www.religiontoday.com.

large of a presence in Latin America."*

The Seventh-Day Adventist Church was organized in 1849 and recently overtook the LDS Church with 13 million members, of whom virtually all are active. In 2004, the LDS Church added an average of 661 converts and 270 children of record each day. Seventh-Day Adventists were adding an average of 3,176 new members each day in 2000[†] and have experienced continued high growth since that time, adding between 900,000 and 1.2 million members each year. The Assemblies of God are growing at approximately 10 percent per year, or over three times the growth rate of the LDS Church, while the Seventh-Day Adventists report growth two to three times LDS rates at 5.6 to 8 percent per year. There are over 570,000 active Seventh-Day Adventists in Kenya alone. This is more than the official number of Latter-day Saints in all of continental Europe, Asia, and Africa combined, less than 200,000 of who are active.

Rodney Stark and Laurence Iannaccone noted: "Except for the years immediately following the prophetic disappointment of 1975, [Jehovah's] Witness growth has consistently outpaced Mormon growth. In 1954, there were 7.7 Mormons per Witness publisher. By 1994, this had been reduced to 1.9. Given that the Mormons are generally viewed as the world's most successful new religion and had about an 80-year start on the Witnesses, this is an astonishing achievement."[‡] It is even more astonishing when we consider that there are far more participating Jehovah's Witnesses than Latter-day

---

*   Young, Lawrence A, "Confronting Turbulent Environments," in *Contemporary Mormonism Social Science Perspectives*, eds. Marie Cornwall, Tim Heaton, and Lawrence Young, Chicago: University of Illinois, 1994, 56–60.

†   "Adventist Church Membership Continues to Climb, Says Secretary," *Adventist News Network*, September 27, 2000, http://news.adventist.org.

‡   Stark, Rodney and Laurence R. Iannaccone, "Why the Jehovah's Witnesses Grow So Rapidly: A Theoretical Application," *Journal of Contemporary Religion*, May 1997: 140.

Saints, since Jehovah's Witness statistical reports consistently cite attendance rates far above official membership, while only a fraction of nominal LDS members are active. In 1935, there were 56,000 Jehovah's Witnesses worldwide and 746,384 Latter-day Saints. Since 1935, the number of active Jehovah's Witnesses has increased more than a hundredfold, while LDS membership has increased by a factor of twenty, with only a fraction of those members remaining active. After more than fifteen years of proselyting in Russia with the largest full-time missionary force of any denomination, LDS membership has risen to only 17,000, and only a minority of those members participates. The same period has seen the number of active Jehovah's Witnesses in Russia rise to over 140,000, with some 300,000 individuals attending conferences. There are more active Jehovah's Witnesses in the countries of Georgia or Armenia than active Latter-day Saints in all of Eastern Europe, Central Asia, and Russia together. There are over 1.4 million proselytizing Jehovah's Witnesses in Europe and 2.7 million who attend Jehovah's Witness conferences, compared to fewer than 100,000 active Latter-day Saints in all of Europe, including the United Kingdom. One Austrian saint observed: "A friend of mine is a Jehovah's Witness.... When he came to Vienna with his family at age eight, there were forty Jehovah's Witnesses in Vienna. That was all for Austria. Now, twenty years later, there are 20,000 active Jehovah's Witnesses. Twenty years ago we had 400 LDS members in Vienna and some more in other cities of Austria, and now, we only have about 750 in Vienna. Whenever we talk about missionary work in Church, we always hear those saying 'it's so hard, and the Austrians are an irreligious people.' That cannot be entirely true, or else the Jehovah's Witnesses would not have had such a growth!"

While still growing faster than stagnant mainline churches, the

LDS Church is one of the slowest growing outreach-oriented Christian faiths in most of Eastern Europe, the former USSR, and India and has one of the lowest rates of membership in Africa. Latter-day Saints are not competing with other denominations, yet these figures can provide a glimpse of the possibilities and a context in which to evaluate our own growth.

INCREASING OPPORTUNITY, DECLINING GROWTH

The average missionary in 1989 brought 8 people into the church, while the mean number of annual baptisms per missionary averaged between 6.0 and 6.5 between 1985 and 1999. From 2000 to 2004, the average missionary experienced 4.5 convert baptisms. When one accounts for actual activity and retention rates, approximately 1.2 of the 4.5 converts baptized annually by the typical missionary will remain active. LDS annual growth has declined from 5 percent in the late 1980s to less than 3 percent from 2000 to the present, even though the absolute number of missionaries has considerably increased over this period. The sharp decline in LDS growth rates occurred even at times with record numbers of missionaries serving. This declining growth comes in spite of unprecedented increase in opportunity. From 1990 to 2000, the LDS Church opened an additional fifty-nine nations to proselyting. Opportunities for growth are time-sensitive. Brigham Young University sociologist James T. Duke conclude from extensive research: "I believe the insight to be gained is that when conditions are ripe, as they were in Mexico, the Philippines, Brazil, Chile, and all of Central America in recent years, we must strike while the iron is hot and do our best job to convert many people. We also must realize that these favorable conditions do not last forever and that the rate of conversions will decline in later years, as seems to be the case in Mexico, Japan, South Korea, and the United States. If a sizable membership can be built up during the good years, the Church will be able to maintain a strong membership when conditions are less favorable."*

---

*   Duke, James T, "Latter-day Saints in a Secular World: What We Have Learned about Latter-day Saints from Social Research," Martin B Hickman 1999 Lecture, Brigham Young University College of Family, Home, and Social Sciences, March 4, 1999, http://fhss.byu.edu/adm/hickman_lecture.htm.

NATURAL GROWTH

CHILDREN OF RECORD

B ENNION AND YOUNG NOTED, "Although Mormons reject infant baptism, they count as members any 'children of record' blessed and named soon after birth. Thus unbaptized children of members (until age eight) make up an important share of the LDS population (about 15 percent among Americans)."* Demographic data contradict the popular belief that the LDS Church is growing rapidly because of large families. Annual LDS statistical report data show that increase of LDS children of record was 98,870 in 2004 and 99,457 in 2003 (0.8 percent of membership).† This represents a modest rebound from lower increases in prior years that had bottomed out with 69,522 new members of record in 2001 (0.6 percent of membership), which was lower than any increase of children of record reported in since 1973. In 1982, the increase in LDS children of record was 124,000. Since then the increase of children of record has progressively declined in spite of increasing LDS membership in high birthrate regions of the world, particularly Latin America. Recent years demonstrate annual increases of LDS children of record between

---

*   Bennion, Lowell C. and Lawrence Young, "The Uncertain Dynamics of LDS Expansion, 1950–2020," *Dialogue*, Spring 1996: 8–32.

†   Annual LDS statistical reports are published in the General Conference edition of the *Ensign* magazine in May of each year, http://library.lds.org.

0.6 percent and 0.8 percent of overall membership.

The increase of children of record is not the same as a birthrate but provides the only public indicator of LDS growth through births. The annual increase of LDS children of record between 0.61 and 0.82 per 100 members weigh in between 28 and 37 percent of the average world birthrate of 2.18 per 100,[*] corroborating LDS activity estimates in the low thirtieth percentiles. Per capita figures for LDS children of record relative to total membership weigh in at 40 to 52 percent of the annual per capita birthrate in communist China (1.57 births per 100), 50 to 68 percent of that in a stagnant industrial nation failing to reproduce itself (France 1.168 births per 100), one-fifth that of Pakistan (3.43 births per 100), and one-sixth to one-eighth of the birthrate in the Gaza Strip or Mali (4.5 to 5.0 births per 100).[†] These statistics demonstrate that we are facing a crisis of low natural LDS growth.

The category of "baptisms of children of record" (children on membership rolls who go on to be baptized) was dropped from LDS statistical reports after 1997. A review of statistics from years when both figures were published demonstrates that the number of children of record baptized is always significantly less than the increase of children of record. The unreported discrepancy between the increase of children of record and those that go on to baptism suggests that the crisis of low natural LDS growth is even more severe than that suggested by children of record statistics alone.

The Church reported 11,315 U.S. units at year-end 1999. The 2000 Glenmary study reported data from 11,515 U.S. LDS congregations, so we can be confident that Glenmary investigators were given member-

---

*   *The State of the World's Children 2001: Early Childhood*, New York: United Nations Publications, 2000, 116.

†   U.S. Central Intelligence Agency, *2001–2006 CIA World Factbooks*, http://www.cia.gov/cia/publications/factbook.

ship figures from virtually all U.S. congregations. The study's definition of "adherents" included members age fourteen and up, regardless of activity status. The Glenmary study found 4,224,026 individuals age fourteen and above on U.S. LDS congregational rolls, compared to 5,113,409 U.S. members at year-end 1999, leaving 889,383 LDS members (17.9 percent of the total) unaccounted.[*] This difference presumably represents unbaptized children of record under age eight and baptized youth between ages eight and thirteen. Bennion and Young's figure of children of record representing 15 percent of LDS members in the early 1990s would lead us to expect approximately 765,000 children of record in the United States, leaving only 124,000 membership records for the entire number of baptized youth between ages eight and thirteen—a number which seems unrealistically low. Data harmonization suggests that the number of U.S. children of record has declined to closer to 10 percent of total membership. The lack of any additional buffer suggests that Glenmary statistics almost certainly include LDS "lost address file" members not affiliated with any congregation, although it is not clear why this is the case for a study reportedly based on congregational data alone.

THE DECLINE OF NATURAL GROWTH

At least three major factors have contributed to low rates of natural LDS growth. First, fractional annual proportional increases in LDS children of record relative to growth rates of healthy populations around the world correlate closely with low activity rates, suggesting that a large majority of inactive members rear their children outside of the Church.

Second, many active international members marry outside the

---

[*] "Religious Congregations & Membership: 2000," Glenmary Research Center, September 20, 2002, http://www.glenmary.org.

Church, while many others remain unmarried. The vast majority of children in part-member homes are brought up outside of the Church. The *Encyclopedia of Mormonism* documents: "The percentage of adults in a temple marriage varies from about 45 percent in Utah to less than 2 percent in Mexico and Central America.... For all of South America, with 2.25 million members, less than 1.8% of the total adult membership has been married in the temple."[*] Sociologist Tim Heaton noted that Latter-day Saints in Mexico have fewer children than the national average.[†] The construction of many small temples worldwide may positively impact temple marriage and sealing rates, yet the problems of few potential worthy marriage partners and low activity remain.

Finally, birthrates have declined considerably among the core North American LDS membership. The average active U.S. LDS family has three children, just one more than the average non-LDS family. A fertility rate of 2.1 children per couple is required for population replacement. With only 22 percent of Latter-day Saints born to U.S. active families remaining active lifelong and another 44 percent returning to the Church after periods of inactivity,[‡] the natural growth of Latter-day Saints in the United States appears to be below the level required to sustain a stable population.

U.S. Latter-day Saints with temple marriages have higher fertility rates than those with civil marriages, and those who attend the temple more regularly have larger families than those who attend less regu-

---

[*]   Ludlow, Daniel H., ed., *Encyclopedia of Mormonism*, New York: McMillen, 1992, vol. 4:1531–32.

[†]   Heaton, Tim B., "Religious Influences on Mormon Fertility: Cross-National Comparisons," in James T. Duke, ed., *Latter-day Saint Social Life*, Provo, UT: Religious Studies Center, 1998, 425–440.

[‡]   Albrecht, Stan L., "The Consequential Dimension of Mormon Religiosity," in James T. Duke, ed., *Latter-day Saint Social Life*, Provo, UT: Religious Studies Center, 1998, 253–292.

larly.* Dr. Heaton documented that the U.S. LDS divorce rate lags only 5 to 10 percent behind the 50 percent national average.[†] Demographic data demonstrate that fewer Latter-day Saints follow the counsel of LDS prophets that mothers should remain at home with their children in most cases. Brigham Young University sociologist Marie Cornwall observed of U.S. Latter-day Saint women: "As a group, they have one more child than the national average, [and] are in the labor force at the same rate as other women but [are] more likely to be in low-paying jobs."[‡]

Tim Heaton reported that rates of contraceptive use between U.S. LDS and non-LDS populations are exactly the same at 80.5 percent.[§] Dr. Robert Romney observed that at least 80 percent of young women seen at the Brigham Young University health center for premarital exams request some form of contraception.[¶] Although most Mormons have traditionally believed that the purpose of the nineteenth century era of polygamy was to "raise up posterity," most LDS couples today choose to limit their families to three children or fewer under far more prosperous circumstances. While birth control was heavily discouraged by LDS Church leaders during the 1960s and 1970s, this stance has been de-emphasized in recent years.

The decrease from 60,850 full-time missionaries in 2001 to 51,067

---

*   Duke, James T., "Latter-day Saints in a Secular World: What We Have Learned about Latter-day Saints from Social Research," Martin B Hickman 1999 Lecture, Brigham Young University College of Family, Home, and Social Sciences, March 4, 1999, http://fhss.byu.edu/adm/hickman_lecture.htm.

†   Moore, Carrie A, "Statistics Offer Good and Bad News for LDS," *Deseret News*, August 11, 2002.

‡   Stack, Peggy Fletcher, "How Do LDS Women Live Their Lives?" *Salt Lake Tribune*, October 5, 2002.

§   Heaton, Timothy, "Dealing with Demographics," 2002 FAIR Conference, http://www.fairlds.org/pubs/conf/2002HeaT.html.

¶   Farnsworth, Kira, "LDS Church Not Opposed to Birth Control," *BYU Newsnet*, January 21, 2004, http://newsnet.byu.edu.

in 2004 reflects both a decline in LDS natural growth, with proportionately fewer young men and women arriving at mission age, and higher standards under the "raising the bar" program. The decrease in children of record provides us with a glimpse into the future of the missionary force. While missionary numbers are expected to rebound in future years, the rate of increase will be much slower than in the past when Latter-day Saints had larger families. Falling LDS birthrates are therefore a primary cause not only of the decline in children of record, but also of convert-based LDS growth. Since approximately 80 percent of all LDS missionaries come from North America, current trends suggest that increased recruitment of new converts and international members will be necessary to meaningfully augment the LDS missionary force in coming years.

CONGREGATIONAL GROWTH

INCREASE IN CONGREGATIONS
AS AN INDICATOR OF GROWTH

INCREASE IN CONGREGATIONS IS one of the best indicators of church growth. Church planter James Moss wrote: "It has long been accepted that beginning new churches is a requirement for long-term numerical growth for a regional body. This is a simple truth that can be born out by study after study."* Protestant church planting guru C. Peter Wagner explained: "New churches are a key to outreach. I have affirmed time and again that planting new churches enhances evangelism. Much research has been done to confirm this.... Lyle Schaller, who is highly regarded as perhaps the most knowledgeable person in America about church dynamics, wrote this: 'Every denomination reporting an increase in [active] membership reports an increase in the number of congregations. Every denomination reporting an increase in the total number of congregations reports an increase in members. Every denomination reporting a decrease in membership reports a decrease in congregations. Every denomination reporting a decrease in congregations reports a decrease in members.' This is a highly significant finding.† Churches that are growing rapidly also

---

* Moss, James W., Sr., "Contrasting Church Renewal and Church Planting," *People Spots*, 4/1 (January 2001): 12.

† Wagner, C. Peter, *Church Planting for a Greater Harvest*, Ventura, CA,: Regal

report large increases in the number of congregations, and churches which are growing slowly report smaller increases in the number of congregations. Schaller is referring to denominations that count only active members. Lyle Schaller observed: 'The first step in developing a denominational strategy for church growth should be to organize new congregations.'"

TRENDS IN LDS CONGREGATIONAL GROWTH

Congregational growth trends are particularly important in evaluating LDS growth, since LDS membership statistics have no obligatory correlation with member activity, and new congregations require active, participating members to be sustainable. From 1999 to 2004, the number of LDS wards and branches rose from 25,793 to 26,670 (+3.4 percent), and the number of LDS stakes increased from 2,542 to 2,665 (+4.8 percent). This represents an annual increase of 0.68 percent for wards and branches and 0.97 percent for stakes—both figures well below world population growth rates. This finding of low increases in the number of church units is not an isolated anomaly, but the continuation of a pattern of declining unit growth rates over the past decade. Between 1994 and 2004, 4,838 new LDS wards and branches were organized, for an average of just 1.32 new congregations created worldwide each day. Those who insist that the low number of new LDS units being formed is a result of policy changes influencing unit size are uninformed: the average number of LDS members per unit has remained relatively stable over long periods, going from 439 per unit in 1973 to 432 in 1991 and 437 in 2001.

Books, 1990.

GROWTH OF LDS STAKES

The 1980 *Ensign* projected growth from 4,625,000 members in 1980 to 11,142,000 members in 2000 and from 1,190 stakes in 1980 to 3,600 in 2000.* While the number of members in 2000 came close to the projected value, there were only 2,602 LDS stakes worldwide at the end of 2002. New stakes of 2,410 were projected, but only 1,412 stakes were formed. Of all of the officially reported church growth statistics, the number of stakes is the only indicator with any obligatory relationship to actual member participation or activity, since stakes cannot be formed without a requisite number of active Melchizedek Priesthood holders.

The low number of congregations and stakes being formed reflects fractional retention of converts. President Gordon B. Hinckley noted in 1997: "Last year there were 321,385 converts comprised of men, women, and children. This is a large enough number, and then some, in one single year to constitute 100 new stakes of Zion."[†] He then cited the imperative need to help new converts "find their way." Certainly it would be a large enough number of converts, if they became or remained active members. Yet a net of just 119 new stakes were formed between year-end 2000 and 2005 (23.8/year). The fact that stakes have been formed at a rate of less than one hundred every four years rather than one hundred or more each year demonstrates that only a fraction of converts become participating members. Respected LDS sociologist Dr. Armand Mauss observed: "The key to the church's future growth will be at least as much a function of retention as conversion. While our numbers continue to grow, the rate at which we are creating new stakes has noticeably slowed down. That

---

*   "A Statistical Profile: What Numbers Tell Us about Ourselves," *Ensign*, April 1980: 15.

†   Hinckley, Gordon B., "Converts and Young Men," *Ensign*, May 1997.

is a clear indication of a retention problem."*

CONGREGATIONAL GROWTH IN PERSPECTIVE

At year-end 2004, the LDS Church reported 12,256,000 nominal members in 26,670 congregations (460 members per congregation). For the same year, the Seventh-day Adventist Church had 12,894,000 baptized adult members in 117,020 Sabbath Schools (congregations) meeting in 53,502 churches (110 members per congregation),[†] while the 6.5 million Jehovah's Witnesses met in 96,894 congregations (67 members per congregation).[‡]

On paper, it would appear that the LDS Church must have very large congregations compared to these other faiths. Yet the average world-wide weekly congregational attendance for all three faiths is very similar, in the range of 120 to 150 individuals. The discrepancies result from widely different membership policies. The Jehovah's Witnesses, who count as members only those who participate regularly in member-missionary work, enjoy a weekly attendance nearly double their official membership figures, while Seventh-day Adventists count as members only active, baptized adults and also experience attendance in excess of membership. Latter-day Saints membership figures convey nothing about member participation, and only a fraction of members are active.

While membership statistics imply that the LDS Church is nearly as large as the Adventist church and nearly twice as large as the Jehovah's Witness organization, congregational data convey the reality that membership figures do not. The latter two organizations

---

*   Stack, Peggy Fletcher, "Growing LDS Church Goes Global," *Salt Lake Tribune,* February 10, 1996.

†   *2003 Seventh-day Adventist Statistical Report,* http://www.adventiststatistics.org.

‡   *Jehovah's Witnesses: Membership and Publishing Statistics, 2004,* http://www.jw-media.org/people/statistics.htm.

are both far larger in terms of the total number of committed, active, and contributing members than the LDS Church.

Although all three denominations experience considerable variations in congregational size, very similar congregational attendance averages in spite of widely different membership reporting practices validate the concept that transdenominational sociologic and organizational principles govern the congregational dynamics of faiths that rely heavily on lay member participation.

Through the application of basic church planting principles, many Protestant and evangelical denominations have experienced exponential and sustained international growth. The Seventh-day Adventist Church experienced a 70 percent increase in the number of congregations worldwide in the course of its explosive growth during the decade of the 1990s and is on track to more than match that rate in the current decade.[*] K. P. Yohannan's Protestant Gospel For Asia group organizes over six new congregations in India and South Asia each day, over twice as many as the LDS Church organizes anywhere in the world.[†] The number of Southern Baptist congregations among some interior peoples of India, Cambodia, and many other nations has almost doubled every year since 1993.[‡] Over 1,000 new churches were organized among one interior Indian people in 2000 alone. Causes of current low LDS congregational growth rates and opportunities for improving congregational growth are discussed in detail in the chapter on church planting.

---

[*]   "Number of Adventist Congregations Worldwide Increases 70 Percent, Says Office of Global Mission," *Adventist News Network*, October 24, 2000, http://news.adventist.org.

[†]   Yohannan, K. P., *Revolution in World Missions*, Carrollton, TX: GFA Books, 2000. See also http://www.gfa.org.

[‡]   Garrison, David, *Church Planting Movements*, Southern Baptist International Mission Board, October 1999, http://www.imb.org/CPM/default.htm.

TRENDS IN LDS MEMBER ACTIVITY AND CONVERT RETENTION

MEMBER ACTIVITY AND CONVERT RETENTION RATES TODAY

The number of Latter-day Saints who attend church, or even identify themselves as Latter-day Saints, is a more meaningful indicator of church growth and strength than total membership figures. While any member who attends church at least once in a quarter is officially considered "active," no official reports of LDS activity rates are published. The *Encyclopedia of Mormonism* notes: "Attendance at sacrament meeting varies substantially. Canada, the South Pacific, and the United States average between 40 percent and 50 percent. Europe and Africa average about 35 percent. Asia and Latin America have weekly attendance rates of about 25 percent."* By multiplying the number of members in each region by the regional activity rate and summating the data, one comes up with a worldwide LDS activity rate of 35 percent, or approximately 4 million individuals. An Associated Press article observed: "While the church doesn't release statistics on church activity rates, some research suggests participation in the church is as

---

*   Ludlow, Daniel H., ed., *Encyclopedia of Mormonism*, New York: McMillen, 1992, vol. 4:1527–28.

low as 30 percent."*

Sociologist Armand Mauss stated that "75 percent of foreign [LDS] converts are not attending church within a year of conversion. In the United States, 50 percent of the converts fail to attend after a year."† This postbaptismal attrition is heavily front-loaded. Elder Dallin H. Oaks noted that "among those converts who fall away, attrition is sharpest in the two months after baptism,"‡ and missionaries report being told in the MTC that up to 80 percent of inactivity occurs within two months of baptism. In some parts of Latin America, 30 to 40 percent of new converts do not even return to church after baptism to be confirmed.§ In contrast, Adventist News Network reported in 2001 that worldwide Seventh-day Adventist member retention rates had fallen from 81 percent in previous years to a still very impressive 78 percent at present.¶

UNITED STATES

Studies investigating church growth through independent parameters document that real LDS growth is modest, with high attrition. The CUNY American Religious Identification Survey (ARIS) queried the self-identified religious affiliation of a large cohort of U.S. citizens in 1990 and 2001.** The study found that the LDS Church had one of the

---

* Henetz, Patty, "Latter-day Saints Urged to Help Retain New Converts," *San Francisco Chronicle*, April 5, 2003.

† Willis, Stacy A., "Mormon Church Is Funding Its Future," *Las Vegas Sun*, May 4, 2001.

‡ Oaks, Dallin H., "The Role of Members in Conversion," *Ensign*, March 2003.

§ Hancock, Wayne (Europe East Area President) at Russia Moscow Mission Conference, December 2000, as cited by Ivan Makarov.

¶ Annual Adventist reports are available at www.adventiststatistics.org.

** Mayer, Egon, Barry A. Kosmin, and Ariela Keysar, *American Religious Identification Survey*, City University of New York, http://www.gc.cuny.edu/studies/aris. pdf.

highest turnover rates of any U.S. faith. The CUNY authors observe: "Some groups such as Mormons … appear to attract a large number of converts ('in-switchers'), but also nearly as large a number of apostates ('out-switchers')." Because of high turnover, the actual growth rate in the number of Americans identifying themselves as Latter-day Saints between 1990 and 2001 was found to be similar to the overall population growth rate, for a proportional net growth rate of close to zero. The study found that just fewer than 2.8 million Americans age eighteen and over identified themselves as Latter-day Saints. There are 5.3 million U.S. citizens officially on LDS membership rolls, although this includes a declining percentage of minors under age eighteen as well as many inactive and disengaged adults. In contrast, the ARIS survey reported that 1.33 million adults in the U.S. identify themselves as Jehovah's Witnesses, while the Jehovah's Witnesses claim only 980,000 U.S. members. An independent survey conducted by *USA Today* in March 2002 demonstrated similar findings, with the percentage of individuals identifying themselves as Latter-day Saints weighing in well below official membership percentages in almost every state.* While nominally identifying oneself as a Latter-day Saint does not necessarily imply church activity, it would be difficult to claim that those on the rolls who do not identify themselves as Latter-day Saints are active or contributing members.

CANADA

The 2001 Canadian census reported a 3.9 percent increase in self-identified LDS members from 100,700 in 1991 to 104,750 in 2001, compared to an official membership increase of 25 percent (125,000

---

* Grossman, Cathy Lynn, "Charting the Unchurched in America," *USA Today*, March 7, 2002.

to 156,575) from 1990 to 2000.* During this same ten-year period, the number of Seventh-Day Adventists identified on the census increased by 20.4 percent, and the Evangelical Missionary Church increased self-identified membership by 48.4 percent. The 3.9 percent LDS increase over an entire decade represents an annual increase of less than 0.4 percent. This is less than half of the annual Canadian growth rate of 0.96 percent, meaning that self-identified LDS membership is losing ground in proportion to the total Canadian population.

Only 67 percent of Canadian members identify themselves as Latter-day Saints on the census (a significant decline from 80 percent in 1991), but this rate is remarkably high compared to the international trends noted in other nations. Religious data on the Canadian census come from random proportional sampling, with only one household in five being sent the long form that included questions on religious affiliation. This sampled data is extrapolated to the entire population and is therefore not as precise as other national censuses that query every individual. In spite of the limitations, the Canadian census suggests declining rates of self-identified religious affiliation among nominal Latter-day Saints and growth rates well below that of the overall population.

LATIN AMERICA

Mexico, Brazil, and Chile, the countries with the second, third, and fourth largest LDS populations, all demonstrate trends of low member activity and poor convert retention. National censuses have provided reality checks that contrast markedly with official LDS membership figures. The *Arizona Republic* reported on the 2000 Mexican census: "The current Mexican Mormon Church ... claims just under 850,000

---

*   "Selected Protestant Denominations, Canada, 2001 and 1991," *Statcan Press Release*, May 2003, http://www.statcan.ca.

members.... However, figures from the 2000 Mexican census, based on self-reported data, place [self-identified] membership at 205,229."[*] The 24 percent LDS self-identification rate derived from a comparison of the 2000 Mexican Census to official membership data is comparable to the 25 percent activity rate for Latin America cited in the *Encyclopedia of Mormonism*, although religious self-identification does not necessarily imply church activity.

The 2000 Brazilian census reported that 199,645 individuals identified the Church of Jesus Christ of Latter-day Saints as their faith of preference, or 26.8 percent of the 743,182 claimed by the Church at year-end 1999.[†] These data harmonize with Peggy Fletcher Stack's report: "According to several Brazilian leaders, the LDS activity rate here is between 25 percent and 35 percent. That means for every three or four converts, only one stays."[‡]

The 2002 Chilean census reported that 103,735 Chileans over age fifteen (0.92 percent of the population) identified themselves as Mormons or Latter-day Saints.[§] In spite of strong encouragement from the pulpit to LDS members to identify their religious affiliation on the census, just fewer than 20 percent of the 520,202 individuals claimed on official LDS membership rolls identified themselves as Latter-day Saints. Individuals under age fifteen (who were not asked for religious affiliation) represented 25.7 percent of the Chilean population. However, the Church has a solid base among young people who repre-

---

[*] Borden, Tessie, "Mexico Mormon Flock Grows," *Arizona Republic*, July 10, 2001.

[†] 2000 Brazilian Census, Instituto Brasileiro de Geografia e Estatistica, Censo Demográfico 2000, http://www.ibge.gov.br/english/estatistica/populacao/ censo2000.

[‡] Stack, Peggy Fletcher, "Brazil Leaves Impression on LDS Church," *Salt Lake Tribune*, April 5, 2003.

[§] 2002 Chilean Census, Chilean National Institute of Statistics, http://www.ine. cl/cd2002/religion.pdf.

sent the nation's future. As for the population of youth ages fifteen to twenty-nine, 1.1 percent identify themselves as Latter-day Saints, compared to only 0.5 percent of the population over age 75. Brigham Young University professor Ted Lyon, who served as a Chilean mission president and the president of the Chilean Missionary Training Center, noted that of the nominal 535,000 Latter-day Saints in Chile, only 57,000 attend church on an average week.[*] More Latter-day Saints attend church each week in Provo, Utah, than in the entire nation of Chile.

The problem of inactivity reaches crisis levels across Latin America. *Deseret News* religion editor Carrie Moore wrote: "Although the church does not provide statistics on activity rates, the number of inactive members in some areas eventually outpaced those who were active by a substantial margin."[†] Brigham Young University Latin American Studies professor Mark Grover acknowledged "a wide gap between the number of people baptized and the number attending church." Former Brazilian mission president Brad Shepherd observed: "Before we arrived (in 1996) there had been a lot of youth baptized without family support. While some of them have gone on and done great things, many others had slipped away and retaining current members was a challenge. We spent a lot of time working on retention and reactivation. In fact, there was time spent every week by missionaries just devoted to that effort. The result was kind of a mixed bag with reactivation. There were some great success stories and others were very challenging."[‡]

---

[*]   Stack, Peggy Fletcher, "Building Faith. A Special Report: The LDS Church in Chile," *Salt Lake Tribune*, March 31, 2006.

[†]   Moore, Carrie, "Flood of Converts Alters the Face of LDS Church," *Deseret News*, October 5, 2002.

[‡]   Moore, Carrie, "Flood of Converts Alters the Face of LDS Church," *Deseret News*, October 5, 2002.

Rushed baptism of inadequately prepared investigators represents a major reason for low retention rates in Latin America. Dr. Lyon noted that low activity rates arose at least in part because "too many people were baptized before they had made the commitments to pay tithing or to attend church."* John Hawkins, who has studied LDS growth in Guatemala, noted: "There has, in the past, been this notion (among missionaries) that if they are not willing to commit to baptism in two weeks, you drop them and keep going…. Members found that oppressive because conversions were happening so rapidly that once the missionaries moved on to other areas, the people they baptized were left without a support system and the local members were overloaded trying to keep up with all the new converts. Many simply gave up and waited to see 'who the good ones were' that would come to church on their own and make a contribution without a lot of nurturing from the congregation."†

Growing awareness of low retention has led to some changes. *Deseret News* Reporter Tad Walch wrote: "In April 1999, President Hinckley visited Chile and delivered a strong message to missionaries on their new area of focus. 'The days are past, the days are gone, the days are no longer here when we will baptize hundreds of thousands of people in Chile and then they will drift away from the church,' President Hinckley said. 'When you begin to count those who are not active, you are almost driven to tears over the terrible losses we have suffered in this nation.'"‡ Apostle Jeffrey R. Holland confirmed that combating low activity and convert retention rates was a major goal of his assignment in Chile, stating: "Every LDS general authority is

---

*   Stack, Peggy Fletcher, "Building Faith. A Special Report: The LDS Church in Chile," *Salt Lake Tribune*, March 31, 2006.

†   Moore, Carrie A., "Flood of Converts Alters the Face of LDS Church," *Deseret News*, October 5, 2002.

‡   Walch, Tad, "LDS Surge in Latin America," *Deseret News*, March 21, 2003.

aware of the challenges that skyrocketing church growth has created in Latin America in the past 20 years. The list includes a large percentage of LDS converts who initially embraced the faith and then fell away shortly thereafter.... We know we have the baptisms. We want to make sure we have the church growing proportionately in strength right along with it." * While overseeing Church efforts in Chile from 2002 to 2004, Elder Holland "revised policy to insist that converts attend church three weeks in succession" and taught missionaries to focus on building the Church rather than simply adding numbers.[†] He noted that these efforts have led to substantial improvement, with more converts remaining active and greater numbers of Chileans serving missions.

EUROPE

European LDS activity rates appear to have fallen well below the older 35 percent figure cited in the *Encyclopedia of Mormonism*. In "Issues in Writing European History and in Building the Church in Europe," Wilfried Decoo reported: "1996 estimated Church membership in Western Europe [is] ... 347,000 members represent[ing] 0.09 percent of the total population ... about one out of four members is active. Our effective membership in Europe [including the UK is] ... about 87,000 or 0.02 percent."[‡] The 2001 Austrian census reported 2,236 citizens who identify the LDS Church as their faith of preference,[§] compared to 3,917 members listed in the 2003 LDS Church

---

* Moore, Carrie A., "Elder Holland 'a Student' in Chile," *Deseret News*, October 13, 2002.

† Stack, Peggy Fletcher, "Building Faith. A Special Report: The LDS Church in Chile," *Salt Lake Tribune*, March 31, 2006.

‡ Decoo, Wilfried, "Issues in Writing European History and in Building the Church in Europe," *Journal of Mormon History*, Spring 1997: 164.

§ 2001 Austrian Census, http://www.statistik.at/presse2002/religion.pdf.

Almanac at year-end 2000 (57 percent). Local members report that actual LDS activity in Austria runs at about 43 percent, one of the highest rates in Europe. Gary Lobb wrote that activity rates of members in large cities of Western Europe vary from 20 to 30 percent.[*] These data correlate closely with my research gathered from traveling to twenty nations. In 1999, LDS activity rates were reported by mission offices, local members, and full-time missionaries as 25 percent in the Czech Republic, 28 percent in Hungary, 20 percent in Estonia, and 20 percent in Poland.

AFRICA

Former African mission president Dale LeBaron noted "during the year 2000 sacrament meeting attendance in the West Africa Area was 54 percent, second only to the Utah South Area."[†] The fact that an activity rate just above 50 percent ranks as the second highest among the Church's twenty-nine areas underscores how low activity rates are in many other areas. How much of this high activity rate in West Africa can be attributed to affinity for LDS teachings and how much is due to cultural factors remains to be elucidated. The 1997 University of Michigan study on rates of weekly church attendance worldwide found that 89 percent of Nigerians surveyed reported attending organized religious meetings of some kind at least weekly—the highest rate of reported church attendance in the world.[‡] The West Africa area represents the only convert-based area in the Church reporting over

---

[*] Lobb, Gary C., "Mormon Membership Trends in Europe among People of Color: Present and Future Assessment," *Dialogue*, 33/4 (Winter 2000).

[†] LeBaron, Dale E., *Devotional*, as cited in Ricks College News Release, April 5, 2001.

[‡] Study of Worldwide Rates of Religiosity, Church Attendance, Press Release, University of Michigan, Institute for Social Research, December 10, 1997, http://www.umich.edu/news/index.html?Releases/1997/Dec97/chr121097a.

50 percent member activity today, yet this feat has been achieved not by North American MTC-trained missionaries, but by native African missionaries who had little or no formal missionary training until the construction of the Ghana MTC in 2002.

LDS member retention has presented major challenges in other regions of Africa. Reporting on a black branch in South Africa, Peggy Fletcher Stack wrote: "Of 23 people baptized into Guguletu Branch of The Church of Jesus Christ of Latter-day Saints during 1997, only three were men age 18 or older. Of these three, only one remains active in the church. The branch has 253 members on the rolls, but an average weekly attendance of about 65. Seldom are there more than two married couples. Five married men attend regularly, four have jobs."* She quoted Guguletu Branch President Nigel Giddey: "I do not think that the missionaries read much beyond a few key scriptures to the potential converts or possibly a few pages of the Book of Mormon."

THE PHILIPPINES

Brigham Young University *Newsnet* quoted senior missionary Dave Brinsfield: "Out of the 49,000 converts who joined the church in 2001 and 2002 [in the Philippines], only 1,000 remain active."† He continued: "The mission was averaging 120–170 baptisms a month two years ago, but only do around 80 now. Even if the numbers are lower, the church members are stronger." The retention statistic is likely misprinted, since 10 to 20 percent retention rates in the Philippines have been reported with a few missions dipping below 10

---

*   Stack, Peggy Fletcher, "African Culture Presents Challenges for Mormon Converts,"_Salt Lake Tribune_, April 4, 1998.

†   Ware, Veeda, "Missionary Work in Philippines Emphasizes Convert Retention and Member Reactivation," *BYU Newsnet*, September 3, 2003, http://newsnet. byu.edu.

percent, but never to 2 percent. In any case, the article is a remarkable admission of the magnitude of the retention problem and the
inadequacy of conventional quick-baptize methods. With a focus on
ensuring that prospective converts are regularly attending church and
have established other gospel habits prior to baptism, a few missions
in the Philippines have greatly improved their convert retention rates.
Many other missions have continued accelerated baptism practices,
perpetuating catastrophic rates of convert loss.

JAPAN

Jiro Numano, an experienced LDS leader in Japan and editor of
a pro-LDS Japanese-language publication, analyzed the seemingly
impressive Japanese LDS membership figures published in official
sources: "Several problems are not apparent from these favorable
numbers. First, the active membership of the church is only a fraction
of the official membership. As recently as 1992, after forty-five years
of post-war missionary effort, only 20,000 members could be counted
as active out of a total membership of more than 87,000, or about
23 percent. Depending on how strict a definition one uses of 'active
member,' the figure could range from 15 percent active, with a strict
definition, to as much as 30 percent.... I estimate 25 percent active
as a realistic figure for the country in general. This means that three-
fourths of church members in Japan are inactive, having nothing to
do with the church. A second problem is the decreasing rates in recent
years both of baptisms themselves and of activity on the parts of new
converts. As an illustration, although 50,000 people were baptized
from 1978 through 1990 (including some children of members),
the increase in active membership was only 10,000, with virtually no
growth in Melchizedek priesthood holders. Since 1981, furthermore,
attendance at sacrament meetings, priesthood meetings, and Relief

Society meetings have all remained fairly level, despite thousands of new convert baptisms. In general, the growth in nominal membership has outstripped the growth in activity by either men or women."[*]

THAILAND

In 2003, there were over 13,000 LDS members in Thailand, of whom approximately 2,100 (16 percent) were active according to estimates from returned missionaries.

AUSTRALIA

Of the 1991 Australian census, Marjorie Newton observed: "While the official membership figure was 78,000 in 1991, the Australian census that year showed only 38,372 Latter-day Saints. A letter from the area presidency urging members to respond to the voluntary census question on religious affiliation was read in every ward sacrament meeting before the census, making it unlikely that many active Latter-day Saints would have refused to answer. When we consider that the census figure also includes those of the 4,000 RLDS members who responded (the Australian Bureau of Statistics does not distinguish between the two churches), the conclusion seems inescapable that well over half the nominal Mormons in Australia no longer regard themselves as Latter-day Saints."[†] The 1996 Australian census (which did distinguish between the LDS and RLDS churches) showed that 42,158 individuals identified themselves as members of the Church of Jesus Christ of Latter-day Saints,[‡] compared to 87,000 official members

---

[*]   Numano, Jiro, "Mormonism in Modern Japan," *Dialogue*, 29/1 (Spring 1996): 224–225.

[†]   Newton, Marjorie, "Towards 2000: Mormonism in Australia," *Dialogue*, 29/1 (Spring 1996): 193–206.

[‡]   Australian National Census, 1996 and 2001, http://www.crc.nsw.gov.au/statistics/Sect1/Table1p06Aust.pdf.

at year-end 1995. The LDS Church statistics show 102,773 Australian members at year-end 2001, while 48,775 individuals reported LDS affiliation in the 2001 Australian census (47 percent of official membership).

NEW ZEALAND

From 1991 to 2001, New Zealand LDS membership statistics demonstrated an 18.6 percent increase from 77,000 (year-end 1991) to 91,373 (year-end 2001). Over this same period, the number of individuals identifying themselves as Latter-day Saints or Mormons on the official New Zealand Census fell from 48,009 in 1991 to 41,166 in 1996 and 39,915 in 2001.[*] Almost all regions of the country showed this decline. Religious groups such as Pentecostals show census increases during this same period. As the 2001 survey allowed individuals to specify up to four religious affiliations and those reporting multiple affiliations were counted in each group, it is unlikely that any significant number of individuals identifying themselves as Latter-day Saints were not counted. The significant decline in the percentage of individuals on LDS membership rolls reporting religious affiliation with the LDS Church from 62 percent in 1991 to 43.7 percent in 2001 suggests that the Church accumulated many nominal members, but retained very few, and may even have experienced a net loss of previously active members to other faith communities.

ADDRESS UNKNOWN FILE

The LDS address unknown file or "lost address file" consists of church members who cannot be located. In Utah, the "address unknown file" consists of 180,000 names, or 10 percent of LDS

---

[*]   1991, 1996, and 2001 New Zealand Census, Statistics New Zealand, http://www.stats.govt.nz.

membership in the state.* Approximately 50,000 individuals in Utah are added to the lost address file each year. Ninety percent of those are found within the next year, while those on the list longer than one year (and located less frequently) constitute over 70 percent of lost address file members. Ted Lyon reported that 200,000 of the 535,000 nominal members in Chile—over 37 percent—are in the "lost address" file.† With over 380,000 lost address file members between Utah and Chile alone, the total number of LDS lost address file members is unlikely to be much less than 2 million.

Elder Merrill Bateman agreed that many of the members on the "lost address file" list are less-active, especially those on the list for more than twelve months.‡ Individuals in the address unknown file are counted as full members and included on statistical reports until the age of 110 or until proof of death can be located. With an average life expectancy of 77.5 years in the United States and significantly less in many developing nations, the address unknown file may result in an overcount of LDS membership. Since lost address file members are not included on unit rolls, activity calculations based on congregational attendance rates may significantly overestimate LDS activity.

DOUBLE AFFILIATION

The phenomenon of double affiliation presents researchers with a major difficulty in determining the true religious makeup of each nation.§ Double affiliation is when the same individual is claimed as

---

* Canham, Matt, "Church Won't Give Up on 'Lost Members,'" *Salt Lake Tribune*, October 17, 2005.

† Stack, Peggy Fletcher, "Building Faith. A Special Report: The LDS Church in Chile," *Salt Lake Tribune*, March 31, 2006.

‡ Canham, Matt, "Church Won't Give Up on 'Lost Members,'" *Salt Lake Tribune*, October 17, 2005.

§ Zoll, Rachel, "The Numbers Game: Accuracy Elusive When Counting Followers

an adherent by more than one religious group. This implies that some faiths claim as members many individuals who express preferences for other denominations. If the raw membership statistics reported by each faith were taken at face value, the summed value in many cases would be greater than the nation's population.

The international LDS population has an especially high rate of "double affiliation," because the majority of members claimed by the Church express other religious preferences, as census data demonstrate. Nations like Tonga and Western Samoa with the world's highest rates of LDS membership (42 percent and 28 percent of population, respectively) have some of the world's highest rates of double religious affiliation (21 percent and 24 percent of the population, respectively), due mainly to the large number of LDS converts who return to their former denominations and beliefs without ever having experienced meaningful LDS activity.[*] In the United States, where Latter-day Saints constitute approximately 2 percent of the population, the double affiliation rate is 7 percent, and most European nations, with LDS populations below 0.1 percent, have double affiliation rates of 0 to 3 percent.

The problem of double affiliation further demonstrates the need to focus on participating or self-identified church membership rather than relying exclusively on denominational membership claims. For denominations for which membership reports do not reflect actual participation, data from other sources such as national censuses, sociologic studies, or attendance reports are necessary to determine the true number of religious adherents.

---

of Religion," *Shawnee News Star Online*, November 10, 2001.

[*]   Johnstone, Patrick, and Jason Mandryk, *Operation World*, Harrisonburg, VA: Paternoster, 2005.

Evaluating Growth
and Retention

Are Census Data Valid?

OFFICIAL LDS GROWTH REPORTS present nominal membership figures without consideration of member activity or participation. The large disparities between official and participating membership figures have often made it difficult for members and leaders to identify, let alone correct, the root problems. The Church's use of the euphemism "less active" to describe those who do not attend church at all understandably arises from the desire to avoid further alienating often already disgruntled inactives but makes it difficult for members and even leaders to fully grasp the magnitude of activity and retention problems.

Some have attempted to discredit census data demonstrating fractional correlation to official membership figures, speculating that many active LDS members may have chosen not to identify their religious preference.[*] Census reports and other sociologic studies are subject to varying margins of error and potential methodological problems. Yet there are good reasons to believe that census data accu-

---

* Stack, Peggy Fletcher, "Keeping Members a Challenge for LDS Church," *Salt Lake Tribune*, July 26, 2005.

rately reflect religious preferences. First, the number of individuals identifying themselves as Latter-day Saints on census reports is far greater than the number that attend LDS meetings. The comparison between the 57,000 members attending church in Chile each Sunday* and the 103,735 self-identified Latter-day Saints reported on the 2002 Chilean census suggests that far from short-changing the strength of the Church, census religious affiliation data vastly outstrip member participation. Second, consistent correlations between census data and official membership claims of high-commitment religious groups provide a control. Census data report self-identified affiliation of 175 to 206 percent of the number of official Jehovah's Witnesses in Latin American nations (reflecting both baptized adults and unbaptized affiliates), while more individuals identified themselves as Seventh-Day Adventists on the census than are officially claimed in each country. Such data contrast with LDS official membership to census correlations of 20 percent (Chile), 24 percent (Mexico), and 27 percent (Brazil). The consistently low correlation between LDS membership claims and self-identified census data across many nations, the high correlation between membership and census data for other denominations in these same countries, and the close relationship between census data and other research on member self-identification and participation all provide strong reasons to believe that census data are reliable. Third, strong official requests by LDS church leaders for local members to register the LDS Church as their faith of preference have been made from the pulpit in virtually every nation where the census has included religious affiliation data. Fourth, the LDS Church enjoys a relatively positive reputation in these nations, and so it is unlikely that Mormons would be less likely than members of marginal groups

---

*   Stack, Peggy Fletcher, "Building Faith. A Special Report: The LDS Church in Chile," *Salt Lake Tribune*, March 31, 2006.

such as Seventh-Day Adventists or Jehovah's Witnesses to express their true religious preferences. Finally, only a small number of individuals in any country refused to answer questions about religious affiliation.

While imperfect, census data provide a more meaningful measure of church growth and strength than official membership numbers. Fractional rates of self-identification provide compelling evidence that most individuals on international LDS rolls do not consider themselves to be members, demonstrating that the challenge of inactivity runs far deeper than economic hardship or transportation problems.

A HISTORICAL PERSPECTIVE

Those who claim that poor retention is a natural or inevitable result of rapid growth are uninformed. Ammon and his brethren baptized thousands but achieved 100 percent convert retention: "As the Lord liveth, as many of the Lamanites as believed in their preaching, and were converted unto the Lord, never did fall away" (Alma 23:6). In modern times, convert retention rates approaching 100 percent were achieved in the British Isles for more than half a century. Between 1840 and 1890, 89,625 of the 92,465 converts (over 97 percent of the total) in Britain immigrated to the United States to gather to Zion, leaving only 2,770 behind.* The converts who left their lands, homes, and families to undertake the perilous transatlantic journey and travel across the plains to join the Saints were dedicated and committed to the Church. Functioning congregations remained in the United Kingdom, demonstrating that many of those who stayed behind also remained active.

---

*   Stark, Rodney, "The Basis of Mormon Success: A Theoretical Application" in
       James T. Duke, ed., *Latter-day Saint Social Life: Social Research on the LDS Church
       and Its Members*, Provo, UT: Religious Studies Center, Brigham Young Univer-
       sity, 1998, 29–67.

During the early twentieth century, most LDS members lived in Utah and the Mountain West, but participation rates were low. In 1976, President Spencer W. Kimball compared church attendance rates to lower figures at the beginning of the twentieth century: "I can remember when we were getting only about 19 percent attendance at sacrament meetings. Of course, that included all members of the Church, children and infants, but it was very low. Today many stakes and missions have reached nearly 50 and 60 percent of their total membership in attendance at sacrament meetings, and there are many units that have a much higher attendance record."[*] There were many semiactive Latter-day Saints who participated irregularly. However, most of these semiactives and even inactives had strong ties to the LDS community. Most were descendents of pioneers and other early church members and lived in communities with a strong or dominant LDS influence. Most identified themselves as Latter-day Saints. Most members lived in rural areas in the early twentieth century, and transportation to church was often time-consuming and expensive. The shift of LDS membership toward urban areas by the mid-twentieth century, as well as the convenience of modern personal transportation, resulted in a significant increase in church participation among believing but previously semiactive members in Utah and the Mountain West. Some changes in church programs led to the return of many part-active members to full activity. The first seminary buildings for youth were constructed in 1912, and the institute program was organized in the 1920s. Both programs expanded greatly during the twentieth century to involve more youth. Young single adult wards and social programs for single adults were organized only in the 1970s, and the more convenient consolidated meeting schedule was introduced in 1980. Contemporary research has shown that all of these programs play a

---

[*]   Kimball, Spencer W., "A Report and a Challenge," *Ensign*, November 1976.

vital role in strengthening and retaining youth.

MODERN TRENDS IN CONVERT RETENTION

While it is commonly claimed that over thirteen million members believe in the Book of Mormon and the prophetic mission of Joseph Smith, data suggest that only a fraction of those nominally on LDS membership rolls share the core beliefs, values, and practices commonly associated with Latter-day Saints. Most international LDS members are not believing semiactives who are simply undersocialized, but completely disassociated, inactive, or hostile individuals with no ongoing connection or commitment to the Church. National censuses and other studies suggest that only a small fraction of international members consider themselves to be "Mormons" in any way. Few attended church for even two months after baptism, and some attended far less.

It is a matter of grave concern that the areas with the most rapid numerical membership increase today, Latin America and the Philippines, are also areas with extremely low convert retention. Many other groups, including the Seventh-Day Adventists and Jehovah's Witnesses, have consistently achieved excellent convert retention rates in the same cultures and societies where LDS missions have experienced only fractional retention, and so LDS retention problems cannot be attributed to deficiencies of local cultures. Some committed believers cannot attend church regularly because of extenuating health problems or extreme hardships, although data suggest that this group represents only a small percentage of infrequent attendees.

Today's catastrophic losses of never-active and inactive converts almost immediately following baptism compare unfavorably with historical convert retention in the era before accelerated baptism programs and appear to be unprecedented in church history. Since most modern inactives lack even nominal belief or identification with the LDS Church, the Church social programs and changes that led to the dramatic increase in member participation in the early twentieth century Utah Church are having only a minor impact on international activity rates today. While over 97 percent of nineteenth century British converts mustered the commitment to cross the Atlantic and travel to Utah after joining the Church, today many of our missionaries fail to teach and prepare converts adequately to even attend church two or three times before or after baptism. The long-term dedication of the Church to its members underscores the need for full preparation of prospective converts and discerning prebaptismal interviews, since the baptism of uncommitted or insincere individuals who do not remain active presents a lifetime liability to the Church.

WHAT IS GROWTH?

Study after study demonstrates a vast discrepancy between official LDS membership claims and participating or self-identified membership. I am not aware of a single large population-based, self-identified affiliation study or national census that has come anywhere close to demonstrating parity with church membership claims. Nominal membership increases that far outstrip gains in active membership beg the question: what is growth? When individuals are baptized but do not attend church, do not identify themselves as members of the Church, and do not believe or live the teachings of the Church, has the Church grown? In nations where total membership figures have increased but the number of individuals attending church is stagnant or even in decline, has the Church grown? When so few converts become participating members that durable new church units cannot be organized and some existing units are collapsed because of the loss of previously active members, has the Church grown?

Most media sources convey the impression that all of these scenarios constitute growth, since LDS growth is measured and reported almost exclusively in terms of raw membership numbers, while activity rates are never officially disclosed. The reader of LDS periodicals comes away with the impression that the Church is growing and flourishing as never before and that the missionary effort throughout the world has been a story of unmitigated success, dynamic growth, and constantly inspired programs and policies.

An understanding of what membership numbers represent is a prerequisite for drawing conclusions about growth or strength. For Jehovah's Witnesses and Seventh-Day Adventists, every number represents an active, participating member. LDS membership figures are based on a one-time baptismal event and do not imply that a "member" attends or participates in church at all, considers the LDS Church one's faith of preference, believes or accepts LDS doctrines, or lives in harmony with LDS teachings. In the case of children of record, membership status does not necessarily imply that one has been baptized or has made a conscious decision to be affiliated with the Church.

Faiths with high convert retention rates are candid and realistic in their measurement of growth. Jan Paulsen, president of the rapidly growing Seventh-Day Adventist church, observed: "A growing church is not primarily identified by the increase in numbers. Growth must also be in depth of understanding … it must also be in depth of commitment both to the Lord, to the truth, and to the church; as well as in increased capacity to unite and bond as a family of believers. Lack of attention to this will produce Adventist mutations, which would be an unacceptable development. [Evangelism] … is effective because the new members have been taught and nurtured over many months, they know who they are and what they believe, and they have a network of friends in the church. When this does not happen, 'growth' is just a play on numbers and does not reflect the reality we want to see. The very word 'growth' means to become bigger, stronger, healthier, and more capable of functioning effectively."* President Paulsen criticized quick-baptize evangelists: "When I hear that 80,000 names have to be deleted from the records of our church in one country simply because they came in en masse, they cannot be traced, they do not come to church, they may not even exist, that troubles me greatly ... something is wrong. Evangelism in these circumstances becomes a carnival. This is not growth." These comments were carried widely in the Adventist press. Yet the Adventist church retains as long-term, participating members not approximately one-quarter of its new converts, like the LDS church, but 75 to 80 percent of them. The 80,000 nonparticipating or "lost members" Paulsen refers to in a country where local evangelists had been engaged in singularly questionable practices compares favorably to any of at least ten countries in Latin America alone with between 80,000 and 800,000 inactive or lost LDS members. If we examine the actual growth rates of the Seventh-Day Adventist Church (2.5 to 3 times LDS rates) and the convert retention rates (also 2.5 to 3 times LDS rates), we find that the real growth rate of the Seventh-Day Adventist Church is six to nine times that of the LDS Church. Their no-nonsense focus on "real growth," rapid intervention in problem areas, and refusal to pad their numbers with even modest numbers of inactives are key factors in maintaining a vibrant faith community where member statistics closely reflect reality.

Rodney Stark and Laurence Iannaccone noted of Jehovah's Witnesses: "Are Witness statistics reliable? There are three excellent and independent reasons to trust them. First ... they often report 'bad

---

*   Paulsen, Jan, Opening Address, General Conference of the Seventh-Day Adventist Church, October 7, 2002.

news'—declines as well as increases in membership. A second reason is that even very critical ex-members ... accept and publish these statistics. Finally, these statistics stand up very solidly when compared with the Canadian Census and the American National Survey of Religious Identification"* and with national censuses and sociologic research from many nations. Not one of these points holds for LDS membership statistics. Because of the combination of accelerated-baptism programs that rush converts to baptism with only minimal commitment and official policies that keep inactive members on the rolls indefinitely, LDS membership figures have continued to report annual increases even in areas where attendance has actually declined.

It has often been stated euphemistically "growth is our biggest problem." Yet it is not real growth based in deep-rooted conversion to the gospel that is unhealthy and problematic, but that so little LDS "growth" is real. Many speak of great future harvests, when the all too frequent reality is that the majority of those currently being baptized are leaving out the back door of the Church almost as quickly as they are being brought in the front. Elder M. Russell Ballard noted: "We cannot establish the Church unless we have real growth—not simply numbers on paper."† The Church cannot be built up by revolving-door practices that rapidly accumulate inactives but do not result in a corresponding increase in participating membership.

We must measure, report, and discuss Church growth in terms of active, faithful, and participating members and focus on building strong, vibrant units, rather than lauding paper membership increases that do not reflect true strength or commitment. There is a scriptural duty to

---

*   Stark, Rodney and Laurence R. Iannaccone, "Why the Jehovah's Witnesses Grow So Rapidly: A Theoretical Application," *Journal of Contemporary Religion*, May 1997: 140.

†   Ballard, M. Russell, Conversion and Retention Satellite Broadcast, August 29, 1999.

look after those who have become part of the flock. However, it is also difficult to make real progress without objective acknowledgment of the present situation. Occasional stories of a longtime disaffected individual returning to the fold are repeatedly cited as evidence of success, yet the far greater trend is that of losing those for whom intervention could make a difference—new converts and receptive semiactives—because member time and resources are spread so thin trying to reactivate everyone instead of focusing on the receptive.

DO ACTIVITY RATES INEVITABLY INCREASE WITH TIME?

Some have claimed that the current low activity rates are an inevitable result of the process of establishing the Church and that these activity rates will rise as the Church becomes more established, citing higher activity rates in Utah and the Mountain West than in surrounding areas. This is an "apples and oranges" comparison which is not supported by data. It is true that activity rates are higher in areas where active members have many children and where there are few convert baptisms, but this observation provides no insight into the problem of catastrophic convert losses that have continued to occur in international areas. The Church entered Mexico, Chile, and Japan well over a century ago, but activity rates in all three countries hover between 20 and 25 percent, and the passing of decades has done little to rectify the crisis. In contrast, some newly opened areas, such as West Africa and Eastern Europe, have activity rates that are somewhat higher. Rampant inactivity cannot simply be waited out. Missions that have applied appropriate scriptural teaching standards have almost immediately achieved very high convert retention rates, while missions that have not have continued to lose the overwhelming majority of their converts even as unit rolls have swelled. The causes and solutions to retention problems are discussed in later chapters.

IS SLOW GROWTH INEVITABLE?

Some have suggested that a slowdown in growth is inevitable as the Church faith becomes more established and claim that rapid growth is a characteristic of small but not of large organizations. This claim fails to explain why LDS growth in the fifty-nine new nations opened for missionary work in the 1990s has been slow in spite of high receptivity and exceptional opportunity and provides no explanation for the accelerating growth of larger faiths with high membership requirements like the Seventh-Day Adventist Church. Some claim that the time of great harvests is over and that now is a time of gleaning. Those who give credence to such claims are not literate in the scriptures or do not believe them. The Lord's statement that "the field is white already to harvest" is repeated at least eight times in scripture, and the Lord promises those of great faith "it shall be given unto such to bring thousands of souls to repentance" (Alma 26:22). The Lord's assertion that the harvest field is ripe has been reiterated by modern-day prophets. Ezra Taft Benson declared: "It is a time of harvest and not a time of gleaning,"[*] and Bruce R. McConkie taught: "We live in that day, the day when the harvest is ripe. We have deluded ourselves long enough that this is a day of gleaning only. This is not a day of gleaning but of harvest."[†] President James E. Faust stated that "there are greater opportunities to build the kingdom of God than ever before."[‡] The time of the "great harvests" is only just beginning for those who are willing to heed God's words.

---

[*]   Benson, Ezra Taft, New Mission Presidents' Seminar, June 25, 1986.

[†]   McConkie, Bruce R., Mission Presidents' Seminar, June 21, 1975.

[‡]   Faust, James E., CES Fireside, Marriott Center, November 1, 1998.

SECTION II

Church Growth Solutions

UNDERSTANDING THE TRUE CAUSES of low LDS growth and poor convert retention is a prerequisite to finding solutions. Many false and unhelpful rationalizations for poor performance have achieved wide circulation. Donald McGavran noted: "Commonly alleged reasons for lack of church growth are ... erroneous or invalid.... Sometimes, of course, 'a resistant field' is indeed the true reason; but often it is not, as is abundantly proved by the growth in that very field of other [churches]. Nongrowth also frequently means that growth is not being sought, or is being sought in resistant rather than responsive segments of the population."* We must recognize the fallacies of widely circulated explanations for poor growth and low retention to avoid directing our efforts in ways that do not produce the desired results.

Church growth and retention ultimately derive from God's grace through the Holy Spirit. The Spirit works in harmony with natural and spiritual principles. For those who do not understand these principles, church growth is a mysterious and frustrating "black box," while those who understand and apply correct principles find that high growth and excellent retention are predictably achievable in virtually any cultural setting. Success results from the consistent application

---

*   McGavran, Donald Anderson, *Church Growth and Christian Mission*, New York: Harper & Row, 1965, 17–18.

of correct principles. The specific principles are discussed in detail in subsequent chapters on member-missionary work, planning, finding, teaching, convert retention, and similar topics. For most topics, the divine mandate in scripture and from the words of modern prophets is first defined. Then actual performance (typically well below the divine mandate) is documented. Finally, principles achieving dramatically improved results are expounded.

Once specific obstacles and opportunities have been identified, we must distinguish between those that we cannot significantly alter and those that we can. Undue focus on uncontrollable external factors often exaggerates their importance and distracts attention from our own opportunities for improvement. We may not be able to eliminate political or cultural barriers, yet we can optimize our outreach efforts in each land according to the freedoms and opportunities available. We cannot readily improve the receptivity of society at large, but we are far more likely to find the honest in heart if we share the gospel with many people rather than with few. We may not be able to prevent every member from being lost to inactivity due to lifestyle choices, but we can ensure that prospective converts are properly taught and prepared so that attrition does not occur due to lack of commitment or understanding. When focused effort is made wholeheartedly to improve that which lies within our own power, the results are astounding, and individuals find that results depend far more on their own effort than they had realized. Shakespeare penned, "Our remedies oft in ourselves do lie which we ascribe to heaven." Only as we make the effort to cleanse the inner vessel and bring our own efforts into full harmony with the Lord's mandates can we expect the fulfillment of the Lord's promises.

THE MEMBER-MISSIONARY
MIRACLE

MEMBER-MISSIONARY WORK IS ONE of the most frequently mentioned but least understood gospel topics. Member-missionary work occupies a central role in church doctrine and is vital to church growth. Members are repeatedly exhorted from the pulpit and in the classroom to share the gospel, yet few active members ever participate in member-missionary work at all.*,† Missionaries spend more time than ever soliciting referrals, but the relative and absolute number of referrals has declined. Numerous programs, initiatives, and gimmicks—from "set a date" to missionary dinner programs—have occupied large amounts of missionary and member time while generating scant results. The Church has overhauled member-missionary programs more sweepingly and frequently than any other major church program, dissolving local seventies quorums, disbanding stake missions, and commissioning local bishops as the head of local member-missionary efforts in recent

---

*   Ballard, M. Russell, "Members Are the Key," *Ensign*, September 2000. The figure of 3 to 5 percent given by Elder Ballard in the August 1999 Conversion and Retention Fireside is incorrectly reported as 35 percent in the *Ensign* article. I have verified with the Church Missionary Department that 3 to 5 percent is the correct figure.

†   Barna, George, "Protestants, Catholics and Mormons Reflect Diverse Levels of Religious Activity," *Barna Research Update*, July 9, 2001, http://www.barna.org.

years. Yet such repeated and drastic reforms have not changed the underlying dynamics of stagnant member-missionary programs in which few members ever make the effort to share the gospel.

While LDS growth rates have declined in spite of unprecedented opportunity, other faiths that have more successfully involved members in proselytism have experienced spectacular growth. The Seventh-Day Adventist Church baptizes between 700,000 and one million new converts each year, due largely to high member-missionary participation. The Jehovah's Witness faith, established only in 1890, now has far more active and participating members than the LDS Church worldwide because of the direct involvement of the average members in proselyting for sixteen hours each month.

A successful member-missionary program requires an understanding of basic outreach principles, vision and leadership, and consistency. I have found that a simple program of scripture-based member-missionary principles can multiply effectiveness in any congregation. The impact of these principles is remarkable. I have often been told by lifelong church members that member-missionary work was an incomprehensible "black box" for them until hearing my presentation, but that afterward missionary work started to make sense for the first time. I have consistently seen member-missionary efforts and successes multiply when these principles are applied. Some have noted that the application of these principles generated seemingly miraculous results. Yet in contrast to so many member-missionary initiatives, this program is simple and scripture-based, with nothing contrived and no gimmicks. The program makes no demands of members except to follow basic scriptural teachings. Many individuals have noted that once these self-evident principles were explained, they wondered how they could ever have viewed member-missionary work any other way.

MEMBER-MISSIONARY LEADERSHIP

This program requires the leadership of a motivated ward mission leader and supportive bishop. Without good organization and leadership, member-missionary programs never amount to more than the sporadic and isolated efforts of a few participating members. Leadership with vision, purpose, understanding, and consistency is essential to raise member-missionary participation from the level of a few isolated members to a cooperative effort of the entire ward.

MEMBER-MISSIONARY PROGRAM OVERVIEW

This member-missionary program involves several key elements. The first is an initial meeting, typically conducted as a fifth Sunday joint Priesthood/Relief Society lesson. The purpose of the initial meeting is to break down barriers to sharing the gospel and to educate members regarding member-missionary work. The content of this lesson differs in many ways from traditional less effective talks and lessons on missionary work. Second, practical three-minute messages on missionary work are given each Sunday in the opening exercises of Priesthood, Relief Society, Young Women's and Primary. Third, a well-stocked table of missionary resources is maintained in the chapel foyer. These steps may seem bland and uninspiring. Yet when correctly implemented, they consistently multiply long-term member-missionary participation. In this chapter, I will explain why each step is crucial, how each point differs from less effective models, and how to implement each most effectively.

VISION AND GOALS

The purpose of this program is not to generate a short burst of member-missionary activity leading to a few more referrals or baptisms, only to quickly taper off to the prior stagnant baseline. Rather, the goal is to change basic member behaviors in a way that will increase referrals and baptisms for years to come by making sharing the Good News a regular part of their life and by providing weekly training to help members refine their member-missionary skills.

Righteous habits are the essence of gospel living. We are commanded to feast daily upon the scriptures, to attend church weekly, and to keep the Sabbath Day holy. Similarly, the central goal of an effective member-missionary program is to encourage members to initiate at least one gospel discussion each week with a nonmember. This goal is far short of the scriptural admonition to open our mouths about the gospel and stand as witnesses of Christ in all places and at all times, yet it is a good starting point that any member can achieve and represents an exponential improvement over current performance. Some members may be able to share the gospel much more frequently than this. Goals centered on numbers of referrals or baptisms are counterproductive to the establishment of the gospel habit of "opening one's mouth." When members are sharing the gospel regularly, referrals and baptisms naturally follow without gimmicks or imposed quotas, and without this habit, scant member-missionary results are ever achieved.

THE STARTUP LESSON

Most members acknowledge the importance of sharing the gospel and have repeatedly been instructed to do so, yet have never been educated or mentored in basic practical elements of the process. Many face barriers of fear or a lack of understanding. Jim Rohn stated, "Education must precede motivation.... If someone is going down the wrong road, he doesn't need motivation to speed him up. What he needs is education to turn him around." Many member-missionary programs fail because they start with motivation rather than training, attempting to inspire members to share the gospel with their acquaintances when most do not know how or are not comfortable with doing so. Apprehension must be changed to enthusiasm, ignorance to understanding, and avoidance to implementation.

While this process takes time, a startup lesson to break down barriers and educate members can dramatically increase member-missionary participation immediately. Members are not instructed to follow a protocol or to implement a narrow program but are taught scriptural principles that can help them to utilize everyday opportunities to share the gospel. I prefer to give this lesson as a concise Power Point presentation which requires approximately twenty minutes, but it can be presented in different ways depending on local needs and resources. The next chapter covers the "Witnesses of Christ" lesson material, which can be modified depending on the audience.

HARNESS THE POTENTIAL OF YOUR MEMBER-MISSIONARY PROGRAM

Most member-missionary programs run at only a fraction of their potential. The Church *Handbook of Instructions* and the *Stake Missionary Manual* state that the missionary program is to be integrated into all programs of the Church. Yet in most wards, efforts of the ward mission leader and ward missionaries are almost exclusively confined to priesthood meetings, with Relief Society and youth meetings being almost entirely neglected. A member-missionary program that functions in this manner is like a car running on only one cylinder. Some data suggest that sisters may be more likely than brethren to share the gospel and to provide member-missionary referrals. Elder M. Russell Ballard stated: "Bishops, engage the whole ward in proclaiming the gospel. You will see that the Lord will bless you and your members with many more converts and many more who will return to full activity. Missionary work should not only be on the ward council agendas but also on Elders Quorum, Relief Society, and other quorum, group, and auxiliary agenda."* A major role of stake and ward missionaries is to make sharing the gospel a natural outgrowth of church membership for all members. Making assignments which are accepted by only one or two members, such as passing out a copy of the Book of Mormon each week for a volunteer to place, is less effective and generates only sporadic involvement of a minority of members. The goal of an effective member-missionary program is for all members to share the gospel all of the time and not for a few members to share the gospel some of the time.

Even after a well-received initial presentation, member-missionary involvement will taper off without regular follow-up and ongoing teaching. Ongoing involvement and continued improvement are best done with a three-minute practical missionary message shared each Sunday in Priesthood meeting, Relief Society, and Young Women's opening exercises.

THREE-MINUTE MEMBER-MISSIONARY EDUCATION

Superior results are achieved when a missionary message focused on practical implementation is given in Priesthood, Relief Society, and Young Women's and Primary opening exercises each week. Weekly three-minute messages should be coordinated in advance by the ward mission leader and can be presented simultaneously by the ward mission leader, ward missionaries, and full-time missionaries in the various opening exercises. A brief missionary tip should be

---

* Ballard, M. Russell, "The Essential Role of Member Missionary Work," *Ensign*, May 2003: 37.

conveyed that helps members to better understand and implement personal member-missionary activities. These messages should be informational, concise, well-organized, practical, and strategic. Each message should end with a specific call to action. Messages can periodically include an interactive segment that includes follow-up from the previous week, finding out and addressing concerns, discussing problems and challenges, and sharing experiences, although the time must be carefully watched. To respect the time of the teacher, full-time and ward missionaries must keep each weekly missionary message within the three-minute time limit. If messages go too long, teachers or quorum presidencies will object and the opportunity to present the messages at all may be retracted.

These messages should be given every week, since infrequent or inconsistent member-missionary lessons fail to promote sustained member-missionary improvement because of inconsistent reinforcement and sketchy follow-up. Member-missionary performance improves when individuals recognize that missionary work will be a weekly topic of discussion for which they will be accountable. Individuals are free to share the gospel in whatever manner they prefer, but every member is expected to share the gospel regularly.

The precise topics depend upon local needs, challenges, and member feedback. A few weekly message topics I have successfully used include:

1. Conversational openers for gospel discussions, including the "golden questions" and other approaches.
2. Ways to handle common concerns or objections, such as responses that individuals believe in nothing beyond the Bible or that they believe in God but do not see a need to attend church.
3. Helping members to understand their responsibility to share the

gospel spontaneously without waiting for special experiences and avoiding prejudging of others.

4. Considering individual needs and situations and responding to feedback and verbal and nonverbal cues in sharing the gospel.

5. Dealing with rejection gracefully and leaving the door open for future discussions.

6. Times of special receptivity: major life change, birth or death in the family, marriage, change of job, or a move.

7. Educating members about different resources for sharing the gospel and the circumstances under which each can be used most effectively.

RESOURCES

A well-stocked supply of missionary resources should be maintained in the foyer. Every additional step required to obtain a missionary resource—asking stake or ward mission leaders, calling full-time missionaries, and so forth dramatically reduces the number of individuals who will use that resource. A prominently displayed table of resources can help keep various tools for sharing the gospel in member consciousness and provides a no-stress environment in which members can examine and select resources that they feel may be most helpful for their acquaintances. These varying resources—Joseph Smith pamphlets, 23 Questions Answered by the Book of Mormon, "Tell Me About Your Family" cards, copies of the Book of Mormon, temple brochures, family resources, family cards, church videos, and so forth—are constantly available for members and nonmembers alike. Missionary resources should be made as widely and easily available as possible to promote maximum utilization. Many people will spontaneously use missionary resources if they are made easily accessible and awareness of these resources is constantly emphasized.

WITNESSES OF CHRIST

THE DIVINE MANDATE

THE BAPTISMAL COVENANT INCLUDES the promise "to stand as witnesses of God at all times and in all things, and in all places that ye may be in, even until death, that ye may be redeemed of God, and be numbered with those of the first resurrection, that ye may have eternal life" (Mosiah 18:9). Joseph Smith declared, "After all that has been said, the greatest and most important duty is to preach the Gospel."*

Sharing the gospel is one of the primary missions of the Church. It is also the area where we have the opportunity to make the greatest difference. The Lord has repeatedly declared that sharing the gospel is the activity of the most worth to our personal salvation: "For many times you have desired of me to know that which would be of the most worth unto you. I say unto you, that the thing which will be of the most worth unto you will be to declare repentance unto this people, that you may bring souls unto me, that you may rest with them in the kingdom of my Father" (D&C 15:4,6; D&C 16:4,6).

Why did the Lord declare that sharing the gospel is the most important work of the Church? While important, the completion of

---

*   Burton, Alma P., ed., *Discourses of the Prophet Joseph Smith*, Salt Lake City, UT: Deseret Book, 1977, 172.

genealogy and vicarious ordinances is inevitable. Vicarious temple work does not change outcomes—it only affects timing. The individuals for whom vicarious work is done have already lived their lives and are in the "night of darkness wherein there can be no labor performed" (Alma 34:33). They may have accepted or rejected the missionaries and are already approaching the judgment stage. In contrast, missionary work alters outcomes. It offers the possibility to change the eternal destiny of souls. The Lord's brother James wrote: "He which converteth the sinner from the error of his way shall save a soul from death, and shall hide a multitude of sins" (James 5:20).

LDS prophets have repeatedly emphasized that member-missionary work is one of the central obligations of church membership with slogans such as "every member a missionary." Brigham Young taught, "There is neither man nor woman in this Church who is not on a mission. That mission will last as long as they live, and it is to do good, to promote righteousness, to teach the principles of truth, and to prevail upon themselves and everybody around them to live those principles that they may obtain eternal life."* He further observed:

> I wish to make this request: that the Elders who return from missions consider themselves just as much on a mission here as in England or in any other part of the world.... We frequently call the brethren to go on missions to preach the gospel, and they will go and labor as faithfully as men can do, fervent in spirit, in prayer, in laying on hands, in preaching to and teaching the people how to be saved. In a few years they come home, and throwing off their coats and hats will say, Religion, stand aside, I am going to work now to get something for myself and

---

*   Young, Brigham, *Discourses of Brigham Young*, Salt Lake City, UT: Bookcraft, 1988, 322.

my family. This is folly in the extreme. When a man returns from a mission where he has been preaching the Gospel he ought to be just as ready to come to this pulpit to preach as if he were in England, France, Germany, or on the islands of the sea. And when he has been at home a week, a month, a year, or ten years, the spirit of preaching and the spirit of the gospel ought to be within him like a river flowing forth to the people in good words, teachings, precepts, and examples. If this is not the case he does not fill his mission.*

Ezekiel recorded the word of the Lord:

Son of man, speak to the children of thy people, and say unto them, When I bring the sword upon a land, if the people of the land take a man of their coasts, and set him for their watchman: If when he seeth the sword come upon the land, he blow the trumpet, and warn the people; Then whosoever heareth the sound of the trumpet, and taketh not warning; if the sword come, and take him away, his blood shall be upon his own head. He heard the sound of the trumpet, and took not warning; his blood shall be upon him. But he that taketh warning shall deliver his soul. But if the watchman see the sword come, and blow not the trumpet, and the people be not warned; if the sword come, and take *any* person from among them, he is taken away in his iniquity; but his blood will I require at the watchman's hand. So thou, O son of man, I have set thee a watchman unto the house of Israel; therefore thou shalt hear the word at my mouth, and warn them from me (Ezekiel 33:2–7).

---

* Young, Brigham, *Discourses of Brigham Young*, Salt Lake City, UT: Bookcraft, 1988, 328–329.

Our responsibility as witnesses does not depend on others' receptivity (Mormon 9:6). We are commanded to share the gospel, not simply to provide referrals for the missionaries or to build the church, although these aims are also important. Sharing the gospel is essential for our own salvation and brings us great spiritual benefits, even when others do not accept our invitations. The extent and regularity with which we share the gospel is one of the most sensitive indicators of our spiritual health. Christ taught regarding members of His church: "Inasmuch as they are not the saviors of men, they are as salt that has lost its savor, and is thenceforth good for nothing but to be cast out and trodden under foot of men" (D&C 103:10).

Gordon B. Hinckley noted: "I wish I could awaken in the heart of every man, woman, boy, and girl here this morning the great consuming desire to share the gospel with others. If you do that you live better, you try to make your lives more exemplary because you know that those you teach will not believe unless you back up what you say by the goodness of your lives."[*] He further declared: "I think every member of the Church has the capacity to teach the gospel to nonmembers. I was told the other day of a crippled woman, homebound, who spends her days in a wheelchair, who has been the means of bringing thirty-seven people into the Church.... We need an awareness, an everyday awareness of the great power that we have to do this thing. Second, a desire.... I am as satisfied as I am of anything that with that kind of prayerful, conscientious, directed effort, there isn't a man in this Church who could not convert another.... Third, the faith to try. It is so simple."[†]

---

[*]   Hinckley, Gordon B., Alaska Anchorage Regional Conference, June 18, 1995.

[†]   Hinckley, Gordon B., "Ready to Harvest," *Improvement Era*, July 1961: 508.

ACTUAL PERFORMANCE
VERSUS THE DIVINE MANDATE

The mandate of consistent lifetime involvement in missionary work as taught by almost every LDS prophet has been internalized and practiced by very few LDS members. Elder M. Russell Ballard cited Church Missionary Department research that only 3 to 5 percent of active Latter-day Saints in North America regularly participate in missionary work.[*] In 1987, member referrals accounted for 42 percent of a cross-section of the population of investigators in North America being taught by missionaries. In 1997, that figure had fallen to 20 percent, and members account for only one in ten referrals. The absolute number of referrals has also dropped, in spite of a significant increase in total membership. Elder Dallin H. Oaks reported in 2003 that the average ward or branch in the United States and Canada provided an average of only two member referrals per month.[†] These trends are of particular concern in light of Missionary Department research findings cited by Elder L. Tom Perry in 1991 that 86 percent of new converts who remain active have close personal ties to other LDS members.[‡]

Most Latter-day Saints believe strongly that the Church is growing rapidly, but have made no attempt to share the gospel with a non-member within the last year. Christian researcher George Barna found that only 26 percent of Latter-day Saints reported making any attempt to share their faith within the past year, compared to 61 percent of Pentecostals, 61 percent of Assemblies of God members, and 57 percent of nondenominational Christians.[§] The 26 percent figure for

---

[*]   Ballard, M. Russell, "Members Are the Key," *Ensign*, September 2000.

[†]   Oaks, Dallin A., "The Role of Members in Conversion," *Ensign*, March 2003.

[‡]   Perry, L. Tom, *LDS Church News*, June 21, 1991.

[§]   Barna, George, "Protestants, Catholics and Mormons Reflect Diverse Levels of

Latter-day Saints is not significantly different from the 24 percent of all adults nationwide who report making some attempt to share faith, but it is significantly lower than that of many outreach-oriented faiths. These other groups all report annual worldwide growth rates two to three times higher (6 to 10 percent) than LDS growth rates (2.6 to 3.0 percent), paralleling their higher rates of member-missionary mobilization. George Barna found that 30 to 35 percent of all the U.S. adult Christian population share Christian beliefs with others and that most of these do so at least monthly.* Barna's studies do not include the Jehovah's Witnesses, who average sixteen to eighteen hours of member-missionary work each month.

It is stunning that the average LDS member in North America spends over one hour per day watching television, but only one-quarter make any attempt at all to share faith over the entire year. It seems odd that the average Latter-day Saint seems so much less inclined to share the vitally important gospel message than Christians of many faiths with far less to offer. LDS member-missionary malaise can be explained only by lack of effort, since these studies asked only whether individuals made some attempt to share their faith and not how successful those attempts may have been.

REASONS FOR LOW MEMBER-MISSIONARY PARTICIPATION

A survey of 166 LDS members I conducted in 1999 found that 73 percent of members reported reasons related to fear as the main barrier to sharing the gospel more frequently with nonmembers. Thirty-one percent of respondents noted that they were afraid of saying the wrong thing, while 23 percent were afraid that they would

---

Religious Activity," *Barna Research Update*, July 9, 2001, http://www.barna.org.

*   Barna, George, *Evangelism That Works*, Ventura, CA: Regal Books, 1994.

not know the answers to questions, and 19 percent cited a general fear of rejection. Ten percent responded that they were not aware of opportunities around them, while 16 percent stated that they had no difficulty sharing the gospel.

I also surveyed eight-six nonmembers about what was the most important to them when individuals of other faiths shared their beliefs. Thirty-eight percent replied that they most valued the sharer's example of righteous living, while 27 percent cited mutual respect for the belief of others. Twenty-six percent cited the sharer's expressions of how his or her faith has helped him or her in life, and 7 percent noted that service was the key factor. Only 2 percent cited the sharer's ability to clearly explain beliefs as being the most important to them.

While these surveys were not scientifically rigorous, the findings are corroborated by other data. Elder M. Russell Ballard cited Missionary Department research that members are generally much more uptight in gospel discussions than nonmembers.[*] The main barriers to sharing the gospel as perceived by members, including fear of not saying the "right thing" or not knowing the answer to complex doctrinal questions, were of little or no importance to the overwhelming majority of nonmembers.

Some members believe that they cannot share the gospel because of personal circumstances which are less than ideal. They think that because of difficulties in their own family situation, personal weaknesses, lack of knowledge of complex doctrinal topics, or other real or perceived shortfalls, they cannot be witnesses of Christ. We must not allow our own imperfections or inadequacies to become excuses for failure to share the gospel message. There is only one perfect example, Jesus Christ. He has called us to be His servants, notwithstanding

---

[*] Ballard, M. Russell, "The Essential Role of Member Missionary Work," *Ensign*, May 2003: 37.

our weakness. We all are in situations that are less than ideal. We are all in need of the atonement of Christ. King Benjamin taught: "For behold, are we not all beggars? Do we not all depend upon the same Being, even God... who has created you, on whom you are dependent for your lives and for all that ye have and are" (Mosiah 4:19,21). The Indian Christian evangelist D.T. Niles stated: "Evangelism is just one beggar telling another beggar where to find bread." The bread of life of the gospel we share is eternal. Great member-missionaries are not perfect people in ideal situations. Rather, they are imperfect people like you and I who do the best they can with the circumstances they have to work with. God has promised that He will give us grace suffi- cient to meet the challenges of our day if we will put Him first in our lives (D&C 17:8).

CORE COMMANDMENTS: THE FOUNDATION OF MEMBER-MISSIONARY SUCCESS

A wise sister missionary stated, "To share the gospel, you have to be receiving blessings from it." People receive blessings from the gospel and want to share it when they are living it. President Kimball taught that the progress made by wards and branches is a reflection of the degree to which each member is living the gospel: "The basic decisions needed for us to move forward, as a people, must be made by the individual members of the Church. The major strides which must be made by the Church will follow upon the major strides to be made by us as individuals."*

One ward mission leader highlighted the importance of gospel living in member-missionary efforts:

---

* Kimball, Spencer W., *Ensign*, May 1979.

Elder Yoshihiko Kikuchi [of the Seventy] told me that he has seen many programs come and go, but there has only been one consistent common denominator for missionary success in a ward: that is the personal righteousness of the ward members.... Because until we are reading and praying consistently—every day—we will not have the presence of the Spirit, and therefore, no true desire to share the gospel beyond mere lip service.... We have a specific plan that we are using to help the members gain the regular companionship of the Holy Ghost.

All effective member-missionary programs focus on helping members to develop and maintain the gospel habits that bring the Holy Spirit, including daily Book of Mormon study, daily family prayer, keeping the Sabbath Day holy, and paying tithing. Without these behaviors in place in the lives of individual members, no member-missionary program will ever reach its potential. Over months and years, the great value of these habits for member-missionary work is unmistakable.

THE WRONG QUESTIONS

Several years ago, an acquaintance told me that she had recently sat next to a man on a plane and felt that he was "ripe for the gospel." She had acquired his name and address and wanted to submit a missionary referral. I asked if she had discussed the gospel with him. Her answer floored me: "I didn't feel prompted to share the gospel."

I wondered: "Did you feel prompted *not* to?" Scriptures are replete with admonitions to share the gospel at all times and in all places. Do we need an angel to appear to us and offer compelling personal revelation each time before we attend church, read scriptures, or pay our tithing? Then why do many wait for spiritual promptings to share the gospel as the Lord has repeatedly commanded?

Unfortunately, my acquaintance's behavior is not atypical. Well-intended but less effective programs such as "set a date" have fostered a false belief in many members' minds that they cannot approach anyone about the gospel without first receiving personal revelation. Members have heard so frequently from the pulpit that they should "listen to the spirit" about who to approach that many believe that they can only share the gospel when they feel powerful spiritual promptings. Many are so afraid of saying the wrong thing that they say nothing at all.

Too many members and missionaries ask the wrong questions: "Which of my neighbors is ready to receive the gospel?" "Which door should I knock on?" As a young missionary, I learned the fallacy of such practices. When I prayed to know what street to tract on or what doors to knock on, I only felt a stupor of thought. I quickly learned that all people have a right to hear the gospel message—not just a select few whom we feel specifically impressed to approach. I learned the truth of the Lord's words: "Go ye and preach my gospel, whether to the north or to the south, to the east or to the west, it mattereth not, for ye cannot go amiss" (D&C 80:3). The Doctrine and Covenants alone contains numerous admonitions to open our mouths about the gospel at all times (D&C 19:29, 24:10, 28:16, 30:11, 33:8–11, 80:3).

There is no scriptural basis for the assumption that members should be able to tell in advance which of their neighbors will be receptive to the gospel message. Attempts to preselect others before even presenting them with an opportunity to hear the gospel message are inappropriate. Christ found more success among the "publicans and sinners" than the outwardly "righteous" Pharisees. I have found that the Spirit often comes only after we demonstrate the faith to sow gospel seeds, and those who wait for divine manifestations before making the effort to share the gospel usually wait in vain.

WHY MOST MEMBER-MISSIONARY PROGRAMS FAIL

Most lifelong members have heard hundreds of talks and lessons about member-missionary work, but few act upon them. Talks and lessons focus primarily on motivating and admonishing members to share the gospel, yet they offer little practical "how-to" information. The few "how-tos" often take the form of contrived programs rather than scriptural principles.

Many member-missionary programs fail because they focus on the wrong goals, emphasizing referrals and baptisms, while neglecting the reality that few members ever initiate a gospel conversation with a nonmember at all. With baptism or referral-based goals, faithful prophets who achieved little success such as Noah and Moroni would be deemed failures. It is appropriate to set goals for our personal effort in sharing the gospel with nonmembers. It is inappropriate to set goals that depend upon the response of others. We cannot control how other people respond to the gospel, and it is manipulative to set goals based on the response of others rather than our own effort.

Ineffective initiatives such as missionary dinners in member homes take missionaries off the street during prime proselyting time when families are home and present the illusion of aiding the missionary effort, while neither the missionaries nor the members are sharing the gospel with nonmembers.

Traditional member-missionary initiatives have focused on planting a very few seeds in carefully selected plots of soil, in conflict with scriptural mandates to offer all people an opportunity to hear the gospel message. How successful would a farmer be who set goals for a large crop yield, but failed to pay any attention to the amount of seed sown? Successful farmers recognize that sowing abundantly is the key to an abundant harvest. Paul declared: "He which soweth sparingly shall reap also sparingly; and he which soweth bountifully shall reap also bountifully" (2 Corinthians 9:6).

HABITS VERSUS EVENTS

Most Latter-day Saints view sharing the gospel as an infrequent event rather than as a consistent behavior, in much the same way that Christmas and Easter Catholics view church attendance. Yet scriptures teach that sharing the gospel must be a consistent habit and not an occasional event. Sharing the gospel is as essential to our own salvation as attending church, praying, studying scriptures, and paying tithing. We all recognize the importance of doing these other things regularly, and would not be satisfied with having read our scriptures last month or having attended church last year. Our responsibility to share the gospel regularly is lifelong and is not limited to full-time missionary service or missionary-related callings.

The desire to share the gospel is a natural outgrowth of faithful membership. It is a joyful activity that must be a regular part of every member's life. Setting a goal to initiate a gospel discussion with at least one nonmember each week provides a good starting point for any member. We must focus on our personal effort and not on our acceptance or rejection by others. Moroni declared: "I fear not what man can do; for perfect love casteth out all fear" (Moroni 8:16).

Members who make a habit of speaking with at least one person about the gospel each day can bring many people into the Church over the course of a lifetime. If a member only speaks with someone about the gospel once or twice per year, it is unlikely that he or she will ever bring another person into the church.

MEMBER-MISSIONARY ATTRIBUTES

Effective member-missionaries share the message frequently with many people in different settings and are undeterred by rejection. Elder Henry B. Eyring observed that effective member-missionaries "are like the sons of Mosiah, 'desirous that salvation should be declared to every creature, for they could not bear that any human soul should perish; yea, even the very thoughts that any soul should endure endless torment did cause them to quake and tremble.' Those who speak easily and often of the restored gospel, prize what it has meant to them. They think of that great blessing often. It is the memory of the gift they have received which makes them eager for others to receive it. They have felt the love of the Savior. For them these words are their daily, hourly reality: 'There is no fear in love; but perfect love casteth out fear: because fear hath torment. He that feareth is not made perfect in love.'"*

WHAT SHOULD I SAY?

Many wonder, "What should I say when I open my mouth?" I do not have a preferred approach, since I find that making the effort to share the gospel consistently is far more important than the approach. There are many ways to share the gospel, but effective approaches incorporate several principles. Keep the message simple, stress its importance to you, and give specific examples of how your faith has helped you. No one can argue with your experience. Elder Ballard observed: "Some members say, 'I'm afraid to share the gospel because I might offend someone.' Experience has shown that people are not offended when the sharing is motivated by the spirit of love and concern. How could anyone be offended when we say something like

---

*   Eyring, Henry B., "A Child and a Disciple," *Ensign*, May 2003: 29.

this: 'I love the way my church helps me,' and then add whatever the Spirit directs. It's when we appear only to be fulfilling an assignment and we fail to express real interest and love that we offend others."[*] The sharer should look for verbal and nonverbal cues and strive to create a two-way discussion, rather than engaging in a monologue.

As we share the gospel, we should focus on the Savior. Nephi wrote: "We talk of Christ, we rejoice in Christ, we preach of Christ, we prophesy of Christ, and we write according to our prophecies, that our children may know to what source they may look for a remission of their sins" (2 Nephi 25:26). We should also focus on Latter-day Saint revelation. What would happen to an honorable person in Noah's day who accepted Adam and Enoch as past prophets but did not heed the counsel of Noah to board the ark? Sharing specific blessings that living the Gospel has brought into your life is the essence of testimony. A living testimony must be radiated in our conduct. It is impossible to testify effectively about a principle which one is not living.

Invite the hearer to take some action, whether to read in the Book of Mormon, to pray to God, to attend a family home evening or church service, or simply to discuss matters of faith another time. Individuals should be invited but never pressured.

LEAVE THE DOOR OPEN

Many lifelong members testify that it took them years to gain a testimony. So why do so many members expect their acquaintances to jump at their first invitation to hear the gospel and label them as unreceptive if they do not accept? Sharers must learn to accept "no" gracefully. If the listener is not ready to take further steps, the sharer should never attempt to guilt or interrogate him or her about his or

---

[*] Ballard, M. Russell, "The Essential Role of Member Missionary Work," *Ensign*, May 2003: 37.

her reasons. This will only make the listener uncomfortable discussing gospel topics in the future. Rather, one should keep the door open for future discussion. Missionary Department research suggests that the average U.S. convert has had between six and twenty contacts with the Church before deciding to join. Very few individuals are ready to accept the gospel the first time. Effective sharers let even uninterested hearers know that they are always available and help them to feel comfortable in bringing up or responding to gospel topics in the future. We should never view the response of others we extend opportunities to as a final judgment upon them.

THE BOOK OF MORMON LOAN PROGRAM

Ezra Taft Benson taught that the Book of Mormon is a great sieve and that the members of the Church are under condemnation for taking it lightly. He taught that the Book of Mormon is the standard we are to use in our missionary efforts. Nephi declared: "And if ye shall believe in Christ ye will believe in these words, for they are the words of Christ, and he hath given them unto me; and they teach all men that they should do good" (2 Nephi 33:10).

Most Book of Mormon gift programs fall short as distributed books are rarely read or followed up on. Fortunately, there is a superior way to utilize the Book of Mormon which avoids the free sample mentality, ensures time-sensitive accountability, promotes follow-up discussion, and utilizes resources efficiently.

The Book of Mormon loan program involves offering contacts or acquaintances a copy of the Book of Mormon as a loan. The sharer asks for the listener's opinion about the book and emphasizes that he or she does not need to read the entire book, but just enough to begin to form an opinion. Copies of 23 Questions Answered by the Book of Mormon or specific passages addressing issues of interest can stimulate reading. The sharer follows up by telephone or in person at an agreed-upon time a few days later. If the individual is not interested, he or she returns the book. If the individual is interested, he or she can continue to read and discuss, with church invitation or eventual missionary referral as appropriate with the individual's permission.

Most people feel an obligation to return other people's property, and so loaning the book is more effective than giving it away. The loaned status of the book also promotes time-sensitive follow-up that is often lost when the book is given away due to the free sample mentality. The Book of Mormon loan program is nonthreatening to the listener, and most members are surprised at how easy it is to implement.

OTHER RESOURCES FOR SHARING THE GOSPEL

Other resources available for sharing the gospel include Joseph Smith testimony pamphlets, pass-along cards, *Gospel Principles* books, church videos, the mormon.org Web site, and other outreach literature. Members should be aware of tools but not limited by them. Remember that your personal witness is still your strongest tool!

SHARE THE GOOD NEWS

Members should make sharing the Good News a regular part of their life and focus on the goal of initiating at least one gospel discussion each week in harmony with scriptural mandates. Our efforts to share the gospel are vitally important to our own salvation and to the salvation of others. Nephi declared: "How great the importance to make these things known unto the inhabitants of the earth, that they may know that there is no flesh that can dwell in the presence of God, save it be through the merits, and mercy, and grace of the Holy Messiah" (2 Nephi 2:8). Elder Henry B. Eyring taught: "I can make two promises to those who offer the gospel to others. The first is that even those who reject it will someday thank us.... My second promise is that as you offer the gospel to others it will go down more deeply into your heart. It becomes the well of water springing up into eternal life for us as we offer it to others."*

At the judgment we will be asked not whether the gospel is true, but whether we were true to the gospel! There are more receptive people in the world than there are Latter-day Saints willing to witness to them. Opportunities are everywhere. Rick Warren stated: "While we wait for God to work for us, God is waiting to work through us!"†

---

*   Eyring, Henry B., "Witnesses for God," *Ensign*, November 1996.

†   Warren, Rick, *The Purpose Driven Church*, Grand Rapids, MI: Zondervan, 1995, 60.

PRINCIPLES OF MEMBER-MISSIONARY WORK

MAXIMIZE IMPLEMENTATION

E LDER M. RUSSELL BALLARD taught: "Do you know what stake mission leaders and stake missionaries spend more time doing than anything else? Our research shows it is attending meetings, planning, and coordinating. These are good things, but sometimes we spend too much time reporting what we have done or planning what we will do. In contrast, stake mission leaders and stake missionaries invest considerably less time in what makes the most difference: personally interacting with their nonmember and less-active member friends and converts."*

President Charles Creel of the Russia St. Petersburg Mission used the analogy: "Who will catch more fish—the fisherman who spends ten hours a day preparing his bait and two hours with his line in the water, or the fisherman who gets his bait together in fifteen minutes and spends ten and a half or eleven hours each day fishing?" While good planning is necessary to establish appropriate and effective courses of action, meetings convert no one and the real difference is made finding and teaching investigators firsthand. Eighty to ninety

---

* Ballard, M. Russell, "Members Are the Key," *Ensign*, September 2000.

percent of missionary and member-missionary time should be spent on the actual implementation of missionary efforts. When meeting and planning consumes more than 20 percent of time, that time is being used inefficiently and should be reallocated to personal interactions with nonmembers. The world is not "fished out": we simply aren't doing much fishing.

CHURCH MEETINGS: THE GOLDEN HOURS

Church meetings and activities represent the "golden hours" for stake, ward, district, and full-time missionaries as well as member-missionaries. From the moment they arrive at church comfortably before the meetings begin to the moment they leave, effective missionaries and member-missionaries are meeting new people and talking to other members about sharing the gospel all of the time that they are not sitting in sacrament or listening to lessons. They ask other members how their efforts to share the gospel are going, learn their experiences, solicit feedback, offer new resources, and follow up on old ones. Be a PPP: a polite persistent pest. Arrive early, stay late, and do not sit down until you have sincerely introduced yourself to any individuals you do not recognize. Do more than say hello—be a real friend, not an assigned one. Your task is to make each person sincerely feel as welcome as possible. Encourage other members to do the same.

FRIENDSHIPPING AND FELLOWSHIPPING

George Barna wrote: "Research among Christians has found that we have an added difficulty in our lives. We tend to associate with other Christians and thus have few significant relationships with nonbelievers. We struggle with evangelism because we are isolated from the very people God has called us to influence. For most Christians, developing meaningful, authentic relationships with non-Christians will be an act of intent, not an act of chance. We probably will have to look for or creatively make opportunities to encounter and interact with nonbelievers."*

Members should look both for opportunities to foster relationships with nonmembers and to fellowship investigators. No one wants to be "assigned a friend" or have only "Sunday friends." Do not just shake hands; get to know the visitors and become involved in their lives. The following helpful fellowshipping suggestions are intuitive and arise naturally from an earnest desire to fellowship others and help them come into the fold of God.

1. One successful mission president told us that his rule is that he does not sit down at Church until he has met all individuals whom he does not know. This is good advice for members and missionaries. More than one individual has told us that they kept coming to Church because they knew that we cared.

2. Create an environment where the person is comfortable by building on common ground. It is helpful to ask about the person's family, background, and so forth to break the ice and to tailor the approach to their needs.

3. Compliment the person for the efforts he or she is making to come to Church, meet with the missionaries, read the scriptures, and do what is right. These steps take courage and deserve praise.

4. Find out what exposure the person has had to the Church: how many missionary discussions (or their topics), what they are reading in the Book of Mormon, and so forth.

5. Identify any questions or concerns the person has about the

---

* Barna, George, *Evangelism That Works*, Ventura, CA: Regal Books, 1995.

Church. Often they will be raised spontaneously after the first three steps.

6. Be a good listener and show genuine interest.

7. Share brief thoughts or testimony about the blessings living the Gospel has brought into your life. This should be more than an abstract assertion that the gospel is true: tell what it has done for you as you have tried to live it. You do not need to be a scriptorian; you just need to be sincere.

8. Tell the individual that you would like to visit with him or her at greater length. Ask if the person would like to visit your house for dinner or home evening or if you can attend one of the missionary or new member discussions.

9. Exchange phone numbers or addresses with the person. Do not simply tell him that you are available; agree on specific plans for follow-up. Set a date and time.

10. Carry through and follow up promptly.

MEMBER-MISSIONARY MENTORING

LDS members typically lack hands-on mentoring in outreach. Involvement of members in missionary splits, teaching and fellowshipping visits with investigators, and role playing are essential elements of member-missionary training. Jehovah's Witnesses are mentored early in proselyting by experienced members, often even before they are formally baptized. The practical, applied focus of the Jehovah's Witnesses has proven far more effective at inspiring member-missionary participation than abstract, theoretical LDS member-missionary exhortations that rarely reach beyond the pulpit or the classroom. For many Jehovah's Witnesses, sharing their beliefs with others is a favorite activity that many perform with a degree of joy that contrasts with the reticence and apprehension of most Latter-day Saints. Latter-day Saints do not need vague admonitions from the pulpit to "do missionary work": they need effective examples that provide practical hands-on mentoring.

QUALITY AND PREDICTABILITY OF TALKS AND LESSONS

Rick Warren, pastor of the fastest-growing Baptist church in U.S. history, stated: "Most churches rarely attract unbelievers to their services because members are uncomfortable bringing them to church. It doesn't matter how much the pastor encourages members to bring friends or how many visitation programs are launched, the results are the same: Most members never bring any lost friends to church. Why is this? There are three important reasons. First, the target of the messages is unpredictable. Members don't know from week to week if the pastor will be preaching an evangelistic message or an edification message. Second, the services are not designed for unbelievers, so much of what goes on in them would not be understandable to an unchurched friend. Third, members may be embarrassed by the quality of the service.... What is the most natural way to increase the number of visitors to your church?... The answer is quite simple: Create a service that is intentionally designed for your members to bring their friends to. And make the service so attractive, relevant, and appealing to the unchurched that your members are eager to share it with the lost people they care about."[*]

The quality of worship services correlates strongly with congregational growth. The Hartsem study, a large-scale study of thousands of congregations (including LDS) throughout the United States, reported that 56 percent of U.S. congregations with "highly inspirational"

---

[*]   Warren, Rick, *The Purpose Driven Church*, Grand Rapids, MI: Zondervan, 1995, 252–53.

services are growing, compared to only 27 percent with low-quality worship services.* While active members can gain personal benefit even from poorly prepared talks through an attitude of worship, a negative impression is made upon visitors, dampening enthusiasm for return attendance. Speakers must use terms that are understandable for non-LDS visitors. Talks and lessons must consistently be inspirational, edifying, and relevant for nonmembers and members alike so that Latter-day Saints are excited to invite their nonmember friends to "come and see" and visitors are excited to return.

SUBMITTING REFERRALS

Members should to ask the permission of nonmembers before sending a referral to the local missionaries. If one does not have the contact's permission, the relationship of trust may be disrupted. If the individual is not interested in learning about the Church when speaking with an acquaintance, it is unlikely that they will react positively to missionaries whom they do not know. It is rarely if ever appropriate to submit a referral without the consent of the person being referred. Some exceptions apply for programs such as missionary "singing Christmas cards," which typically do not include a full teaching invitation but require follow-up by the referring member.

LESSONS FROM "CELL CHURCHES"

Cell or house churches or faith groups that meet in member homes have experienced explosive growth over the past two decades and represent the fastest-growing segment of Christian worship today. LDS membership is growing at just over 2 percent per year, while the Southern Baptists have been growing at 100 percent or more per

---

*   *Faith Communities in the U.S. Today*, Hartsem Institute for Religious Research, Hartsem Seminary, http://fact.hartsem.edu.

year for almost a decade in nations such as Cambodia and some areas of India where they have employed cell churches as their main growth strategy. Without paid clergy or dedicated meetinghouses, the overhead of cell churches is minimal, facilitating rapid expansion with limited resources. The fellowshipping and integration problems which represent major issues for groups meeting in large freestanding churches are almost automatically solved by the dynamics of cottage groups. Many cell churches experience almost 100 percent member-missionary participation and fellowshipping due to their focus on three or four core issues instead of dividing member energies among dozens of programs and activities.

Although some elements of cell church programs are not transferable to an LDS setting, important principles can be learned from groups that have reduced worship to essentials. While members of large congregations with choir, mutual, and other activities may be inclined to look with contempt upon no-frills "cell churches" of some other denominations, it is humbling to remember that these groups have far better rates of member-missionary participation than Latter-day Saints do. Peripheral church activities are not always beneficial, since they can distract member attention away from more important activities. Organized weekly congregational worship plays an essential scriptural role in our faith, yet lessons of the "cell church" can be successfully distilled in the context of LDS cottage meetings.

COTTAGE MEETINGS

A cottage meeting is an informal gospel-based meeting held in a member's home with nonmembers present. Cottage meetings are not a substitute for investigators attending church, but they represent a valuable supplement that facilitates the consistent achievement of vital teaching and fellowshipping tasks that are at times difficult to accomplish by more traditional methods. I find that investigators and new members have consistently given excellent reviews to cottage meetings held in member homes. More significantly, I have found a much higher return rate for investigators who attended both church and cottage meetings than those who attended church meetings alone. Cottage meetings have also played an essential role in laying the foundation for the church in some new areas and nations, including the Russian Far East area, Armenia, Kazakhstan, and Georgia.

In conjunction with regular church attendance, cottage meetings are typically able to foster a higher degree of enthusiasm for the gospel in investigators than attendance at church meetings alone. This is because the problems with many conventional church meetings—the unpredictability of talks, lessons not specifically tailored to investigators, and inconsistent fellowshipping—are almost entirely eliminated in the setting of cottage meetings. Investigators enjoy cottage meetings because they are attractive, relevant, and appealing. Cottage meetings are held weekly on a specific night (other than Monday) in a member's home with predictable teachers and consistent interaction. Quality fellowshipping in cottage meetings is almost inevitable, and the relationships that develop are much stronger than those developed in Sunday meetings by a greeting or a handshake in the hall. All this is achieved while simultaneously reaching multiple people within a limited time.

Following are some specific principles and practices that I have found to be helpful in conducting cottage meetings. Others may have found different approaches to be effective in their area. Individuals are encouraged to try different approaches and discover what works best for them.

1. **Audience**. In addition to the members who will lead the discussion, new members, investigators being currently taught by the missionaries, and a pair of missionaries are invited each week.

2. **Topic**. The goal of cottage meetings is to help the attendees become better people and establish essential gospel habits. Some of the things we focus on include daily personal or family Book of Mormon reading, weekly church attendance, full Sabbath day observance, consistent personal and family prayer, the Word of Wisdom, and family history work. We also address some fundamental doctrinal topics including prophets, the Holy Ghost, the apostasy and restoration, divine authority, and families. If the investigators understand doctrinal issues but are not reading scriptures and attending church, our teaching has failed. Lessons are scripture-based, and questions are answered from the scriptures when possible.

3. **Timing**. Respecting the time and other obligations of investigators is vital, and the lesson should always end before the spirit leaves. We keep our meetings relatively brief so that they can be relevant and powerful. In this way, the investigators are eager to come back for more instead of regretting that their whole evening was soaked up. We aim for sixty minutes and never allow cottage meetings to go past ninety minutes, including time for refreshments and socializing. The purpose of cottage meetings is not to provide detailed doctrinal discourses, but to furnish a simple lesson, provide fellowshipping, address questions and concerns, and demonstrate the gospel in action in the home.

4. **Relevance**. Lessons involve frequent feedback and interaction with participants and are never lectures. The lesson plan must

be flexible and meet investigator needs. If the investigators have multiple questions on topics that are more important to them than the lesson, address those questions and topics instead. One must always keep in mind the goal of giving investigators practical teachings that will make their lives better. I will briefly answer questions on tangential or deep doctrinal issues (but to the listener's satisfaction) before leading the discussion back on topic. If you find yourself facing a question you do not know the answer to, tell the questioner that you will have an answer the next week.

5. **Consistency**. Cottage meetings are most effective when held in the same place at the same time every week. The missionaries know that they are welcome to bring anyone they are currently teaching. The new members and investigators who have attended once know that we will be looking for them the next week. Tuesdays or Thursdays have worked the best for us because Monday is family home evening, Wednesday is our ward activity night with scouts and mutual, and Friday and Saturday are inconvenient for most people for social reasons. When cottage meetings are not held consistently or are held in unpredictable locations, it is difficult to achieve a regular turnout.

6. **Relaxed atmosphere**. Everyone should be involved. Ask open-ended questions, and avoid manipulative or leading queries.

7. **Refreshments at the end**. We find this to be a productive time when investigators will open up even more and share things that they might not share even in the small group setting.

FINDING THROUGH FAMILY HISTORY WORK

Family history can present one of the best inroads for member-missionary work. The *Ensign* article "Family History as a Missionary Tool" shares valuable insights about how family history can succeed as a member-missionary tool where less effective missionary dinner programs and other initiatives have failed.[*] LDS General Authorities have encouraged the effective use of family history as a missionary tool. Elder D. Todd Christofferson of the Presidency of the Seventy noted: "Family history is obviously a crucial tool in redeeming the dead, but it can also play an important role in proclaiming the gospel and strengthening members of the Church. With even minimal coordination between priesthood leaders, family history workers, and missionaries, it will not be difficult to use family history as a tool for conversion and retention of new members and activation of less-active members."[†] While the program's main goal is to make genuine friends and help individuals to understand the LDS emphasis on the family, some individuals become interested in the Church. Stake missionary Charles Wright noted: "Religion is personal to people and many times is closely held. On the other hand, nearly anybody will sit down and talk to you about your ancestors. You can ask people questions about where they're from, and they enjoy letting you know about their heritage."

Members receive "Tell Me About Your Family" cards which help nonmembers to start recording names, places, and dates. The members then invite the interested contact to a family home evening about family history or a family history open house. Open houses are held up to once per month. Stake Mission President Dean Dexter

---

[*]   Bigelow, Christopher K., "Family History as a Missionary Tool," *Ensign*, October 2000: 29–31.

[†]   Christofferson, D. Todd, *Ensign*, February 1999: 77.

of the Huntsville Alabama Stake stated, "The most successful open houses included several elements: one, a brief, spiritual presentation on why Latter-day Saints do family history work; two, a demonstration of FamilySearch software, with the computer screen projected for everyone to see, if possible; three, an opportunity for each visitor to sit down at a table and be assisted in filling out the 'Where Do I Start?' pamphlet and other forms."* He noted that displays of family history work done by other members can be helpful and that having full-time missionaries participate "is the most critical and important part of what we are doing at these open houses." Stake High Councilor Robert Swenson stated: "The key is to have the full-time missionaries sit at tables and work with people one-on-one and establish a rapport. Otherwise it's just another family history seminar. People naturally ask questions that lead to opportunities to share the gospel." Charles Drake, a member who has invited up to seven individuals to an open house, stated: "We try to get the same people to come back by having something new for them each time. We want to get well-acquainted with them so we can invite them to another Church activity and move them toward investigating." President Dexter noted that lessons are brief: "We want visitors to leave hungry for more, not overstuffed."

THE CASE AGAINST
MISSIONARY DINNER PROGRAMS

There is perhaps no member-missionary program as widespread or as ineffective as missionary dinner programs. In many wards, the monthly missionary dinner calendar is circulated with the expectation of a dinner appointment in a member's home almost every night. Some wards even have a special calling for a missionary dinner

---

* Bigelow, Christopher K., "Family History as a Missionary Tool," *Ensign*, October 2000: 29–31.

appointment coordinator. The concept, as described by its proponents, sounds attractive: missionaries can economize time by doing two things at once—building relationships with members and soliciting member referrals while having a nutritious dinner. Economic justifications have also been cited, since members in some areas are instructed that the missionaries' monthly support funds take into account that they will not be buying their own dinner.

The missionary dinner program neutralizes missionaries by taking them off the street during prime finding and teaching time when families are home. Even when dinner visits are brief, missionary travel time ensures that member dinners consume considerable proselyting time each evening. There is no evidence that wards with missionary dinner programs generate more referrals than those without them, and many wards have experienced a revitalization of member-missionary work when dinner programs were terminated. Members of many other faiths are far more likely than Latter-day Saints to share their beliefs with others, yet rarely if ever have denominational missionaries in their homes.

Like many nonscriptural traditions of the ancient Jews that overrode the weightier matters of the law, the ubiquitous missionary dinner program is not mentioned at all in the official *Preach My Gospel* manual. The manual instructs that missionaries should finish with dinner no later than 6 PM and makes no exclusions for dinner in member homes. This rule is ignored in most areas, with the large majority of missionary dinner appointments not even being scheduled to start until 6 PM or later. It is difficult to justify a program that consumes vast missionary time while failing to reliably improve member-missionary participation. The missionary dinner program is perpetuated not because it is effective, but because it is comfortable. It provides members with a false sense of contributing to the missionary effort without requiring the courage or effort to approach nonmember acquaintances about the gospel. It provides missionaries with the comforts of home while avoiding the frequent rejection involved in contacting nonmembers. It spins the wheels and generates motion without progress while missionaries and members talk about missionary work instead of doing it. These points inevitably evoke objections from members who have become attached to the missionary dinner program while doing little missionary work themselves. They cite enjoying the spirit that the missionaries bring into their home. Yet missionaries are not called to be surrogate home teachers for active members. We must not be selfish and deny numerous nonmembers the chance to be contacted by the missionaries in the time consumed by every missionary dinner appointment. While occasional well-planned member visits to address specific needs can be valuable, regular dinner visits to member homes when investigators are not present are rarely as productive as alternative finding and teaching activities.

MISSION PREPARATION

PREPARING TO SERVE

President Spencer W. Kimball declared:

When I ask for more missionaries, I am not asking for more testimony-barren or unworthy missionaries, I am asking that we start earlier and train our missionaries better in every branch and ward in the world. That is another challenge—that the young people will understand that it is a great privilege to go on a mission and that they must be physically well, mentally well, spiritually well, and that the Lord cannot look upon sin with the least degree of allowance. I am asking for missionaries who have been carefully indoctrinated and trained through the family and the organizations of the Church, and who come to the mission with a great desire. I am asking for better interviews, more searching interviews, more sympathetic and understanding interviews, but especially that we train prospective missionaries much better, much earlier, much longer, so that each anticipates his mission with great joy.*

---

* Kimball, Spencer W., *Ensign*, October 1974: 7.

PROTESTANT MISSION MOBILIZER DONALD McGavran noted: "The first requirement for church growth on the mission field is for the Church at home to produce and send forth the right kind of seed abroad.... The missionary, as the first seed of the Church, will reproduce his own type of faith and spiritual vigor in the life of his converts.... Vigorous Christians produce vigorous converts.... The first step in church growth is to have missionaries who are vital Christians, who will inspire in converts a true spirit of sacrifice for the Gospel and a burning passion for souls."* Alma taught "every seed bringeth forth unto its own likeness" (Alma 32:21). One must be fully converted before one can convert others, and one cannot instill a greater degree of conversion in others than one has personally experienced.

Being an effective missionary requires an integrated balance of gospel attributes, including obedience to God, selflessness, love of the people, ability to understand and relate, and an inexhaustible drive to contact, teach, truly convert, and reap an abundant harvest. The Lord proclaimed: "No one can assist in this work except he shall be humble and full of love, having faith, hope, and charity, being temperate in all things, whatsoever shall be entrusted to his care" (D&C 12:8). While it is possible to complete a full-time mission or serve actively in the Church without these attributes, in their absence we "cannot assist in this work": the fruits will not endure and our efforts will be for naught. As fractional retention and activity statistics from many areas of the world demonstrate, until we develop the required scriptural attributes and "an eye single to the glory of God," we are only deceiving ourselves and playing games at the expense of others. The most important commandment for us is the one with which we have the most trouble. Similarly, the attributes that are the hardest for us

---

* McGavran, Donald Anderson, *Church Growth and Christian Mission,* New York: Harper & Row, 1965, 113.

deserve the most attention since they are usually the ones that are limiting our progress.

A LOVE FOR THE LOST

It has often been said that 90 percent of a mission president's job is motivating missionaries. I may not be in strict agreement with that, but the importance of motivation is undeniable. A wise bishop stated: "Any mission president will tell you candidly that 20% of the missionaries do 80% of the work. Those are the 20% of the missionaries who go to preach the gospel. For the other 80%, the mission is the main experience—gaining a testimony."[*] Some missionaries have a strong, nearly inexhaustible inner drive for faithful and fruitful service, while some others who have attended the same church meetings and seminary meetings and sometimes have even been reared in the same family go through the motions while demonstrating little energy or initiative. The first group carries their motivation and resolve within themselves, while even the most inspiring talks and impassioned pleas from mission leaders produce little more than a short burst of energy in the second. I have often observed missionaries from fine families who give moving talks and doctrinally solid lessons and appear in social situations to be ideal "Mormons" in every way, yet squander time in the mission field and never fully overcome their fear of approaching strangers about the gospel. Truly many are called, but few are chosen.

LDS Missionary Department studies document that missionary work ethic and productivity in the mission field correlate highly with having a mother who does not work and with mission expenses that are paid largely or in full by the missionary himself. As many young

---

[*]   Bishop James Donaldson, Crestmoor Ward, Denver Colorado Stake, circa. 1996.

men approach mission age, the question is frequently whether to serve at all. If one is preoccupied with the question of whether or not to serve, instead of the question of how to serve effectively from youth, the delay undermines both spiritual and financial preparation for missionary service. Those who have made major personal financial sacrifices by working to fund their missions throughout their adolescence, generally retain greater vision and motivation in the mission field than those who serve missions as the result of a last-minute decision with little planning or sacrifice. While most converts and youth in developing nations cannot fully fund their own missions, there are few reasons for lifetime members in developed nations to arrive at mission age without being able to pay most or all of their personal missionary expenses.

What makes the difference between the missionaries and members who experience a fading burst of energy after inspirational pep talks and those who hold within themselves a deep and constant drive to share the gospel? The secret of motivation is charity. Those who have it in sufficient degree do not require external motivation; those who lack it respond only transiently to external motivators. Charity banishes the fear of man that impedes missionary outreach. John taught: "There is no fear in love; but perfect love casteth out fear: because fear hath torment. He that feareth is not made perfect in love" (1 John 4:18). Charity is love based on Christ rather than on human relationships. It instills perspective and does not allow our caring to be monopolized by a few investigators making little progress while many other individuals have never been approached with the gospel message. Moroni taught that "charity is the pure love of Christ, and it endureth forever; and whoso is found possessed of it at the last day, it shall be well with him" (Moroni 7:47).

Each Latter-day Saint must develop charity, which leads us to share the gospel. The number of unreached individuals in the world is virtually unlimited, while each of us has finite time and energy. Jim Rohn stated, "Without a sense of urgency, desire loses its value." As any procrastination on our part will result in the loss of opportunities to our fellow men, the work of sharing the gospel cannot be compartmentalized into brief periods of life when we are serving as full-time missionaries or are assigned to missionary-related callings. Love is the foundation from which all other missionary attributes arise. Wolfgang Amadeus Mozart stated: "Neither a lofty degree of intelligence nor imagination, nor both together, go to the making of a genius. Love, love, love: that is the soul of genius." A love of the Lord, a love of missionary work, and a love of people are prerequisites for both the understanding and effective implementation of missionary efforts. George Washington Carver observed: "There is nothing that will not reveal its secrets if you love it enough."

Few individuals who have grown up in active families in the Church of Jesus Christ of Latter-day Saints can fully appreciate the depth of spiritual need of the unreached. For many, the gospel and the support system of faithful families, scripture, and church have been a constant rock in life providing meaning, counsel, and direction. Those who converted to the Church at considerable personal sacrifice, as well as those who have experienced the loss of a loved one or serious personal setbacks, may appreciate at least to a small degree the breadth of anguish and depth of need caused by the absence of the gospel message. The love which is central to missionary work requires a change of heart which is contrary to the natural man, "for all seek their own, not the things which are Jesus Christ's" (Philippians 2:21).

The burning desire to reach the unreached can be developed only through obedience and great personal sacrifice. The practices of studying the scriptures daily and keeping a journal can keep charity alive in our hearts by helping us to remember our own nothingness and eternal debt to God. The welfare of our fellow men should be a constant object of thought and prayer. Nephi, Enos, Alma, Mormon, and others prayed fervently for the welfare of their brethren (2 Nephi 33:3, Alma 38:14, Enos 1:11, Words of Mormon 1:8, Mormon 8:24). Some of the greatest missionaries of scripture, including Alma, the sons of Mosiah, and the Apostle Paul, developed a love for the lost through personal suffering. Alma wrote: "There could be nothing so exquisite and so bitter as were my pains ... on the other hand, there can be nothing so exquisite and sweet as was my joy" (Alma 36:21). A proper understanding of the gospel, combined with charity, generates a compelling desire to share the gospel with others. The Book of Mormon records that the sons of Mosiah "were desirous that salvation should be declared to every creature, for they could not bear that any human soul should perish; yea, even the very thoughts that any soul should endure endless torment did cause them to quake and tremble" (Mosiah 28:3). Similarly, many of the great missionaries of the modern era describe the burning desire to reach the lost keeping them awake at night. Each of us must vicariously feel the suffering of those who have not had an opportunity to receive the full gospel.

We are commanded to "pray unto the Father with all the energy of heart, that ye may be filled with this love, which he hath bestowed upon all who are true followers of his Son, Jesus Christ" (Moroni 7:48). Christ taught that we develop His love by sustained obedience to God: "If ye keep my commandments, ye shall abide in my love; even as I have kept my Father's commandments, and abide in his love" (John 15:10). The reverse is also true: "If you keep not my commandments, the love of the Father shall not continue with you, therefore you shall walk in darkness" (D&C 95:15). When we stray from God's commandments, even in seemingly small things, our love of God—and of our neighbor—inevitably wane and our vision becomes clouded, although the change at the time may be imperceptible to us.

The love of God is closely tied to love of our neighbor. LDS leaders have taught that our love for others is measured by the sacrifice we make for them. Christ taught that love is a yardstick of discipleship: "By this shall all men know that ye are my disciples, if ye have love one to another" (John 13:35). There is perhaps no greater missionary than John the Beloved, who modern revelation teaches has remained on the earth to bring souls to Christ (D&C 7:1–8). He taught: "If we love one another, God dwelleth in us, and his love is perfected in us.... If a man says, I love God, and hateth his brother, he is a liar: for he that loveth not his brother whom he hath seen, how can he love God whom he hath not seen? And this commandment have we from him, that he who loveth God love his brother also" (1 John 4:12, 20–21). John taught that the love of the world and the love of God are ultimately mutually exclusive: "If a man love the world, the love of the father is not in him" (1 John 2:15). In this sense, we might better understand the Parable of the Rich Young Man who asked the Savior what he must do to inherit eternal life. The Savior replied: "Go and sell that thou hast, and give to the poor, and thou shalt have treasure in heaven: and come and follow me." Matthew records that the young man "went away sorrowful: for he had great possessions" (Matthew 19:16–22). The young man had many virtues, but he lacked the most important one of all: charity, the abiding and unfailing love of Christ. Paul taught: "And now abideth faith, hope, charity, these three; but the greatest of these is charity" (1 Corinthians 13:13). The Savior taught: "Thou shalt love the Lord thy God with all thy heart, and with all thy soul, and with all thy mind. This is the first and great commandment.

And the second is like unto it, thou shalt love thy neighbour as thyself. On these two commandments hang all the law and the prophets" (Matthew 22:37–40).

Charity can flourish only when barriers cutting us off from the Holy Spirit are removed by surrendering to God the piece of our heart that we have been holding back. A deep love of the unreached, combined with sacrifice, prayer, and hard work, can open the doors for the Spirit to work. Alma taught: "He that repenteth and exerciseth faith, and bringeth forth good works, and prayeth continually without ceasing—unto such it is given to know the mysteries of God; yea, unto such it shall be given to reveal things which never have been revealed; yea, and it shall be given unto such to bring thousands of souls to repentance, even as it has been given unto us to bring these our brethren to repentance" (Alma 26:22).

DOING THE RIGHT THINGS

When I started my surgical residency, a friend gave the advice: "Always do the right thing for your patient, no matter how tired you are." A memorable faculty surgeon taught the motto "TTLYM"—treat them like your mother. These counsels are just as applicable to the mission field as to medicine. Problematic scenarios that generally lead to predictably poor results, such as a poorly prepared investigator being rushed to baptism to meet an artificial baptismal date, a monthly goal, or a missionary transfer date or the baptism of itinerants shortly before they leave an area, all sacrifice the investigator's ultimate spiritual welfare for personal considerations. In each of these examples, the missionaries demonstrate a lack of charity. When we have charity, we are driven by a desire to always do the right thing for our investigators. Our investigators' best interests are never sacrificed for programs, goals, quotas, or secondary gain. We treat each individual in the manner that we would like our mother, our best friend, or ourselves to be treated under similar circumstances.

BECOME A MISSIONARY

The true test of a missionary is not simply in accepting the mission call, but in the dedication with which he or she serves daily. The decision to serve diligently should be made once and adhered to, rather than having to be decided each day. Elder David A. Bednar noted that "our rather routine emphasis on *going* misses the mark.... The issue is not going on a mission; rather, the issue is becoming a missionary and serving throughout our entire life with all of our heart, might, mind, and strength. It is possible for a young man to *go* on a mission and not *become* a missionary, and this is not what the Lord requires or what the Church needs. My earnest hope for each of you young men is that you will not simply go on a mission—but that you will become missionaries long before you submit your mission papers."[*]

THE BETTER PART

When many missionaries think of mission preparation, one of the first questions is what to bring. This question is primarily self-centered with the focus on personal comfort. The physical aspects can dominate and crowd out the "weightier matters of the law." Christ taught: "Take no thought, saying, What shall we eat? or, What shall we drink? or, Wherewithal shall we be clothed? (For after all these things do the Gentiles seek).... But seek ye first the kingdom of God, and his righteousness; and all these things shall be added unto you" (Matthew 6:31–33). Many well-meaning parents, friends, and family members, like Martha in the New Testament, worry more about serving physical

---

[*]   Bednar, David A., "Becoming a Missionary," *Ensign*, November 2005.

needs or wants than the better part: the Gospel of Jesus Christ. Few things are less significant to missionary work than personal belongings. Instead, we must "treasure up in [our] minds continually the words of life" (D&C 84:85). The Lord warns us of the consequences of focusing on the temporal: "Behold, there are many called, but few are chosen. And why are they not chosen? Because their hearts are set so much upon the things of this world" (D&C 121:34–45). The question that newly called missionaries should be asking instead of "what should I bring" is "how can I be most effective in bringing souls to Christ?" For the devoted missionary, no bed is too hard and no culture is too challenging. All energies are directed toward the task of reaching souls.

DETERMINATION AND MINDSET

By one's mindset and determination, much of the foundation for missionary success or failure is laid before one arrives in the mission field. Those determined to reap an abundant harvest can typically do so, while those who lend credence to the myths that "it doesn't really matter how many conversions there are" or that "the Lord is in control, so it isn't so important how I work" are easily neutralized. It matters a great deal how effective we are in proclaiming the gospel when the lives of our brothers and sisters are changed through repentance and conversion. If our own souls are precious, surely the souls of our fellow men and women are as precious as our own, not as statistics, but as unique individuals precious in the sight of our Heavenly Father. How successful would Ammon have been if he had decided that he already had too many member visits and discussions on his schedule to go out and do more contacting? Elder Bruce R. McConkie stated: "We are not getting the results we ought to get. We are not getting the numbers of baptisms that in my judgment the Lord expects us to get. To a degree, at least, we are grinding our wheels without going forward.... Perhaps what is wrong is that we have not desired faith with all our hearts to bring souls into the kingdom. Perhaps we have not made up our minds that we can and will bring people into the Church. Now, very frankly, whether we gain many converts or few depends in large measure upon our frame of mind."[*]

President Ezra Taft Benson declared: "New missionaries need to know exactly the purpose for being in the mission field which is to save souls, to baptize converts, and to bring families into the church."[†] Similarly, President Gordon B. Hinckley taught missionaries: "Behold how great is your calling (D&C 112:33)... You are not sent here to take pictures. You are not sent here to play. You are sent here to find and teach. That's our opportunity, our challenge, and our responsibility. You'll never rise higher in all your lives than you will do while you are in the mission field. That may sound like a strange thing. I said that once in Argentina many years ago, and about ten years later I received a letter from a young man who said, 'When I was on a mission in Argentina, you came there and you put a hex on me. I haven't been able to lift it. I have been no good ever since. I failed in school, I failed in my work, I failed in my marriage.' I didn't put a hex on him. I simply told him that he would never stand taller, never rise higher, than while in the service of the Lord, and his subsequent life demonstrated that."[‡]

WORDS, THOUGHTS, AND DESIRES

Words and thoughts reflect true priorities and desires. A dedicated

---

[*]   McConkie, Bruce R., Mission Presidents' Seminar, June 21, 1975.

[†]   Benson, Ezra Taft, Mission Presidents' Seminar, June 1976.

[‡]   Hinckley, Gordon B., *The Teachings of Gordon B. Hinckley* , Salt Lake City, UT: Deseret Book, 1997, 362.

missionary consistently centers his desires and thoughts on the Lord's work and always seeks to be more effective. An astute missionary companion noted that "you can tell a lot about missionaries by the things they talk about when they get together." Effective missionaries share experiences, information, and ideas about missionary work, while others talk about entertainment, meals at nice restaurants, or postmission plans. Self-improvement comes naturally when the Lord's work is put above one's own. Our willingness to sacrifice personal desires and think the Lord's thoughts rather than our own is a strong indicator of personal conversion.

SCRIPTURE STUDY

The time to learn the scriptures is long before the mission call. Missionaries who seriously study the doctrines of the restoration, master the scriptures, and memorize hundreds of verses before their missions as President Benson instructed are able to hit the ground running. Missionaries who have not consistently studied the scriptures prior to their missions lose much valuable time in the field in search of basic understanding. Righteous habits and correct understanding of the gospel are not acquired overnight. Many individuals accept and promulgate a philosophy that spiritual needs can be met by reading only one or two verses of scripture per day. The intent may be to encourage those who are not reading scriptures regularly to read some small amount, but the usual effect is to generate complacency with little or no real effort at scripture study. Full nourishment is necessary for us to endure the heat of the day of mortal challenges and temptations. We cannot abide the conditions of salvation or teach them to others without understanding them ourselves.

It is not enough simply to read the scriptures. They must be written on our hearts and guide our conduct and actions. Missionaries must become fluent with the scriptures in the local language. A missionary's knowledge of scriptures is of little benefit to others if he cannot freely share passages with investigators and members.

FOLLOW THE SPIRIT

The Spirit speaks both to mind and heart (D&C 8:2) and can no more speak to the mind in an environment of illogic than it can speak to the heart in an environment of contention and dispute. Exclusive focus on reason at the expense of spiritual feeling is equally ineffective. True spirituality demands both mind and heart, reason and feeling, logic and love. Truth, reason, and enlightenment come from the same divine spirit as the burning within the heart. The Lord can fully answer our prayers only when we have made an earnest attempt to study, contemplate, and understand. The Spirit can enlighten us to its full potential only when we have done our part to investigate, study, and ponder and when we sacrifice our personal desires to God's will.

OBEDIENCE: THE KEY TO TESTIMONY

Developing a testimony takes time, and testimonies exist in varying degrees and strengths. Elder Heber J. Grant stated: "I may know that the Gospel is true, and my wife may know it; but I do not imagine for one moment that my children will be born with this knowledge. We receive a testimony of the Gospel by obeying the laws and ordinances thereof; and our children will receive that knowledge exactly the same way; and if we do not teach them, and they do not walk in the straight and narrow path that leads to eternal life, they will never receive this knowledge."* The real measure of testimony is the extent to which obedience to the gospel is reflected in our daily lives. The

---

*   Grant, Heber J., as cited in *Collected Discourses*, vol. 4, April 6, 1894.

Savior taught that a testimony is acquired through obedience: "If any man will do his will, he shall know of the doctrine, whether it be of God or whether I speak of myself" (John 7:17). The best and only way to come to understand the truth of any gospel principle is to live it. Alma describes how our faith can grow from belief into a perfect knowledge by nurturing the word through obedience to the gospel (Alma 32). There is a greater difference between the missionary who is 100 percent obedient and a 95 percent missionary than between a 95 percent missionary and a 50 percent missionary. The Lord can trust missionaries who are consistently faithful to work miracles like Paul, Nephi, and Ammon, while those whose obedience is inconsistent never reach their full potential in bringing souls to Christ.

TRUE FAITH, EXPECTATIONS, AND REALITY: EMOTIONAL PREPARATION FOR SERVING EFFECTIVELY

Emotional preparation for frequent rejection is one of the most important preparations for missionary service. The scriptures are replete with directives to share the gospel without regard for the fear of man, and all those who heed the ridicule of those in the "great and spacious building" stray from the straight and narrow path (1 Nephi 8:33–34). Many missionaries are discouraged that more people do not accept their message. Frequently, the problem lies not in their techniques, but in unrealistic expectations and in not meeting enough people. Most missionaries expect to baptize a relatively high percentage of those whom they meet and teach. Many state that they have "faith" that all of their investigators will desire to be baptized, that all of those who commit to baptism will carry through, and that all those who are baptized will remain active and strong members of the church throughout life almost regardless of the quality of teaching or demonstrated level of commitment. "Faith" that does not allow for the moral agency of others is deficient. Inspirational stories of miraculous success with seemingly little effort can fuel unrealistic expectations.

Missionaries can become discouraged when results do not measure up to their expectations, and many slacken their efforts to minimize further rejection. When missionaries have excessive expectations for early acceptance and are poorly prepared to cope with rejection, they often waste valuable time by repeatedly visiting investigators who are not keeping commitments, while failing to put forth adequate ongoing contacting efforts. Beyond a certain point, additional effort with the same individuals generates diminishing returns. Missionaries who are content with contacting a handful of people each day never rise above mediocrity.

While much can be done to improve finding and teaching effectiveness, frequent rejection is a fact of life for even the best missionaries in almost every mission. Traditionally, only a fraction of investigators at each major decision point typically progress. Only a small fraction of those who promise to attend church actually show up, and most missionaries find that 40 to 70 percent of first and second discussions fall through. In the early 1990s, the Church Missionary Department reported that only about one-fifth of first discussions lead to second discussions, only a fraction of investigators commit to baptism, and only one-fifth of baptismal commitments are carried through. Other research demonstrates that only one-quarter of international converts remain active for any meaningful period. Much can be done to improve progression at the later points. I have consistently found that over 80 percent of baptismal commitments are accepted, a similar percentage materialize, and 80 to 90 percent of baptized converts remain active with application of the principles described in this book, leading to exponentially greater long-term success. Yet virtually all missionaries experience a high degree of rejection in the early stages as part of the scriptural "sifting" of those who hear the gospel message.

All effective missionaries are undeterred from sharing the gospel and maintain consistent high effort in the face of frequent rejection. They expect to contact thousands and teach many in order to bring a single contact into the church. The Savior taught that we will experience rejection just as He did: "If they have persecuted me, they will also persecute you; if they have kept my saying, they will keep yours also" (John 15:20). Mission President Charles Creel instructed missionaries: "If you aren't being rejected many times each day, you aren't doing much missionary work." The gospel polarizes people, and those who accept or reject the gospel are passing judgment on themselves and not on the messengers. We must be sensitive to local customs and individual needs and feelings so that the rejections that inevitably come will be for the gospel's sake rather than because of our own lack of preparation or sensitivity.

Elder Neal A. Maxwell noted: "Too many of us seem to expect that life will flow ever smoothly, featuring an unbroken chain of green lights with empty parking places just in front of our destinations!"* President Howard W. Hunter taught: "This faith and hope of which I speak is not a Pollyanna-like approach to significant personal and public problems. I don't believe we can wake up in the morning and simply by drawing a big 'happy face' on the chalkboard believe that is going to take care of the world's difficulties. But if our faith and hope are anchored in Christ, in his teachings, commandments, and promises, then we are able to count on something truly remarkable, genuinely miraculous, which can part the Red Sea and lead modern

---

*   Maxwell, Neal A., *Ensign*, November 1989: 82.

Israel to a place 'where none shall come to hurt or make afraid.'"*

The real faith is in persistently putting forth our best effort, come what may, to teach others to love and live the gospel. With consistent effort over time, such effort is inevitably rewarded. In facilitating the miracle of conversion, the most important lessons are those that prepare our hearts and minds to put our hands to the plough and to serve with all our might. Jim Rohn stated: "Don't wish it was easier; wish you were better. Don't wish for less problems; wish for more skills. Don't wish for less challenge; wish for more wisdom."

---

*   Hunter, Howard W., *Ensign*, October 1993.

GOAL SETTING

WISE GOALS CAN PROMOTE increased productivity, skill development, and gospel service. President Spencer W. Kimball taught: "We do believe in setting goals ... we must have goals to make progress, encouraged by keeping records.... Laboring with a distant aim sets the mind in a higher key and puts us at our best.... Goals should always be made to a point that will make us reach and strain."* Without goals, confusion of purpose ensues. Thomas Carlyle wrote: "A man without a goal is like a ship without a rudder." Goals can expand vision and provide greater awareness of opportunities. Jim Rohn observed: "The ultimate reason for setting goals is to entice you to become the person it takes to achieve them." Goals can help us to overcome past limitations. Elder Neal A. Maxwell stated: "Our goals should stretch us bit by bit. So often when we think we have encountered a ceiling, it is really a psychological or experimental barrier that we have built ourselves. We built it and we can remove it. Just as correct principles, when applied, carry their own witness that they are true, so do correct personal improvement programs. But we must not expect personal improvement without pain or some 'remodeling.' We can't expect to have the thrills of revealed religion without the theology. We cannot expect to have the soul stretching without

---

* Kimball, Spencer W., Regional Representatives' Seminar, April 3, 1974.

Christian service."*

Some goals are more helpful than others, and improper goals can be as detrimental as good goals are helpful. Ezra Taft Benson noted: "We cannot do everything at once, but we can do a great deal if we choose our goals well and work diligently to attain them."[†] To harness the full power of goals, we must choose goals that are both appropriate and suitable to our situation. Before we can formulate helpful goals, we must understand the principles of goal-setting.

GOALS VERSUS QUOTAS

Quotas, or numerical goals established for individuals other than oneself, are inappropriate. Spencer W. Kimball taught: "Now somebody also got mixed up and they thought goal was spelled, 'q-u-o-t-a,' and it isn't; that's another word. Now there's a tremendous difference between a goal and a quota."[‡] Elder James E. Faust stated: "Missionaries should have goals but they should not be imposed by the mission president, his assistants or the zone leaders. I am persuaded that the missionaries will be more dedicated to their work, will be more committed, if they have set their own goals, and happier in their labors than if goals are imposed upon them. The best motivation is self-motivation."[§] In spite of this counsel, some missions continue to impose monthly and weekly mission quotas for baptisms, discussions, inactive visits, member visits, and other items. Effective leadership does not impose quotas. Returned missionary Kevin Buell explained the leadership model of the late President Viacheslav Efimov of the

---

*   Maxwell, Neal A., *Deposition of a Disciple*, Salt Lake City, UT: Deseret Book, 1976, 33–34.

†   Benson, Ezra Taft, Mission Presidents' Seminar, June 27, 1974.

‡   Kimball, Spencer W., Regional Representatives' Seminar, April 3, 1974.

§   Faust, James E., New Mission Presidents' Seminar, June 21, 1996.

Russia Yekaterinburg Mission, who set new records as the highest-baptizing mission president in Russia at the time of his service: "He didn't have a lot of goals for us. Districts and zones set their own goals. He just encouraged and continued the work atmosphere." Baptismal quotas lack credibility, since the leaders who impose such goals have rarely if ever consistently achieved these same goals themselves for any sustained period. More helpful goals such as members speaking with at least one nonmember about the gospel each week or missionaries contacting a minimum number of people each day allow leaders to lead by example and to expand their own understanding and insight into the challenges experienced by others and their solutions. Good leadership is not fostered by imposing vicarious quotas on others but by mentoring others in effectively finding, teaching, and retaining converts.

GOALS AND AGENCY

Time management guru Jeffrey Meyer noted: "set goals for activities, not for results, and the results will take care of themselves," as long as the chosen activities are appropriate. Goals contingent on the responses of others are inherently manipulative and often lead to false feelings of guilt, unworthiness, and discouragement when hard-working missionaries and members fail to achieve them. Missionaries are sometimes taught that reaching their monthly baptismal goals is an indicator of personal obedience. This is contrary to the scriptural principle of moral agency, since missionaries can control only their own conduct and not how investigators react to the gospel message. Noah preached for 120 years, yet no conversions are recorded in scripture. Mormon and Moroni describe their own vigorous preaching efforts that seemingly produced few visible results. Mormon wrote:

"And now, my beloved son, notwithstanding their hardness, let us labor diligently" (Moroni 9:6). Yet monthly baptismal goal initiatives would have branded these prophets as failures.

Monthly baptismal goals introduce subversive incentives and lead to tragic results by eclipsing the investigator's personal needs and shortchanging the repentance and conversion processes in the rush to baptize. The collapse of hundreds of LDS congregations throughout Latin America between 2001 and 2004 due to rampant inactivity and fractional convert retention demonstrate the catastrophe incurred by runaway baptismal goals uncoupled from the conversion process. Thousands of missionaries met monthly goals while neglecting the eternal ones, resulting in impressive statistical reports while leaving behind the emotional and spiritual wreckage of lost souls. What consolation can we derive from statistical reports of numerous baptisms that do not result in convert retention or activity? The wheel was spinning, but the gerbil was dead.

On my mission, the official policy requiring missionaries to establish arbitrary monthly baptismal goals produced considerable frustration, since many monthly goals went unmet in spite of our best efforts. We therefore abandoned the process of setting arbitrary baptismal goals and focused on things we could control, such as the number of individuals contacted with the gospel each day and the quality of prebaptismal teaching and preparation of investigators. Our happiness level, confidence, and spirituality rose dramatically, and our success increased to levels that had never been achieved with baptismal goals.

Goals to teach a certain number of discussions often lead to missionaries forging ahead with discussions that the investigators are not prepared to hear. Teaching an investigator the next discussion is not in the investigator's best interest when significant concerns remain unresolved or commitments from past lessons remain unfulfilled.

Goals for members to bring one individual into the Church each year or to set a date to find someone ready to be taught by the missionaries put the cart before the horse. These programs are demoralizing for members, who in spite of their best efforts to regularly share the gospel are counted the same as members who make no attempt to share the gospel at all, if they are not able to produce referrals or baptisms. A focus on secondary outcome measures such as referrals or baptisms rarely, if ever, results in sustained improvement without members first establishing regular habits of sharing the gospel with nonmembers.

We must choose goals that facilitate our true purpose, rather than false endpoints that do not reflect our eternal aims. We must understand what our goals actually measure and be aware of any potential for abuse. Real growth is subverted when the considerations of quality teaching, repentance, and conversion become secondary to numerical baptism or discussion goals.

HELPFUL GOALS

Helpful goals focus on putting forth a strong effort on a consistent basis and do not depend on the response of others. These goals can be achieved consistently by anyone with application of adequate effort. President Gordon B. Hinckley noted: "If you will work hard, the matter of converts will take care of itself. I am satisfied of that. Give it your very best."* Good goals are based firmly in gospel principles, while unhelpful goals are arbitrary. Helpful goals are not manipulative and never sacrifice the needs of souls. Helpful goals start small and help us to progress from our current state. By focusing on work

---

* Hinckley, Gordon B., *Teachings of Gordon B. Hinckley*, Salt Lake City, UT: Deseret Book, 1997, 357.

ethic rather than results, good goals ultimately generate much greater benefits to the real growth of the church than unrighteous or improper goals, while simultaneously helping us to become better people. They lift our character and enrich the lives of others.

The best goals are gospel-oriented habits or simple daily acts that can be performed consistently. In the small, quiet, daily acts unseen by most of the world, the real battles are won or lost. Once a challenging but consistently achievable level of performance is reached, it is not necessary to continue raising the goal indefinitely. Good goals are stable and sustainable and focus on improvement through consistent performance. Good habits generate regular progress that, over time, facilitates the conversion of others. My preferred goal for member-missionary work is to approach at least one nonmember per week about the gospel and for missionaries to contact at least fifty to one hundred nonmembers each day. These goals involve the direct fulfillment of scriptural mandates rather than participation in contrived programs and are directly within the power of each person to accomplish.

Planning and
Time Management

J IM ROHN ADVISED: "NEVER begin the day until it is finished on paper.... At the end of each day, you should play back the tapes of your performance. The results should either applaud you or prod you." Every evening following the missionaries' return to the apartment, the schedule for the following day is reviewed and calls are made to confirm existing appointments, establish new ones, and follow up with contacts, investigators, and members. The current day is also reviewed to recognize both successes and opportunities for improvement. The schedule for the coming week should be planned at a set time each week and then reviewed and updated daily. It is often easiest to do this after finishing proselyting at 9:30 pm on Sundays, with the knowledge of which investigators have attended church and who is available to be taught. The existing appointments are reviewed along with the needs of each investigator. Gaps in the schedule are considered, and telephone calls are made first to investigators and second to new members to set additional appointments. To minimize travel time, appointments close to each other should be scheduled consecutively when possible. In areas of high receptivity, consideration should be given to improving time efficiency to allow more people to be taught. Investigators can be taught in small or medium-sized groups rather than as individuals, or investigators can be scheduled in a location convenient for the missionaries, such as a chapel or designated member home, in sequential time slots. Consideration must be made to the alternative activities available at various time slots. An effective missionary will harvest the power of prayer in planning. Ezra Taft Benson noted, "In the work of the Lord there should be no serious mistakes. The most important point of your planning should be on your knees."*

Evening and weekend time when families are home usually constitutes prime time for missionary work. Because standard business and school hours are often more difficult to fill with productive teaching and finding activities than evenings or weekends, appointments should preferentially be scheduled during the day when possible. Evening and weekend appointments should ideally be scheduled only for individuals who are unavailable during daytime hours.

Several common planning mistakes can impair productivity. One common mistake of inefficient planners is to schedule few widely spaced appointments and view those time slots as inflexible. For most missionaries, only 30 to 60 percent of scheduled discussions with contacts and investigators actually materialize due to investigator no-shows, initially receptive contacts who become disinterested, and invalid or wrong addresses. The prudent missionary overschedules every day, recognizing that many appointments will inevitably fall through, creating gaps. If most or all visits turn out, the missionary must be flexible in delivering powerful but concise teaching to allow the schedule to be kept.

A second mistake is to lack a suitable backup plan. Some missionaries are repeatedly caught unprepared when appointments fall through and return to their apartments or engage in other fruitless

---

*   Benson, Ezra Taft, *Ensign*, May 1977.

activities stating that there is "nothing to do." The prudent missionary anticipates that many appointments do not materialize, especially with new contacts and investigators who have had less than three discussions. Tracting, street contacting, and brief drop-in visits to members or other contacts in the area often make excellent short-notice backup plans. Backup activities are planned in advance: tracting or street contacting in the area, brief stop-ins to other contacts or members in the area, and so forth. By anticipating trends and being prepared with a backup plan, the disappointment and frustration of broken appointments can be turned into fruitful opportunities. Over the course of a mission, missionaries who lack backup plans will lose hundreds of hours of productive work and tens of thousands of gospel contacts compared to missionaries who plan for contingencies.

A final mistake is to fail to schedule daily contacting time. Maintaining daily exposure to many new contacts and keeping an active turnover of investigators are essential to developing a strong, high-quality teaching pool. Contacting is the foundation of missionary productivity and brings greater vitality to all other endeavors. Schedules should include daily time for tracting, street contacting, or other methods of finding through the missionaries' own efforts. Incidental time spent contacting while in transit to appointments is typically not nearly as productive as dedicated contacting activities and so should be done in addition to and not as a substitute for dedicated contacting time. Two hours of tracting every evening or street contacting during the day represent a far more fruitful use of time than return visits to investigators who are not progressing or dinners with members. If pursued as a resolute goal, 50 to 200 individuals can be approached about the gospel every day in most areas in addition to keeping a nearly full teaching schedule.

SPECIAL PRIORITIES

Following up on contacts and referrals is one of the most productive missionary activities relative to the time spent and should be viewed as an urgent priority by all missionaries. On several occasions, I have contacted missionaries to pass on referrals and was told that they did not have time to teach new people, even though they had not had a baptism in months. In other cases, I have followed up a week or later on contacts I referred only to find out that the missionaries in their area had never contacted them. Referrals should be followed up on within forty-eight hours when at all possible, since most are time-sensitive. Mission-level follow-up can be helpful to ensure that referrals have been contacted by the assigned missionaries.

Sunday church meeting hours are the most important time of a missionary's week. It is crucial to meet all new contacts and investigators, record addresses and telephone numbers, and establish appointments when possible. I have been surprised at how frequently some missionaries fail to ask first-time visitors for contact information or to schedule follow-up appointments with them. There is little value in diligent contacting during the week when individuals that show up to church slip through the cracks through poor prioritization or neglect.

THE SECRET OF MISSIONARY WORK

President Ezra Taft Benson stated that the secret of missionary work is work. Besides obedience, work is the most important factor in gaining and keeping the companionship of the Holy Spirit. Remarkable spiritual experiences come the way of those who tirelessly serve and not to those who sit back waiting for experiences to come to them. The Lord needs hands that do His work more than lips that pray. While visiting missionaries in Japan, President Heber J. Grant stated that missionaries should work at least as hard as those who earn salaries, implying that this was often not happening. I felt the most powerful manifestations of the Spirit as a missionary when my companion and I had worked very hard putting in twelve and thirteen hour days bringing the word face to face.

In most missions, there are seventy-five hours set aside for proselyting in a missionary week (9:30 AM to 9:30 PM six days per week and 6:30 PM to 9:30 PM on preparation day). Almost any missionary who observes basic mission rules, used efficiently, maintains a vigorous work ethic, economizes travel time, keeps lunch to only one hour or less, and uses preparation day for preparation can consistently reach over sixty hours of proselyting each week. Optimally, at least fifty hours per week or 80 percent of total working time should be spent in actual proselyting activities, contacting and teaching nonmembers firsthand.

PROSELYTING HOURS

Webster's dictionary defines proselytizing as: 1. to induce someone to convert to one's faith; 2. to recruit someone to join one's party, institution, or cause. Many missions include time spent visiting active members, writing talks or lessons for members, attending meetings, and travel time in reported proselyting hours, although none of these activities meet the definition of proselyting. Some of these activities can represent legitimate uses of missionary time, at least on an occasional basis, but working with contacts and investigators face-to-face are the primary activities that build the kingdom of God. When all nonproselyting activities are excluded, it is often surprising how little time is being spent contacting and teaching the gospel firsthand. A large amount of time spent in nonproselyting activities is a sign of inefficient time utilization. It is often difficult for missionaries and mission leaders to recognize and troubleshoot such inefficiencies without a specific breakdown of what reported proselyting hours represent. To avoid numbers inflated by nonproselyting activities, it is valuable to separately report and track the number of hours spent making fresh contacts and teaching investigators.

PREPARATION DAY

Preparation day is the "missionary Sabbath," since it must be spent properly for the rest of the week to run in good order. Sightseeing and other diversions should be enjoyed only after preparation is done. When preparation day time is not utilized appropriately, shopping, personal errands, and other nonproselyting activities spill over into the rest of the week to the detriment of finding and teaching opportunities.

TEACH THOSE WHO ARE READY NOW

In areas of high receptivity, missionary productivity is frequently limited by the ability of local missionaries to effectively manage their time. Ammon and his brethren could not have experienced high success without good time management skills, regardless of the receptivity of those around them. Many missionaries today continue to visit investigators as long as they will accept visits, even if they are not keeping commitments or making progress. Such visits are typically based primarily on personality and other interests rather than the gospel message. While investigators should never be pressured to be baptized, it is imperative that investigators put forth regular effort toward the development of gospel habits including Book of Mormon reading and church attendance to justify repeated missionary visits. Missionaries should not schedule time with individuals who are consistently unwilling or unable to keep basic commitments. Missionaries must find those who are prepared to observe gospel commitments now, while leaving the door open for those who may be ready later. An active turnover of investigators is essential to keeping the finding and teaching pools vibrant.

LANGUAGE LEARNING

LANGUAGE LEARNING HAS ONLY a modest relationship to intelligence, but a strong relationship to consistency of effort. Continued daily language study is necessary to move from rudimentary communication to speaking correctly and mastering a full range of expression. Some find the challenge of studying a new language overwhelming, while others slacken their study after reaching a basic comfort zone. Brigham Young University professor Dilworth B. Parkinson stated: "One of the clearest results of language teaching research is that when a student becomes satisfied with what he knows, when he feels he 'knows the language,' he almost immediately ceases to make progress. We call this the 'returned-missionary syndrome.'" * This syndrome is not restricted to returned missionaries: many missionaries overestimate their own language proficiency and fail to progress after only a few months into the mission. Dr. Parkinson continued: "[Those] who manage to keep in mind how little they know and how much they have still to learn end up being the ones who make the most ultimate progress and find the most joy in the journey. Being reminded of the huge gulf between one's own language abilities, no matter how advanced, and those of a native speaker appears to be a prerequisite for further progress."

---

* Parkinson, Dilworth B., "We Have Received, and We Need No More," BYU Devotional, March 2, 2004.

When one first arrives in a foreign country, one may feel that he or she knows little and may not understand the people well. For some, there is a temptation to stay in the apartment and study during proselyting hours. It is important to study the language diligently during scheduled study hours. It is also essential to get out of the apartment and work diligently to make new contacts during proselyting hours. There is always time in the "cracks in the day" to enhance study. I would read a pocket dictionary on the bus and listen to language cassettes when preparing meals, showering, or cleaning up. Opportunities for study can be found any time, while opportunities to proselyte and share the gospel are limited to daylight and evening hours. One can learn much about a language by interacting with people that cannot be learned from books, cassettes, or CDs. Missionaries who lose proselyting time to other activities, no matter how well-intentioned, lose the spirit and feel that something is missing in their work. The best feeling in missionary work is to come home after putting in a long day of well-used time, regardless of whether people have rejected you or invited you back, knowing that you did your best.

Small children learn languages by listening. They learn intonation and pronunciation first, then vocabulary, and grammar last of all, achieving relative fluency before they can even read or write. Most North American schools teach languages by focusing first on grammar, then vocabulary. Pronunciation is learned later, and intonation is learned last if at all. This style of teaching typically leads to a strong accent and limited conversational ability. This style reflects academic needs rather than practical utility. It is easier for instructors who may not have full mastery of the language themselves to assess spelling and grammar than evaluate pronunciation or conversational ability.

Time is much better spent learning vocabulary, phrases, and dialogues from cassettes or CDs recorded by native speakers than from written lists. Learning a word on paper does not give one the ability to pronounce or use it correctly. Hearing the words and repeating them is less mentally taxing than reading from paper and is retained better. One should repeat the words or phrases and compare one's own pronunciation and intonation to that of a native speaker. At first, it may be difficult to hear important differences in pronunciation or intonation. Learning to listen accurately is vital to achieving language mastery. Large numbers of adult speakers of other languages with severe accents demonstrate that it is often difficult to unlearn bad habits of pronunciation or intonation once they become established, and it is much more efficient to learn a language correctly from the beginning with a focus on acquiring proper pronunciation and intonation. Diligent study of the written language is vital, yet this study should occur on top of a foundation of good pronunciation and intonation from listening.

Many missions employ a Speak Your Language (SYL) policy, requiring missionaries to speak the local language among each other when out of the apartment. While such programs can have some positive benefit when appropriately employed, the foreign language discussions by two missionaries who both speak the language badly can reinforce habits of poor pronunciation, improper intonation, and erroneous phrasing that can be difficult to overcome. Jim Rohn stated: "You cannot speak that which you do not know.... You cannot translate that which you do not have. And you cannot give that which you do not possess. To give it and to share it, and for it to be effective, you first need to have it. Good communication starts with good preparation." For languages that are not as simple for English speakers to learn as are Spanish or Portuguese, few missionaries are adequately proficient to effectively mentor each other in language skills. I have often found that college students who live in an immersive environment abroad typically master the local language faster and better than most missionaries. Missionary language learning is best facilitated by a constant focus on listening in an immersive environment, with language cassettes and CDs in the apartment and consistent attention to careful listening and analysis in conversations with natives. While Book of Mormon recordings are available in few languages, the New Testament is available on cassette or on audio CD in hundreds of languages from firms such as Hosannah: Faith Comes by Hearing* and Audio Scriptures International. These audio resources allow missionaries to achieve exceptional scriptural fluency in the mission language.

On-demand multilingual news broadcasts are available online from sources including BBC World Service, Deutsche Welle, and Voice of America. Words used most frequently become a part of the user's active vocabulary, while words used less frequently become a part of one's passive vocabulary. News broadcasts generally employ practical, commonly used words that are much more useful than the specialized vocabulary of great literature. Audio news broadcasts present invaluable language learning tools for those who do not have the opportunity to constantly be around native speakers. Additionally, many broadcasts are focused on local events that shed insight into cultural issues. General audience newspapers are similarly useful. For languages such as Russian and Ukrainian with variable syllable stress and stress changes with declension, an orthographic dictionary is an essential companion to a standard dictionary to ensure that one can correctly pronounce the words one reads.

One should keep a dictionary handy and write down all unfamiliar words to look up later. Some missionaries feel that they can understand the "essence" of a conversation without understanding certain

---

* Hosannah: Faith Comes by Hearing, http://www.hosanna.org.

words. On closer questioning, I have found that those who make this claim usually did not understand or misunderstood the speaker's meaning. There is no place for bluffing one's way through a conversation. Looking up unfamiliar words goes a long way toward ensuring accurate comprehension and communication.

After the mission, it is much easier to keep up on a language than to re-learn it in later years. "It is always easier to keep up than to catch up." More young elders and sisters are needed who are already fluent in a foreign language, and older couple missionaries who are fluent and have kept up on another language can usually accomplish much more than those who do not speak the language of the country in which they serve.

Contextualizing the Gospel
to the Culture

CULTURE REQUIRES SPECIAL STUDY by foreigners to avoid misunderstandings and to present the gospel in the most relevant and appropriate ways. In his essay "On Liberty," John Stuart Mill remarked on the widely different values and assumptions of different cultures: "No two ages, and scarcely any two countries, have decided it alike; and the decision of one age or country is a wonder to another. Yet the people of any given age and country no more suspect any difficulty in it, than if it were a subject on which mankind had always been agreed. The rules which they obtain among themselves appear to them self-evident and self-justifying." The Apostle Paul recognized that different groups of people had different needs and concerns: "For the Jews require a sign, and the Greeks seek after wisdom" (1 Corinthians 1:22). He integrated an understanding of local culture and contemporary needs into his preaching and demonstrated similarities between the gospel teachings and cultural ideals in his discourse to the Athenians on Mars Hill by citing the work of Greek poets: "For in him we live, and move, and have our being; as certain also of your own poets have said, For we are also his offspring" (Acts 17:28). He wrote: "For though I be free from all men, yet have I made myself servant unto all, that I might gain the more. And unto the Jews I became as a Jew, that I might gain the Jews; to them that are under the law, as under the law, that I might gain them that are under the law; To them that are without law, as without law, (being not without law to God, but under the law to Christ,) that I might gain them that are without law. To the weak became I as weak, that I might gain the weak: I am made all things to all men, that I might by all means save some" (1 Corinthians 9:19–22).

Paul could not have tailored his message to different cultures without careful study of cultural values, priorities, and real and perceived needs. Similarly, the gospels of Matthew, Mark, Luke, and John were all directed to different audiences—Jews, Romans, Greeks, and "all the world," respectively—with each version presenting Christ's teachings and ministry in a manner most convincing and relevant to the target culture. Would the early church have experienced the same initial growth if the authors had presented the gospel message to everyone in the same fashion without regard to cultural considerations, local conditions, or personal needs? Yet Jews, Romans, and Greeks were all united under the single government of the Roman Empire. If each of these groups required a different approach to maximize receptivity, how great a need do we have today to contextualize the gospel message to the tens of thousands of people groups and cultures in over 250 nations around the world?

FIND OUT ABOUT THE PEOPLE IN YOUR COUNTRY AND AREA

Evangelist Rick Warren wrote: "Targeting for evangelism begins with finding out all you can about your community. Your church needs to define its target in four specific ways: geographically, demographically, culturally, and spiritually.... I must pay as much attention to the geography, customs, culture, and religious background of my community as I do to those who lived in Bible times if I am to faithfully communicate God's Word."* A missionary should consider: What are cultural beliefs that share common ground with the gospel? What approaches are considered to be appropriate or inappropriate within this culture? What do people consider to be their greatest needs? What cultural beliefs might present obstacles for potential investigators, and how can they effectively be addressed? When missionaries are fully aware of local needs, beliefs, and opportunities, they are able to direct their time and energies much more effectively.

CULTURAL ISSUES TODAY

Brigham Young University sociologist Lawrence Young noted: "Mormonism attempts to take the form of a community that was developed in a specific place—where the Mormon Church is one of the most powerful social actors—and to transport that community to other host societies that are not well matched."† Sociologist Tim Heaton reported that by the late 1980s, 80 percent of church growth occurred outside of the United States, and Utah accounted for only 3 percent of membership growth—overwhelmingly from baptisms of children of record rather than convert baptisms.‡ In 1987, Elder Boyd K. Packer reminded a group of Church leaders that "we can't move [into various countries] with a 1947 Utah Church! Could it be that we are not prepared to take the gospel because we are not prepared to take (and they are not prepared to receive) all of the things we have

---

* Warren, Rick, *The Purpose Driven Church*, Grand Rapids, MI: Zondervan, 1995, 150.

† Young, Lawrence A., "Confronting Turbulent Environments," in Contemporary Mormonism Social Science Perspectives, eds. Marie Cornwall, Tim Heaton, and Lawrence Young, Chicago: University of Illinois, 1994, 56–60.

‡ Heaton, Tim B., "Vital Statistics," in *Encyclopedia of Mormonism*, ed. Daniel H. Ludlow, New York: McMillen, 1992, vol. 4:1522.

wrapped up with it as extra baggage?"*

The universality of the gospel message does not eliminate the need to present this message in a culturally relevant and understandable fashion. Neither a 1947 Utah Church nor a 2007 Utah Church can be readily transplanted to other cultural settings without differentiating between the principles of the everlasting gospel and American cultural baggage. This mismatch is often perpetuated by missionary research that continues to be conducted primarily in English-speaking areas under the assumption that U.S. outreach findings will be applicable to the rest of the world because "there is one gospel is for all people." The large discrepancy between LDS convert retention in the United States (approximately 40 percent) and international areas (20 to 25 percent) suggests that LDS programs developed in North America unwittingly draw too much from the cultural setting of the American church and, at least in part, fail to tailor approaches in a fashion appropriate for other cultures and conditions.

In many nations, slow church growth has been related in part to a failure to present the gospel in a culturally relevant manner, rather than to hard-heartedness of local people. German LDS member Peter Wollauer pointed out the problems of exporting Utah-based missionary paradigms to other cultures: "German missionary work was slow for a long time because mission presidents from the United States used American methods of contacting and teaching potential converts. With more German mission presidents, stake and ward leaders 'emancipated' from U.S. leaders, the conversion rate has picked up. That does not mean that we ignore the counsel and suggestions of General Authorities, but it does mean that we feel free to find our own German and Austrian way to put these suggestions into practice."† He

---

*   Packer, Boyd K., as quoted in *Dialogue*, 21 (Fall 1988):97.

†   Stack, Peggy Fletcher, "As Mormon Church Grows, Global Challenges Arise,"

noted that all Church instruction manuals and videos are produced in the United States and are often less relevant or understandable for those of other cultures: "The videos intellectually bring the message, but emotionally there is a lack of identification—high school, problems with dating, a teaching moment in the desert. The young people are not able to feel the situation, because the school system is very different, the tradition of dating is very different, and there is no desert in Germany." Former German missionary Helmut Lotz wrote: "When I served a mission in Germany in 1985, I was called to a committee that had to review the missionary discussions for cultural adaptation... To date, the church has not even corrected the grammatical mistakes. Nor has anybody made an effort to use illustrations that would be compatible with German culture...There is no gospel reason why every Mormon needs to become half an American. Evangelicals and Pentecostals seem to adapt to non-American cultures more effectively."* Similar difficulties have been noted by members from many other cultures. In an age where increasing numbers of LDS members live outside of the United States, this transfer of Utah culture along with the gospel message may help one to understand why the LDS Church is still commonly regarded as an "American Church" by most of its own international members, even in English-speaking nations.[†]

If Utah-based materials and methodologies are less relevant in Germany, which shares Western heritage and close ties with the United States, the challenges of transplanting them into non-Western cultures are even greater. For example, the *Missionary Guide* (1986–2004) carried role-playing dialogues suggesting that approaching nonmembers with

---

Salt Lake Tribune, August 20, 1994.

*   Lotz, Hellmut, personal communication, July 14. 2004.

†   Newton, Marjorie, "Towards 2000: Mormonism in Australia," *Dialogue*, Spring 1996, 193–206.

tangential small talk and then leading into a gospel conversation was universally more effective than a direct approach. Yet as a missionary in Russia, I found that an indirect approach by strangers was often perceived as being evasive or even dishonest, while a direct approach was more effective.

The new *Preach My Gospel* manual offers no specific insights into different cultures, but it removes many of the U.S. culture-based tactics found in past editions that were unsuitable in other cultural settings and encourages missionaries to develop and use their own cultural insights rather than following a formula. Better research, careful study, and involvement of local members will be required to develop effective ways of presenting LDS beliefs in non-Western cultures and among Muslims, Hindus, Buddhists, and other non-Christians.

Principles of Finding

THE IMPORTANCE OF FINDING

I T HAS BEEN SAID that almost anyone can teach a truly "golden investigator" but that finding such investigators in the first place is much more challenging. Missionary Department studies estimate that finding represents at least two-thirds of missionary work. Elder Dallin H. Oaks stated that the average LDS missionary in North America spends only nine hours per week teaching investigators.* Teaching skills and many other elements of missionary preparation often do not even come into play until missionaries have found investigators willing to listen to their message. Missionary success therefore depends greatly upon correct understanding and diligent implementation of principles of finding.

The most notable distinction between great missionaries such as Dan Jones, Brigham Young, Wilford Woodruff, Paul, the Sons of Mosiah, and less effective missionaries is not in their teaching program, but in their finding program. Effective missionaries reach vast numbers of people by utilizing every opportunity to share the gospel. Whether in receptive or resistant areas, missionaries who understand and apply correct finding principles can multiply their effectiveness.

---

* Oaks, Dallin A., "The Role of Members in Conversion," *Ensign*, March 2003.

REACHING EVERY SOUL FOR CHRIST

The Savior commanded His disciples: "Go ye into all the world and preach the gospel to every creature" (Mark 16:15). Those who accept the baptism covenant "stand as witnesses of God at all times and in all things, and in all places" (Mosiah 18:9). The Doctrine and Covenants contains numerous admonitions to open our mouths about the gospel at all times (D&C 19:29, 24:10, 28:16, 30:5, 30:11, 33:8–11, 61:3, 71:1, 80:3). The Lord instructs us: "go … from house to house"(99:1), "search diligently [for receptive people] and spare not" (84:94), "thrust in your sickle" (31:5), "deliver [His] words" (5:6), "[do not] hide the talent"(60:2), "bear testimony in every place" (66:7, also 58:47,59), "publish it upon the mountains" (19:29), "lift up your voice" (34:6), "labor in the vineyard" (50:38), "speak freely to all" (19:37), "warn the people" (88:81), "declare glad tidings" (31:3), and "go and proclaim my everlasting gospel with a loud voice, and with great joy" (124:88). The New Testament, Book of Mormon, and Doctrine and Covenants all teach that the opportunity to accept or reject the gospel must be presented to all people. Christ taught that the task of reaching each soul with the gospel must be approached urgently because of the limited time available: "But when they persecute you in this city, flee ye into another: for verily I say unto you, Ye shall not have gone over the cities of Israel, till the Son of man be come" (Matthew 10:23).

Modern prophets have reaffirmed our scriptural mandate to reach each soul with the gospel message. Joseph Smith taught that the responsibility to open our mouths will not be discharged until the gospel trump has sounded in every ear and "the great Jehovah says, 'the work is done.'"* David O. McKay stated: "The best means

---

*   Burton, Alma P., *Discourses of the Prophet Joseph Smith*, Salt Lake City, UT:

of preaching the gospel is by personal contact."* Ezra Taft Benson declared: "We are to take the gospel to every person. Without exception, without excuse, without rationalization, we are to go 'unto all the world and preach the gospel to every creature'" (Mormon 9:22).[†] Gordon B. Hinckley stated: "It is wonderful what we can do as we practice a little ingenuity. You ought to take advantage of every opportunity in the world to speak with people about why we are there and what we are doing and give them some taste of a gospel message."[‡] Elder Tingey instructed missionaries: "Speak to everyone: shopkeepers, passengers riding buses, people on streets, and everyone you meet."[§]

ACTUAL PERFORMANCE VERSUS THE DIVINE STANDARD

While the admonitions to "open our mouths," "lift up our voice," and "thrust in our sickle" by speaking with others about the gospel at all times are the most frequent instructions on missionary work found in the scriptures, the implementation of these scriptural mandates is the rare exception rather than the rule. Missionaries I have surveyed in numerous U.S. missions reported spending an average of less than five hours per week tracting or finding through their own efforts, even though most had fewer than five active investigators. As a missionary in Russia, I was shocked when the mission president stated after collecting contacting data from missionaries that the average missionary was approaching only five to ten new people each day. In 1999, only 2 to 4 percent of people I surveyed in two Eastern European capitals

---

Deseret Book, 1977, 172.

*   McKay, David O., *Conference Report*, October 1969.

†   Benson, Ezra Taft, Regional Representatives' Seminar, April 5, 1985.

‡   Hinckley, Gordon B., *LDS Church News*, July 4, 1998.

§   Tingey, Earl C., *Ensign*, May 1998.

reported ever being approached by Latter-day Saints or "Mormon" missionaries. Over 70 percent reported being personally approached by Jehovah's Witnesses, often multiple times. Many LDS missionaries felt that they had all the time in the world to eke a handful of referrals out of a few new members, while the Jehovah's Witnesses and other more rapidly growing faiths recognized the urgency of reaching large numbers of people quickly.

While I have occasionally found missions where the majority of missionaries are contacting large numbers of people daily, I have more frequently found that missionaries are approaching only a fraction of the number that one would reasonably expect from those whose full-time obligation is to share the gospel. One wonders how receptive nonmembers are to experience conversion when little effort is being made to offer them the gospel. Paul asked, "How will they believe in him of whom they have not heard? And how shall they hear without a preacher?" (Romans 10:14–15). The Lord declared: "With some I am not well pleased, for they will not open their mouths, but they hide the talent which I have given unto them, because of the fear of man. Woe unto such, for mine anger is kindled against them" (D&C 60:2). Full-time missionaries represent the church's primary mechanism of growth. When missionaries are not meeting their scriptural duties to "open their mouths" in all places and at all times, many souls are lost, and church growth is stunted.

I have found little awareness of low contacting rates. Of the hundreds of missionaries and dozens of mission presidents I have interviewed about growth problems in poorly productive areas, external factors such as materialism, atheism, local culture, and anti-Mormon activity have been repeatedly cited. In contrast, not one has cited low missionary contacting rates as a major cause of slow growth. While it should seem obvious that missionaries who contact only a handful of people each day are unlikely to be very successful, the number of individuals approached by missionaries each day— perhaps the most essential single statistical indicator of missionary effort—has traditionally not been recorded or reported at all. Many mission leaders with little involvement in frontline missionary activities assume that missionaries are making far more contacts than is actually the case. In recent years, directives to increase time spent with members and inactives have resulted in fewer convert baptisms since missionaries have spent less time approaching nonmembers about the gospel. Such directives have further decreased awareness of low contacting rates and have made it easier for missionaries to rationalize feeble contacting efforts.

ARE PEOPLE UNRECEPTIVE?

The idea that people are less receptive to the LDS church than to other proselytizing denominations is a common rationalization for slow growth. My analysis strongly suggests the opposite. Data reported by Jehovah's Witnesses[*] and by numerous evangelical denominations[†] suggests that these other faiths typically have to provide tens of thousands or even hundreds of thousands of exposures and thousands of proselyting hours to make a single convert. My research suggests that the number of total nonmembers contacted about the gospel per conversion in most LDS missions is in the low thousands and sometimes far less. While the methodologies may be slightly different, the response rate to the message of the restored gospel is one of the highest reported for any denomination, opposition to the Church

---

[*]   Jehovah's Witness Annual Statistical Reports, http://www.watchtower.org/statistics/worldwide_report.htm.

[†]   Barrett, David and Todd Johnson, World Christian Trends, William Carey Library, 2001.

notwithstanding. This higher receptivity is the result of the true message of the restored gospel, the confirmation of the Holy Spirit, and an enthusiastic missionary force.

In most areas, LDS difficulties finding people to teach reflect poor member and missionary effort far more than any lack of local receptivity. Only 3 to 5 percent of active LDS members in North America are regularly involved in missionary work,[*] and just 26 percent of Latter-day Saints report engaging in a gospel conversation with a nonmember within the past year.[†]

Contacting is the lifeblood of missions. There is no missionary mandate in scripture more frequently repeated than the command to "open your mouth at all times" and to sound the gospel in every ear, yet LDS missionary contacting efforts in many areas are surprisingly low. As a missionary in Russia in the early 1990s, I found that foreign evangelical preachers with no knowledge of the local language could consistently achieve high attendance at their meetings, while many LDS missionaries proficient in the local language struggled to get one or two investigators to church each week. Some argued that evangelicals experienced greater success because of lower standards and that little was required of members of many churches beyond mere attendance. Yet attendance represents an obligatory first step, and most of the commonly cited "higher standards" of the LDS faith—tithing, the Word of Wisdom, and so forth—were not officially even brought up until after investigators had already completed several discussions and were committed to baptism. Nor can public opinion be cited as a major factor: most Russians at that time did not know

---

[*]   M. Russell Ballard, Conversion and Retention Satellite Broadcast, August 29, 1999.

[†]   Barna, George, "Protestants, Catholics and Mormons Reflect Diverse Levels of Religious Activity," *Barna Research Update*, July 9, 2001, http://www.barna.org.

"Mormons" apart from any other foreign religious group. A year later, an enlightening survey conducted by my mission president found that the average missionary was approaching an average of only five people per day about the gospel. While there were many excuses for poor contacting, most missionaries abdicated responsibility for the finding process to members instead of putting forth the effort to contact large numbers of people on their own.

I have since conducted surveys of nonmembers in various cities of Eastern Europe and the United States and have found that surprisingly few people report ever being approached by LDS missionaries, even in areas with a large missionary presence. My surveys of missionaries in most areas have found daily contacting rates that are remarkably low, far below the 50 to 200 contacts a day that I found necessary to sustain productivity as a missionary. Most missionaries consider contacting an undesirable chore to do when they have "nothing else to do," and many fill in schedules with "make-work" visits to members and stagnant investigators in order to avoid contacting whenever possible. Interviews with missionaries demonstrate that many expect an unrealistically large percentage of those they contact to accept the gospel and are disappointed when dramatic results are not achieved with little effort.

Christ taught that the task of outreach is urgent and that spending large amounts of time with the unreceptive cannot be justified while the ripe harvest remains unreaped: "But when they persecute you in this city, flee ye into another: for verily I say unto you, Ye shall not have gone over the cities of Israel, till the Son of man be come" (Matthew 10:23). The Apostle Paul taught, "He which soweth sparingly shall reap also sparingly; and he which soweth bountifully shall also reap bountifully" (2 Corinthians 9:6). "How shall they hear without a preacher?" he asked (Romans 10:15). The scant sowing of the gospel seed is a primary cause of slow growth in many LDS missions. Many other faiths have experienced more rapid growth because they understand the need to contact many thousands or tens of thousands to make a single proselyte, while many LDS missionaries and members expect miraculous results with token effort.

A MESSAGE FOR ALL THE WORLD

As new missionaries, my companion and I prayed fervently to know where we should tract. We yearned sincerely for the Lord to lead us to the "right door," yet we did not receive any specific direction. While we were working hard to be fully dedicated and obedient and were blessed to find and teach some wonderful converts, we felt that something was missing. Where did we go wrong?

As a new missionary, I was guilty of the same misunderstanding as Oliver Cowdery, thinking that the Lord would enlighten me through the Spirit while taking little thought except to ask (D&C 9). I had overlooked the Lord's words spoken to elders preaching the gospel early in this dispensation: "Go ye and preach my gospel, whether to the north or to the south, to the east or to the west, it mattereth not, for ye cannot go amiss" (D&C 80:3). I quickly came to understand that the Lord expected me to knock on every door and present the opportunity to hear the gospel message to all people and not just to a select few that I felt especially prompted to approach.

As we worked tirelessly, contacting one hundred or more people each day, the Spirit came in a measure I had never felt while on my knees, and missionary successes multiplied. I have consistently found that the Spirit is often received only after we put forth the faith to share the gospel. While prayer is vital, its primary role is not to determine to whom we should offer opportunities to hear the gospel.

Most of us are unable to discern ahead of time who will be ready to receive the gospel message. Assumptions that missionaries and members should be able to do so are out of harmony with scriptural mandates that every soul is to be reached with the Good News. Those who accepted the gospel were rarely individuals that I felt a burning spiritual impression to approach or with whom I had particularly memorable initial conversations. They were simply those who put forth the effort to nourish a seed of faith when others did not.

Many members and missionaries are overly concerned with finding the perfect plot of soil to plant their few seeds in and dedicate much effort to attempts to alter the nature of the soil instead of planting more seeds. The Parable of the Sower teaches that the selection process occurs once seeds have been abundantly sown and not by the sower choosing to plant only a few seeds (Matthew 13).

All people are entitled to an opportunity to hear the Lord's words. The selection process is to occur in the heart of the hearer and not in the mind of the sharer. Our role is to knock into all the doors, to reach all people, and to offer the gospel message universally. Who accepts the gospel message is in God's hands. Any goal short of providing all people with an opportunity to accept or reject this message is unsatisfactory.

A VISION FOR THE UNREACHED

The Lord declared that "this is a day of warning, and not a day of many words" (D&C 63:58). Many less effective missionaries contact few new people each day while repeatedly visiting a few friendly but lukewarm investigators who have read little in the Book of Mormon and are not regularly attending church. Such missionaries often express touching emotions about the deep responsibility they feel to give their nonprogressing investigators yet another chance, yet seem to feel little if any responsibility toward the countless individuals whom they have never presented with a single opportunity to learn about the gospel at all. Great inequity exists when a few noncommittal individuals are allowed to monopolize vast amounts of missionary time, while millions of others have never been offered the opportunity to hear the gospel message. It is natural to feel strong emotional ties to individuals we have worked with and prayed for, but greater perspective is required to maintain a sense of responsibility toward those we have not yet met.

Successful missionaries maintain a constant vision of responsibility to the unreached. Every activity, whether meeting with members or returning to visit nonprogressing investigators, is carefully weighed against the opportunity to meet fresh contacts. They schedule several hours of contacting time daily, regardless of how busy they may be with other activities. The burning desire to offer the gospel message as widely as possible overrides the desires of the "natural man."

THE PRINCIPLE OF SELF-SELECTION

In areas of exceptional receptivity, many missionaries find that time limitations seemingly do not allow them to teach all of those who are willing to accept visits with conventional approaches. Under such circumstances, missionaries often make arbitrary decisions about who to teach. Many missionaries become saturated with low-yield visits while receptive individuals remain untaught. In these cases, the limiting factor in Church growth is not the lack of receptive individuals in the community but the time management skills and work ethic of the missionaries. A missionary who does not understand when it is time to move on will never be able to bring large numbers of quality converts into the Church regardless of local receptivity.

Many ineffective missionaries require prospective investigators to demonstrate commitment rather than effort as a prerequisite for initial or ongoing teaching. Missionaries serving in some areas of Latin America would drop investigators if they were not ready to accept baptism within two weeks of the first contact. Many educated and contemplative investigators were abandoned by missionaries in favor of more impulsive individuals who were willing to accept baptism quickly but experienced high rates of relapse and inactivity. Instead of building a strong core of committed members, this practice fostered revolving door patterns of quick baptism followed by almost immediate inactivity. There is no scriptural basis for the expectation that quality investigators should be ready to accept baptism within an arbitrary period, only that they put forth continuing effort to learn, study, and implement gospel principles. In some Eastern European missions experiencing an initial wave of receptivity, arbitrary guidelines were imposed requiring that individuals attend church, often several times, before they could even receive a copy of the Book of Mormon. Without an opportunity to read and understand God's word, a sincere investigator would have no reason to demonstrate denominational commitment to the LDS Church any more than to the numerous other faiths that provided religious literature more accessibly.

In view of the eternal importance of the gospel message, the decision of who to teach out of many potentially receptive people cannot be rightly based on arbitrary factors. We must ensure that threshold self-selection criteria represent reasonable expectations of the pure in heart and are not unscriptural or unfair.

The key to the appropriate allocation of missionary resources lies in the scriptural principle of self-selection: "Mine elect hear my voice, and harden not their hearts" (D&C 29:7). Instead of taking it into one's own hands to decide who is "prepared" to receive God's word, the effective missionary makes the gospel message widely available and invites receptive individuals to participate in activities that can lead to teaching, such as attending church and reading in the Book of Mormon. Investigators who continue to put forth independent effort to attend church and study the Book of Mormon should be worked with patiently, even over prolonged periods, since these gospel habits eventually lead to conversion in the large majority of cases. Some of the strongest mission converts I correspond with are individuals who studied the Book of Mormon and attended church for several months before making the decision to join. The effective missionary does not place deadlines on conversion. Rather, he focuses on helping investigators to develop the habits of daily scripture reading, church attendance, and obedience to other gospel laws that allow the conversion process to occur by facilitating a change of heart through the spirit.

Individuals who do not demonstrate a willingness to attend church and are not diligent in studying the scriptures should not continue to be taught but should be invited to attend church or contact the missionaries when they are willing to study the gospel more earnestly. Those without root or depth of soil sort themselves out, placing the responsibility for selection on the investigator instead of the missionary.

Learning when to let go of those who are not ready to receive the gospel and move on is an essential element of missionary maturation, as is the recognition that moving on from a nonprogressing investigator does not represent a final judgment on him or her and does not close the door to future opportunities. In our desire to give one more chance to a recalcitrant soul who is progressing slowly if at all, we must not lose the vision of our divine mandate to reach those yet unreached. By making the gospel message widely available and letting the faithful manifest themselves through their actions, scriptural self-selection practices ensure that missionaries spend their time teaching the most receptive individuals. This results in more committed, higher quality converts, maximizing the benefit to both the investigator and the Church.

Rick Warren wrote: "It is a waste of time to fish in a spot where the fish aren't biting. Wise fishermen move on. They understand that fish feed in different spots at different times of the day. Nor are they hungry all the time. This is the principle of receptivity.... At certain times, unbelievers are more responsive to spiritual truths than at other times. This receptivity often lasts only briefly, which is why Jesus said to go where the people would listen. Take advantage of the responsive hearts that the Holy Spirit prepares. Notice Jesus' instructions in Matthew 10:14 (NCV): 'If a home or town refuses to welcome you or listen to you, leave that place ...' This is a very significant statement that we shouldn't ignore. Jesus told the disciples they were not supposed to stay around unresponsive people. We aren't supposed to pick green fruit, but to find the ripe fruit and harvest it."* He further stated: "Is it good stewardship to continue badgering someone who has already rejected Christ a dozen times when there is a whole community of receptive people waiting to hear the gospel for the first time?... The apostle Paul's strategy was to go through open doors and not waste time banging on closed ones. Likewise, we should not focus our efforts on those who aren't ready to listen. There are far more people in the world who are ready to receive Christ than there are believers ready to witness to them."

UNDERSTANDING THE ROLES
OF FINDING METHODS

Under "Finding," the white LDS *Missionary Handbook* states: "The

---

* Warren, Rick, *The Purpose Driven Church*, Grand Rapids, MI: Zondervan, 1995, 187–88.

most effective sources of finding are members and investigators. Plan to use these and the following sources (listed in order of effectiveness). 1. Recent converts. 2. Baptismal services. 3. Stake missionaries' contacts with members and nonmembers. 4. Part-member families. 5. Members in general. 6. Former investigators. 7. Current investigators (referral dialogue). 8. Media, visitors' centers, and Church headquarters referrals. 9. Activation efforts (unknown address file). 10. Service activities. 11. New move-ins. 12. Special interest contacts. 13. Tracting. 14. Street contacting. 15. Speaking with everyone."

From the time they enter the Missionary Training Center, missionaries are repeatedly taught that finding activities based on their own efforts are the very least effective, weighing in at numbers eleven through fifteen. Not surprisingly, many missionaries quickly come to believe that their success at finding people to teach depends little upon their own initiative or effort. Many individuals cite the preceding list as rationalization for neglect of repeated scriptural admonitions to open their mouths about the gospel at all times.

Results are often widely discrepant with the sweeping claims of effectiveness presented in this list. Many missionaries achieve far greater success through tracting and street contacting than by soliciting referrals from members; others find reactivation efforts and service projects less fruitful than their own contacting efforts. Over 98 percent of baptisms on my mission came from tracting or street contacting, since there were few members from whom to solicit referrals. A heavy reliance on member referrals may produce acceptable results in areas such as Utah with very high member to missionary ratios and high member involvement but fails to produce similar results in nations without such favorable ratios. Conversely, street contacting and local media efforts that produce dramatic response in some newly opened areas of the world where few individuals have had an opportunity to hear the gospel may not generate such exuberant responses in areas of Western Europe or North America that have been saturated with evangelistic messages of different faiths for decades.

MEASURING THE EFFECTIVENESS OF FINDING METHODS

Elder Dallin H. Oaks reported that "of investigators found through media campaigns, about 1 to 2 percent are baptized. Of investigators found through the missionaries' efforts, about 2 to 3 percent are baptized. Of investigators found through the members, 20 to 30 percent are baptized."[*] This is valuable information, although it is based on North American studies that cannot be extrapolated to other areas. Many international missions experience baptism rates well above the 2 to 3 percent U.S. rate for investigators found by the missionaries' efforts.

Some individuals point to such data to justify missionary finding programs that consist exclusively of soliciting referrals from members. Since member referrals are ten times as likely to be baptized as those found through the missionary efforts, they argue why even bother with other contacting methods at all? Why not concentrate missionary finding efforts soliciting referrals from members rather than dissipating effort on tasks with only a fraction of the yield?

While such reasoning may sound appealing, it is erroneous. These data are helpful in assessing teaching success rates once referrals are in hand, but they do not consider the average amount of time necessary to obtain referrals or establish an investigator in the first place and therefore do not answer the question of what finding method is the most effective.

Most missionaries I have surveyed cite an average of at least seven

---

[*]   Oaks, Dallin A., "The Role of Members in Conversion," *Ensign*, March 2003.

to ten member visits to obtain a single referral, and sometimes far more. When visitation and travel time are included, the amount of time needed to procure a single member referral is considerable. Nor are all referrals of the same quality: some members give referrals to the missionaries without the individuals' permission or knowledge, with success rates that are little better than those of "cold call" street contacts, while other members provide better quality referrals. Since only a fraction of individuals referred by members become active investigators, the amount of missionary time needed to generate a single investigator from member referrals is typically much greater than is recognized. Because hundreds of street contacts can usually be made in the time it takes to obtain a single member referral—let alone an investigator—and because success at soliciting referrals is unpredictable, the effectiveness of working through member referrals and street or tracting contacts cannot be validly compared at an individual level.

When measuring the effectiveness of finding approaches, results must be assessed per unit time, rather than per contact. If it takes ten member visits requiring ninety minutes each when travel time is included to obtain a single member referral and one referral in five becomes an investigator, it would take seventy-five hours of missionary time to generate one investigator from member referrals. If one can contact thirty people in an hour by tracting or street contacting, over two thousand individuals can be contacted in the average time needed to obtain a single investigator from member referrals. Even if only one individual in one hundred contacted became an investigator, the missionaries' time in this example is far more effectively used contacting nonmembers through their own efforts rather than visiting members to solicit referrals. The precise figures vary in different areas, but careful analysis often favors the missionaries' own finding efforts over member visits to solicit referrals without prior leads.

Contacting may seem less productive because it involves speaking with many people at a low response rate and because the near-constant rejection is emotionally taxing. The natural psychological bias against contacting results in a strong tendency to underestimate results from contacting efforts and to overestimate results of referral solicitation. Except in areas with overwhelming member to missionary ratios, the mental gymnastics invoked by many to rationalize a primary or exclusive focus on member visits as the basis of finding efforts typically do not result from an unbiased evaluation of the data, but from a desire to avoid the hard work and rejection of contacting in favor of more comfortable activities.

The scriptural mandate of reaching every soul with the gospel message deserves independent consideration in every finding program. Even if the productivity of tracting or street contacting efforts and working through member referrals were the same, the independent contacting efforts would be preferable because they offer exposure to the gospel message to hundreds or thousands of people in the time that would offer such opportunities to only one or a few individuals when working through member referrals. It cannot be surprising that missions where missionaries choose to do little independent contacting typically fall far short of their growth potential. Greatly increased productivity is achieved when one abandons the mindset that contacting is an undesirable task to be done when there is "nothing else to do" and reorients one's thinking to focus on the divine mandate to reach every soul in one's area and to reach them repeatedly.

THE VALUE OF CONTACTING
FOR CHURCH GROWTH

President David O. McKay taught that "the best means of preaching the gospel is by personal contact,"* yet many missionaries and even some mission leaders insist that missionary contacting efforts are so ineffective as to scarcely be worth the bother. It seems unfortunate that the value of independent missionary finding efforts continues to be controversial. Some missionaries express the deterministic view that God will inevitably guide the elect into His Church, regardless of member or missionary effort. Scriptures flatly contradict such erroneous beliefs and teach that the effort put forth by members and missionaries to share the gospel makes a tremendous difference in the lives of nonmembers and in the growth of the Church.

While some converts possess a high degree of discernment and insight and might perhaps come into the Church under any circumstances, for most the road to membership is more situational than theological. Most converts had not embarked on a systematic search to find the one true Church but accepted an invitation from a missionary or member when they felt something important was missing from their lives. The divine word rang true, and they received their own spiritual witness of the restored gospel as they exercised faith and made sacrifices.

The value of independent missionary contacting efforts can be appreciated by examining areas where such efforts are not permitted. In the Ukraine Donetsk mission, local law allowed proselytizing in Donetsk and Kharkov but prohibited foreign missionaries from approaching nonmembers without invitation in Dnipropetrovsk, where missionaries relied on strongly emphasized member-missionary efforts to

---

*   McKay, David O., Conference Report, October 1969.

find investigators. All cities had a similar missionary complement throughout their early histories. In 2001, there were approximately 700 members each in Donetsk and Kharkhov, the two cities allowing missionary outreach, and only 250 members in Dnipropetrovsk.

In Minsk, Belarus, there were about 150 active members in 1994, when contacting by full-time missionaries was prohibited. Since that time, investigators have been found almost exclusively through member referrals. In 2001, there were approximately twenty full-time LDS missionaries in Minsk, but still only about 150 active members. Although well over one hundred man-years of full-time LDS missionary labor had been expended in Minsk during this period, Church growth was slow, and existing members were lost to inactivity nearly as fast as new converts were baptized. In both Minsk and Dnipropetrovsk, finding programs based exclusively on member referrals resulted in drastically stunted growth compared to that which occurred in other areas where missionaries found investigators both through their own efforts and through referrals, even though independent missionary contacting efforts in the latter areas were far from optimal. Many other case studies could be cited demonstrating similar results.

Advocates of finding through member referrals alone frequently cite the example of Utah missions. Utah missions have among the highest annual baptism rates in the United States, with the overwhelming majority of baptisms coming from member referrals. Proponents conveniently neglect to mention that the three Utah missions encompass less than 1 percent of the LDS missionary force but draw referrals from more than 1.7 million LDS members in Utah, representing one-seventh of the world LDS population, as well as benefiting from the Church's foremost tourist attractions. Utah experiences an average of only 1.5 convert baptisms per ward per year, well below the world LDS average. This represents an annual growth rate of 0.2 to 0.5 percent when baptisms of member children and move-ins are subtracted. Relative to the number of members, Utah member-missionary efforts are among the least effective in the world.

Some also support member-only finding methods by citing the spectacular Church growth in Mongolia in spite of restrictions on contacting. Research demonstrates a high degree of spontaneous interest, with many self-referrals spontaneously requesting teaching or baptism. Such growth patterns do not reflect poorly on contacting, since there has been no opportunity for direct local comparison, but rather reflect circumstances of exceptional receptivity under which almost any kind of finding effort would be successful. While missionaries in highly receptive areas sometimes find more abundant teaching opportunities than their time management skills allow them to utilize, such remarkable levels of spontaneous interest cannot be extrapolated to other cultures.

Low growth rates are understandable in situations where contacting is not permitted by law and missionaries are working as diligently as they can under local conditions. However, stunted growth is much less acceptable in the far larger number of cases where missionaries have wide freedom to contact but choose not to fully utilize the opportunities that the Lord has provided.

LIMITED VERSUS UNLIMITED METHODS

Finding methods that depend on the referrals of others are intrinsically limited. In contrast, the potential of contacting is virtually unlimited and is restricted only by the missionaries' work ethic and motivation. I have repeatedly been surprised at how many missionaries and mission presidents, even in areas with few members, expect the local members to bear almost the entire burden of finding people to teach without effective independent missionary finding methods.

Missionary productivity has progressively declined in spite of greatly increased time spent soliciting member referrals. Only a small minority of active LDS members have made any attempt to start a gospel conversation with a nonmember over the past year in spite of frequent missionary exhortations. In most areas, it is not feasible for hard-working missionaries to occupy their time productively working through referral sources alone. Members, new converts, and investigators should certainly be asked for referrals, but this can often be done efficiently at church meetings or other scheduled activities with telephone follow-up, without having to divert vast amounts of time away from scripturally mandated outreach activities.

OPTIMIZING FINDING PROGRAMS

Which finding method is best? Finding through members? Contacting? Working through media? Given the wide discrepancy in results among the same methods in different areas, or even among similar categories implemented in different ways, the only tenable answer is that the effectiveness of an approach depends on local circumstances and that the "best" approach varies among areas. Any generalization that one method is always "more effective" than another conveys a misunderstanding of the dynamics of finding methods. It would seem foolish to ask a carpenter whether the hammer, the saw, or the measuring tape is the best tool. All of these tools have different uses, and the carpenter who goes through his career using only a single tool will encounter many difficulties not experienced by those who know how to utilize a variety of tools for their most appropriate functions. It is a disservice to claim that certain finding methods are categorically "more effective" or "less effective," rather than teaching the underlying principles by which each finding method can be optimally employed.

Most missionaries have strong views about which finding methods are more or less "effective," yet have little or no training on how to implement each method most effectively. Sweeping claims that one finding method is always more effective than another only obscure the reality that there are more and less effective ways to implement any given finding method and that different methods are complementary rather than conflicting when properly implemented. One can make frequent and lengthy visits to members' homes to solicit referrals, or one can speak to members individually at church and telephone during the week to follow-up or drop by when already in the area. One can stand passively by a park display or sign board waiting for someone to approach, or one can boldly approach passersby.

Nearly a century ago, President B. H. Roberts observed: "If tracting is the backbone of missionary work, how is it that we do not have some treatise or instruction on the subject, some manual; or some definite course of training in it? There was no answer to the question except to confess to the neglect of the subject; and that, of course, was no answer."* Today, modern missionary manuals offer little insight into such basic topics.

PRINCIPLES OF FINDING

With unlimited needs and limited resources, good stewardship requires not only that we share the gospel regularly, but that we also employ the best approaches in the most effective fashion. Effective missionaries use a balance of finding approaches, although the optimal balance depends greatly upon local circumstances. Each finding method has a valuable role, and each method can be employed in effective or ineffective ways. The real question is not whether to

---

*   Roberts, Brigham H., "On Tracting," circa 1920.

find through members, through one's own finding efforts, or through media, as all are needed, but how to employ each approach most effectively. Attention must be given not only to choosing the optimal finding methods for local conditions, but also to implementing each finding method as effectively as possible.

There are no substitutes for hard work and creativity. The innovative missionary enthusiastically applies a variety of finding methods and modifies approaches based on observations and results. Here are some principles to consider in determining how and when to best employ each finding technique.

TIME UTILIZATION AND PLANNING

Every missionary should allocate daily time for finding and contacting, regardless of how busy he is teaching discussions and visiting members. This principle is crucial to long-term missionary success. One should never think in terms of filling up one's schedule, but in terms of reaching souls. Priorities and approaches must be reconsidered if missionaries are spending less than 80 percent of work hours contacting and teaching the gospel face to face. Meetings, personal errands, and other nonproselyting activities provide no one with the opportunity to hear the gospel.

In an era when missionaries are taught from official sources that their own efforts are the least productive of all finding methods and some believe that contacting is so unproductive as to almost not be worth bothering with at all, it is easy for many to avoid contacting by filling schedules with additional member visits and trips to old investigators who fail to keep commitments. Missionaries who shirk scriptural mandates in this fashion fall far short of their potential. The litany of rationalizations and false philosophies many contrive in attempts to excuse themselves from scriptural contacting obligations defies both reason and inspiration.

Finding methods should be scheduled in a complementary fashion at the times when each is most effective. Some finding methods are more effective at some times than others or are only available at certain times. An overreliance on one or two methods frequently results in finding missionaries wasting time when their finding method of choice is not available. Street or park contacting is usually most productive during the day, but much less effective at night, and is often slightly more effective on weekends when families are together and individuals are less rushed. Tracting has low yield during business hours, but a higher yield in the evenings and on weekends when families are home. Member visits are best scheduled so that they do not take missionaries off the streets during prime proselyting and teaching time when nonmember families are home. The holiday season in Christian nations provides special opportunities for presenting messages about the Savior. Schedules for free English lessons for international college students are often best attended during the school year.

Some finding methods offer the predictable opportunity to approach many people about the gospel in a short time, while others require far more time to make a single contact and are less predictable. Some approaches require significant advance planning, while others do not. Media efforts, community presentations, family history workshops, and so forth can be effective with appropriate planning and preparation. Tracting and street contacting can be done almost anywhere with little preparation or notice and make excellent backups when teaching plans fall through.

RESPONSE PATTERNS

Different audiences experience varying patterns of responsiveness to finding methods. When my companion and I tracted in Russia, most people who let us in for conversation were young or middle-aged. When we placed church invitations in several thousand apartment mailboxes, the average age of church visitors the next week was significantly older. Elderly people, who were often reluctant to open their doors to strangers, responded better to invitations they could read and study on their own, while younger people usually responded better to personal contact. Broad societal outreach requires the implementation of complementary finding methods, each of which is most effective at reaching a specific audience.

GEOGRAPHIC CONSTRAINTS

Finding methods face geographic considerations. Most residences can be reached by tracting, although locked apartment buildings and gated communities create limitations. Street contacting is most effective in high traffic areas such as parks or metro stations, but varying governmental policies in different nations allow missionary contacting in some locations while restricting it in others.

Finding methods and locations also affect contact distribution. Missionaries serving in central areas of large cities often find that many individuals contacted in public areas live remotely, leading to greater follow-up travel time or requiring referrals to be passed off to missionaries in other areas. Tracting often offers geographic advantages because most individuals live where they are contacted, and travel time can be economized by tracting through adjacent areas. When tracting contacts do not keep an appointment, time can be used to stop by on other contacts or investigators in the same area or to continue tracting nearby.

SATURATION AND DIMINISHING RETURNS

Directives to spend more time soliciting referrals from members and less time contacting nonmembers are based on the untested assumption that spending twice the time with members will generate twice the number of referrals. Both field data and an analysis of referral dynamics suggest that this assumption is inaccurate. Missionaries today spend more time than ever working with members, yet the percentage of a cross-section of U.S. investigators being taught as a result of member referrals fell from 42 percent in 1987 to 20 percent in 1997.[*] Most full-time missionaries spend dozens of hours each month visiting members, participating in missionary dinner appointments, and soliciting member referrals in other ways, but the average North American LDS congregation produces only two member referrals each month.

Except in areas where the member base is extremely large, attempts to solicit member referrals reach a point of saturation and diminishing returns, meaning that incremental effort results in a progressively smaller increase in the number of referrals received. Even diligent members who are good referral sources eventually run out of fresh leads, while the majority of members never provide a referral, no matter how frequently missionaries visit. While much can be done to improve member finding effectiveness, this depends much more upon the presence of an effective member-missionary program in the local congregation than on missionary visits. Every effort should be made to solicit referrals that are easily obtainable, yet care should be taken to ensure that member visits do not detract from primary proselyting

---

[*]   Ballard, M. Russell, "Members Are the Key," *Ensign*, September 2000.

responsibilities without producing corresponding practical results. The precise point of saturation depends on number of members (active and inactive making varying contributions) and the relative obedience to the gospel and motivation of the members. Saturable finding methods are most helpful when combined with a balance of other finding approaches, but typically produce suboptimal results when used as the main or sole finding method.

In contrast to referral-based finding, tracting and street contacting are unsaturable except in very small towns, with two to three times the effort typically generating two to three times as many contacts. Such unsaturable finding methods generate linear returns that are limited only by the missionaries' work ethic and should represent the primary finding method in most areas.

Programs that directly involve missionaries or members in sharing the gospel with nonmembers almost always produce superior results to indirect methods that involve merely exhorting others to do so. Effective finding programs make the gospel message available to large numbers of people on a consistent basis, fulfilling the gospel mandate to sound the gospel in every ear. It is usually much more effective to make large numbers of fresh contacts each day than to dedicate large amounts of time to visits attempting to solicit referrals. It is more effective to mentor members in sharing the gospel on splits or in teaching situations than to exhort them to share the gospel over dinner.

PROCESS IMPROVEMENT

One should work hard, listen to the spirit, and evaluate progress objectively and regularly. Missionaries should set reasonable expectations and realize that rejection is the most common response at every step. Nonetheless, one should not persist in approaches that are not effective after adequate trials. Effective missionaries use ingenuity and try new finding methods that they feel are more likely to be successful than their current ones. If an approach is not working, they determine why, modify the approach as needed, and reevaluate later for fine-tuning.

CONTACTING GOALS

While contacting is hard work and involves near constant rejection, I have repeatedly found that missionary success over the course of a mission is determined more by the number of people contacted each day than by any other single factor. Paul taught: "He which soweth sparingly shall reap also sparingly; and he which soweth bountifully shall also reap bountifully" (2 Corinthians 9:6). The habit of approaching at least one hundred new people each day about the gospel is perhaps the most vital single trait that a missionary can acquire.

Even at return rates per contact that seem extremely low, contacting can still be a very effective church growth tool when missionaries and their leaders have the vision and discipline to make consistently large numbers of gospel contacts. My companion and I had to contact over one thousand people to find a single individual who was ready to join the Church, yet we averaged one baptism per week for the last eight months of my mission because we contacted 100 to 200 people each day. Jim Rohn taught: "This little equation, when understood and acted upon, is perhaps the most powerful equation there is in regards to long-term achievement and accomplishment.... Your short-term actions multiplied by time equals your long-term accomplishments." Just as the spiritual benefits of daily scripture reading may be barely perceptible after a few sessions but accrue to great levels over time, the results of diligent daily contacting may not be obvious in one week or even one month but become vast over sustained periods.

With the possible exception of particularly resistant areas of Western Europe, low contacting effort is almost always a major cause of poor missionary success. Almost any missionary companionship willing to put forth adequate effort can contact one hundred new people per day, with abundant time remaining for teaching discussions. In some small towns where distances between homes are large, missionaries may find a minimum of fifty contacts each day to be more realistic. There is almost never any valid reason for a companionship to average fewer than fifty gospel contacts in a day, except in nations where contacting is prohibited.

A missionary who consistently contacts one hundred people per day can reach over 70,000 people over the course of a mission, while one who contacted only five per day would reach only 3,600. In a relatively receptive area that averaged one baptism per five hundred contacts, a missionary with the simple habit of contacting one hundred people each day could achieve approximately 140 baptisms over the course of a mission. If an average of 5,000 gospel contacts were needed to achieve one baptism in a highly resistant area, a missionary who approached one hundred contacts each day could bring fourteen people into the Church.

A continuing flow of investigators through the finding and teaching pools is essential both to productivity and to refinement of missionary skills. More importantly, the best and often only way for missionaries to consistently receive the Holy Spirit is by contacting large numbers of people daily. Missionaries who make few new contacts find that it is difficult to receive or maintain the companionship of the Holy Spirit, regardless of their sincerity.

EXPECTATIONS AND REALITY

Many missionaries expect that a relatively high percentage of contacts and investigators they teach will be baptized and are therefore content with making few contacts. Even under the most favorable circumstances, only a small fraction of individuals contacted and taught will be ready to accept the gospel, since not everyone is willing to adhere to gospel laws. Yet it is not enough even for us to reach each individual once. We must present individuals with multiple and frequent opportunities to receive the gospel. Multiple contacts are often required even for sincere individuals to develop a desire to investigate the Church. U.S. research suggests that the average convert has had between six and twenty exposures to the Church before deciding to join. Since people are receptive to the gospel at different times and often require multiple exposures to the gospel before accepting it, we cannot consider our duty to be done when each individual has had a single gospel opportunity. We must offer the gospel widely so that it is available to individuals when they are ready and not simply when we finally decide to make the effort to share it with them.

OVERCOMING THE FEAR OF MAN

The burning desire to share the gospel felt by servants of Christ is replaced by fear in the carnal man. Beyond the theoretical understanding that contacting is important, effective contacting requires a driving sense of responsibility to reach the unreached and a high tolerance for rejection. Developing these traits is one of the most difficult emotional and psychological tasks many missionaries face, and many never develop them over their entire missions. Missionaries must prepare themselves mentally and spiritually to be undeterred by rejection. President James E. Faust taught: "Missionaries still need to have the right attitude in contacting people. They need to cast aside all fear and be positive about the great message which is here."* He further taught that missionaries should "fear not and doubt not. We have a leader who fears not and doubts not." Moroni wrote: "I fear not what man can do; for perfect love casteth out all fear" (Moroni 8:16).

Participating in the first contact of nonmembers with the Church is the most exciting part of missionary work for me. Initially, I contacted diligently out of a sense of the importance and urgency about the gospel message, although I found contacting challenging. Later in my mission, I came to greatly enjoy contacting. Different individuals offer such a variety of experience and perspective that contacting can be very rewarding when approached with the proper attitude. Even when people are not interested in the Church, I am enriched by the experience. By varying in one's approach, trying out new words in the mission language, and working to build on common beliefs, one can turn contacting from a chore into an exciting and enjoyable activity.

THE BOOK OF MORMON LOAN PROGRAM

Missionaries can economize time while increasing their productivity by using the Book of Mormon as a sieve, allowing the honest in heart to self-select. Ezra Taft Benson taught: "The Book of Mormon is the great standard we are to use in our missionary work. It shows that Joseph Smith was a prophet. It contains the words of Christ, and its great mission is to bring men to Christ. All other things are secondary. The golden question of the Book of Mormon is 'Do you want to learn more of Christ?' The Book of Mormon is the great finder of the golden contact. It does not contain things which are 'pleasing unto the world,' and so the worldly are not interested in it. It is a great sieve (see 1

---

*   Faust, James E., *LDS Church News*, June 26, 1999.

Nephi 6:5)." He taught that the wicked are offended at it, the worldly are not interested in it, and the righteous delight in it.

In many missions, missionaries do not allow contacts to receive a copy of the Book of Mormon until they have already received the first discussion. In other cases, congratulatory articles celebrate wards that have distributed copies of the Book of Mormon indiscriminately to anyone who will accept one, often with little or no follow-up. Fortunately, there is a program that is superior in virtually every way to the extremes of inadequate use of the Book of Mormon or of indiscriminate distribution without meaningful follow-up.

The Book of Mormon loan program is an effective finding method for both missionaries and members that involves offering a copy of the Book of Mormon as a loan to individuals with the request that they read just enough to form an opinion. If the acquaintance has specific questions or interests, reading passages can be recommended. A copy of 23 Questions Answered by the Book of Mormon can help the acquaintance find portions that may stimulate his or her interest. The missionary or member mentions that he would like to meet with the contact to discuss the principles of the book at greater length if he or she finds the contents to be interesting. For a book to be loaned, the contact must agree to read in the book and to return it if he or she is not interested. A tentative follow-up within the next several days should be agreed upon, and individual's telephone number and address are obtained. If the individual wishes to borrow a copy of the Book of Mormon but is reluctant to provide his or her telephone number or address, a commitment to return the book during Sunday church meetings can be obtained and local church address and meeting times can be provided. One should not give out a church invitation before requesting the individual's telephone number since the person may subsequently decide not to provide personal contact information that is often necessary for follow-up.

The recipient is told that the Book of Mormon is not being given as a gift, but is being loaned and that he or she will be expected to return it. When the book is given as a gift, many people feel no sense of accountability or urgency for reading it due to the prevalent free sample mentality. However, most individuals do feel a sense of obligation about returning other peoples' property. After a few days, the missionary or member calls or stops by to follow up at the agreed time. If the individual is interested or would like to discuss the book, the Book of Mormon has worked as a sieve increasing the value of the missionary's time and discussion ensues. If the individual is not interested, the book is picked up (for follow-up in person), or he or she is asked to return the book at a church meeting or at another convenient agreed-upon time (if follow-up is by telephone). The Book of Mormon has acted as a sieve and that individual has sifted himself out, saving the missionary considerable time. While not every uninterested person may return the book, many do. Because of the opportunity cost of time, missionaries do not need to spend their time picking up books unless it is convenient. They can be left in the home of investigators at the missionaries' discretion. The individuals brought into the Church through the Book of Mormon loan program have a high rate of continued activity because they are truly converted to the gospel message and not to the missionaries or to the social programs of the Church.

CASE HISTORY

In one Brazilian mission, my father as a missionary divided his time equally between morning and afternoon and divided the city into two halves, and one of the halves into two quarters.

For three hours each morning, he would go to one quarter and go door to door with his briefcase full of copies of the Book of Mormon. At each house, he would say: "Here is a book. It is not for sale. It is a loan. It is for your husband to read to you. We will return in two days to see how you like it."

For three hours each afternoon, he would go to the other half of the city and do conventional tracting, namely, introducing himself and his companion as missionaries of the LDS Church and offering to present a missionary discussion.

On even days he would go to one quarter in the morning, and on odd days he would go to the other quarter.

Each copy of the Book of Mormon was underlined in passages where the basic points of the gospel leading to conversion were indicated. At the bottom of the page, the reader was pointed to the next reference: "Go to page —."

During the time this experiment was conducted, one person was baptized by conventional tracting. Ten people were baptized by the Book of Mormon loan program.

My father did not have time to mark all of the copies. He printed up a marking chart and found that not only members, but also even nonmembers were often very happy to mark the books for him. Some of them confessed that they stopped to read the passages as they were underlining them.

In this manner, my father was able to distribute copies of the Book of Mormon in Portuguese, Spanish, French, Italian, and German and tracts in Russian and Japanese because the book was not available at that time in those languages.

The book was left with the family for as long as they continued reading it. The books were picked up from disinterested families and loaned out again to new contacts.

Whenever a book was left with a Jewish family, he would refuse to take the book back. His mission President, Wayne Beck, assured him that some day they would not be able to resist the temptation to read it. "The Jews are great readers," he said.

My father spent all the money ever sent to him on his mission by well-wishers on copies of the Book of Mormon. Upon leaving the mission, he had one hundred copies of the Book of Mormon in the hands of people who said they were still reading them. He affirms that if he were ever called on another mission, he would spend all his daylight hours doing nothing but loaning copies of the Book of Mormon. Evenings, of course, were always reserved for teaching.

FAMILY TO FAMILY BOOK OF MORMON PROGRAM

Ezra Taft Benson cited the Family to Family Book of Mormon Program as one of the most effective missionary approaches, noting the need for families to send copies of the Book of Mormon on missions for them.* I have found that many investigators give positive feedback about the value of the following measures:

1. A photo of the individual or family. An address should also be included if the family desires to correspond.

2. The book should include a copy of a printed personal or family testimony which focuses not simply on assertions that the Book of Mormon is true, but on the blessings one has received through following its principles.

3. A copy of 23 Questions Answered by the Book of Mormon, complete with page references, to stimulate meaningful reading.

4. Local contact information for the Church. Individuals who

---

* Benson, Ezra Taft, *Come Listen to a Prophet's Voice: To the Elderly in the Church*, 74.

enjoy reading the Book of Mormon receive limited benefit if they cannot find the Church.

WORKING WITH MEMBERS EFFECTIVELY

There are effective and ineffective ways to work with members. Some missionaries believe that one cannot find through members without a long period of building trust, often through frequent visits and excessive socialization. Ezra Taft Benson taught:

> Too many missionaries are neutralized and occasionally lost (excommunicated) because of over-solicitous members, member sisters who "mother" the missionaries, and socializing occurring between missionaries and members. Because of the importance of members and missionaries working effectively together on the member missionary program, it is vital that missionaries maintain the proper missionary image and have the reputation as great proselyting elders and not simply "good guys." The greatest help members can be to a missionary is not to feed him, but to give the names of their friends so that he can teach them with the spirit in their homes and challenge them, with the wonderful members helping to fellowship. [*]

Frequent missionary transfers and more pressing scriptural responsibilities make it impractical and inappropriate for each member to get to know each missionary well socially, nor does socialization alone generally result in the generation of productive referrals. Visits can be counterproductive when missionaries stay too long or visit too frequently. The utilization of all opportunities to speak with members at church meetings and functions and close follow-up with appropriately timed telephone calls can save many needless trips and fruitless visits.

---

[*]   Benson, Ezra Taft, Mission Presidents' Seminar, June 21, 1975.

Effective finding through members involves at least three factors. First, missionary visits to members are centered on helping members to develop and continue basic gospel habits that generate spiritual growth, including reading the Book of Mormon daily, saying prayers, sharing the gospel, observing the Sabbath Day and Word of Wisdom, attending the temple, and the habit of regularly initiating gospel discussions with nonmembers. Members with these habits are much more likely to participate in member-missionary work. Righteousness is the precursor of effective missionary work and the source of self-motivation. When the objectives of missionary visits are nebulous, social, or centered exclusively on soliciting referrals, little is accomplished.

Second, missionaries must work hard at independent finding methods and teach investigators appropriately to build trust. When missionaries successfully find, teach, and baptize quality converts who remain active, members gain confidence and are more willing to invite their acquaintances with less prompting. Conversely, when missionaries are unable to regularly get new investigators to church or when poorly committed "converts" are quickly lost to inactivity because of being rushed to baptism prematurely, member confidence in missionaries is seriously damaged.

Finally, missionaries must ensure that their referral expectations are reasonable based on the ratio of members to missionaries and past performance. The cliché that "if members were doing their job, missionaries wouldn't have to tract" is neither scripturally sound nor realistic in most areas. The belief that finding people to teach is "someone else's job" is attractive to human nature but obscures personal responsibility and dampens independent effort.

FINDING THROUGH MEDIA

Latter-day prophets have taught that we have an obligation to share the gospel through media. Spencer W. Kimball taught: "When we have increased the missionaries from the organized areas of the Church to a number close to their potential, that is, every able and worthy boy in the Church on a mission; when every stake and mission abroad is furnishing enough missionaries for that country; when we have used our qualified men to help the apostles to open these new fields of labor; when we have used the satellite and related discoveries to their greatest potential and all of the media—the papers, magazines, television, radio—all in their greatest power; when we have organized numerous other stakes which will be springboards; when we have recovered from inactivity the numerous young men who are now unordained and unmissioned and unmarried; then, and not until then, shall we approach the insistence of our Lord and Master to go into all the world and preach the gospel to every creature."[*] Of his media interviews, President Gordon B. Hinckley stated: "We have something that the world needs to hear about, and these interviews afford an opportunity to give voice to that."[†]

Elder Dallin H. Oaks noted that in North America "studies show that about 6 out of 10 of adult converts said that they were positively influenced by our media messages before deciding to be baptized."[‡] This figure does not apply to international areas, where relatively few converts have been exposed to church media messages. Little LDS media outreach is conducted in areas of the developing world where costs are low and response rates are high. George Barna has found that

---

[*]   Kimball, Spencer W., "When the World Will Be Converted," *Ensign*, October 1974.

[†]   Hinckley, Gordon B., *Ensign*, May 1996.

[‡]   Oaks, Dallin A., "The Role of Members in Conversion," *Ensign*, March 2003.

in the United States "more people use Christian media than attend church" and that large numbers of non-Christians listen to Christian radio.[*] The impact of media messages even on the relatively stagnant North American religious scene suggests that the potential for media messages in the developing world is immense. I have often found that the use of outreach media is the primary difference between the finding program of Protestant missionaries and pastors who do not speak the local language but succeed in assembling large congregations and that of LDS missionaries who speak the local language yet have few investigators to teach. Many of the best media opportunities are at the mission level and below. Local media opportunities are often both more effective and less expensive than national ones and can be fine-tuned based on local needs and results.

CHURCH MEDIA OUTREACH

The value of religious feature stories run by major news networks is usually diluted by the simultaneous presentation of inaccurate or opposing views. Press interviews with church leaders, feature articles, and public service advertisements without specific contact information and a call to action may generate some positive feelings but rarely inspire individuals to investigate the Church or accept the missionary discussions. Positive publicity in the lay press is often only weakly positive, while negative articles are often strongly negative. Many network television stations in the United States and Western Europe now categorically refuse to run evangelistic advertisements, making it more difficult for churches to conduct outreach through secular media. Many churches have found that their efforts are better directed

---

[*] Barna, George, "More People Use Christian Media Than Attend Church," *Barna Research Update*, March 14, 2005, http://www.barna.org/FlexPage.aspx?Page=BarnaUpdate&BarnaUpdateID=184.

toward developing their own media outreach venues than attempting to achieve wide positive exposure through the lay press. Churches that do their own religious broadcasting and printing can proclaim the gospel message without the content being altered or attacked by third parties before even reaching its audience.

OPTIMIZING MEDIA PROGRAMS

LDS media messages can directly generate referrals, or they can exert a positive influence that may increase receptivity in future LDS contacts. In receptive or newly opened areas, direct-response media messages that invite contacts to attend church, read the Book of Mormon, or visit with the missionaries are much more effective than image messages that promote a positive view of Latter-day Saints but do not invite to action. Effective media programs should be sustained over time. With few exceptions, ongoing media programs that achieve modest but constant exposure usually produce superior long-term results to large, one-time media events.

Awareness of the principles of threshold effort, response rate, and respondent receptivity can help to optimize media outreach for any area. Threshold effort is the personal effort that the respondent must put forth to act upon the media invitation, such as making a telephone call, inviting the missionaries, or attending a church meeting. The response rate is the number of individuals who respond to the media message, typically measured per thousand exposures. Respondent receptivity is the rate at which respondents become investigators or progress in other ways toward church membership.

Media programs generate different response rates and reach different audiences based on the content of the message and the effort required from the respondent. The response rate is inversely proportional to the threshold effort. However, the average respondent receptivity is directly proportional to the threshold effort. Free literature or video offerings increase the response rate but lower respondent receptivity. LDS-specific media content, such as Book of Mormon, typically lower response rate but increase respondent receptivity compared to content that is not unique to Latter-day Saints, such as the Bible. Programs that require greater threshold effort, such as attending church, will receive fewer responses than those that require less effort or offer free materials, but those who do respond will be more likely to become serious investigators.

The message content and required threshold effort must be balanced against the response rate and productivity of visits achieved to optimize results in the context of community receptivity and missionary availability. Media programs with threshold-commitment ratios that are mismatched to local needs can dissipate time and resources better utilized in more productive ways. One elder in the southern United States stated that his companionship received an average of three referrals per day from the Lamb of God video program but that the program had resulted in very few converts across his mission. He noted that more baptisms resulted from talking with nonmembers on the way to and from media referral appointments than from visiting the media referrals themselves, explaining that "many people here just want free stuff."

Media programs in areas of high community receptivity and abundant teaching opportunities should favor a high threshold effort such as church attendance or reading in the Book of Mormon. Such initiatives reach modest numbers of individuals who are more likely to progress to conversion and Church membership, ensuring that missionary time is utilized as effectively as possible. This is especially crucial in missions with low missionary to population ratios. In contrast, low-threshold, high-response rate programs offering free books or videos to be brought to an investigator's home may be useful in less receptive areas where missionaries face major difficulties trying to find anyone to teach at all.

If a media initiative does not produce the desired outcome, the message content and the initial required effort can be modified to produce a locally appropriate balance between the number of referrals and contact interest level. If the number of referrals generated is high but few individuals become converted, the media program should be modified to require greater investigator effort, leading to fewer but more productive teaching opportunities.

MEDIA EXAMPLES

Media opportunities should be utilized to increase positive church exposure. In one city, I wrote an article on the Church in Russian that was published in a local newspaper. We had many discussions and several baptismal commitments due to publicity from the article. We also paid for an attractive signboard with information about the Church with our meeting time to be posted near a bus stop. Several individuals came to church as a result of the sign and were baptized. Since many people had seen the sign, contacting efforts were more successful. We presented local libraries with a copy of the Book of Mormon and *Gospel Principles* book with the church addresses and times pasted inside. The *Gospel Principles* book was well received because of its accessible format and organized and well-referenced overview of LDS doctrines. Small newspaper advertisements provide an inexpensive way to increase public awareness. One mission companion was baptized after attending church meetings he found through a newspaper advertisement with nothing but the Church's name, location, and meeting time.

REFERRAL PROCESS IMPROVEMENT

My follow-up audits have found that not all missionaries consistently attempt to reach referrals. Addresses are not always valid, telephone numbers are often not provided, and much time can be lost attempting to visit contacts that are not home. Referrals are time-sensitive, since receptivity often wanes with time. It is necessary to ensure that receptive referrals are reached promptly, while avoiding the dissipation of large amounts of time in repeated attempts to locate hard to reach contacts with only minimal interest.

The challenge begins with referral forms that allow submission of only name and contact information. Additional information can economize missionary time and increase the likelihood of successful contact. Important questions include: What is the best time to visit or call? What exposure have you had to the Church? Do you have LDS friends or acquaintances? What interests you about the LDS Church?

This additional information allows missionaries to reach the individual and establish rapport much more effectively than is possible by cold-calling with nothing more than a name and address. Such information can also provide missionaries with the impetus to make repeated or exceptional attempts to contact difficult to reach but potentially high-yield contacts, while avoiding repeated and often fruitless efforts to reach low-yield ones. A contact who has attended church in another area, has close member friends, has studied the Book of Mormon, and has expressed a strong interest in receiving the discussions warrants far greater effort to reach than an individual who has expressed only a casual curiosity or an individual referred by a member without his knowledge or permission. Systematic mission-level audits are valuable to ensure that referrals disbursed to missionaries are followed up promptly.

TEACHING FOR TRUE CONVERSION

IMPORTANCE OF TEACHING

GORDON B. HINCKLEY TAUGHT: "[If missionaries could really convey the gospel message], at least twice as many people would come into the Church.... I hope this improvement will continue until we learn to really speak to the world."* One mission companion had a gift for teaching gospel principles in a simple and personal yet profound way that could convey the insight of the Holy Spirit to both the new contacts and longtime members. He was able to teach and baptize individuals whom I never would have thought it was possible to reach. I had never dreamed that hearing about faith or repentance for the thirtieth time could be so fascinating. The great Christian apologist C. S. Lewis, who inspired millions with his practical insight on Christianity, wrote that if you cannot convey a principle of faith in simple terms, "then either you don't understand it or you don't believe it."† Walter Hooper called Lewis the "most thoroughly converted man I ever met." To a great extent, our ability to convey gospel principles is a direct reflection of our own personal conversion and the meaning of these principles in our own lives.

---

* Hinckley, Gordon B., New Mission Presidents' Seminar, *LDS Church News*, July 4, 1998.

† Hooper, Walter, ed., *C. S. Lewis: Readings for Mediation and Reflection*, New York: Harper Collins, 1992, p. xiv.

PREPARE TO TEACH

We are commanded to pray for the Spirit before each visit (2 Nephi 32:9). A prayer within the home can also help bring the Spirit. If we do not receive the Spirit, we are commanded not to teach (D&C 42:14). It is better to reschedule an appointment than to teach without the Spirit.

Upon entering the investigators' home, distractions should be minimized. One should ask to turn off the television or radio at the start of each visit. Eating at investigators' homes is usually counter-productive. Missionaries should let investigators and members know ahead of time that they will not have time to eat. It is difficult to keep the Spirit when individuals are preoccupied with serving or eating rather than directing all energies to the one needful thing, the message of the gospel (Luke 10:38-42). Serving meals can also present a major economic burden to those in developing nations and can be a source of unseen tension in the home. If the investigators still insist on serving something, tell them that a light snack will suffice.

Introductions should be brief. On a first visit, a few open-ended, nonthreatening questions can often help the missionaries to gain insight into how to best meet the investigator's needs. What is the individual's vocational and religious background? What interests the individual about the Church or about faith and spirituality in general? Does the investigator have LDS friends or acquaintances? What are the investigator's goals in life? These and other relevant questions can be asked initially or at a more opportune time, depending on missionary rapport and verbal and nonverbal cues. The home or apartment can also provide clues about the individual's interests and priorities.

At subsequent visits, the investigator's understanding and preparation must be assessed before beginning a lesson. Open-ended questions are asked to find out how the investigators understand the material covered at the last visit, what progress they have made on interim scripture reading, church attendance, and any other commitments, and whether they have any questions or concerns. The investigator's scripture reading should be discussed as specifically as possible. Individuals who claim to have read but state that they cannot remember what the reading was about have usually not read or have made only a cursory attempt. Discussing the reading as specifically as possible helps the missionary to understand how much reading is really occurring and helps the investigator to realize that the missionaries are serious about the commitment to study the scriptures. Missionaries who skip over investigator's statements about scripture reading without specifically discussing the material often face unpleasant surprises and will find that their investigators and converts rarely develop the habit of daily scripture reading.

The major highlights of the last lesson should be briefly reviewed. If the investigator does not accurately understand or remember the material covered in prior lessons, has significant unresolved concerns, has not read scriptures or attended church, or has not observed other commitments, it is generally ill-advised to proceed with the full discussion. Discussions should only be given when investigators are adequately prepared to receive them. If one chooses not to give a discussion, a short lesson or brief follow-up visit focusing on the issues of concern is usually appropriate. It is important to attempt to stay on topic, but it is also important to ensure that investigator questions and interests are adequately addressed.

Once the baptismal commitment has been accepted, the investigator's progress toward each of the core commitments (reading scriptures daily, praying daily, attending church weekly, and observing the Word of Wisdom and law of chastity) is discussed at the beginning of each visit. This provides a very good idea of the investigator's overall status and a window into what issues may represent current or potential future challenges. The discerning missionary finds very few surprises, while the less effective missionary is frequently caught off guard with unanticipated disappointments.

Teaching lays the foundation for how investigators will act as members. It takes time and effort for investigators to absorb and apply the teachings and principles presented in the discussions. Few investigators can adequately incorporate the information and commitments from more than one formal discussion per week. Programs in which all of the lessons are crammed into brief intervals of three weeks or less have inevitably been associated with major deficiencies in the teaching process and low convert retention rates. There should be no pressure as to the pace at which investigators are taught, nor should there be any incentive for rushing investigators beyond the pace with which they feel comfortable.

TEACHING TIME

Wide variation exists in missionary teaching patterns. I knew many missionaries serving in Russia who routinely took two to three hours to teach a discussion due to language difficulties and habits of eating large meals in investigators' homes with every visit. Some Latin American missions experience the opposite extreme, with brief five- to ten-minute "doorstep discussions" that make passing mention of key discussion points to contacts who usually fail to understand or incorporate the whirlwind information overload. While this tactic succeeded in running up discussion numbers, the actual meaning of this increase is dubious, since few "converts" taught with this method remained active or acquired even a rudimentary grasp of the principles being taught. The *Preach My Gospel* manual instructs missionaries that lessons should take only thirty to forty-five minutes and that multiple small visits may be necessary to cover discussion material adequately. The *Preach My Gospel* manual provides short outlines of the discussions that can be taught in as little as three to five minutes. While such abbreviated summaries can be useful when discussing beliefs with street contacts, when time is short, or when reviewing past lessons, they are not a substitute for full-length discussions and should not be counted or reported as such.

I find that few investigators are able to comprehend adequately and incorporate the discussion material in less than sixty to ninety minutes. With the new four-discussion program, teaching the officially recommended thirty to forty-five minutes results in less instructional time between the missionaries' initial contact with an investigator and baptism than in a single three-hour Sunday meeting block. Most missionaries try to complete the discussions within the allotted thirty to forty-five minutes, since the prospect of return visits to complete a single lesson disrupts continuity and lacks appeal. Few find-out questions are asked as the missionaries race to complete the discussion, leaving the typical investigator with major unresolved issues that are quickly apparent to an experienced observer. At follow-up, investigator hang-ups expectedly relate to unresolved issues and misunderstandings that should have been recognized and addressed in the prior discussion. This highly abbreviated teaching schedule most commonly results in the rushed baptism of investigators who do not adequately grasp the lesson material. If investigators cannot find the time or muster the attention to sit through sixty- to ninety-minute discussions during their initial acquaintance with the Church, how will they possibly find the discipline to attend the full Sunday block meeting schedule for life? Limiting maximum teaching time to only forty-five minutes is also inefficient, especially in areas where missionaries cover large areas and may require considerable travel time.

I believe that sixty- to ninety-minute lessons are most adequate and appropriate. Follow-up and member visits should not take more than one hour. Staying beyond that time is usually counterproductive. A cardinal rule of missionary work is always to leave before the Spirit does so that the investigators eagerly anticipate the next visit instead of feeling anxious for the missionaries to leave.

The missionary discussions contain many essential principles that are new for many investigators and frequently require appropriate find-out questions, explanations, and examples. Investigators must be taught for true conversion and not for deadlines. Shortchanging the teaching of receptive investigators is false economy and fails to adequately prepare investigators for membership. Missionaries have no greater responsibility than to teach the gospel. Receptive and committed investigators deserve to be taught adequately.

Some missionaries teach fine lessons, only to misjudge their time and then ask to be excused at a critical point in the discussion when the allotted lesson time expires or the evening curfew approaches. The Spirit, which has been carefully built up to witness to an essential point, is lost, and the atmosphere upon returning to resume the discussion is not the same. While most such episodes can be avoided by remaining time-conscious, staying on a lesson schedule, and stopping the discussion on a suitable noncritical point if the lesson must be split, missionaries should keep in mind that their investigators' needs usually represent the "weightier matters of the law." It is unwise to abandon a highly spiritual discussion with a receptive investigator before a major commitment or crucial teaching point simply to stay within an arbitrary allotted time.

INVOLVE MEMBERS

For serious investigators, it is essential to arrange for members to be present for at least two and preferably more discussions or visits before baptism in order to ensure that meaningful fellowshipping begins long before baptism. In this way, the investigators develop friendships with active members with whom they will have long-term contact and benefit from their teaching and testimony. Local members also receive many benefits, including spiritual blessings, hands-on mentoring in sharing the gospel, and lasting friendships. I find that it is less helpful to bring members on the first discussion unless they are personal friends of the investigator, since the large majority of first discussions never result in a second, and the presence of a member is of questionable benefit for first-time investigators who are likely to have other hang-ups.

FOCUS ON THE SAVIOR

We must focus on Jesus Christ as we teach the gospel. Nephi taught: "We talk of Christ, we rejoice in Christ, we preach of Christ, we prophesy of Christ, and we write according to our prophecies, that our children may know to what source they may look for a remission of their sins" (2 Nephi 25:26). All gospel principles ultimately go back to the Savior.

TEACH THE UNIQUENESS
OF LATTER-DAY DOCTRINES

Recognizing that acceptance of Christ's work today through His chosen messengers is vital to our becoming modern disciples of Christ. Bruce R. McConkie stated: "Until we get involved with latter-day revelation, the process of conversion does not begin to operate in any substantial degree in the heart of an investigator. The Lord said to Joseph Smith: 'this generation shall have my word through you ...' (D&C 5:10). That is His decree. They either get it through Joseph Smith or they do not get it, and our whole perspective is: Joseph Smith and the Book of Mormon, the Book of Mormon and Joseph Smith."* Missionaries must take every opportunity to emphasize that the doctrines they are teaching, while found in ancient scripture, are understood only because of Latter-day revelation given to Joseph Smith and other prophets in our time. When investigators claim that their church teaches the "same thing," they often betray a lack of awareness of the true beliefs of their prior faith. To the world of sectarian Christianity, basic doctrines of the gospel such as the nature of God, the true definition of faith, the identity of the Savior as the Old Testament Jehovah, the requirements for salvation, the nature of repentance, and the Holy Ghost are all mysteries. Grant Von Harrison wrote of the responsibility to teach investigators to gain a love for the Book of Mormon and the prophet Joseph Smith: "If you fail in this basic responsibility, you will see many people accept the basic doctrines that you introduce, but they will not be inclined to join the Church."†

TEACH WITH THE BOOK OF MORMON

Jesus Christ personally appeared to all of the main editors and authors of the Book of Mormon and instructed them what to write in the limited space they had to convey a message of infinite importance. In this sense, the Book of Mormon is unique among scripture

---

*   McConkie, Bruce R., Mission Presidents' Seminar, June 21, 1975.

†   Von Harrison, Grant, *Tools for Missionaries*, Orem, UT: Keepsake Paperbacks, 1989, 217.

in that Christ Himself was the Editor in Chief. The Book of Mormon was written for our day. Moroni wrote: "I speak unto you as if ye were present, and yet ye are not. But behold, Jesus Christ hath shown you unto me, and I know your doing" (Mormon 8:34–35). Having seen our day and having been personally instructed by the Savior Himself, Book of Mormon prophets provide the guidance for our times. Nephi testified that the sincere followers of Christ will recognize the voice of Christ in the Book of Mormon: "And now, my beloved brethren, and also Jew, and all ye ends of the earth, hearken unto these words and believe in Christ; and if ye believe not in these words believe in Christ. And if ye shall believe in Christ ye will believe in these words, for they are the words of Christ, and he hath given them unto me; and they teach all men that they should do good. And if they are not the words of Christ, judge ye—for Christ will show unto you, with power and great glory, that they are his words, at the last day; and you and I shall stand face to face before his bar; and ye shall know that I have been commanded of him to write these things, notwithstanding my weakness" (2 Nephi 33:10–11). He wrote that the Book of Mormon "speaketh harshly against sin, according to the plainness of the truth; wherefore, no man will be angry at the words which I have written save he shall be of the spirit of the devil" (2 Nephi 33:5). The way in which individuals receive the Book of Mormon determines whether they are able to receive additional divine truths. Mormon records: "These things have I written, which are a lesser part of the things which he [Jesus] taught the people. And when they shall have received this, which is expedient that they should have first, to try their faith, and if it shall so be that they shall believe these things then shall the greater things be made manifest unto them" (3 Nephi 26:8–9).

President Ezra Taft Benson declared: "The Book of Mormon is the instrument that God has designed to 'sweep the earth as with a flood, to gather out His elect unto the New Jerusalem.' This sacred volume of scripture has not been, nor is it yet, central in our preaching, our teaching, and our missionary work."* He taught that the Church is still under condemnation for taking the Book of Mormon lightly and that "the Book of Mormon must be the heart of our missionary work in every mission of the Church if we are to come out from under this condemnation (see D&C 84:56–57)." President Benson emphasized that "we must flood the earth with the Book of Mormon." He noted: "A missionary who is inspired by the Spirit of the Lord must be led by that Spirit to choose the proper approach to be effective. We must not forget that the Lord Himself provided the Book of Mormon as His chief witness. The Book of Mormon is still our most powerful missionary tool. Let us use it."† He challenged us: "Would not the progress of the Church increase dramatically today with an increasing number of those who are spiritually reborn? Can you imagine what would happen in our homes? Can you imagine what would happen with an increasing number of copies of the Book of Mormon in the hands of an increasing number of missionaries who know how to use it and who have been born of God? When this happens, we will get the bounteous harvest of souls that the Lord promised. It was the 'born of God' Alma who as a missionary was so able to impart the word that many others were also born of God. (See Alma 36:23–26.)"‡

In almost every case where true conversion has occurred, much of the converting power has come from the scriptures. President Benson taught: "There is a difference between a convert who is built on the rock of Christ through the Book of Mormon and stays hold of the

---

*   Benson, Ezra Taft, Salt Lake City, UT, March 5, 1987.

†   Benson, Ezra Taft, *Teachings of Ezra Taft Benson*, Salt Lake City, UT: Bookcraft, 1988, 204.

‡   Benson, Ezra Taft, Mission Presidents' Seminar, June 25, 1986.

iron rod, and one who is not. I promise you that you will have more and better converts in every mission of the Church if you will teach and inspire missionaries to effectively use the Book of Mormon as the great converter."* President Benson stated that social, educational, or other converts will not endure the heat of the day, while those built on the rock of Christ through the Book of Mormon will endure. Bruce R. McConkie noted: "When you get into the active operation of your proselyting program, this is a concept you absolutely must have. It has been our traditional course in days past, unfortunately all too frequently, to say, 'Here is the Bible, and the Bible says this and this, and therefore the Gospel has been restored.' Well now, there is no person on earth that believes the Bible more than I do. I read it and ponder its words. I know that what is in it is true. But let me tell you, it is not the Bible that brings people into the Church; it is the Book of Mormon and latter-day revelation."†

I substitute Book of Mormon passages for Bible passages whenever possible in the discussions and in teaching, because they are clearer and more powerful than Bible verses, as investigators frequently attest. For the last eight months of my mission, I did not carry a Bible, using the investigators' own Bible on rare occasions when it was necessary to refer to it at all. It was not by chance that this was by far our time of greatest success.

It is almost always better to find an appropriate Book of Mormon scripture in answer to a question rather than to answer in one's own words. Investigators have a right to receive divine instruction rather than personal opinion. When missionaries integrate Book of Mormon scriptures consistently, investigators and members come to realize that they can find their own answers by reading God's word and develop

---

*   Benson, Ezra Taft, Mission Presidents' Seminar, June 25, 1986.

†   McConkie, Bruce R., Mission Presidents' Seminar, June 21, 1975.

a greater desire to study the Book of Mormon on their own. When passages from the Book of Mormon are read frequently with investigators from the moment they meet the missionaries, many gain a partial testimony and love for the Book of Mormon even before reading commitments are extended.

Overreliance on the Bible and underutilization of the Book of Mormon will fail to teach and inspire investigators adequately. I have seen many converts taught by missionaries with Bible-centric methods begin to question the importance of the Book of Mormon soon after baptism, usually without ever seriously studying it, and fall away shortly thereafter. This relates to several problems with the teaching process.

The prior missionary discussions encourage investigators to "contemplate that which you have read, comparing truths in the Book of Mormon with truths in the Bible." This instruction implies that the Bible is used as a standard for verifying the truth of the Book of Mormon and, by implication, constitutes a superior authority. While the *Preach My Gospel* manual no longer contains this instruction, some missionaries continue this practice which presents a stumbling block for many investigators. Scriptures teach us that this approach is exactly backward, since the Book of Mormon establishes the veracity of the Bible (1 Nephi 13:40). As a fourteen-year-old boy, Joseph Smith recognized that "the teachers of religion of the different sects understood the same passages of scripture so differently as to destroy all confidence in settling the question by an appeal to the Bible" (JS-H 1:12). The Book of Mormon is the only book of scripture that the Lord endorses as independently containing the "fullness of the gospel" (D&C 20:9, D&C 27:5).

Joseph Smith stated: "If Mormons believe in the Bible, we are the only people on earth who do, for there are none of the other sects of the day that do." Studies have shown that a large proportion of sectarian ministers do not believe in the literal resurrection of the Lord Jesus Christ and other fundamental doctrines of the Bible. Many ministers proclaim that the Bible contains the final word of God and represents the ultimate authority, while they simultaneously deny or ignore basic Biblical teachings. Many basic doctrines such as the degrees of glory and vicarious baptism, while mentioned in the Bible, are not taught or understood by other faiths. Sectarian views of the Bible are filtered through the orthodoxy of the apostate church and its creeds. Scriptures warn us not to underestimate the power Satan has over many because of false interpretations of the Bible. Nephi saw in his vision of the latter days: "Because of the many plain and precious things which have been taken out of the book [the Bible], which were plain unto the understanding of the children of men, according to the plainness which is in the Lamb of God—because of these things which are taken away out of the gospel of the Lamb, an exceedingly great many do stumble, yea, insomuch that Satan hath great power over them" (1 Nephi 13:29). When we use the Bible as the foundation of our teaching, investigators can go to priests, ministers, or acquaintances and receive widely different interpretations of the same passage. Sectarian churches purport to show by taking selected, often poorly translated, Bible verses out of context and twisting their interpretation that the Book of Mormon does not agree with the Bible. Why would we want to increase Satan's power by perpetuating misconceptions about the Bible? We must instead direct attention to the source of Bible writings: the Savior and his ongoing revelations to mankind. When we teach with the powerful passages of the Book of Mormon, there can be no appeal except to God.

Many Bible verses represent poor choices for explaining doctrine. In both the old and new discussions, John 3:16 is the first scripture cited: "For God so loved the world that he gave his only begotten Son, that whosoever believeth in him should not perish, but have everlasting life." The *Preach My Gospel* manual omits the second part of verse 16 and skips to verse 17, although the whole passage is often read by missionaries and investigators in actual teaching situations. While the intention is to demonstrate God's great love and to build on common beliefs with investigators, missionaries are unwittingly pulling the carpet out from under their feet. This same verse is widely used by Protestant denominations to "prove" that all that is required for eternal life is to express belief. Investigators who understand the verse in this manner may interpret it to mean that there is no need to belong to a specific church, obey the commandments, or have the missionaries return. While the gospel writer used the word belief to describe a degree of commitment and obedience far greater than implied in modern uses, misunderstandings can be avoided by using scriptures from the Book of Mormon that speak powerfully of God's love but cannot be perceived to trivialize the conditions of salvation.

Prior discussion protocols advocated that missionaries recommend the story of Christ's visit to the Americas in 3 Nephi 11–14 as the investigator's initial Book of Mormon reading. Proponents typically reason that Christ's visit to the Americas represents the highlight of the Book of Mormon. I have found that recommending these chapters for initial reading is often problematic. First, it may convey to investigators that other portions of the Book of Mormon that do not involve the direct teachings of Christ are less important than those that do. This is untrue and may make the investigator less inclined to read other portions of the Book of Mormon. Nephi, King Benjamin, Mosiah, Moroni, and other prophets talk about Christ far more than the epistles of the New Testament. The Lord proclaims: "Whether by mine own voice or by the voice of my servants, it is the same" (D&C 1:38). Helping investigators to understand this initially can prevent considerable difficulties down the road with those who pretend to acknowledge Christ while disregarding His prophets. The second and more serious problem with this approach is that chapters 12 to 14 are almost verbatim for chapters in the New Testament with only subtle differences, which for many investigators does nothing to help them develop a testimony of the Book of Mormon. Some intelligent, well-read investigators to whom I recommended the standard Third Nephi selection quickly concluded that many parts of the Book of Mormon were simply copied from the New Testament with minor changes. While in fact Christ gave some common teachings to his disciples in Israel and in the Americas because of their importance, one can understand how an investigator could get the impression that passages were simply copied with minor alterations. It is at best an anticlimax, and at worst testimony-threatening, to build investigators up for reading the Book of Mormon by emphasizing that it contains new witnesses of Jesus Christ, only to recommend passages that cite the old witnesses of the Bible almost verbatim. Only a tiny fraction of Book of Mormon chapters are redundant with the Bible, and recommending chapters for initial reading of which the large majority are redundant leaves investigators with an unfortunate and misleading impression. For these reasons, I do not suggest recommending 3 Nephi 12–14 early on for investigators with Christian backgrounds. I have found it to be much more effective to recommend powerful and unique sections such as King Benjamin's speech (Mosiah 2–5), Alma's discourse (Alma 5), the seed of faith (Alma 32), and many others. Try recommending a variety of selections throughout the Book of Mormon, and develop your own recommendations based on what works best for you and your investigators. It should always be kept in mind that the Savior

Himself designed the sequence of material in the Book of Mormon. Do you suppose that there is a reason for the very first account given in the Book of Mormon being of a prophet prophesying the destruction and captivity of the people if they did not repent? Of a man therefore praying in behalf of his people and thereupon receiving his own testimony?

The effectiveness of missionaries in motivating investigators to read the Book of Mormon is a largely a reflection of the conviction of the missionaries themselves. Missionaries can testify all day about their belief in the Book of Mormon, but if they do not extensively integrate Book of Mormon scriptures into their teaching and finding dialogues, they are unlikely to be successful in inspiring investigators to diligently read and study the book for themselves. Testimonies of the power of the Book of Mormon should be specific and personal. When some missionaries describe how they began to seriously read and study the Book of Mormon only shortly before their missions or after arriving in the mission field, they unwittingly demotivate investigators and undermine gospel teaching. If missionaries who were raised in the Church did not have the conviction or drive to study the Book of Mormon earnestly until their missions became imminent, one wonders how investigators they teach could gain a deep and immediate desire to become lifelong students of the Book of Mormon.

FOCUS ON COMMANDMENTS

Keeping the commandments is and must be the main difference between members of the Lord's true Church and members of other churches or social groups. If investigators are not faithful in keeping small commitments, such as reading the Book of Mormon daily and attending Church each week, will they be faithful when their faith is tried by more serious challenges? Missionaries should take every opportunity to reinforce the commitments and emphasize that they are not one-time events but require daily effort and consistency. Only as investigators put forth effort to consistently adhere to gospel laws do true conversion and subsequent spiritual growth occur.

The core commitments that form the basis of faithful gospel living and are the basis for every missionary visit, whether with investigators, new converts, members, or inactives, include:

1.   Daily prayer morning and evening and, where possible, midday also
2.   Daily reading in the Book of Mormon for half an hour (Ezra Taft Benson)
3.   Weekly church attendance and participation
4.   Keeping the Sabbath Day holy (this involves much more than simply attending church)
5.   Living the Word of Wisdom
6.   Living the Law of Chastity (in words, thoughts, and deed)
7.   Repentance of sins
8.   Paying tithing and serving in the Church (for members)

When these commitments are not vigorously emphasized and enforced as requirements for baptism, many converts become content with nominal social activity in the Church while failing to observe other gospel laws. While activity in the Church is vital, little is achieved by building congregations of members who are not studying scriptures daily, keeping the Sabbath day holy, and living other commandments that are necessary to gain and retain the guidance of the Holy Spirit. Such individuals may demonstrate the appearance of growth by mastering church jargon and procedural tasks, while in fact failing to draw close to Christ. A new convert who practices consistent habits of meaningful daily family scripture reading, daily prayer, and full observance of the Sabbath is spiritually light-years ahead of a lifelong member who has been active in the Church for decades, served a mission, held many leadership positions, but neglects daily scripture reading and other gospel habits. The true strength of our testimony is demonstrated by our daily sacrifices.

SHARE TESTIMONY EFFECTIVELY

There is a difference between testimonies born of righteous living and deep conviction which motivate us to action and those that merely go through the motions. Effective testimony bearing generally incorporates the following features:

1. Effective testimony is directed not simply to convincing the listener that the Church, or some principle, is true, but toward motivating the listener to keep specific commandments.
2. Effective testimonies tell how the bearer received a personal knowledge that the principle is true.
3. Effective testimonies share a witness of specific fruits that living the principle has brought into one's own life.
4. A "living testimony" must be radiated in our conduct. It is impossible to effectively testify about a principle which one is not living. Our lives must glorify the Savior and give powerful evidence of our faith.

FIND OUT: ASSESS UNDERSTANDING AND CONVICTION

Current discussions cover large concepts of the gospel in a very

abbreviated format that require the addition of personal testimony,
scriptures, experiences, examples, and discerning find-out questions
on the part of the missionary and effort on the part of the investigator.
When the discussions are presented without expanded clarification
of important points and very specific, discerning find-out questions,
it is unlikely that investigators will adequately understand or implement the principles taught. Before moving on, the investigator's
understanding of each principle should be assessed with open-ended
questions.

Due to the emphasis on building from common beliefs, many
assume that investigators with a Christian background understand
many gospel principles because of the use of a shared nomenclature.
In reality, the restored gospel teaches a far greater depth to these principles than most members of other faiths appreciate. These principles
should not be glossed over, since missionary teaching serves as the
foundation of understanding for new members. When investigators
state that they "already know" about faith, repentance, and other principles, this usually demonstrates not that they have mastered the topic,
but that they do not understand it.

Investigators may demonstrate one of three levels of understanding:

1. Vague or inaccurate understanding. The investigator cannot
   accurately restate the pertinent points of the principle which
   was taught. The investigators may give vague answers parroting
   some of the major themes which were discussed but without
   adequate detail, or the answer may contain erroneous information.
2. Abstract understanding. The investigator can accurately restate
   the pertinent points but is unable to apply them to mean-

ingful real-life situations or give original examples.
3. Understanding with insight. The investigator can accurately restate the points which were discussed and can give original examples and apply his understanding to real-life situations.

Anything less than understanding with insight is inadequate. One should never assume that the investigator has understood or incorporated a teaching point simply because he has heard it and has not asked questions or raised objections. Such assumptions are often unfounded and frequently lead to disappointment. Missionaries who are skilled in find-out techniques rarely face unpleasant surprises, while those who make unfounded assumptions are constantly bewildered as to why they are having difficulties with their investigators.

Effective missionaries ask specific find-out questions to accurately assess the investigator's understanding and acceptance of doctrines taught. When areas of lack of understanding are identified, they focus on remedying these deficiencies and help investigators to develop the gospel habits of daily scripture study and regular church attendance, rather than pressing onward in spite of unresolved issues.

When multiple investigators are being taught, it is necessary to ensure that each individual understands the principles. This does not need to take an inordinate amount of time, nor should each person be asked every question. When investigators demonstrate varying levels of interest, understanding, or acceptance, the missionaries must determine whether it is most appropriate to focus on the most interested individuals or to attempt to accommodate everyone. Often missionaries will be able to pick up on nonverbal cues if certain individuals are uninterested or feel uncomfortable when asked questions in a group setting, and the wishes of such individuals should be respected. If one individual is particularly skeptical or disruptive and not responsive to missionary explanations, focusing on the most receptive individuals can allow progress and avoid confrontation or disruption. If the investigators are on track for baptism, it is imperative to ensure that each individual fully understands the principles taught, agrees with them, and is implementing them. It is more important to ensure that each individual is fully prepared and worthy for baptism than to meet arbitrary goals for families or friends to be baptized simultaneously.

ADAPT TO INVESTIGATOR NEEDS

The prudent missionary does not simply follow a cookbook but adapts the lesson as appropriate for the investigator's needs, background, interests, and time available. He is alert to verbal and nonverbal cues that help him to assess the investigator's interest and understanding and to identify challenges. He is respectful of the investigator's time and other responsibilities. He actively assesses the situation and is flexible in changing plans as necessary during the visit to best meet the investigator's needs. After each teaching session, he and his companion evaluate what went well and where opportunities for improvement exist. They carefully discuss each investigator to identify potential hang-ups and to determine how to best meet that individual's needs on future visits.

BAPTISM

As a missionary, I found that most investigators would sail smoothly through most of the second of the six discussions at the time, which emphasized the role of Jesus Christ and the first principles and ordinances of the gospel, culminating in a challenge for baptism. The investigators would typically express agreement with all points of the discussion until we arrived at the crucial question: "Will you be baptized on [date]?" The common reaction was one of bewilderment: "But I've already been baptized!" Upon investigation, most other missionaries in my mission, as well as many acquaintances who served in other areas of the world, reported the same problem with alarming frequency.

Many of our investigators with Christian backgrounds were familiar with the basic concepts of faith, repentance, and baptism, although they may have understood them somewhat differently. They agreed with the concept that baptism was necessary but did not understand why they had to be baptized in the LDS church after accepting baptism in another denomination. The principles of priesthood authority, apostasy, and restoration were not taught until the third discussion at that time, while the baptismal commitment was presented in the second. The discussions failed to lay a logical foundation for other Christians, who felt violated or threatened when asked to make a membership commitment to the LDS Church without first being taught and accepting the principles of apostasy, restoration, and divine authority.

The error of asking investigators who did not understand and accept these concepts to commit to baptism on the second discussion was in most cases unrecoverable once the investigators built up barriers with the surprised reply that they had already been baptized. Our solution was to switch the order of the second and third discussions, teaching the principles of apostasy, restoration, and divine authority at least one visit before the baptismal question was ever asked, to address potential concerns preemptively. We extended the baptismal commitment only in the third discussion and emphasized that baptism performed by those without authority was not recognized by God, before ever reaching the baptismal commitment. The results were remarkable; the percentage of our investigators who accepted the baptismal commitment rose dramatically. I never again heard an investigator respond to the baptismal commitment with the statement that he or she had already been baptized.

More than a decade later, the official lessons have placed the principles of authority, apostasy, and restoration in the first discussion, as it had been half a century earlier, so that investigators are taught these principles before the baptismal commitment is presented. The problem of investigators stating that they "have already been baptized" has become less common, but it still occurs when investigators are inadequately taught or when missionaries have not appropriately verified understanding and agreement. Clear and proper teaching of these principles is necessary to help the investigator gain an appreciation for the blessings of the restored gospel and to diffuse concerns preemptively.

WHEN SHOULD THE BAPTISMAL COMMITMENT BE EXTENDED?

Most missionaries using the *Preach My Gospel* manual still report low acceptance rates when they ask investigators to commit to baptism. Missionaries are instructed to extend the baptismal commitment at the end of the second discussion unless they specifically feel guided by the Spirit not to do so. Yet no attempt is made to help missionaries understand or evaluate the factors that impact responsiveness, and so such failures are not surprising.

The instruction to solicit the commitment for baptism at the end of the second discussion may be premature for most investigators. My research has found that few investigators have read more than several pages in the Book of Mormon or have prayed and received a testimony at the time missionaries ask for a baptismal commitment. Very few have any meaningful idea of the expectations of Church membership and are ill prepared to "count the cost" as the Savior instructed prior to committing to follow him (Luke 14:27–33). Most investigators have not attended church even once before the baptismal commitment is extended. How many would propose marriage to an acquaintance before even going on a date? Then why do we ask investigators to be baptized before they have attended church? These factors contribute to both low response rates to the baptismal commitment and to low retention rates even when baptism occurs. While the ostensible intent of such approaches is to ensure that missionaries are consistently inviting investigators to follow Christ, premature invitations to lifelong commitment before the conversion or repentance processes have begun in earnest typically backfire and lead to the loss of receptive people who could be baptized and retained with more and better preparation.

I have found that it is rarely appropriate to extend the baptismal commitment until investigators have attended church, read in the Book of Mormon, received a divine witness by the Holy Spirit, and demonstrated understanding of the principles of divine authority, apostasy, restoration, and one true and living Church. Missionaries should know whether investigators understand that the Church is true and are willing to observe divine commandments before extending the baptismal commitment.

At the time a baptismal commitment is requested, the basic expectations of Church membership should be discussed (see the previous Focus on Commandments section). If missionaries have been teaching the message of repentance, most of these points should have been covered well before the baptismal commitment is presented. If missionaries begin teaching the discussion with the baptismal commitment and determine with preliminary find-out questions that the investigators are not ready for the baptismal commitment, it is appropriate to defer the baptismal commitment to a later discussion and adapt the lesson to focus on foundational principles and basic gospel laws.

It is not necessary to set a baptismal date at the time the commitment is extended. The major issue is the investigator's desire to work toward baptism by living gospel laws. If a tentative date is agreed upon, the investigators should understand that this date will be adjusted depending on their consistency in implementing the gospel habits that demonstrate the fruits of repentance. By implementing these principles, my companion and I found our acceptance rate for the baptismal commitment rise from less than one-quarter to over 80 percent. With appropriate preparation and insight, the investigator's response to the baptismal commitment should almost never be a surprise.

LESSONS FROM THE AREA BOOK

Several times on my mission, I was assigned to serve in areas where previous missionaries had little success. After reviewing the area books where prior missionaries kept records of their activities, I began to understand many other reasons for low missionary success besides the "hardness of people's hearts." Records were revealing about what missionaries had or had not been doing, revealing four red flags in areas where missionaries had experienced low success:

1. Poor record keeping in general. What the missionaries had been doing was not clearly documented. Schedules were largely empty with only a few appointments, mostly with members and stale investigators, while very little contacting was being done.

2. The relative paucity of fresh contacts. There were often only a handful of contact telephone numbers, even in areas where

missionaries had served for many months. Even these had often not been followed up promptly. I sometimes wondered what the missionaries had been doing with their time, since few discussions had been taught and there was scant evidence of finding or contacting activities.

3. Few investigators relative to the time the missionaries had served. Some area books might appear thick, but usually these went back many months.

4. A pattern of inappropriate discussions that was obvious even from the sparse documentation. Often, missionaries would push ahead with the discussions with investigators who had not resolved prior concerns or observed earlier commitments. Investigator records frequently contained notes like these:

"We finished the last discussion. John is still having trouble believing that there is a God who loves him."

"Mary had difficulty accepting the principle of tithing ... she has not yet been to church."

"We talked about eternal progression [4th discussion] with the Jones family. They are not reading regularly in the Book of Mormon and are having trouble believing in modern prophets."

Major investigator hang-ups should have been resolved early. When such difficulties were not resolved, the missionaries should have invited the investigators to come to church to learn more when they were willing to put forth greater effort, rather than pressing forward without resolving the underlying issues.

Many missionaries were frustrated at completing all of the discussions with investigators who were not attending church or regularly reading scriptures and who had never accepted the baptismal commitment. One exasperated elder asked, "We've taught them all that we have and they still haven't committed to baptism. What now?" The problem was rooted in the practice of improperly teaching discussions for which the investigators were not prepared. It is inappropriate to continue with new discussions when more basic material is not accepted or commitments are not being kept. Introducing new material generally overwhelms doubtful investigators further, rather than resolving existing concerns.

These practices were adopted by missionaries who are interested in filling up their schedules with visits of any quality rather than acting in the best interest of the Lord and the people they were called to serve. The proper question when scheduling discussions is not "how can we fill up our schedule to minimize or avoid contacting," but rather "are the investigators adequately prepared to hear and accept the next lesson." If we will "treasure up in our minds continually the word of life," it will be given to us "that portion that shall be meted unto every man" (D&C 84:85). The portion that is meted is "according to the heed and diligence which they give unto [Christ]" (Alma 12:9). It is counterproductive and contrary to the spirit of the Lord to mete out to individuals more than the portion that their heed and diligence allow.

After a few telephone calls to determine the level of interest of old investigators and contacts, we generally had the area book down to a fraction of its former size. Many individuals were sad that elder or sister so-and-so was gone but expressed no real interest to continue learning about the gospel. Such responses are indicative of inappropriate teaching centered on personal relationships rather than on the gospel of Jesus Christ. In areas that prior missionaries had labeled as "hard-hearted," my companions and I always found it remarkable how much more receptive we found the local people to be as we consistently got out of doors to make new contacts and kept an active turnover. Increased contacting, appropriate teaching, and prayer were associated with greater success, and the congregations started to grow again.

ADDRESSING CONCERNS OF CRITICS

Anti-LDS literature and concerns of critics need to be addressed, because they are ubiquitous and are encountered repeatedly by missionaries worldwide. The impact of critics on Church growth is small compared to the impact of our own faithfulness, obedience, and implementation of correct principles in our own missionary efforts, as suggested in D&C 103:5–10. My research suggests that the implementation of appropriate and effective finding and retention programs founded in gospel principles can each increase real growth by three- to fourfold (and approximately tenfold in combination), while the detriment of anti-Mormons can be generously estimated at less than 50 percent. Nonetheless, the Book of Mormon prophet Nephi attributes the small size of the worldwide Latter-day Saints Church to the activities of the "great and abominable church" (1 Nephi 14:10–12), which undoubtedly encompasses anti-LDS agitators.

Just as Book of Mormon missionaries experienced far greater success among the Lamanites than among the Nephite dissenters, attempts to reclaim hostile ex-members are rarely successful today. This is not because the claims of critics are difficult to answer; to the contrary, I have not found a single significant claim of critics that can endure the scrutiny of honesty, sound reasoning, full historical context, and scripture. It is rather because those affected by critical literature have often closed their minds to any possibility of a faithful solution before allowing an audience. Following King Lamoni's miraculous conversion, all those who heard his testimony believed and were converted, but many refused to listen (Alma 19:31–32). Even the Savior experienced little success in his ministry among the Pharisees.

Anti-LDS literature is problematic precisely because it dissuades many individuals before they even allow defenders of the faith an audience. One former mission president observed that once the poison of anti-Mormonism gets into the system, it is very difficult to reverse. Even when individuals are willing to discuss concerns, answering one concern often results only in the presentation of a litany of others. When concerns are addressed to the individual's satisfaction, most disaffected members still fail to return to church. Alleged concerns sometimes have little to do with the real difficulties. Some individuals like to drink beer or to spend Sundays playing golf and cite criticisms to rationalize chosen behavior patterns.

Yet scriptures also teach that many honorable men and women have been "blinded by the craftiness of men" (D&C 76:75) and misled by church critics. It is not for us to judge the worthiness or motives of those willing to seek answers to their questions. Some of the most destructive "answers" I have ever seen have come from committed but insensitive members who seemed to be more intent on "proving" that the questioner had some underlying spiritual problem than in providing a rational reply. The fact that an individual is willing to seek out and listen to a reply places him far ahead of most of those troubled by the claims of critics.

Prevention is the first line in dealing with anti-Mormonism. This includes a focus on each member and investigator's daily study of the Book of Mormon, with families where possible, personal and family prayer, church attendance, and personal worthiness. When these habits are not in place, individuals are unlikely to have the guidance of the Holy Spirit and are much more vulnerable to the false claims of critics. Those with limited spiritual maturity and historical knowledge of the Church, such as investigators, are particularly vulnerable to anti-LDS claims. Investigators preparing for baptism and new converts should also be prepared for adversity by being made aware that there are many false accusations circulating about the Church.

Austin Farrar noted: "Though argument does not create conviction, lack of it destroys belief. What seems to be proved may not be embraced; but what no one shows the ability to defend is quickly abandoned. Rational argument does not create belief, but it maintains a climate in which belief may flourish."* While the practice of reducing all questions to a testimony of Joseph Smith and the Book of Mormon can be a valid starting point, the inability to provide specific answers to repeated questions can be unsettling.

The average member or missionary does not need to know the answer to every question of critics, nor do criticisms and their answers usually represent a good use of study time. However, it is valuable to be aware of resources for dealing with such concerns. When one does not know the answer to a question, local members or leaders may be helpful. The Foundation for Apologetics Information and Research (FAIR) maintains a Web site at www.fairlds.org with answers to critics, extensive resources for defending faith, and an online response team that can provide assistance with addressing difficult concerns. FAIR has no administrative connection to the Church, and answers may be helpful but should not be viewed as official.

Awareness of some of the tactics used by critics of the Church can be helpful in understanding how to combat them. Such points are

---

* Farrer, Austin, "The Christian Apologist," in *Light on C. S. Lewis*, ed., Jocelyn Gibb, New York: Harcourt, Brace & World, 1965, 26.

nicely addressed in the book *Guess Who Wants to Have You for Lunch? A Missionary Guide to Anti-Mormon Tactics & Strategies* published by FAIR.* Wider awareness of challenges in defending faith and the resources available for answering them are necessary to achieve faster and more accurate responses to investigators and members tainted by anti-Mormon literature during the very limited time window in which some receptivity to faithful answers may be preserved.

---

*   Denison, Alan and Darryl L. Barksdale, *Guess Who Wants to Have You for Lunch? A Missionary Guide to Anti-Mormon Tactics & Strategies*, Redding, CA: Foundation for Apologetics Information and Research, 2002.

Teaching Points
from the Discussions

T HE FOLLOWING POINTS ARE not intended to provide a comprehensive overview of the discussions but offer practical observations on selected topics.

BELIEF IN GOD

Belief in God is a long-term issue with deep roots, which can only rarely be changed by missionaries. There are many witnesses in the world to the existence of God (Alma 30:44), and the testimony of missionaries can rarely overcome an individual's lifelong rejection of the witnesses of nature all about him. However, there are many good people like King Lamoni who acknowledge the existence of a greater power, yet have thought little about God. To the sectarian world, the nature of God is a mystery. Many denominations preach an incomprehensible God who is everywhere and yet nowhere in particular, in whose image nothing could be created, and for who man can be only a distant servant rather than a friend. Without an understanding of God's attributes and perfections, as Joseph Smith noted in *Lectures on Faith*, there is no means to develop true faith in Him. Our belief in a good, merciful, and just God is unique and empowering. The ancient pagan faiths believed in gods who were often capricious and unjust.

Many Christian denominations also preach an unjust god, who they believe will save them in iniquity because they acknowledge their creed as a one-time event or with a deathbed confession after a life of sin, while condemning to eternal punishment unbaptized children and just and honest individuals of other faiths who live more righteously. Some good men and women of other faiths may understand God's justice and perfection, but to the extent that they do, it often represents a divergence from the official teachings of their denominations.

CONTINUING REVELATION THROUGH PROPHETS

Investigators should understand that revelation must be an ongoing process and that the word of God to ancient peoples as contained in the Bible, while it is very important to us, is not fully adequate for us today. We need a living prophet to receive God's ongoing word. The living prophets have never been popular or widely accepted by the world. The creed of apostate religions has always been to pretend to follow dead prophets while persecuting the living ones. The Pharisees of Christ's day claimed to be disciples of Abraham and Moses, while rejecting the living Christ. Christ pointed out that they would have accepted Him if they had truly understood and obeyed the teachings of Abraham and Moses (John 5:45–46). Christ taught that whosoever accepts His representatives on earth accepts Him, and whosoever rejects His earthly representatives rejects Him also. It is easy to nominally acknowledge long-dead prophets, since they are not here to admonish to repentance. False religions can readily take out of context the words of dead prophets who are not there to object. It requires much greater effort to conform one's life to the Lord's teachings through modern prophets, since living prophets ask us to obey specific commandments today.

The need for continuing revelation through prophets can be demonstrated by asking investigators what would have happened to an individual living in the time of Noah who tried to live righteously and claimed to accept the teachings of Adam, Enoch, and other prior prophets but refused to listen to Noah. If he rejected the living prophet and did not board the Ark, what would have happened to him when the floods came? Today we have many challenges and circumstances which are different from those of ancient peoples. It is as vital for our salvation that we follow the guidance of the Lord's living prophet on the earth today as it was for individuals to follow Noah and board the Ark at the time of the Great Flood. It is not adequate simply to acknowledge the prophet's divine calling: we must obey his words. We should be anxiously engaged in learning and implementing the counsel of the living prophet, the Lord's mouthpiece on earth.

JOSEPH SMITH

Wilford Woodruff taught: "Those who have been acquainted with the Prophet Joseph, who laid the foundation of this Church and kingdom, who was an instrument in the hand of God in bringing to light the Gospel in this last dispensation, know well that every feeling of his soul, every sentiment of his mind, and every act of his life, proved that he was determined to maintain the principle of truth, even to the sacrificing of his life."[*] The Joseph Smith testimony pamphlet is an excellent proselyting tool, because it teaches most of the points of the first three discussions, from the nature of God and the central role of Christ in the plan of salvation to the apostasy, restoration, and priesthood authority. For this reason, I have often found it helpful to give selected contacts a copy of the pamphlet and ask their opinion

---

[*] Woodruff, Wilford, *Journal of Discourses*, 2:192.

about it when I call to follow up.

While teaching the discussions, it is important to establish whether the investigator, like Joseph Smith, has been confused by the multitude of churches teaching discordant principles while proclaiming their own precepts to be true. The conflicting creeds of the more than 30,000 nominally Christian denominations cannot all be true or of God. Does he understand that although a variety of faiths may have varying fragments of truth, only one church can be completely true and that there should be one church for all nationalities and cultures? If so, is it important for them to find the true church? How can they find out which it is? If the investigator does not understand or agree that there can be only one true church and that it is important for us to find that church and obey Heavenly Father's teachings, it is unlikely that significant progress toward conversion can be made until understanding and agreement are achieved.

Many grown men and women have never considered or contemplated the essential and self-evident principle that the fact that there should be one true church for all people was apparent to Joseph Smith as a fourteen-year-old boy. Many declare of their national or cultural church that "we have our own church," betraying nondivine origins. Like Joseph Smith, the pure in heart seek to conform their lives to the will of Christ through divine instruction in His one true Church, rather than seeking a faith built on the works of man that conforms to personal aims instead of God's.

APOSTASY AND RESTORATION

Two visual aids are particularly helpful in conveying the concepts of apostasy and restoration. The first demonstrates the Lord's model of communication with mankind through the process of ongoing revelation linking heaven and earth. A timeline representing the history of the world is drawn from left to right on the bottom of a paper turned so that width is greater than length. The words "Heavenly Father" are written centered at the top of the page. Starting at the beginning of the timeline, the names of selected prophets such as Adam, Enoch, Noah, Abraham, Moses, Nephi, and Alma are written. The investigator is asked whether Heavenly Father communicated with these prophets and then how He communicated with them (through revelation). Lines are drawn from the title "Heavenly Father" to the names of each of the prophets, representing revelation. The missionary explains that God sent His son, Jesus Christ, whose name is written on the time-line followed by the label "apostles." It is explained that after Christ's crucifixion and resurrection, the apostles were sent into all the world, but after a short time, they were persecuted and killed. The line of revelation ends, and a break is drawn. For many centuries, there was no true church upon the earth. Because people relied on their own wisdom for understanding of doctrine, contentions arose, and many separate movements were founded. Lines representing the apostate church are drawn branching into many offshoot denominations. It is explained that in our time, God called a prophet and spoke to him just as He spoke with Moses and other ancient prophets. Joseph Smith's name is written further down the timeline, and lines of revelation from Heavenly Father to Joseph Smith and other modern prophets are drawn. Revelations have continued with inspired prophets called after Joseph Smith up to the current prophet, Gordon B. Hinckley, and beyond. Once you are convinced that the investigators understand the model, ask them to explain the apostasy and restoration in their own words.

The second visual aid teaches the concept of the only true and living church. The outline of a temple picture is cut out from an old *Gospel Principles* book or another source. The picture is cut into five pieces, with three on the top and two on the bottom. The three top pieces are labeled "revelation," "divine authority," and "teachings." The bottom two pieces are labeled "Jesus Christ" and "living apostles and prophets." The pieces are stored in an envelope for convenience when not in use. The temple representing the Church of Jesus Christ is assembled, and it is explained to investigators that the Church is more than just a building, an organization, or a collection of teachings. The Lord's true church is built upon the foundation of (1) Jesus Christ as the chief cornerstone (Ephesians 2:20) and (2) living apostles and prophets with (3) revelation, (4) divine authority, and (5) teachings. The temple is taken down step by step during the discussion principle on the apostasy and rebuilt during the subsequent discussion of the restoration of the gospel.

This model demonstrates that the difference between the true Church and other churches is far greater than simply a few missing pieces of doctrine. Other churches have no living apostles and prophets, no ongoing revelation, no divine authority, and therefore no direct link with Jesus Christ. They have only some teachings, a small fragment of the complete church, which are corrupted because of the absence of the first four principles and by intermingling with the philosophies of men. Once you are convinced that the investigators understand these essential features of the true Church, ask them to explain the importance of each.

ASKING OF GOD

Like Joseph Smith, each investigator must receive a witness of truth by asking of God. Does the investigator understand why one's neighbor, friend, or pastor may not be an accurate or objective source of divine truth? If Heavenly Father is the source of divine truth, only He can confirm truth through the Holy Spirit and His prophets. Joseph

Smith took real effort first to study out truth by study and contemplation. When he prayed, he prayed sincerely with willingness to obey the Lord's answer to his prayer, regardless of how difficult it might be. When we pray to know truth, we must be willing to live in accordance with the answer we receive.

On many occasions I have heard missionaries instruct investigators to continue to pray for an answer, while failing to recognize the quiet promptings of the Holy Spirit that had already borne witness to the investigators. While some receive remarkable revelatory manifestations, for most the witness of the Spirit comes as a "still small voice." A discerning missionary can tell when investigators are feeling the Spirit and help investigators to recognize its manifestations.

PRAYER

Whether the investigators pray vocally at the end of the first discussion is an important predictor of future success. If missionaries cannot get investigators to pray at the conclusion of the first discussion, chances for a return visit and for future progress with the investigator are significantly reduced. Therefore, every effort must be made to help the investigator to pray at the end of the discussion. Few missionaries are able to get more than a minority of their investigators to pray at this time, generally because the investigators are not prepared adequately and the commitment is not presented properly. I have found that the application of a few simple steps can consistently increase the percentage of investigators who pray verbally at the conclusion of the first discussion to over 80 percent.

A chart of the four steps of prayer (addressing Heavenly Father, giving thanks, asking for blessings, and closing) is introduced to the investigator. The missionary asks the investigator who we pray to (Heavenly Father). Then we give thanks. The investigator is asked what he or she is thankful for, and several responses are written down on a piece of paper following the respective prayer steps. Common responses include one's family, work, health, life, the day, the gospel, and so forth. The investigator is then asked what blessings he or she needs in his life, and a few of the mentioned blessings are jotted down. Many investigators mention needs such as blessings for their family, help in finding or learning truth, health, safety, and so forth. The investigator is then asked how we close a prayer (in the name of Jesus Christ, with "amen" signifying agreement). The investigator is encouraged for his or her replies. At the end of the discussion, it is easy to encourage the investigators to pray. The common objection that they do not know how to pray has been preemptively diffused. The missionary can remind the investigator that they have already come up with all of the elements of prayer. Missionaries must exude confidence that the investigator can pray. Although the investigator is not limited to his list, he can use this as a reference. The investigator may need to be prompted slightly, but the overwhelming majority will offer a prayer. The investigator should then be commended for praying.

FAITH

Investigators must be taught the distinction between true faith and mere belief. Joseph Smith taught that faith is a principle of power that requires sacrifice and commitment that transcend mere belief. Ezra Taft Benson taught: "Unless we do His [Christ's] teachings, we do not demonstrate faith in Him."* My father defined faith as "the will to do right." I believe it is, even when it requires great personal sacrifice.

---

*   Benson, Ezra Taft, *Come Unto Christ*, Salt Lake City, UT: Deseret Book, 1983, 132.

GIFT OF THE HOLY GHOST

Investigators should be taught to distinguish between the Holy Ghost, the Light of Christ, reason, and personal feelings and emotions. Knowing that something is right or wrong is not a function of the Holy Ghost, but of the Light of Christ: one's conscience. The Holy Ghost distinguishes between true and false (Moroni 10:5) and provides other gifts of the spirit. The Holy Ghost is not automatically received when the gift of the Holy Ghost is conferred on us. The scriptures provide some examples of exceptional individuals who were sufficiently prepared that they immediately received the Holy Ghost after confirmation. Most of us have to work hard after baptism to receive and retain the Holy Ghost. The Holy Ghost is not commanded to come to us: we are commanded to actively "receive the Holy Ghost," or to seek, find, and keep it through our diligence and obedience.

SABBATH DAY

Observance of the Sabbath is a core commandment that should be taught to all investigators at the time that they express a desire to work toward baptism, since obedience to this law is necessary for the investigators to receive the Holy Spirit. Observance of the Sabbath includes more than simply attending church meetings. It means that we do not buy or sell things on Sunday, work in our garden, or engage in paid employment when at all possible. Harold B. Lee taught: "May we not hope that in addition to our worshipful activities on the Lord's Day we might also on that day reduce the drudgery of the home to a minimum, and that outside the home only essential chores will be performed. Make this a day of prayerful, thoughtful study of the scriptures and other good books.... My experience has taught me that the prompting of the conscience to a faithful Church member is the safest indicator as to that which is contrary to the spirit of worship on the Sabbath Day."*

Prospective converts should understand that the spiritual necessity of attending church meetings transcends the value of the information conveyed. Christ taught that taking the sacrament regularly is vital to salvation: "Except ye eat the flesh of the Son of man, and drink his blood, ye have no life in you. Whoso eateth my flesh, and drinketh my blood, hath eternal life; and I will raise him up at the last day" (John 6:53–54). Spencer W. Kimball taught: "We do not go to Sabbath meetings to be entertained or amused; we go there to worship the Lord. It is an individual responsibility, and regardless of what is said from the pulpit, if one wishes to worship the Lord in spirit and in truth, he may do so by attending his meetings, partaking of the sacrament, and contemplating the beauties of the Gospel. If the sacrament meeting is a failure to you, you are the one that has failed. No one can worship for you, you must do your own serving of the Lord."†

THE WORD OF WISDOM

Elder Dallin H. Oaks noted: "According to one study, 75 percent of adult converts in North America had to give up at least one of these substances mentioned in the Word of Wisdom—tobacco, alcohol, coffee, or tea—and 31 percent had to give up smoking, a very addictive habit. The study also showed that almost all converts—over 90 percent—had a very high desire to avoid these substances after their baptism. However … one third to one half of them reported that they had experienced 'occasional,' 'frequent,' or 'complete' lapses into their

---

*   Lee, Harold B., *Decisions for Successful Living*, Salt Lake City, UT: Deseret Book, 1973, 148.

†   Kimball, Spencer W., *Conference Report*, April 1944.

abstinence."* Tobacco use is much more prevalent in Europe, Asia, and Latin America than in the United States, while tea is ubiquitous in Europe and Asia. Most investigators acknowledge that smoking and drinking are wrong but cite the force of addiction.

Word of Wisdom problems represent a major obstacle to baptism and to long-term convert retention. In the old discussion series, Word of Wisdom issues were brought up only at the end of the fourth discussion, when the investigator had already completed two-thirds of the entire discussion series and two discussions after the baptismal commitment was obtained. In the *Preach My Gospel* discussion series, Word of Wisdom issues are typically brought up only in the final discussion before baptism! These issues often take time for investigators to overcome. Many missionaries run out of material to teach while the investigator continues to struggle with overcoming an addiction, and some investigators are never baptized in spite of completing a full series of discussions.

I often find it helpful to bring up the Word of Wisdom restrictions on smoking and alcohol on the first or second visit with an interested investigator, recognizing these habits as potentially serious stumbling blocks that must be addressed early. Substance addictions also impair the spirit, and progress is often limited when the investigator has numbed his spirit with nicotine or other drugs. There is no point in sailing smoothly through the early discussions only to find out much later that the investigator wants to take several months to try to stop smoking. Mentioning the Word of Wisdom early also saves face for the investigator, because they have a longer time to quit and are able to get more support along the way. Most individuals know from their conscience that alcohol and tobacco abuse are wrong, and so raising these issues even before investigators have gained a testimony rarely

---

*   Oaks, Dallin A., "The Role of Members in Conversion," *Ensign*, March 2003.

leads to objections.

In most cultures, abstinence from tea or coffee should not be pushed until the baptismal commitment is obtained, although some individuals will discontinue drinking them as soon as they learn that the missionaries abstain. These substances, while still addictive, are usually significantly easier for investigators to give up than alcohol and tobacco. It is also more difficult for many people to understand the need to give up these substances until they have received a testimony.

Because many investigators never conquer substance addiction, no baptismal commitment should be considered firm until the Word of Wisdom is being fully observed for sustained periods. All prospective converts should be expected to abstain from substances forbidden by the Word of Wisdom for at least four weeks prior to baptism to ensure that addictions are firmly overcome. Shorter periods lead to high relapse rates.

Missionaries serving in Europe or Asia where tea is widely consumed should be aware that many of the commercially available "herbal teas" are actually mixtures of herbs with yellow, black, or green tea. Many missionaries have unwittingly consumed large quantities of forbidden tea in investigators' homes by assuming that all "herbal tea" is safe. If an investigator offers "herbal tea," the missionary should always look at the box to ensure that tea extract is not one of the ingredients before accepting.

The Word of Wisdom offers benefit to all. Heber J. Grant taught: "No man who breaks the Word of Wisdom can gain the same amount of knowledge and intelligence in this world as the man who obeys that law. I don't care who he is or where he comes from, his mind will not be as clear, and he cannot advance as far and as rapidly and retain his power as much as he would if he obeyed the Word of Wisdom."[*]

---

[*]   Grant, Heber J., *Conference Report*, April 1925.

Convert Retention

THE SAVIOR'S TEACHINGS
ON CONVERT RETENTION

THE RESURRECTED CHRIST COMMISSIONED His disciples: "Go ye therefore, and teach all nations, baptizing them in the name of the Father, and of the Son, and of the Holy Ghost" (Matthew 28:19). The Savior taught that if we abide in Him, we will bring forth "much fruit" (John 15:5) which is to endure: " I have chosen you … that ye should go and bring forth fruit, and that your fruit should remain" (John 15:16). Christ's disciples are not sent forth to baptize individuals who lack commitment or understanding in order to generate long lists of nominal but overwhelmingly inactive members, but to build a living church of committed and participating believers who have undergone real and life-changing conversion. The Savior taught that individuals must count the cost of discipleship before deciding to follow him: "And whosoever doth not bear his cross, and come after me, cannot be my disciple. For which of you, intending to build a tower, sitteth not down first, and counteth the cost, whether he have sufficient to finish it? Lest haply, after he hath laid the foundation, and is not able to finish it, all that behold it begin to mock him, saying, This man began to build, and was not able to finish. And this he said, signifying there should not any man follow him, unless he was able to continue; saying, Or what king, going to make war against another king, sitteth not down first, and consulteth whether he be able with ten thousand to meet him that cometh against him with twenty thousand? Or else, while the other is yet a great way off, he sendeth an ambassage, and desireth conditions of peace. So likewise, whosoever he be of you that forsaketh not all that he hath, he cannot be my disciple. Wherefore, settle this in your hearts, that ye will do the things which I shall teach, and command you" (JST Luke 14:27–35). Missionaries must help prospective converts to count the cost to ensure that they will be able to continue long-term in full Church activity, even in the face of significant challenges or hardships.

Christ taught that investigators must already be keeping the basic commandments at the time of baptism, rather than merely promising to do so: "Bring forth therefore fruits meet for repentance…. And now also the axe is laid unto the root of the trees: therefore every tree which bringeth not forth good fruit is hewn down, and cast into the fire" (Matthew 3:8,10). The Savior declared: "Ye shall know them by their fruits. Do men gather grapes of thorns, or figs of thistles? Even so every good tree bringeth forth good fruit; but a corrupt tree bringeth forth evil fruit. A good tree cannot bring forth evil fruit, neither can a corrupt tree bring forth good fruit. Every tree that bringeth not forth good fruit is hewn down, and cast into the fire. Wherefore by their fruits ye shall know them" (Matthew 7:16–20). Christ also taught "he that will not hear my voice, the same shall ye not receive into my church, for him I will not receive at the last day" (Mosiah 26:28). Other language translations clarify this passage with words equivalent to "hearken" or "heed" instead of "hear." If desiring baptism alone were adequate for church membership, the Lord would not have needed to give Alma these instructions. Prospective converts must not only passively hear, but also must actively heed the Lord's word to qualify for baptism.

Christ taught that no constructive role is filled by recalcitrant inactives and members who do not live the gospel: "Salt is good: but if the salt have lost his savour, wherewith shall it be seasoned? It is neither fit for the land, nor yet for the dunghill; but men cast it out. He that hath ears to hear, let him hear" (Luke 14:34–35). In modern revelation, the Lord affirms: "If ye will not abide in my covenant ye are not worthy of me" (D&C 98:15). It is incongruous with intelligence to believe that an investigator is willing to forsake everything for Christ and even to give up his or her own life if necessary, when he or she has been unreliable in making even the petty sacrifices of weekly church attendance, daily scripture reading, and so forth for even four weeks before baptism. When the disciples could not cast a devil out of an afflicted man, Christ admonished them: "Howbeit this kind goeth not out but by prayer and fasting" (Matthew 17:21). Similarly, helping investigators to become genuinely converted and to fully repent before baptism requires sustained preparation, meditation, and prayer.

SCRIPTURAL TEACHINGS
ON PREBAPTISMAL PREPARATION

The prophet Moroni emphasized that individuals are worthy for baptism only when they bring forth not promises, not sprouts, not leaves, but the actual fruits of full repentance, habits of consistent obedience to gospel principles, and righteous living: "Behold, elders, priests, and teachers were baptized; and they were not baptized save they brought forth fruit meet that they were worthy of it. Neither did they receive any unto baptism save they came forth with a broken heart and a contrite spirit, and witnessed unto the church that they truly repented of all their sins. And none were received unto baptism save they took upon them the name of Christ, having a determination to serve him to the end" (Moroni 6:1–3).

Paul's admonition to "lay hands suddenly on no man" (1 Timothy 5:22) is commonly interpreted as a caution only against suddenly bestowing the Melchizedek Priesthood and high leadership callings upon green converts, but Greek manuscripts suggest differently. The Greek word "medeis" used in the phrase is not gender-specific to men, but means simply "no one": "Lay hands suddenly on no one." As the gift of the Holy Ghost is conferred during the confirmation of members of both genders shortly after baptism, Paul's prohibition encompasses and was likely directed primarily toward the rushed baptism and confirmation of unproven investigators. In 220 AD, Origen taught baptismal candidates: "Go and repent, catechumens, if you want to receive baptism for the remission of your sins.... No one who is in a state of sin when he comes for baptism can obtain the remission of his sins."*

The Book of Mormon provides an example of a spirit-led missionary program achieving 100 percent convert retention on a large scale. Of the efforts of Ammon and the sons of Mosiah, the Book of Alma states: "Thousands were brought to the knowledge of the Lord, yea, thousands were brought to believe in the traditions of the Nephites; and they were taught the records and prophecies which were handed down even to the present time. And as sure as the Lord liveth, so sure as many as believed, or as many as were brought to the knowledge of the truth, through the preaching of Ammon and his brethren, according to the spirit of revelation and of prophecy, and the power of God working miracles in them—yea, I say unto you, as the Lord liveth, as many of the Lamanites as believed in their preaching, and

---

*   Danielou, Jean, *Origen*, trans. Walter Mitchell, New York: Sheed & Ward, 1955, p. 54, Homily on Luke 21.

were converted unto the Lord, never did fall away" (Alma 23:5–6). This example of 100 percent convert retention is not included in the Book of Mormon to tease us as an impossible goal: it is the standard we are to emulate.

MODERN PROPHETS ON CONVERT RETENTION

President Gordon B. Hinckley reaffirmed that full retention is both possible and expected, stating: "I believe it is totally unnecessary that we lose [any of] those who are baptized" (brackets in original).[*] Quality is never an accident, and full convert retention does not occur by chance. In order to achieve the enduring fruits spoken of by the Savior, the Book of Mormon, and President Hinckley, we must follow the instructions the Lord has given us through both ancient and modern prophets. Retention requires a combination of proper teaching, strong fellowshipping which is firmly in place well before baptism, and full prebaptismal preparation. President Faust noted: "President Hinckley's strong, continuing challenge to us is retention, which requires full cooperation between the missionary, the leaders and members."[†]

Missionaries and mission leaders have a responsibility to ensure that new converts are fully prepared and worthy for baptism. President Gordon B. Hinckley has instructed: "A convert is a 'precious person.' He or she will make a tremendous decision in coming into the Church. Retention will primarily be the work of the local wards and branches. However, you have a very, very important part in this. Your missionaries must be sure that conversion is real, that it is life-

---

[*]   Hinckley, Gordon B., New Mission Presidents' Seminar, *LDS Church News*, July 4, 1998.

[†]   Faust, James E., New Mission Presidents' Seminar, *LDS Church News*, June 26, 1999.

changing, that it is something that is to last forever and go on through generations.... There is no point in baptizing people if they do not become solid members of the Church. Actual harm, he said, may be done to those who leave old friendships and old ways of doing things only to be allowed to slip into inactivity."* President Hinckley challenged missionaries in Bolivia: "Will you please see that every convert who comes into the Church while you are here on this mission is so taught that he or she will grow in faith and that a year after baptism he or she will be ready to get a temple recommend, and as soon as the temple is completed will be eligible to go to the house of the Lord?"† The implication is that proper missionary teaching can ensure that almost all converts remain active and qualify for temple recommends. President James E. Faust taught: "Who should be baptized? The answer would seem easy. Should we not baptize all those who want to or are willing to be baptized? The answer is not that simple. It is a great responsibility to bring someone into this Church who has not been adequately taught and who has not received of the Spirit so that through baptism they may become a new person through repentance. Moroni gave a solemn warning about this in Mormon 9:29: 'See that you are not baptized unworthily ...' Some of our young missionaries are so hungry for baptisms they may urge people to be baptized before their investigators understand what they are baptized for. Peter said, 'Repent and be baptized' (Acts 2:38). We must be certain the repentance process is at work. Investigators have a responsibility on their own as they hear the message of the restored gospel, but what I wish to emphasize today is our responsibility to them because it is

---

*   Hinckley, Gordon B., New Mission Presidents' Seminar, *LDS Church News*, July 4, 1998.

†   Hinckley, Gordon B., Bolivia Cochabamba Missionary Meeting, November 10, 1996.

under the authority of the priesthood that they are baptized and come into the Church."*

SCRIPTURES CANNOT
JUSTIFY FRACTIONAL RETENTION

In spite of the repeated mandates from ancient and modern prophets to achieve full or near-full convert retention, some Latter-day Saints dismiss even very low convert retention and member activity rates as part of a natural and allegedly unavoidable sorting process without even a cursory investigation into the causes and solutions, absolving both missionaries and members of any responsibility for quality teaching, adequate preparation, and fellowshipping of new converts. Adherents of quick-baptize approaches often cite the Parable of the Sower (Matthew 13:18–23), claiming that the falling away of many converts is inevitable. Yet the Savior gives no indication that the seeds sown on stony ground or among thorns in this parable represent converts baptized into the Church. To the contrary, the Savior describes them only as those who "hear the word": the Parable of the Sower is a parable of sharing the word with nonmembers of the Church. When the Savior is speaking of the Church, He typically refers to it as the "Kingdom of Heaven," a phrase absent in the Parable of the Sower.

Christ's parables of the "Kingdom of Heaven" imply that he is referring primarily to the active membership of the Church as being divided among "wheat and tares" (Matthew 13) and "wise and foolish virgins" (Matthew 25). Even the "foolish virgins" at least showed up to the wedding of the bridegroom, indicating that Christ was speaking about active members. Christ refers to the wheat and tares in the Church

---

* Faust, James E., New Mission Presidents' Seminar, *LDS Church News*, June 29, 1996.

"growing together" until the end of the world. In ancient scripture, church history, and the contemporary church, we can find abundant evidence of both wheat and tares among active church membership. While the Church provides teachings and ordinances that are essential to our salvation, simply participating in the social structure of the Church does not make us celestial people. As modern data indicate, only a fraction of active LDS members consistently observe central directives of ancient and modern prophets to share the gospel regularly, pay a full tithe, read the Book of Mormon daily, and so forth. Christ tells us that we cannot accurately discern between the wheat and tares in our midst, again suggesting that He is referring primarily to the active membership of the Church rather than to inactives. His statement that they will "grow together" until the "end of the world" again suggests that both represent active members, as even the tares have vitality that inactive and never-active members lack.

Knowing that the word will quickly wither in the stony ground of many listeners, it would be foolish to rush individuals to baptism before those who lack even the commitment to attend church for three or four weeks have sorted themselves out from those who have undergone a "life-changing conversion" that will "last forever and go on through generations." The need for the main sorting to occur before baptism is a key reason why the Lord instructs us to preach the word "not in haste" (D&C 60:8,14) and to gather "not in haste, lest there should be confusion, which bringeth pestilence" (D&C 63:24), why the apostle Paul instructs us to "lay hands suddenly" on no one, and why Christ taught of the need for listeners to first "count the cost" and be willing to forsake all that they have before embarking on the path to discipleship. (Luke 14).

There are a few occasions recorded in early Church history and even in the New Testament when individuals were baptized after what appears to be only a brief acquaintance with the Church, as in the case of Philip and the Ethiopian eunuch. These events occurred at a time of intense persecution during which accepting the Christian faith often meant facing a very real threat of death. Members often had to leave home and belongings to gather with the Saints, and tremendous sacrifice was implied in the act of joining the Church. Many converts came from the Jewish faith and other devout groups that were striving to carefully observe divine laws. Vast populations to reach over wide distances, limited time and resources, and persecution provided temporal urgency. The Bible is missing key portions, and the full background and follow-up of the stories of Philip and others are not presented. The scripture records: "And when they were come up out of the water, the Spirit of the Lord caught away Philip, that the eunuch saw him no more" (Acts 8:39). The dismal retention rates associated with quick-baptism policies suggest that if the Ethiopian eunuch became active in the Church following his baptism, this was likely a greater miracle than Philip being carried away by the Spirit. Missionaries today who employ quick-baptize techniques can simi-larly expect in many cases that they will "see their converts no more," not because of being miraculously carried away, but because of the rapid inactivity that almost always follows quick-baptize tactics. The teachings of Christ, Moroni, and many ancient and modern prophets teach compellingly that robust and thorough prebaptismal prepa-ration is required. How can one possibly claim that a convert has brought forth the "fruits of repentance" and has a determination to serve Christ to the end when he has not even made the effort to attend church for several weeks and study scriptures daily?

The counsel of President Hinckley and the example of the sons of Mosiah on achieving full convert retention are possible and expected. My personal experience is also that 100 percent convert retention at one year and 90 percent convert retention at two to five years can be consistently achieved by the application of scriptural principles. I have seen excellent retention rates in areas that have previously struggled with "revolving door baptisms" with the implementation of such guidelines. Such results can be achieved anywhere with careful cooperation between missionaries and members and adherence to essential standards.

THE COST OF INACTIVITY

ONLY AS CONVERTS BECOME active members does missionary work satisfy its divine purposes. Efforts to improve convert retention are often undermined by widespread misconceptions that low retention rates are either unavoidable or inevitable. One missionary shrugged off the catastrophic inactivity of quick baptism tactics with the reply: "At least these people are on the rolls so that now we can keep track of them better and look after their home teaching." If one hundred converts are baptized but only twenty or thirty are still active one month later, this performance is generally viewed as a resounding success. The missionaries met their statistical goals, a few converts remained active, and the responsibility for dealing with the other 70 to 80 percent is shifted to overwhelmed local members. Convert loss is not inevitable, nor does rampant inactivity represent only minor collateral damage on the way to meeting monthly baptismal goals. It is possible to generate large numbers of inactives in a relatively short time, yet even years of intensive fellowshipping and reactivation work are rarely able to fully reverse the damage done by prior accelerated baptism programs.

THE COST TO THE CONVERT

The cost of inactivity is devastating and immense. President Gordon B. Hinckley stated: "Nobody gains when there is baptism without retention. The missionary loses, and while the Church gains statistically, the membership suffers, really, and the enthusiasm of the convert turns to ashes."* He further noted: "Actual harm may be done to those who leave old friendships and old ways of doing things only to be allowed to slip into inactivity." He taught: "What does it profit the missionary to baptize someone who leaves the Church within six months? Nothing is accomplished; in fact, damage is done. We have pulled them away from their old moorings and brought them into the Church, only to have them drift away."[†] Those who lapse in fulfillment of solemn covenants find their eternal prospects worse than if they had never met the missionaries at all. Wilfried Decoo, an experienced Belgian church leader who became the president of a branch of 200 members with only 10 percent activity as a twenty-two-year-old convert, reflects on his work with inactives over more than three decades: "This is far more than a problem of organizational failure. If we take our religion seriously, we are talking about the prospect of a kind of spiritual death for those millions whom we have lost.... For many the suffering begins already in this life. I know, from years of experience in working with inactive members, of the agony—some of it lifelong—involved in the process of leaving the church. Here are people who once joyfully discovered the gospel, gained testimonies, and then turned their lives upside down and even severed relationships with families and friends to follow gospel principles, only to sink back eventually into the bitter pool of disillusionment."[‡]

---

*   Hinckley, Gordon B., *LDS Church News*, July 4, 1998.

†   Hinckley, Gordon B., Woods Cross Utah Regional Conference, January 10, 1998.

‡   Decoo, Wilfried, "Feeding the Fleeing Flock: Reflections on the Struggle to Retain Church Members in Europe," *Dialogue*, 29/1 (Spring 1996): 97–113.

THE COST TO THE CONGREGATION

I have been inundated with messages from members around the world who have long noted problems with the widespread revolving-door quick-baptize approaches. Such stories have come not from critics, but from faithful members, including bishops, high counselors, stake presidents, branch presidents, CES teachers, ward mission leaders, stake mission presidents, and returned missionaries. They cite the tremendous burden of recent and ongoing quick-baptize practices to the work of the Church. Wilfried Decoo noted the cost to the congregation of disillusioned inactives: "Probably every unit of the church has some of these sad souls, and they are not all converts, of course. In the larger wards or branches they can be assimilated and their potential for disruption can be contained. In the mission field, however, both their presence and their influence can be disproportionately large, partly because a small branch might not be large enough to integrate them readily, and partly because branch presidents and bishops are not allowed to evaluate the readiness for baptism of even seriously troubled and eccentric converts if missionaries and mission leaders are determined to baptize them."[*] High activity empowers a ward or branch, while inactivity saps vitality. The disproportionate number of poorly committed and troubled individuals rushed to baptism in some areas can overwhelm and cripple previously healthy units.

THE COST TO OUTREACH

Low activity and retention rates contribute to poor member-missionary participation among actives, since self-absorption with

---

[*]   Decoo, Wilfried, "Feeding the Fleeing Flock: Reflections on the Struggle to Retain Church Members in Europe," *Dialogue*, 29/1 (Spring 1996): 97–113.

internal problems hinders mission outreach. Which congregation is better suited to reach out to the community: one with 75 actives and 25 inactives or one with 75 actives and 300 inactives? The first is able to meet its own needs and reach out to the community. The second is chronically unable to meet even its own home teaching needs and remains forever self-consumed by internal troubles, unable to effectively reach out to the larger community. Outreach to lost members is time and resource intensive, and Christ refers to the shepherd leaving the ninety and nine to find the one that is lost. One might contemplate how Christ's "ninety and nine" to one compares to the ratio of approximately thirty "found" sheep to seventy "lost" sheep in today's church.

Just as faithful, testifying members represent a great asset to church growth, nonobservant inactives and disgruntled former members present a liability. One leader in an area recovering from the effects of longstanding quick-baptize tactics stated: "Today we spend a majority of our time attempting to rehabilitate those members that were baptized years ago without adequate preparation. Essentially, what we did then was open a hospital for the sick ('the whole have no need of the physician') without having any doctors on staff. The result was predictable. Everyone got sicker. We are paying dearly for it at this time, because our time is consumed in an effort to reactivate." The considerable missionary time that is diverted from contacting and teaching investigators to reactivation efforts in low-retaining areas significantly slows growth. It is far more efficient to teach converts correctly and ensure that they are fully converted in the first place than to rush unprepared individuals to baptism and attempt to pick up the pieces later.

THE COST TO FELLOWSHIPPING

Soldiers in major military conflicts report that they are afraid to grow close to newcomers because of the tremendous emotional expense and coping problems they face when friends are killed in battle. Aloofness and withdrawal become natural defense mechanisms for survival. Similarly, most members find that it is too emotionally draining to repeatedly attempt to warmly fellowship new converts and develop close friendships, only to have the large majority vanish into inactivity or outright hostility within a short time of baptism. I have known many members who have tried earnestly to fellowship investigators and converts, only to find their enthusiasm for fellowshipping and member-missionary work irreparably damaged as they witnessed the overwhelming majority of poorly prepared converts rapidly become disinterested or hostile due to the lack of a testimony, relapse to old habits, or family pressures. Rush baptisms, low retention, and poor fellowshipping become a vicious cycle, and the few converts with genuine commitment to the Church may find their friendship needs unmet. The emotional scars from even a brief period of low-retaining accelerated baptism programs can demotivate fellowshipping efforts for years. Repeated exhortations to members to increase fellowshipping in such areas rarely leads to sustained improvement.

In elucidating these dynamics, I do not imply that there is any valid excuse for failures of fellowshipping, even in accelerated baptism areas. A small percentage of members are able to consistently fellowship new converts in spite of the tremendous emotional burden of revolving door inactivity. Yet if we are to correct definitively the underlying issues and foster a widespread, sustained increase in member fellowshipping, accelerated baptism programs and other missionary initiatives that place converts at great spiritual risk and undermine member confidence must be abolished. The credibility of local missionary efforts must be rebuilt by consistently responsible teaching and baptizing tactics and improved prebaptismal preparation, leading to more consistently positive interactions among active members, investigators, and new converts. This in turn leads to a surge in member enthusiasm for missionary work and fellowshipping.

PREVENTION: THE BEST MEDICINE

President Thomas S. Monson taught that we must "start at the headwaters to ensure activity."[*] Many missions have elaborate plans for reclaiming inactives, but no clear plans for improving the quality of prebaptismal preparation and stopping the loss of converts to inactivity. Is it good stewardship to persevere in bailing water out of a leaking ship without first plugging the hole? An ounce of prevention is worth a pound of cure, and extra effort to teach new converts correctly before baptism and establish firm gospel habits often does far more good than hundreds of hours spent working with inactives. For those who feel that it is too difficult to prepare converts properly for baptism, try home teaching hostile or disaffected individuals every month for the rest of their lives and attempting to remedy the enormous personal, social, and spiritual problems that inactivity inflicts upon individuals and the Church. It is much more honorable to leave individuals without adequate understanding and commitment unbaptized than to rush them into a lifelong obligation for which they are not prepared.

---

[*]   Monson, Thomas S., *LDS Church News*, April 10, 1999.

GROWTH AND STANDARDS

ARE QUALITY AND QUANTITY COMPETING AIMS?

M ANY VIEW QUALITY AND quantity as competing or even mutually exclusive aims. One missionary who served in a large Latin American country with many nominal members but few actives acknowledged: "The quality of prebaptismal teaching was never much of a focus. Many hoped that by simply baptizing large numbers of people, enough of them would remain active to build the Church." Many others cite little quality control in the prebaptismal teaching process, leading to "revolving door" retention problems with new converts going inactive almost as quickly as they are baptized. A missionary in a low-retaining area of the United States conveyed an attitude I have heard expressed by hundreds: "Our job is just to teach and baptize. What happens after is the members' job." Such beliefs lead missionaries and leaders to write off convert losses as inevitable or to blame failure upon local members without making any genuine effort to evaluate and improve the gaping deficiencies in their own teaching and prebaptismal preparation of converts. Many proponents of accelerated baptism programs actually believe that the fractional retention rates such methods incur are compensated for by a modest alleged increase in baptismal numbers associated with rushed baptisms and low standards and express that high attrition is simply the cost of having a "productive" mission.

On the other hand, some attempt to excuse poor performance by claiming that slow growth is an inevitable result of a focus on quality. Over the past fifteen years, I have frequently heard mission and area leaders concerned about poor convert retention instruct missionaries and members that convert retention must be improved through a focus on quality teaching. They claim that achieving quality growth requires diverting large amounts of time and attention away from finding activities, rationalizing the decline in baptisms. Yet much of the talk about quality has been so vague that it is difficult to distill practical lessons. Most leaders have been reluctant to establish or enforce meaningful standards beyond attendance at one to three sacrament meetings and affirmatively answering a list of questions that deal primarily with belief.

My interviews with investigators and new converts in many areas where missionaries pride themselves on "quality teaching" have produced little evidence to support their claims. While missionaries may have conducted more social visits or engaged in more small talk with the investigators, I have found that converts have still attended church only irregularly before baptism, have failed to establish habits of daily scripture reading, and have been abstinent from forbidden substances for only a brief period before baptism. Not surprisingly, such areas continue to suffer from low retention rates that represent only a meager improvement. Guidelines that prospective converts should abstain from alcohol and tobacco, attend church, and read scriptures become more nominal than real when there is no minimum period of observance before baptism. Without clear standards which are consistently enforced, of what can quality possibly consist? With missionaries facing continuing pressure to baptize investigators quickly to meet arbitrary goals, the quality of convert preparation reflects primarily the minimal accepted standards.

When daily scripture reading, consistent church attendance, and adherence to other basic gospel laws are optional for baptism, we cannot be surprised that convert retention remains the exception rather than the rule. At a mission conference in Brazil in 1965, a visiting authority taught: "Don't hide behind the mask of quality. If you say 'we are baptizing fewer people because we are baptizing quality converts,' then the question is: what were you doing before?"

QUALITY AND QUANTITY

President Gordon B. Hinckley has affirmed that the Lord wants both quality and quantity, rather than one or the other or, as has most often been the case, neither. The scriptures teach that both quality and quantity, both faithfulness and fruitfulness are expected. The "field is white, already to harvest." Disciples of Christ are sent not to generate paper lists of inactive members, but to establish a living, vital Church. The Savior emphasized both missions: "I have chosen you, and ordained you, that ye should go and bring forth fruit, and that your fruit should remain" (John 15:16)

Ammon and his brethren succeeded at both baptizing thousands and achieving full retention: "As many of the Lamanites as believed in their preaching, and were converted unto the Lord, never did fall away" (Alma 23:6). Early missionaries of the modern era such as Dan Jones, Wilford Woodruff, and Brigham Young also baptized thousands in the British Isles while achieving retention rates above 90 percent. Most of these great missionaries also built the Church "from scratch" in new areas and were able to achieve rapid growth and excellent retention without the benefit of an established member base.

A great lesson of my mission was that quality and quantity are simultaneously achievable. During the last six months of my mission, my companions and I taught and baptized approximately 25 percent of all of the converts in the mission. Over 90 percent of the converts were still active two years later. Almost all of these individuals were contacts with no friends or family in the Church, and some were baptized in areas with few or no other active members. So their retention cannot be attributed merely to social relationships. This growth can be credited to the application of specific principles learned from insightful companions, as well as to diligent work and the Holy Spirit. Since that time, I have carefully studied exceptional missions around the world where high growth and retention were both achieved. In every case, I find the application of common principles of growth and retention that are deficient in less productive missions.

IS POOR RETENTION AN INEVITABLE STEP IN MATURATION?

Some claim that a so-called "critical mass" of members is essential for rapid growth and optimal retention and that current low activity rates are an inevitable result of the process of establishing the Church in new areas. They claim that activity rates will rise as the Church becomes more established, citing higher activity rates in Utah and the Mountain West than in surrounding areas. This is an apples and oranges comparison which is not supported by existing data. The observation that activity rates are higher in areas where active members have many children and where there are few convert baptisms provides no useful insight for rectifying the problem of catastrophic convert losses that have continued to occur in both international areas and in regions of North America that rely primarily on convert growth. The Church has been established in Mexico, Chile, and Japan for well over a century, but activity rates in all three countries hover between 20 and 25 percent, and the passing of many years has done little to rectify the crisis of inactivity. In contrast, some newly opened areas, such as West Africa and Eastern Europe, have activity rates that are somewhat higher. Rampant inactivity cannot simply be waited out. Poor retention is no more a necessary part of the growth of the Church than sickness is a prerequisite to health.

Public discourse on LDS convert retention centers has traditionally centered so overwhelmingly on the need for fellowshipping of new converts that it is easy to lose sight of other factors which play a similar or even greater role in retention. If it were true that member fellowshipping represented the key factor in convert retention, it would not have been possible for Ammon, Dan Jones, Brigham Young, and other highly effective missionaries to organize from scratch large congregations with excellent retention in areas without preexisting Church infrastructure. On my mission, I also found that it was possible to organize healthy congregations and consistently achieve very high convert retention in areas with few or no members. In contrast, programs that focus on fellowshipping as the primary or exclusive means of convert retention typically achieve only slight gains. As a ward mission leader in an area of the United States where missionaries systematically rushed unprepared converts to baptism, I found that even the most diligent fellowshipping efforts only marginally improved very low retention rates. Explanations of retention problems solely in terms of member fellowshipping focus on superficial social issues while ignoring much deeper spiritual ones.

Missions that have applied appropriate scriptural teaching standards have almost immediately achieved very high convert retention rates, while missions that have not have continued to lose the overwhelming majority of their converts even as unit rolls have swelled. The principles that can uniformly ensure excellent convert retention in any area are discussed in detail in the Convert Retention chapter.

DO HIGH STANDARDS HINDER
GROWTH AND RETENTION?

Many members and critics alike have unquestioningly accepted the assumption that high membership expectations are detrimental to LDS growth, claiming that the church is "incapable of growing exponentially" and that "the strict lifestyle that the church promotes, eschews alcohol, premarital sex and even coffee, prompts many converts to drift away."* They claim that rapidly growing faiths attract members easily because they require little, while attributing stagnant LDS growth rates even under circumstances of great opportunity and receptivity to "high standards." There is nothing helpful or developmental about such claims, which blame slow growth on the "hard-heartedness" of local people while ignoring any opportunity for improving our efforts.

Sociologists have long observed that the world's rapidly growing missionary churches are not those that require little (Catholic, Orthodox, and mainline Protestant churches experience few conversions), but faiths with high membership requirements, such as the Seventh-Day Adventists (growing at 8 to 11 percent annually) and Jehovah's Witnesses. The "Hartsem Faith Communities Today" study, the largest study of religious congregations in the United States in history, found that strictness of member expectations contributes to high growth rather than dissuading prospective converts.[†] Sixty-four percent of U.S. congregations with strict member expectations are growing, compared to only 37 percent with low member expectations. Congregations with explicit and high member expectations are

---

*   Gerstein, Josh, "Mormons Rising in Government, Business, Schools," *New York Sun*, October 18, 2005.

†   "Faith Communities in the U.S. Today," Hartsem Institute for Religious Research, Hartsem Seminary, http://fact.hartsem.edu.

also much less likely to experience conflicts that sap vitality. Many other studies demonstrate the correlation between high standards and high growth and retention. In a landmark paper entitled "Why Strict Churches Are Strong," Laurence R. Iannaccone of Santa Clara University presented evidence that free-rider members, or individuals who maintain nominal membership while failing to contribute, weaken any religious body and result in the fruitless dissipation of resources.[*] He wrote: "Any attempt to directly subsidize the observable aspects of religious participation (such as church attendance) will almost certainly backfire." Low standards, or subsidization of commitments, foster maladaptive dynamics that hamper church growth. Rapidly growing denominations understand that converts who join with the expectation of giving active service strengthen a church, while those who join expecting to be passively served weaken it.

HIGH STANDARDS, STRONG CONVERTS

I have consistently found that prebaptismal preparation practices correspond highly to convert retention. In areas with excellent retention, missionaries have consistently ensured that converts have firmly established the habit of meaningful daily reading in the Book of Mormon well before baptism. The investigator has consistently attended church every week for one month or more. He has fully overcome substance addictions, with at least four weeks of full abstinence from substances forbidden by the Word of Wisdom. The missionaries have actively involved members in at least two formal discussions or visits prior to baptism, facilitating the development of friendships that extend beyond handshakes and hallway greetings at church.

---

[*]   Iannaccone, Lawrence R., "Why Strict Churches Are Strong," *American Journal of Sociology*, 99/5 (1994): 1180–1211, updated version online at http://lsb.scu.edu/econrel/Downloads/Strict-D.PDF.

The baptismal interview is insightful and helpful, and the baptism of candidates who have not demonstrated consistent adherence to basic gospel laws throughout the teaching period is delayed until such habits have been firmly established and demonstrated.

A common pattern is also found in most low-retaining missions. The typical investigator has attended church only once, twice, or several times with gaps before baptism. He has rarely read more than ten pages in the Book of Mormon and has not developed the habit of consistent daily scripture reading. Little or no effort has been made to involve members in the teaching and fellowshipping process prior to baptism. Investigators have often been abstinent from tobacco or alcohol for two weeks or less and experience catastrophic relapse rates after baptism. The baptismal interview represents little more than a rubber stamp focusing on nominal belief and future promises, while making little if any effort to ascertain the investigator's consistency in adhering to commitments over the teaching period. Converts often feel unprepared for baptism but report feeling pressured by the missionaries to be baptized quickly.

Faiths that achieve high convert retention rates require high prebaptismal standards. Seventh-Day Adventists and Jehovah's Witnesses have lifestyle, commitment, and time requirements that are comparable and in some ways more demanding to those required for LDS membership. Seventh-Day Adventists follow a law of health that is stricter than the LDS Word of Wisdom, requiring not only abstinence from alcohol, tobacco, coffee, and tea, but also a near-vegetarian diet. Seventh-Day Adventists also worship on Saturdays rather than Sundays, which presents social and cultural challenges. Even with these commitments, the Seventh-Day Adventist church is growing rapidly and retains 78 percent of new members. The average Jehovah's Witness proselytizes nonmembers for an average of fifteen to twenty hours each month.

Jehovah's Witnesses must also give up birthday parties, Christmas and Easter celebrations, and more. Jehovah's Witnesses and Seventh-Day Adventist investigators are typically expected to attend church regularly, often for months, to complete Bible-study courses, and to adhere consistently to membership requirements prior to baptism.

Faiths that require little offer little and fail to mobilize the commitment and dedication that are prerequisites for sustained rapid growth. Individuals experience the blessings of faith only as they put forth effort and make sacrifices, and so the failure of low-commitment quick-baptize programs is predictable. Joseph Smith taught: "A religion that does not require the sacrifice of all things never has power sufficient to produce the faith necessary unto life and salvation."* Faiths with low expectations often fail to even get their existing members to church and experience few voluntary conversions. Strictness is not a barrier but an asset to growth and retention.

WHO BENEFITS FROM HIGH PREBAPTISMAL STANDARDS?

Some suggest that high prebaptismal standards are unlikely to have much impact on retention. They claim that standards may weed out a few grossly unprepared or insincere individuals but are unlikely to make much difference for the sincere converts. They also express concern that the higher teaching standards could result in a sharp drop in total baptisms and speculate that accelerated baptism programs may lead to greater growth.

Data contradict such claims. The consistent success of appropriate prebaptismal requirements in elevating convert retention rates from 20 to 30 percent prior to their implementation to 80 to 90 percent afterward demonstrate that benefits are experienced by the over-

---

* Smith, Joseph, *Lectures on Faith*, Salt Lake City, UT: Deseret Book, 1985, 6:7.

whelming majority of prospective converts. While some insincere and uncommitted individuals are "weeded out," this difference in total baptisms is far more than made up over time by a stronger long-term membership base and by the application of principles discussed in the Principles of Finding chapter. I have found that the vast majority of prospective converts are sincere and genuinely want to succeed in the Church but find themselves severely disadvantaged when rushed to baptism without having developed essential gospel habits. Many converts who have gone on to become branch and district presidents and serve faithfully in other callings have reported that holding them back from baptism until they were well prepared was the best thing anyone did for them and made a formative difference in impressing upon them the seriousness of gospel covenants. Quality retention programs do not improve retention only for marginal converts. They dramatically improve retention rates for the entire spectrum of sincere converts who desire to succeed in the Church but require proper training and habituation in order to become spiritually self-reliant.

Some have presented examples of converts baptized after a very brief period of teaching who remained active in the Church and went on to serve in leadership callings as "proof" that accelerated baptism programs are effective and appropriate. Few would consider the stories of survivors of an airline that delivered only 25 percent of its passengers safely as documentation of an acceptable safety record, nor would an anecdote of an acquaintance who survived unscathed after speeding through red lights demonstrate that such a practice is appropriate or advisable. Most such examples presented by accelerated baptism proponents involve converts with other strong connections to the Church that the claimants fail to recognize as salient factors in promoting ongoing activity, such as a spouse, other family members, or close friends who are active members. Even the 20 to 25 percent retention rates typically reported for accelerated baptism programs often overestimate their success, since the small segment of converts with strong preexisting ties to active Church members make up a disproportionately large number of those who remain active. Retention rates for cold contacts baptized through accelerated baptism programs are even lower.

Understanding
the Conversion Process

THE PROCESS OF CONVERSION through the Holy Spirit occurs in the investigator's heart only to the degree that he or she puts forth consistent effort to obey divine commandments. Contrary to popular misconceptions, conversion is not a passive event that occurs when an investigator's heart is touched and he feels the Spirit. The Spirit can testify to an investigator of truth, but only the investigator can put forth the effort to nourish the seed through repentance and obedience that leads to true conversion and brings forth the fruits of the Spirit. James wrote: "Thou believest that there is one God; thou doest well: the devils also believe, and tremble" (James 2:19). Even Paul and Alma the younger, whose conversion were facilitated through miraculous means, put forth great personal effort. Gospel habits must be firmly in place before baptism, or the converts will never receive the Holy Spirit that is crucial to conversion and retention. Those with gospel habits of daily scripture study, weekly church attendance, and active service are able to maintain their own spiritual nourishment through fellowshipping of the Spirit, while those without them can only rarely be adequately fed spiritually even by the intensive efforts of local members. The Parable of the Wise and Foolish Virgins (Matthew 25:1–11) teaches that lasting conversion cannot be passively conveyed but requires active effort. Habits of obedience to basic gospel laws provide the key to keeping the oil of the Holy Ghost burning brightly in the lamps of both new converts and longtime members.

If there were even a grain of truth to the quick-baptize mantra that we should "baptize investigators quickly and get them the Holy Ghost before Satan gets to them," we would expect to see uniformly excellent retention areas where accelerated baptism tactics are practiced instead of the 20 to 30 percent rates (and sometimes far less) seen in actual practice. Such expressions also convey a deep misunderstanding of the workings of the Spirit. The confirmation prayer does not command the Holy Spirit to come upon new members, but rather commands the members to actively seek after and "receive the Holy Ghost" by living their covenants. Without consistent effort to study scriptures and bring one's life into harmony with divine commandments, most never receive it. The fear of losing the baptism if the investigator "changes his mind" conveys deep insecurity that is a hallmark of poor teaching and inadequate prebaptismal preparation. Proponents of quick-baptize practices understand neither the workings of the Holy Spirit nor the conversion process and are often driven by impure considerations contrary to the desire of those with an eye "single to the glory of God" to build the Kingdom of God through quality teaching leading to lasting conversion. Time is not a threat to true conversion. In view of the consistent history of crisis-level inactivity left by quick-baptize tactics, those who feel that they have been "moved by the Spirit" to baptize converts without a consistent record of obedience to gospel laws and firm gospel habits should ponder whether the spirit they heed is indeed a holy one. To the extent that convert retention rates in a given area, mission, or ward do not measure up to the divine standard of full retention, it almost inevitably reflects a deviation from scriptural principles.

THE MEMBER RESPONSIBILITY

President Gordon B. Hinckley taught: "It is an absolute imperative that we look after those who have become a part of us."[*] He stated: "Every one of us has an obligation to fellowship those (converts), to put our arms around them, to bring them into the Church in full activity. It is not enough just to go to Church on Sundays; we must reach out each day. I wish with all my heart that in Costa Rica every man, woman, and child who was baptized would remain faithful and active. And that can happen if all of you make up your minds to reach out and help the new convert. There is no point in the missionaries baptizing people only to have them come into the Church for a little while and then drift off. You have remained faithful, and I thank you for that, but again urge that you make an extra effort to reach out to those who have recently been baptized.... They need your help. God bless you to fellowship the new convert. That is so very, very important. That is a principle of the gospel of Jesus Christ. Only as we reach out to help others are we truly Latter-day Saints."[†]

Fellowshipping is a vital element of any effective retention program. Inadequately fellowshipped converts may stray from the Church when challenges are encountered that a well-fellowshipped convert could have withstood. Members have a responsibility to offer a good example and warm and timely fellowshipping beginning well before baptism. Delayed or inadequate fellowshipping of the new convert and the poor example of active members who do not live the gospel in daily life can both contribute to convert loss. Early involvement of members in the fellowshipping process requires appropriate communication and initiative from the full-time missionaries.

---

[*]   Hinckley, Gordon B., *Ensign*, May 1997.

[†]   Hinckley, Gordon B., Member Fireside, San Jose, Costa Rica, January 20, 1997.

THE MISSIONARY RESPONSIBILITY

Member fellowshipping, while important, is not enough to retain converts unless they have been properly taught and prepared by the missionaries. The retention process does not start at the moment of baptism and confirmation. It begins much earlier, the moment that missionaries first walk in the door. I have never known of any ward or branch that was able to achieve consistently acceptable convert retention rates even with excellent fellowshipping efforts in spite of accelerated baptism programs practiced by full-time missionaries. With personal knowledge of the converts' challenges and executive decision-making authority about baptismal readiness and other important processes, LDS missionaries play a central role in convert retention. Missionaries control the quality and content of the teaching of converts, the preparation of converts at the time of baptism, the period over which converts are taught before baptism, and the degree to which active members are involved in the teaching and fellowshipping process prior to baptism. Missionaries make the ultimate decision about when investigators are ready to be baptized and perform the baptismal interview. The bishop and ward mission leader are denied any opportunity to evaluate the readiness of prospective converts for baptism, and so the ultimate responsibility for the state of the convert at the time of baptism lies almost exclusively with the missionaries.

For many years, most discussions of convert retention centered so exclusively on member fellowshipping efforts that many lost perspective that any other factors were involved. Many missionaries and leaders in accelerated baptism areas expressed the notion that "our job is just to teach and baptize. What happens after is the members' job." One returned missionary who had served as an assistant to the president in Chile candidly acknowledged: "The quality of prebaptismal teaching was never much of a focus. Many hoped that by simply baptizing large numbers of people, enough of them would remain active to build the Church. My mission president in the late 1990s tried to turn things around and focus on quality prebaptismal teaching and convert retention and not just baptismal numbers, but he was one of the first I know of to do so."

If trained missionaries who have full time to dedicate to the single purpose of finding and teaching potential converts are unable to get the investigators to attend church regularly and obey basic gospel laws for even a few weeks before baptism, is it reasonable to expect overwhelmed and undertrained local members to succeed at getting these "converts" to become active and obey gospel laws for life? Accelerated baptism programs result in converts who require not simple member fellowshipping, but comprehensive teaching and activation. The common rationalization that members should "fellowship new converts into full activity" is problematic, since most of the investigators are not "active investigators" at the time of baptism.

Former ward mission leader Kent Clark wrote:

> Every missionary related meeting I attend is focused on what we can do about [the retention] problem. Unfortunately, it is all directed to efforts after baptism, instead of attacking the root of the problem which begins long before. We must abolish the evils of the spiritual dole and re-enthrone the personal responsibility of the investigator as the ruling principle of missionary work. It has always seemed curious to me that as a church we fervently embrace self-reliance and personal responsibility in matters of money but ignore them in the conversion process. If we pick the investigator up, carry him to the baptismal door, lift his arm and when he makes one feeble knock, i.e. attends

sacrament meeting a single time, and immediately thrust him through, why are we surprised that many don't keep walking?... If we want active converts then we must focus our attention on baptizing active investigators. To me this seems so obvious it hardly bears mentioning, but when I dared express some of these ideas in a stake missionary correlation meeting the arguments and denials from the full-time mission were fervent and passionate. "We're just following the prophet!" they repeated over and over. But page 234 of the official church *Missionary Guide* contains excerpts from a letter sent out from the First Presidency concerning who is qualified for baptism. It states that a prerequisite to baptism is that the investigators "attend regular Sunday church meetings and feel united with Church members." Nowhere does it state that this is accomplished by attending a single time. Indeed, it is hard to imagine anyone feeling such unity after two or even three Sundays.[*]

Missionaries have a responsibility to baptize only active converts who have firmly established gospel habits of weekly church attendance, daily scripture reading, and prayer and have fully overcome substance addictions. There are times when participating members fall away, and dedicated reactivation work is required in such cases. But it is an entirely different situation when converts are baptized without meeting scriptural standards only to fall away rapidly.

[*]   Clark, Kent, "Mission Vision: Personal Thoughts on Missionary Work in the Church Today," Sunstone Symposium, Los Angeles, California, March 5, 1998.

Achieving Full Convert Retention

CONVERT PROFILES

IN MOST LOW-RETAINING LDS missions, the average investigator has attended church only once, twice, or several times with gaps before baptism. He has rarely read more than ten pages in the Book of Mormon and lacks the habit of daily scripture reading. He has not established meaningful friendships with active members prior to baptism and has often been abstinent from alcohol or tobacco for two weeks or less.

In areas with high retention, missionaries have consistently ensured that converts have firmly established the habit of meaningful daily reading in the Book of Mormon well before baptism. The average investigator has consistently attended church weekly for four weeks or more and has been abstinent from alcohol and tobacco for a similar period. They have also established meaningful friendships with active members that extend beyond handshakes and hallway greetings in church. Active members have typically been present for at least two missionary discussions with the investigators.

A key to high retention is to modify the profile of converts being baptized from the quick-baptize, low-commitment profile found in areas of poor retention to the higher commitment profile found in areas with good retention. This is entirely within the control of missionaries who understand these principles and work together with members to ensure the true and lasting conversion of new converts.

THE BEST TIME FOR CHANGE: BEFORE BAPTISM

The quality of prebaptismal teaching and preparation lays prospective converts' spiritual foundation and plays a large role in determining whether they will experience full activity and continued spiritual growth, social membership alone, or inactivity. While new converts are generally willing to make substantial life changes to qualify for baptism in the true Church, much of the impetus and urgency for additional change is lost after baptism, especially if prior commitments remain unmastered. If prospective converts have not achieved consistency in basic gospel habits including daily scripture reading and weekly church attendance before baptism, it is unlikely that they will ever develop these habits.

Elder Henry B. Eyring noted:

Another fallacy is to believe that the choice to accept or not accept the counsel of prophets is no more than deciding whether to accept good advice and gain its benefits or to stay where we are. But the choice not to take prophetic counsel changes the very ground upon which we stand. It becomes more dangerous. The failure to take prophetic counsel lessens our power to take inspired counsel in the future. The best time to have decided to help Noah build the ark was the first time he asked. Each time he asked after that, each failure to respond would have lessened sensitivity to the Spirit. And so each time his request would have seemed more foolish, until the rain came. And then it was too late. *

When inspired counsel is not followed the first time it is heard, the power of the hearer to follow it in the future declines dramatically. The discrepancy between expressed and internalized beliefs grows, and this discrepancy becomes accepted. This explains why prospective converts who are properly taught are often much more inclined to follow inspired counsels than many longtime members. The period of prebaptismal teaching presents the best chance the converts will ever have to assimilate and implement the essential gospel laws they were not taught as children.

BUILDING SPIRITUAL SELF-SUFFICIENCY: HABITS OF FAITH

Living testimonies require constant spiritual nourishment. The most efficacious and dependable form of nourishment is self-nourishment. Those who depend on others to replenish the oil in their spiritual lamps will find that their lamps will inevitably run dry. Those with gospel habits are fortified to remain firm and resilient through adversity while those without them falter on the smoothest of roads. New members who join with established habits of daily scripture reading, Sabbath observance, daily prayer, and others become spiritually self-sufficient in the local congregation. Their habits provide not only for continued activity, but also for cumulative growth. Aristotle noted: "Excellence is an art won by training and habituation. We do not act rightly because we have virtue or excellence, but we rather have those because we have acted rightly. We are what we repeatedly do. Excellence, then, is not an act but a habit." Jim Rohn stated, "Motivation gets you started, and habits keep you going." He further noted:

---

*   Eyring, Henry B., *Ensign*, May 1997.

"Success is nothing more than a few simple disciplines, practiced every day; while failure is simply a few errors in judgment, repeated every day. It is the accumulative weight of our disciplines and our judgments that leads us to either fortune or failure." These same principles apply to spiritual matters. President Heber J. Grant taught: "It is not position, it is not education that gives the Spirit of God; but it is keeping the commandments of Almighty God and being lowly in heart and desiring to fulfill the commandments of God in our daily walk and conversation. I bear witness to you here today that no man ever will fail in this Church, who is honest in his heart, honest in the payment of his tithes and offerings, who obeys the Word of Wisdom, who attends to his family prayers and his secret prayers, and who attends to his quorum meetings. No man will fail who is doing his duty in this Church."[*] Converts with these habits are immediately able to provide service and strength to the Church and the community. In contrast, even intensive postbaptismal fellowshipping and teaching are often inadequate to keep converts without these basic gospel habits from inactivity or nominal social membership with little spiritual progress. A well-prepared new member with firm gospel habits towers spiritually over lifelong members without them.

It is imperative for each new convert to fully overcome harmful addictions before baptism and to firmly establish basic habits of weekly church attendance, daily scripture reading, and obedience to other basic gospel laws. Sociologists estimate that it takes at least three to four weeks for repetitive acts to become habits. Converts do not develop gospel habits by accident. Consistent missionary emphasis and follow-up are vital.

---

[*]   Grant, Heber J., *Conference Report*, April 1901, 64.

FORTIFY PROSPECTIVE
CONVERTS FOR ADVERSITY

Effective missionaries help investigators to anticipate and prepare for adversity and help investigators to focus from the beginning on the need to "endure to the end" to receive eternal life. Ineffective missionaries emphasize the glorious promises of the gospel while underemphasizing personal responsibility and failing to prepare investigators for inevitable adversity, leaving the investigators or converts disillusioned and unable to cope when challenges arise. Some seek success by preaching a "prosperity gospel" promising rapid temporal and social blessings that differs from the message of Christ and His disciples. Christ promised faithful disciples his peace, but noted that this inner peace is "not as the world giveth": he does not promise worldly success (John 14:27). To the contrary, he promises that trials and persecution are the common lot of all believers (John 15:20, 16:33) and that He will test us to see whether we will abide in His covenant. Investigators must be willing to "bear their cross" and "count the cost" before embarking on the path of discipleship to ensure that they have the dedication and commitment to finish (Luke 14:27–33). Heber J. Grant taught: "Do the elders of Israel when they go out into the world to preach the gospel hold out flattering inducements to those whom they meet to become Latter-day Saints? No. On the contrary, they tell them that if they embrace the gospel they may expect that their friends and associates will turn against them, and that their names will be cast out as evil. That is the kind of promise they make to them."[*]

Church membership is the path to sacrifice and in no way represents a "quick fix" to personal issues, financial problems, or gaping

---

[*]   Grant, Heber J., *Gospel Standards*, Salt Lake City, UT: Improvement Era, 1943, 102.

spiritual wounds. The restored gospel of Jesus Christ does hold the answers to life's problems, but answers and blessings are often received only with sustained righteous living. Those who accept the gospel must understand that they will face ridicule and persecution from friends and acquaintances, and often even from family members. How will they respond to this opposition? All those who heed the ridicule of those in the great and spacious building representing the pride of the world fall away from the iron rod of scripture that leads to eternal life (1 Nephi 8:33–34). Investigators should also be taught that Church members, while striving to varying degrees to uphold gospel principles, are imperfect. They must be prepared for the likely eventuality that another member may say or do something that they may perceive to be offensive. Investigators must be taught to join the Church prepared to serve rather than expecting to receive service.

BAPTISMAL DATES

Rather than committing investigators to a firm baptismal date, I find that it is more helpful to make a list of the basic gospel commitments for the investigator, including daily Book of Mormon reading for half an hour, weekly church attendance, observance of the Sabbath, Word of Wisdom observance, and daily and family prayer, with the understanding that the investigator will work toward baptism as he or she makes progress in these areas. When missionaries focus on gospel habits instead of deadlines, investigators realize that the missionaries are there to help them to meet their spiritual needs and develop a relationship with Christ rather than merely attempting to rush them to the font. After obligations are fully disclosed and investigator needs are carefully considered, a tentative timetable may often be mutually agreed upon, with the understanding that the ultimate baptismal date will be moved back if necessary depending on the investigator's diligence in observing core commitments and establishing gospel habits. It is necessary to be firm in standards required for baptism. Failure to attend church consistently, read scriptures, or fulfill other gospel commitments should always result in any anticipated baptismal date being moved back. When the tentative dates need to be pushed back to allow additional opportunity for the development of gospel habits, most investigators are relieved at the opportunity for additional preparation. They understand that it is not the date that is sacred, but the covenant of baptism, which demands earnest preparation. Using the approaches recommended in this book, over 80 percent of investigators who I asked to be baptized accepted the invitation, and over 80 percent of those carried through with the commitment. This compares to approximately 20 percent at each step with traditional programs. This does not imply that most investigators were baptized, but rather that those who were not ready had selected themselves out by a repeated failure to read scriptures, attend church, or put forth effort in other ways before progressing to the appropriate discussion. Some selectivity and discernment are necessary in assessing when to ask for the baptismal commitment. With appropriate preparation, teaching, and missionary responsiveness, there should be very few surprises regarding who accepts the baptismal commitment, and the vast majority of commitments obtained should follow through. Accelerated baptism approaches that demand too much too soon backfire and drive away receptive people, leaving missionaries constantly surprised, bewildered, and disappointed.

Baptism is a wonderful experience for investigators who are properly prepared, but like other gospel ordinances, it is a covenant that brings blessings only when we do our part. Inactives who were rushed to baptism without adequate preparation often disclose that their baptism was a letdown and they did not feel anything special. In contrast, converts who have been well prepared cite burning spiritual feelings and remember their baptismal date as one of the most wonderful days of their life. Many new converts whose baptism was delayed until they were truly ready stated that this was the best thing anyone ever did for them. Baptisms are more meaningful and investigators are far more likely to remain active when missionaries focus on spiritual preparations for baptism rather than the event itself. Investigators who are consistently keeping commitments also need to understand that while gospel habits must be in firmly place before baptism, it is not necessary for preparation to be dragged out indefinitely.

FELLOWSHIPPING

Scriptures and Latter-day prophets have repeatedly emphasized the imperative to nurture prospective converts and new members. President Gordon B. Hinckley stated: "Those who have come into the Church made a great sacrifice, many of them, when they were baptized. They are precious. They are the same kind of people that you are and their generations will become the same kind of people as will your generations if they are nurtured and brought along in the Church. I don't know how to say it more strongly. This is a matter about which I feel so deeply as I go about this Church across the world."[*]

Missionaries have far more influence over the fellowshipping process than is commonly recognized. Many missionaries baptize converts who have attended church only once or twice, and most missionaries do not invite members to discussions even with converts committed to baptism in the push to achieve baptisms quickly. Even the most avid members have little opportunity to fellowship prospec-

---

[*] Hinckley, Gordon B., Woods Cross Utah Regional Conference, January 10, 1998.

tive converts if the missionaries do not invite them, and their only possible contact with the investigators is a brief hello in the hallway at the one or two church meetings the prospective converts may attend before baptism. The missionaries control the teaching schedule and baptismal dates and are therefore the only ones who can reliably ensure that members are involved in the fellowshipping process well before baptism.

Elder L. Tom Perry noted: "According to research, 86 percent of the active converts have close personal ties to other LDS members or relatives."[*] Since only 20 percent of investigators in North America are referred by members, the practice of rushing investigators to baptism before close personal relationships with active members have been established is a recipe for inactivity. Fellowshipping efforts that begin at or after baptism are usually much too late. In order for all new converts to develop "close personal ties to other LDS members," fellowshipping must start long before baptism and be built in to standard teaching protocols. Inviting one or more local members to at least two discussions or visits with the investigators prior to baptism helps to initiate fellowshipping and ensures that the integration process of prospective members into the local congregation is already well underway by the time of baptism. When members are brought into the investigators' homes or the investigators are taught in member homes early in the teaching process, deeper and more personal relationships are developed than occur with superficial church contact. This practice breaks down barriers of unfamiliarity and embarrassment that can occur without this transition when new members may be reluctant to allow home or visiting teachers into their home. Involvement of members with prospective converts long before baptism facilitates a smooth transition of nurturing responsibilities from the missionaries

---

[*]   Perry, L. Tom, *LDS Church News*, June 21, 1991.

to local members that is much more effective than assigning home teachers to cold-call absent converts they have never met. Members and local leaders much prefer being involved early in visiting receptive investigators with missionaries, rather than being assigned to activate uncommitted converts who have established patterns of inactivity almost immediately after baptism.

OUR RESPONSIBILITY

Given the importance of each soul, we cannot be content with approaches that result in anything less than full church activity of each new convert. Missionaries and members have an ethical and moral responsibility to strive to act always in the best interest of their investigators, rather than in the interest of specific programs, monthly baptismal goals, or other considerations. We have a duty to provide each investigator with the best possible prospect of long-term activity through quality teaching and sound preparation. Convert loss shortly after baptism is entirely preventable. A discerning missionary approach, proper teaching, fellowshipping, and emphasis on the basic commitments without excuse or exception provide the best medicine to prevent early inactivity. Later inactivity will likely never be entirely avoided, since the moral agency and obedience of the member in living the gospel are dominant factors in this later period. However, wards and branches can both strengthen active members and reduce the prevalence of inactivity in this period by focusing on consistent obedience to the fundamental principles of the gospel that increase worthiness for the companionship of the Holy Spirit and generate spiritual growth. Full convert retention is never achieved by chance. It occurs when the scriptural principles of conversion and retention are consistently applied.

THE NEED FOR A COMPREHENSIVE PROGRAM

Some have claimed that lengthier periods of prebaptismal teaching make no difference in convert retention. Such claims are faulty both because the "lengthier periods" cited are typically very brief (usually less than three weeks) and because of continued neglect of other major convert needs. A farmer trying to grow crops in a challenging climate recognizes that multiple elements, including sunlight, watering, fertilizer, weeding, and spraying for bugs, are all necessary for an abundant harvest. Would it be fair for an individual attempting to grow crops in the dark with no water to conclude that adding fertilizer makes no difference in crop growth or to claim that sunlight is not important for crop growth when seeds placed under a scorching sun but never watered or nourished fail to thrive? Successful convert retention is achieved only when multiple steps are taken to achieve positive outcomes. Converts who come to church for two months but who fail to read scriptures or abstain from substances prohibited by the Word of Wisdom may still fall away, but this does not mean that consistency in attending church is not important. The full synergistic benefit of each element is achieved only in conjunction with other essential factors. A comprehensive retention program employing multiple essential elements is necessary to achieve optimal convert retention.

ACHIEVING FULL CONVERT RETENTION

During my first year as a missionary in Russia, my companion and I worked diligently and taught many converts. Yet we were troubled by the loss of 20 to 30 percent of our converts within the first year. In retrospect, were able to identify clues of the individuals' need for more rigorous preparation for baptism that we had not picked up on as we followed official teaching protocols. We also served in areas where the majority of converts baptized only a year or two previously by prior missionaries were already inactive. Some had not fully overcome tobacco or alcohol addiction before baptism and experienced relapse. Even sincere converts had been baptized without adequately developing the habits of regular church attendance and daily scripture reading that they needed to succeed as Church members. The loss of many converts and serious difficulties even among active members were causes of great concern to missionaries, mission leaders, and members alike. Serving in an area where the Church was relatively new, we felt a great need to build the Church on the right footing and were troubled by the failures and missed opportunities that were already becoming apparent.

After careful study, fervent prayer, and the input of an insightful companion, we instituted steps not found in the missionary manuals of the time to ensure that our prospective converts had indeed undergone a genuine and life-changing conversion. We wanted converts to join the Church ready to serve, rather than arriving at the gate of baptism with gaping spiritual wounds only to rapidly succumb to inactivity. We wanted to build durable converts who would remain strong in a nascent congregation with few or no members or in an established congregation where active members were not ideal examples. We did not want to build a church with teetering and indecisive souls who could be retained only if all other members in the ward conducted themselves perfectly but would fall away in the real-world setting where the implementation of congregational programs often fell short of the ideal. We wanted to empower our new converts by placing the keys to spiritual growth in their own hands, rather than fostering dependency on other sources from which help was often not forthcoming.

My companions and I implemented these steps, focusing on full disclosure of membership expectations in a no-pressure setting and on the investigators' cultivation of firm gospel habits before baptism. Almost immediately, we began experiencing dramatically greater success in both quality and quantity. We rejoiced as new converts joined the Church better prepared to serve than many longtime members, and the branches we served in became more vibrant and productive. Convert retention, which we had previously viewed as a frustrating "black box," became predictable as we applied basic scriptural principles. Over 90 percent of the converts we taught the second year were still active in the Church two years later. We were thankful to the Lord for answering our prayers and granting greater productivity and improved convert retention, even if the impact was largely limited to our companionship.

Since returning from the mission field, my research has validated the widespread applicability of these principles in many cultures. I have repeatedly found that one-year convert retention rates have exceeded 80 percent in every mission and culture where the principles in this guide have been consistently implemented. One mission president in Latin America observed that when he arrived in the mission field two years earlier, the one-year retention rate in his mission was 18 percent, with 49 percent of converts never returning after the first month. After implementing every point of this program, he noted that the one-year retention rate in his mission climbed to 83 percent. He also observed that the quality of converts being baptized greatly increased and included more professional people, including physicians, engineers, and attorneys. One mission president in the Philippines noted an increase in one-year convert retention from 8 percent to 95 percent with the missionwide implementation of these points. I have received numerous letters from missionaries, bishops, ward mission leaders, and branch presidents who note dramatic and sustained improvements in their local convert retention rates after applying the principles described here.

The 12 Points are discussed in the following section. In the mission field, we implemented points 1 through 8. I believe these points to be the most vital. In 2001, I added points 9 through 12 in response to additional available research on convert retention. I claim no credit for this program, since its principles are scriptural, practical, and intuitive and offer no profound conclusions once one has come to a correct understanding of the nature of the conversion process. I am indebted to excellent missionary companions for their insight, especially to Christopher Eastland.

Retention programs based on similar principles have been independently developed in some missions with considerable success. Almar Pihelgas, former president of Tallinn Estonia Stroomi Branch, explained why convert retention rates in Estonia rose from 20 percent in the early and mid-1990s to over 80 percent in 2001: "In the recent two years, we have centered our missionary work effort to teaching the people first and to make very sure that they indeed understand all things they need to understand before they can be baptized. Things are now much different; we do not lose people anymore because they do not understand the teachings of the Church, only when they decide that they do not want to follow them."

The ongoing difficulty with poor convert retention, which represents perhaps the most serious challenge facing the modern Church, is tragic, since early convert loss is almost entirely avoided when missionaries have the understanding and discipline to properly teach and prepare prospective converts. I have consistently been able to trace the problem in areas with low convert retention to the neglect of these principles. Ward leaders in areas where adequate retention programs have not been applied by local missions note that in retrospect, almost all of their converts who remained active after baptism satisfied at least five or six points of this guide, while quick-baptizees who rapidly fell away satisfied few or none. Jim Rohn observed: "We must all suffer one of two things—the pain of discipline or the pain of regret and disappointment." We can choose to fulfill scriptural mandates and build strong congregations of active members, or we can choose to continue accelerated baptism tactics and then attempt to cope with the consequence of fractional convert retention rates.

The new *Preach My Gospel* manual lists elements of most of the 12 Points in the retention section, although they are not presented as mandatory and no specific time frames are given. I believe that the obligatory nature of each step (especially 1 through 8) as well as the period of observance (at least four weeks) makes a critical difference between success or failure to retain converts.

THE 12 POINTS FOR NEARLY 100 PERCENT CONVERT RETENTION

The 12 Point program can dramatically improve convert retention in any area. The 12 Points listed here are not theories or ideas, but have consistently facilitated one-year convert retention rates between 80 percent and 100 percent across widely different cultures. They are derived from scripture, the teachings of modern prophets, and research. The modest effort and coordination that are required to apply these steps is overwhelmingly in the long-term interest of both the prospective convert and the Church. Some points may not be applicable to every area, such as areas without a temple, where converts cannot perform proxy baptisms, or newly opened areas with no members to fellowship prospective converts. Nonetheless, every point that is possible in one's area should be consistently applied for each prospective convert.

The combination of appropriate prebaptismal preparation and nurturing facilitates the continuing activity of new converts so that missionaries can rejoice as Alma: "And they shall be gathered into the garners, that they are not wasted. Yea, they shall not be beaten down by the storm at the last day; yea, neither shall they be harrowed up by the whirlwinds; but when the storm cometh they shall be gathered together in their place, that the storm cannot penetrate to them; yea, neither shall they be driven with fierce winds whithersoever the enemy listeth to carry them" (Alma 26:5–6).

Seven points involve helping prospective converts to establish essential habits of faith before baptism that lead to ongoing spiritual growth, while five involve appropriate nurturing. Individuals experience conversion and receive the blessings of the gospel only as they put forth the effort to nourish the seed of faith and obey God's laws. No baptismal date should be considered firm until essential gospel habits are in place.

HABITS OF FAITH

For at least four consecutive weeks before baptism, prospective converts should implement habits of faith:

1. Consistently read in the Book of Mormon for half an hour each day.
2. Consistently attend all church block meetings.
3. Observe the Sabbath Day.
4. Hold daily personal and family prayer.
5. Obey the Word of Wisdom and completely abstain from forbidden substances.
6. Obey the Law of Chastity in word, thought, and deed.
7. Receive an adequate baptismal interview centered on basic

gospel habits.

NURTURING

Prospective converts should also be nurtured by missionaries and members:

8. Missionaries should ensure that active members participate in at least two missionary discussions or visits with the prospective convert prior to baptism.
9. Converts should receive a calling within one week of baptism. In most cases, the calling should already be determined by the time of baptism.
10. Home teachers should be assigned, and appointments for the first home teaching visit and first new member visit should be established prior to baptism.
11. New converts should be greeted by the family history coordinator at baptism and started on personal family history work immediately after baptism.
12. In areas where temples are available, converts should be prepared to participate in temple proxy baptisms within six weeks of baptism.

DISCUSSION OF THE 12 POINTS

Now each point will be examined and discussed in turn.

1. Consistent daily reading in the Book of Mormon for half an hour each day for at least four weeks. Ezra Taft Benson taught that individuals and families should read and study the Book of Mormon for half an hour each day and make it a lifetime pursuit. He taught: "There is a power in the book which will begin to flow into your lives

the moment you begin a serious study of the book. You will find greater power to resist temptation. You will find the power to avoid deception. You will find the power to stay on the strait and narrow path."* He reaffirmed that the members of the Church are still under condemnation for taking the Book of Mormon lightly, "and they shall remain under this condemnation until they repent and remember the new covenant, even the Book of Mormon" (D&C 84:54–57). No amount of nurturing from external sources can make up for a failure to consistently study the Book of Mormon in the home. Establishing scripture reading as a consistent habit takes time.

2. Consistent attendance at all church block meetings for at least four weeks. Most investigators are not regular churchgoers in any faith at the time they receive the missionary discussions, and successfully establishing the habit of weekly church attendance requires major life change. Becoming accustomed to the three-hour LDS meeting block may take considerable effort, even for converts previously active in other faiths who have attended shorter worship services. Even simple fellowshipping tasks become much more difficult when converts are not regularly attending priesthood and Relief Society meetings. If a convert has attended church sporadically or has attended sacrament meeting but has not regularly attended the other block meetings prior to baptism, there is no basis to believe that a convert will begin consistently attending all meetings as a member. Missionaries who accept irregular patterns of prebaptismal church attendance should not be surprised when these same patterns continue after baptism and taper off into eventual inactivity.

---

* Benson, Ezra Taft, "The Book of Mormon—Keystone of Our Religion," *Ensign*, November 1986.

3. Observance of the Law of the Sabbath. Sabbath day observance, which extends beyond simply attending church meetings, is vital to the spiritual progress of investigators and members. Isaiah taught: "If thou turn away thy foot from the Sabbath, from doing thy pleasure on my holy day; and call the Sabbath a delight, the holy of the Lord, honourable; and shalt honour him, not doing thine own ways, nor finding thine own pleasure, nor speaking thine own words: Then shalt thou delight thyself in the Lord; and I will cause thee to ride upon the high places of the earth, and feed thee with the heritage of Jacob thy father: for the mouth of the Lord hath spoken it" (Isaiah 58:13–14). The sacrament differs from the food we pray over at every meal in that it is not only blessed, but also is sanctified, or made holy. Similarly, the Sabbath Day is not only blessed, but also is sanctified by the Lord himself (Genesis 2:3), and its observance offers blessings not attainable through other sources. The need to dedicate the Sabbath Day to divine service, without shopping or work activities (where possible), typically requires a major lifestyle change that must be fully impressed upon prospective members and consistently implemented prior to baptism.

4. Regular daily personal and family prayer. The scriptures command: "Pray always, lest you enter into temptation and lose your reward" (D&C 31:12). James E. Faust quoted President Spencer W. Kimball: "In the past, having family prayer once a day may have been all right. But in the future it will not be enough if we are going to save our families."[*] Daily prayer helps investigators and converts to strengthen their relationship with Christ, receive divine inspiration, and resist the temptations of the world. Where possible, we should follow Daniel's example of holding personal and family prayers

---

[*]   Faust, James E., *Ensign*, November 1990.

morning, noon, and evening (Daniel 6:10). My father's family does this by holding family prayers at each mealtime prior to and separate from blessing the food. By linking prayers to meals, this is never forgotten.

5. Obedience to the Word of Wisdom, with consistent abstinence from forbidden substances for at least four weeks before baptism. Elder Dallin H. Oaks reported: "According to one study, 75 percent of adult converts in North America had to give up at least one of these substances mentioned in the Word of Wisdom—tobacco, alcohol, coffee, or tea—and 31 percent had to give up smoking, a very addictive habit ... However ... one third to one half of them reported that they had experienced 'occasional,' 'frequent,' or 'complete' lapses into their abstinence."* Rates of tobacco addiction are even higher in much of Asia and Latin America than in the United States.

In spite of the magnitude of the substance abuse problem, missionaries receive little training on how to help investigators to overcome substance abuse issues. The Word of Wisdom is officially presented only in the last discussion before baptism, and there are no official standards regarding any obligatory period of abstinence to qualify for baptism. When missionaries routinely baptize converts who have been abstinent from highly addictive substances for only a few days, one can appreciate why relapse rates are very high. Mark Twain's quip that "quitting smoking is easy, I've done it a thousand times" takes on tragic significance in areas where missionaries and mission leaders do not have the insight to insist that prospective converts have fully overcome substance addictions before baptism. New converts with substance abuse problems are often embarrassed to divulge their situation to other members and rarely seek help.

---

*   Oaks, Dallin A., "The Role of Members in Conversion," *Ensign*, March 2003.

Missionaries, who are usually the only ones aware of an investigator's Word of Wisdom challenges, are in the best position to ensure that the investigator has fully overcome harmful addictions and prevent relapse by requiring an adequate period of full abstinence from forbidden substances before baptism. Medical studies demonstrate that the relapse rate for smokers abstinent from cigarettes for less than three to four weeks is catastrophic. Missions that have insisted that investigators fully overcome substance addictions by abstaining from all forbidden substances for at least four weeks before baptism have achieved much higher convert retention rates than missions without such policies.

6. Obedience to the Law of Chastity in word, thought, and deed for at least four weeks. Moral transgressions are among the most serious of sins (Alma 39:5), yet also among the most prevalent. Those who even think immoral thoughts cannot be fellowshipped by the Holy Spirit (D&C 42:23). Joseph F. Smith stated: "There appears to be something beyond and above the reasons apparent to the human mind why chastity brings strength and power to the peoples of the earth, but it is so."[*]

The Church, which requires that members refrain from any sexual relations outside of marriage, faces a widening gulf between scriptural standards and secular values. In the United States, 60 percent of all adults,[†] including 54 percent of mainline Christians, 42 percent of weekly church attendees, and 36 percent of born-again Christians believe that premarital cohabitation is morally acceptable.[‡] Sociolo-

---

[*]   Smith, Joseph F., *Gospel Doctrine*, Salt Lake City, UT: Deseret Book, 1978, 274.

[†]   Barna, George, "Morality Continues to Decay," *Barna Research Update*, November 10, 2003, http://www.barna.org/FlexPage.aspx?Page=BarnaUpdate& BarnaUpdateID=152.

[‡]   Barna, George, "Practical Outcomes Replace Biblical Principles as the Moral

gist Stephanie Coontz observed: "People's behavior about marriage changed more in the past 30 years than in the last 3,000."[*] One recent study reported that 95% of Americans born from the 1940s onward had engaged in premarital sexual relations by age 44, with the median age of first premarital relations reaching 17 for those born after 1970.[†] Promiscuity is also spreading rapidly, even in nations which have traditionally fostered strong family values. In China, 70 percent of Beijing residents reported sex before marriage in 2005, compared to just 15 percent in 1989.[‡] Similar trends of growing permissiveness and promiscuity are seen in many other nations.

I have sometimes heard missionaries refer lightly to moral sins, stating that unmarried investigator couples "just need to move out or get married so that they can be baptized." Such attitudes trivialize the repentance process. President Kimball wrote of one young couple: "They were very disturbed when their marriage was postponed to allow time for repentance. They had rationalized the sin nearly out of existence. They pressed for a date, the first possible one on which they could plan their temple marriage. They did not understand that forgiveness is not a thing of days or months or even years but is a matter of intensity of feeling and transformation of self."[§] While missionaries must be sensitive to feelings and should not pry into moral transgressions, they must be firm in ensuring that the repen-

---

Standard," *Barna Research Update*, September 10, 2001, http://www.barna.org/cgi-bin/PagePressRelease.asp?PressReleaseID=97&Reference=F.

[*] Roberts, Sam, "So Many Men, So Few Women," *New York Times*, February 12, 2006.

[†] Finer, Lawrence B. Trends in premarital sex in the United States, 1954-2003. Public Health Reports 122 (Jan-Feb 2007):73-77.

[‡] Beech, Hannah, "Sex Please—We're Young and Chinese," *Time Asia Magazine*, January 23, 2006.

[§] Kimball, Spencer W., *The Miracle of Forgiveness*, Salt Lake City, UT: Bookcraft, 1977, 155–56.

tance process is truly at work and that the requisite transformation has occurred.

7. Every prospective convert should receive an adequate baptismal interview to ensure that he has consistently applied the previously mentioned gospel habits for the requisite period. Appropriate interviews ask open-ended questions to allow the investigator to explain gospel principles as he or she understands them and what he or she is doing to live these principles. Scriptures require that prospective converts must have "a determination to serve him [Christ] to the end, and truly manifest by their works that they have received of the Spirit of Christ unto the remission of their sins" (D&C 20:37). Individuals who have not established consistent gospel habits have not demonstrated the "fruits of repentance" that are required for baptism. Moliere wrote: "All men are alike in their dreams, and all men are alike in the promises they make. The difference is what they do." The baptismal interview represents the best and last opportunity to ensure that converts are living basic gospel laws and are fully prepared for baptism. I have known many converts who have thanked the missionaries or the interviewer for delaying their anticipated baptism, since the delay reinforced the importance of gospel covenants and helped them to become much stronger and more committed members. When the opportunity to ensure that converts are appropriately qualified for baptism is abdicated by missionaries and leaders who are more interested in padding monthly statistical reports than in ensuring the true conversion of converts or building the Church, irreversible damage is done. If the one-year convert retention rate in your area is below 80 to 90 percent, the quality, insight, and discernment of prebaptismal interviews needs to be improved.

8. Missionaries should invite active members to participate in at least two missionary discussions or visits with the prospective convert prior to baptism. Fellowshipping is crucial, and few converts remain active without developing meaningful friendships with active members. The First Presidency mandate that converts must feel unity with local members to qualify for baptism* requires that fellowshipping efforts must begin long before baptism and that prospective converts must be attending church consistently. The traditional pattern of initiating fellowshipping efforts only at the time of baptism is much too late. Missionaries can ensure that meaningful fellowshipping occurs and that friendships are established well before baptism in every case by inviting active members to participate in the discussions in the investigator's home or by teaching the prospective convert in a member's home.

9. Appointments for the first home teaching visit and first new member discussion should be established prior to baptism. The *Church Handbook of Instructions* teaches that home teachers should meet the new members at or before the time of baptism. Accelerated baptism programs arranging baptisms on short notice violate this directive, which requires good coordination and communication between the full-time missionaries, ward and stake missionaries, and local priesthood leaders. New converts must be visited promptly and have the new member discussions started.

Local leaders must ensure that the new converts are assigned reliable home teachers. Ward missionaries and members who have established friendships or participated in the fellowshipping process can also make good home and visiting teachers, although local leaders

---

*   *Missionary Guide*, Salt Lake City, UT: The Church of Jesus Christ of Latter-day Saints, 1988, 234.

must rely upon inspiration in making appropriate assignments. At a minimum, the ward mission leader, quorum president, or missionaries should personally discuss the urgency of the assignment and the status of the individual as a new convert to the assigned home teacher, so that the convert does not fall through the cracks as an unfamiliar name on a long assignment list. Any special needs or interests should also be discussed with the home teacher. The home teacher should attend the baptism. The missionaries or ward mission leader should also follow up closely for several months to ensure that timely and consistent home teaching is occurring.

10. Converts should receive a calling within one week of baptism. The prospective convert should be interviewed by the bishop and discussed in ward council or bishopric meetings well before baptism so that a timely calling can be issued. President Gordon B. Hinckley noted: "With the ever-increasing number of converts, we must make an increasingly substantial effort to assist them as they find their way. Every one of them needs three things: a friend, a responsibility, and nurturing with the 'good word of God' (Moroni 6:4). It is our duty and opportunity to provide these things."[*]

11. Converts should be greeted by family history missionaries at or before the time of baptism and started on personal family history work. This helps the converts to become involved in another mission of the Church. When new converts were started on personal family history immediately after baptism, convert retention rates in one area of Utah rose from 40 percent to 80 percent.[†]

---

[*]   Hinckley, Gordon B., *Ensign*, May 1997.

[†]   As cited at Regional Family History Conference, Vernal, Utah, September 2000.

12. Where possible, converts should be prepared to participate in temple proxy baptisms within six weeks of baptism. Converts who attend the temple within six weeks of conversion to perform proxy baptisms experience increased retention rates. This is especially true when the converts are working on their own family file.

The actual time needed to implement these points for prospective converts varies widely according to individual needs. As a missionary, I found that the average time between the first contact and baptism with the implementation of these points was approximately six to eight weeks. Some missions implementing these points have reported average teaching times of up to three months for investigators to consistently implement all gospel habits and prepare for baptism. While quality teaching and preparation require more effort and discipline than accelerated baptism programs, they meet the investigator's spiritual needs, provide consistent, lasting Church growth, and fulfill scriptural and prophetic mandates in ways that accelerated baptism programs do not.

New converts should also be encouraged to obtain their patriarchal blessings, which provide guidance and strength, and to prepare to attend the temple to receive their own endowments.

SPECIAL CASES IN CONVERT RETENTION

BAPTISM OF CHILDREN
WITHOUT ACTIVE PARENTS

T HE BAPTISM OF MINOR children without parents or other close family members active in the Church demands careful contemplation. Many sixteen- and seventeen-year-olds and some fourteen- and fifteen-year-olds are sufficiently independent to maintain their faith in the absence of family support. Many members baptized in their mid to late teens as the only members of their family have become strong members, served missions, and married in the temple. However, few children under the age of fourteen are able to remain active long-term in the absence of ongoing parental support, example, and teaching. Most young children who remain active have other active Church members in their immediate or extended family, or at a minimum a strong commitment of nonmember parents in ensuring that they attend church each Sunday and adhere to gospel standards.

There are very few instances where baptism without parental involvement is appropriate for children under age fourteen. Cases of fourteen- and fifteen-year-olds must be carefully considered individually to ensure that each prospective convert is attracted not merely to the social elements but to the spiritual offerings of the restored gospel, has demonstrated sustained commitment to the Church, and has firmly established gospel habits. Child baptism proponents present a false dichotomy between immediate baptism and no baptism at all, yet many with genuine commitment are able to remain involved in the Church until reaching the age of emancipation when parental consent is no longer required. If prospective converts truly meet the scriptural requirement of having demonstrated a firm determination to serve Christ until the very end of their lives, they can wait weeks, months, or even a few years for baptism.

Waiting for baptism often helps to solidify conversion and commitment while weeding out uncommitted souls who would not have remained active in spite of baptism. Belgian leader Wilfried Decoo described his own experience: "Since I was a minor when I first expressed a desire for baptism, and my parents would not approve, I was required to wait three years. During that waiting period my knowledge, commitment, and testimony of the gospel only increased, while the sanctity and importance of the baptismal ordinance loomed ever larger in my mind."[*] Another former bishop wrote: "I was in the same situation as a youth, wanting to join the Church, but having parents who were almost hostile toward the Church.... After two and a half years of persistent study and having the lessons with three sets of missionaries, studying pro and anti materials, and interesting my friends and their families to join the Church before me, I finally got my parents' permission and was baptized a week before I turned eighteen. While it was agonizing at the time, I am grateful for the deep study I did while I was a 'dry Mormon.'"

---

[*]   Decoo, Wilfried, "Feeding the Fleeing Flock: Reflections on the Struggle to Retain Church Members in Europe," *Dialogue*, 29/1 (Spring 1996): 97–113.

BAPTISM OF TRANSIENTS

Opportunities to teach and baptize transient students, workers, and visitors planning a return or move to a distant area within the next three months raise difficult issues. Recognizing the vital role of fellowshipping in convert retention, the baptism of an individual who is almost immediately transplanted to an area where he or she has virtually no fellowshipping support is a recipe for failure. Even the baptism of local investigators before an extended vacation or long trip can be problematic. Missionaries often shortchange the teaching process as they rush to baptize investigators before they leave, since they receive no "credit" for baptisms performed in other areas and face no personal consequences if the convert is not retained. My audits have found that few such converts become active or participating members unless there are other family members or close friends who are active in the Church.

I believe that it is rarely appropriate to baptize short-term transients returning to an area where the Church is already established. In most cases, it is best to help the investigators to establish firm gospel habits that will provide spiritual nourishment and transition their teaching to missionaries and members in the new area so that they can be baptized and fellowshipped in the ward in which they will partici-pate. Investigators who have experienced genuine conversion can wait for baptism to be performed in their home area by missionaries and members who will be able to appropriately fellowship, nurture, and involve them. Rare exceptions exist in which baptism can be appro-priate shortly before moving, but such situations should be thought through carefully, and the convert must be thoroughly prepared for the challenges to come.

The question of baptizing transients from areas without established

Church units is more complex. It is not possible for individuals to fully meet the expectations of Church membership without an organized congregation in their home area. The concept of baptizing such individuals in the hope that they will serve as the nucleus of the Church at some future date when a congregation is established in their home area seems attractive, but the desired outcome is rarely achieved. As a missionary in Russia opening a new city for missionary work, I found that none of the members previously baptized in other areas became fully active when a branch was opened in their area, and few attended even occasionally. In case studies of new cities opened in other areas, I have also found that participating membership overwhelmingly comes from new converts rather than previously baptized members. Harm may be done by saddling new congregations with major inactivity problems from their very inception.

Careful consideration and reliance on the Holy Spirit is necessary, since there are situations where the baptism of individuals from areas without congregations is appropriate and necessary. In some countries, the Church must have a certain number of members in a city to receive government approval to open a congregation or send missionaries, and baptism of transients may help permit later Church expansion. Some converts make extraordinary sacrifices to maintain contact with the Church. One of the best missionaries I have known was a young soldier named Igor who was baptized while serving in the Russian Army in Germany. He returned home to a small Ukrainian city named Kirovograd with no missionaries, waited the requisite year, and then submitted his papers after making extraordinary efforts to make contact with a mission headquarters hundreds of kilometers away. He was a wonderful and effective missionary and went on to marry a returned Russian sister missionary in the temple and to serve faithfully in the Church.

In spite of the difficulties, I believe that in most cases, the benefit of the doubt should favor baptism for investigators who live in areas where the Church is not yet established. In every case, it is necessary to ensure that prospective investigators from such areas have undergone a life-changing conversion and are prepared for the challenges they will face.

Understanding Inactivity
and Reactivation

REAL VERSUS ALLEGED CAUSES OF INACTIVITY

THE SAVIOR'S PARABLES TEACH that converts are lost for different reasons. In Luke 15, Christ taught that some inactives willfully stray (Parable of the Prodigal Son), some are lost through neglect or carelessness (Parable of the Lost Coin), and some are lost from a lack of adequate teaching or pastoring (Parable of the Lost Sheep). Some leave because of social issues; others because of family pressure; some because of worthiness problems or difficulty living commandments; and some because of lack or loss of belief in LDS doctrines and teachings. James Duke noted: "Lifestyle issues, which usually involves some degree of disobedience to commandments, are major reasons why people drop into inactivity, but members give many different reasons for their inactivity. Lack of social integration into the ward is also a major cause of inactivity."*

A talk given at the April 2005 General Conference stated that studies showed "that almost all less-active members interviewed believe that

* Duke, James T., "Latter-day Saints in a Secular World: What We Have Learned about Latter-day Saints from Social Research," Martin B Hickman 1999 Lecture, Brigham Young University College of Family, Home, and Social Sciences, March 4, 1999, http://fhss.byu.edu/adm/hickman_lecture.htm.

God exists, that Jesus is the Christ, that Joseph Smith was a prophet, and that the Church is true."[*] The location, methodology, and sample size of the cited study or studies was not disclosed. It seems unlikely that such results could have been obtained outside of Utah, since none of the hundreds of leaders, missionaries, and members I have interviewed outside of the Wasatch Front cite local data anywhere near this favorable. Numerous national censuses and religious self-identification studies around the world have almost invariably found that only a small fraction of international members identify the LDS Church as their faith of preference.

One Missionary Department survey of U.S. inactives reported that "85%+ of all inactives retained active testimonies of the restored gospel" but chose not to attend because of Word of Wisdom issues, a lack of Sunday church clothing, a real or perceived offence by local members, a lack of friends in the ward or branch, or feelings of unworthiness. If an individual stops coming to church for such reasons, one wonders of what an "active testimony" could possibly consist. Because of social acceptability bias, many respondents may cite external reasons deemed acceptable to the interviewer rather than acknowledging issues of personal worthiness, lack of interest, or disbelief, especially when research is conducted by Church employees rather than by independent researchers. A more discerning and meaningful follow-up study would evaluate how many of those who claimed that they did not attend because of the lack of suitable Sunday apparel promptly returned to full church activity after being given appropriate clothes and how many of those who reported staying home because they had no friends at church started attending regularly once diligent fellowshipping and home teaching measures were implemented.

---

*   Whetten, Robert J., "Strengthen Thy Brethren," LDS General Conference, April 2005.

While some few do return, my experience is that only a small fraction of those who claim such reasons are reactivated after the alleged deficiencies are remedied. In most cases, addressing one excuse only brings a litany of new ones. It would be naïve to accept justifications such as the "lack of Sunday clothes" as primary causes of inactivity.

A survey on substance abuse relapse among new converts cited in an *Ensign* article noted that of those who relapsed, over 90 percent stated that they had "a very high desire" to stay abstinent for prohibited substances after baptism.* Like the prior study, this study lacked the discerning follow-up questions that are necessary to ascertain the validity of the assertions. What did the individuals do to translate their "very high desires" into meaningful action? Did they seek help, meet with the bishop, see a physician, or try a treatment program? The effort individuals put forth to achieve their alleged desires is the only valid test of sincerity. Studies show that the large majority of smokers are dissatisfied with the habit and express at least a theoretical desire to quit. But what do they do about it? If one were to ask one hundred people if they desired one million dollars, there is little doubt that well over 90 percent of them would express a "strong desire." Do they put in the requisite effort to study, work, and plan, or do they purchase lottery tickets and sit in front of the television waiting for their big break? The "strongest desire" expressed in words but not backed up by action is only an idle fantasy.

Census data from around the world consistently report self-identified religious affiliation far below official LDS membership numbers, and very low international activity has seen little improvement in spite of the diversion of large amounts of missionary time into reactivation work. Such data should lead us to look beyond flattering but superficial explanations of inactivity as primarily a social phenomenon and

---

*   Oaks, Dallin A., "The Role of Members in Conversion," *Ensign*, March 2003.

to examine its deeper causes. While social factors can play a role in member retention, the tremendous impact of prebaptismal preparation, gospel habits, testimony, and personal effort upon member retention must not be overlooked.

WHY DO MOST REACTIVATION PROGRAMS FALL SHORT?

Having followed the situation in Eastern Europe closely since 1991, I have heard many times of soon-to-be stakes held back only by "reactivation problems." While I was on my mission from 1992 through 1994, it was widely anticipated by both local leaders and visiting authorities that stakes in St. Petersburg, Kiev, and Budapest would be organized within one to three years. I have heard leaders state on numerous occasions that "if only we could reactivate fifty Melchizedek priesthood holders, we could form a stake." It was stated repeatedly that work with members and inactives would represent the key to growth. At the time of this writing, there are no stakes in Russia. A stake was created in Ukraine only in late 2003, nearly a decade later than widely expected. In spite of a strong focus on reactivation for nearly ten years by intelligent, dedicated mission leaders and, according to one general authority, "the best missionaries the church has to offer," the anticipated gains of reactivation remain largely unfulfilled. Some missions experienced slight gains in member activity rates, but most of these areas have subsequently relapsed. The diversion of large amounts of missionary time into member rehabilitation efforts contributed to a sharp decline in convert baptisms since missionaries spent less time proselytizing receptive nonmembers. Even in missions where missionaries spent a full 50 percent of their time with inactives, the vast majority of growth has continued to come from the baptism of nonmembers rather than the reactivation of carnal members.

Reactivation programs failed or produced scant gains, because they were based on erroneous assumptions. The first assumption was that inactives were overwhelmingly individuals with "active testimonies" who had been lost because of the lack of socialization or nurturing who were merely waiting for the invitation to come back. As we have seen, only a small minority of inactives fit this description. Most international inactives are "never-actives" who had been rushed to baptism by the missionaries, often without attending church more than one or two Sundays, without fully overcoming substance abuse habits, and without gaining a solid testimony of the gospel. Many would not have been baptized if scriptural requirements for baptism had been applied. Since many such inactives were never active to begin with, even massive "reactivation" efforts rarely result in any meaningful gains among this group. Many others were active for only a brief period or had made the decision to stop attending due to lifestyle or testimony issues.

The second assumption is that it is easier to reactivate disaffected members than to make new converts. Some argue it must be much easier to reclaim those who have already accepted the restored gospel and are familiar with LDS teachings than to "start from scratch" with nonmembers who know nothing about the Church at all. Such reasoning, however attractive, is not factually supportable. I have consistently found that missions that divert large amounts of missionary time away from proselyting into reactivation work consistently experience a sharp drop in convert baptisms for which the meager number of reactivated members does not come close to compensating.

The dramatic successes of Ammon and his brethren among the nonmember Lamanites compared to the scant results achieved among the apostate Nephites and the considerable growth of the early Church among the Gentiles after its rejection by the Jews should lead one to appreciate that reactivation work is often less fruitful than proselyting. Rick Warren observed: "Growing churches focus on reaching receptive people. Non-growing churches focus on reenlisting inactive people.... It usually takes about five times more energy to reactivate a disgruntled or carnal member than it does to win a receptive unbeliever. I believe that God has called pastors to catch fish and feed sheep, not to corral goats!"* He continued: "Often the local pastor and I would spend the afternoons making evangelistic house calls. Many times the pastor would take me to the same stubborn case that previous evangelists had failed to win. It was a waste of time. Is it good stewardship to continue badgering someone who has already rejected Christ a dozen times when there is a whole community of receptive people waiting to hear the gospel for the first time?... The apostle Paul's strategy was to go through open doors and not waste time banging on closed ones. Likewise, we should not focus our efforts on those who aren't ready to listen. There are far more people in the world who are ready to receive Christ than there are believers ready to witness to them."†

Reactivation work is important, yet the awareness that each soul is precious demands that endless time and resources cannot be dedicated to low-yield activities when more productive alternatives exist. Especially in new areas where resources are limited, resources should be preferentially allocated toward teaching receptive and committed individuals who can strengthen the Church. There is always a role for reactivation work, yet reactivation programs must be held to the same results-based standards as conventional proselyting techniques.

---

*   Warren, Rick, *The Purpose Driven Church*, Grand Rapids, MI: Zondervan, 1995, 183.

†   Warren, Rick, *The Purpose Driven Church*, Grand Rapids, MI: Zondervan, 1995, 188.

A balanced perspective must be kept on reaching those who are receptive, whether they are nonmembers in the community or less-active members.

DIMINISHING RETURNS IN REACTIVATION

The fact that few areas of the international Church have achieved activity rates above 30 to 35 percent after more than a decade of strong worldwide emphasis on work with members and less-actives suggests that none of the widely implemented reactivation programs have been particularly effective or noteworthy. Even with exhaustive effort, most reactivation programs rarely activate more than a small fraction of inactives.

After a certain amount of effort is put forth to reach all inactives, a point of diminishing returns is reached. Continued work with the same people becomes progressively less likely to result in activation. Beyond the point of full saturation, additional reactivation effort produces little or no results. No matter how many opportunities inactives are given to return to Church fellowship, they retain moral agency and must make their own decisions. Even the most powerful teacher cannot convert or reactivate those who refuse to give a fair audience. When King Lamoni preached "as many as heard his words believed, and were converted unto the Lord. But there were many among them who would not hear his words; therefore they went their way" (Alma 19:31–32).

While reactivation efforts can generate slight gains, they should never be allowed to become a black hole that diverts large amounts of missionary time away from more productive efforts to contact and teach nonmembers. Reactivation work is usually a dead end among "never-actives" who were not adequately prepared for baptism in the first place. Sometimes it is better to acknowledge the loss of some individuals to the Church and move on to more fertile pastures instead of continuing to pour vast amounts of resources into reactivation projects producing scant gains at the expense of outreach to nonmembers.

CONCENTRATING EFFORTS TO REACH THE LOST

The Parable of the Shepherd leaving the ninety and nine to reach the one (Luke 15:4–7) and the Parable of the Lost Piece of Silver (Luke 15:8–10) teach the necessity of concentrated efforts to reach the lost. There is no parable of a woman going to simultaneously seek ten lost pieces of silver, nor of a shepherd leaving a handful of found sheep to gather a whole flock of strays.

While one would ideally like to be able to dedicate unlimited resources toward reactivating each inactive member without decreasing nonmember opportunities to hear the gospel, the reality is that we have limited time and resources available in an era when "the harvest is great, but the laborers are few" (Luke 10:2). Understandably, no one wants to be responsible for allocating outreach priorities and potentially denying some individuals opportunities. Nonetheless, good stewardship demands that we prioritize to ensure that limited resources are directed toward the most receptive audiences. Those who refuse to prioritize deny the most receptive people an opportunity to hear the gospel.

FACTORS ASSOCIATED WITH REACTIVATION

The decision of which inactives should receive priority attention depends on both receptivity and resources. While prayerful consideration is vital, the individual who understands what factors impact the likelihood of reactivation is much more likely to be inspired by the Holy Spirit than one who does not.

The following factors improve the likelihood of reactivation:

1. The individual regularly attended church for at least six to twelve months before going inactive.
2. A close family member of the inactive person, especially a spouse, is an active member.
3. The individual has close friends who are active members.
4. The individual has drifted into inactivity relatively recently.
5. The inactive is a teen or young adult.
6. The individual was raised in the Church by an active family.

The following negative factors diminish prospects for reactivation:

1. The inactive did not attend regularly for any meaningful period after baptism.
2. There are no family members active in the Church.
3. The individual has no close friends who are active members.
4. The individual has been inactive for many years.
5. The inactive is an older adult.
6. The inactive is a convert or was raised in an inactive family.
7. The inactive is actively affiliated with another faith.

Personal factors also play a role. Many individuals with a seemingly positive profile never return to church, while some individuals with multiple negative factors are successfully reactivated. Yet understanding the factors associated with reactivation can help us to set realistic expectations and to ensure that those most likely to respond receive priority attention.

Reactivation efforts are most effective when they focus on helping inactives to develop the habits of daily scripture reading, personal and family prayer, church attendance, Sabbath Day observance, and to feel fellowship with the Saints.

UPBRINGING AND ACTIVITY

George Barna noted that most of those in the United States who become Christians do so as children. He wrote: "Children between the ages of 5 and 13 have a 32% probability of accepting Jesus Christ as their Savior. The probability of accepting Christ drops to 4% for those who are between the ages of 14 and 18. Those older than 18 have a 6% probability of accepting Jesus Christ as their Savior."[*] People come into the LDS church at all ages, although young people tend to be the most receptive. Barna reported that 61 percent of U.S. adults who attended church as children are attending church today, compared to 22 percent of adults who did not attend church as children.[†] Barna continues: "Attending church over the course of years appears to have affected the religious practices of people, too. The survey discovered that adults who attended church as a child are twice as likely to read the Bible during a typical week as are those who avoided churches when young; twice as likely to attend a church worship service in a typical week; and nearly 50% more likely to pray to God during a typical week." The study also noted that "denominational loyalty has remained unexpectedly strong among those who were attending church during their early years."[‡]

---

[*]   Barna, George, "Research Archives: Evangelism," *Barna Research Online,* http://www.barna.org/cgi-bin/PageCategory.asp?CategoryID=18.

[†]   Barna, George, "Adults Who Attended Church as Children Show Lifelong Effects," *Barna Research Update,* November 5, 2001, http://www.barna.org/cgi-bin/PagePressRelease.asp?PressReleaseID=101&Reference=D.

[‡]   Barna, George, "Adults Who Attended Church as Children Show Lifelong Effects," *Barna Research Update,* November 5, 2001, http://www.barna.org/cgi-bin/PagePressRelease.asp?PressReleaseID=101&Reference=D.

Being raised by a churchgoing family also increases chances of returning to activity after periods of inactivity. LDS sociologist James Duke cites Stan Albrecht's Activity and Inactivity study: "Of every 100 people born in the Church, only 22% remain active throughout their lives. That means 78% are inactive for a year or more at some time. Most, 44%, return to activity, while 34% remain inactive.... Those who become inactive usually do so during the teenage and young adult years. Those who return usually do so during young adulthood. If young Latter-day Saints grow up in a religious home in which many gospel principles are practiced, 44% will remain active their whole lives.... On the other hand, of the young Latter-day Saints who grow up in an inactive home, 13% of them will remain active."[*],[†] Among those raised in active families, there is a correlation between daily scripture reading and other gospel habits in the home and long-term church activity. Children who grow up in the homes of inactive parents hostile to the Church or completely disengaged from LDS beliefs are far less likely to return to activity than those who grow up in the homes of less-active parents who still acknowledge the truth of the Book of Mormon, who attend church at least occasionally, and who have faithful church members in the immediate or extended family. If a slight majority of lifelong U.S. members who go inactive eventually return to the fold, the prospects for return to activity among international inactives are far less hopeful, because few international converts were raised in LDS homes, and most converts were active only for a brief period if at all.

---

[*]   Duke, James T., "Latter-day Saints in a Secular World: What We Have Learned about Latter-day Saints from Social Research," Martin B Hickman 1999 Lecture, Brigham Young University College of Family, Home, and Social Sciences, March 4, 1999, http://fhss.byu.edu/adm/hickman_lecture.htm.

[†]   Albrecht, Stan L., "The Consequential Dimension of Mormon Religiosity," in James T. Duke, ed., Latter-day Saint Social Life, Provo, UT: Religious Studies Center, Brigham Young University, 1998, 253–292.

INACTIVITY AMONG CONVERTS

Convert inactivity occurs in three main peaks, although some overlap exists. The first peak is within the first two months after baptism and relates primarily to poor teaching and inadequate prebaptismal preparation. Inactivity in accelerated baptism areas is heavily front-loaded, with up to 80 percent of inactivity occurring within the first two months. Inactivity in this period is completely avoidable by ensuring that prospective converts have established firm habits of obedience to gospel laws and have fully overcome alcohol and tobacco addictions and other prohibited behaviors before being considered for baptism.

The second peak occurs from two months to one year after baptism and often relates to deficient fellowshipping or nurturing, although gospel habits of daily scripture reading and weekly church attendance often have not been instilled by the missionaries. Inactivity in this period can usually be prevented by involving members in the teaching and fellowshipping of converts starting well before baptism to ensure that the converts have developed strong friendships with active members before baptism. As with the first peak, ensuring that prospective converts have established the habit of daily scripture reading and weekly church attendance is vital.

The third peak occurs more than one year after baptism and usually relates to the convert's willful choice to stray. Sometimes inactivity is attributed to some real or imagined offense or to difficulty in accepting a specific gospel teaching. It can occur when an individual leaves old friends in a ward or branch and never makes the effort to connect up with the Church in his or her new area. Whatever the ostensible cause, inactivity of this third kind is generally related to personal disobedience of the inactive member. While at times serious transgression may be involved, very often this inactivity is due simply to neglect of daily scripture reading, daily prayer, church attendance, Sabbath day observance, and other basic commandments that shape our character and determine our eternal destiny. Our implementation of these commandments determines whether we make daily progress toward emulating the Savior or stagnate in our growth. While this third peak of inactivity will likely never be entirely avoided, it can be reduced when individuals have been required to develop positive habits of spiritual nourishment before baptism and when obedience to basic gospel laws rather than mere social activity is a constant focus in the local congregation.

Missionaries who have spent large amounts of time working to reactivate inactive converts from prior years typically experience success far below the figures cited in Albrecht's study. While this study provides interesting insight into those born into active LDS families in the United States, it does not apply to converts. Those born in the Church who later lapse into inactivity often have the experience of their entire upbringing as well as a strong family support system to guide them back into the Church, while most adult converts go inactive within several weeks of baptism and lack the family support and background of lifelong members. Reactivation efforts in areas of convert growth generally achieve only slight success and are typically far less successful than efforts to teach new investigators. Converts do not have the benefit of having been taught gospel habits all of their lives, and convert retention drops below activity rates of lifetime members when converts are poorly taught or are baptized without meeting scriptural requirements.

Nonetheless, convert growth has major potential advantages over growth among children of record. Converts make an informed decision to select the LDS Church over other alternatives, while children raised in LDS homes are raised in a tradition with little opportunity to make an independent decision until coming of age. Perhaps for this reason, the highest recorded activity and retention rates have occurred among converts. All of Ammon's converts remained active (Alma 23:6), while over 97 percent of converts baptized in the British Isles between 1840 and 1890 emigrated to join the U.S. saints.[*] Indeed, appropriate teaching and preparation of prospective converts offers the unique opportunity to build new congregations that are stronger and more vibrant than those in established areas. Wonderful and miraculous events occur when converts are prepared to receive the Holy Spirit. Spencer W. Kimball observed that "if there were no converts, the Church would shrivel and die on the vine."[†]

EXTREMES OF INVOLVEMENT

The extremes of lack of involvement and burnout from excessive church-related demands can both contribute to inactivity. The impact of lack of involvement is well-known, while the impact of member burnout has been less extensively studied. Many active international members are assigned multiple church callings and long lists of inactives to home or visit teach. The travel costs of attending church and filling church-related assignments several times throughout the week can be prohibitive for many. Some individuals have gone inactive after years of faithful service in the Church, citing burnout at simultaneously carrying multiple callings and chronic guilt at being unable to

---

[*]   Stark, Rodney, "The Basis of Mormon Success: A Theoretical Application," in James T. Duke, ed., *Latter-day Saint Social Life: Social Research on the LDS Church and Its Members*, Provo, UT: Religious Studies Center, Brigham Young University, 1998, 29–67.

[†]   Kimball, Spencer W., "When the World Will Be Converted," *Ensign*, October 1974, 4, originally presented at Regional Representatives' Seminar, April 4, 1974.

visit all of their numerous assigned home teachees every month. Some of these individuals express that they want "a break," want to be "left alone," or want to "get their life back" of friends and outside interests that they were not able to maintain while all of their discretionary energies were focused on church assignments. The expectations of the Church should be within the reach of every active member and should never be allowed to eclipse personal physical, mental, and spiritual well-being or family needs. Christ taught: "For my yoke is easy, and my burden is light" (Matthew 11:30).

POSTRELEASE INACTIVITY

In areas where the Church is young and members have little familiarity with the natural cycle of congregational leadership change, inactivity frequently follows the release of leaders from callings. My second mission president reported that in our mission area with just over twenty branches, fourteen former and current branch presidents and members of district presidencies went inactive or left the Church over a three-year period.* While leaders are typically viewed as representing some of the strongest members, leaders may be particularly vulnerable to spiritual malnourishment, because administrative time demands are sometimes allowed to crowd out daily scripture reading and other activities essential for spiritual growth. Constant tasks of planning, organization, and administration leave leaders with little opportunity to be taught or edified. Many leaders are caught off guard by the sudden and largely unanticipated nature of their release and are left with a void where they had found fulfillment through service. Some may feel that nonleadership callings are not as honorable or

---

*   Rogers, Thomas F., "Mormonism's First Decade in the Former USSR: Patterns of Growth and Retention," Presentation at Mormon History Association Meeting, Copenhagen, Denmark, June 2000.

important or may mistakenly believe that release from leadership represents a personal disgrace. Others may be offended when those over whom they previously had been given stewardship, often younger or more recent members, become their priesthood leaders.

There is little data on how postrelease inactivity can be avoided. It may be helpful to impress upon local leaders that at the time that the calling is given that callings are temporary and that release is inevitable. Church callings do not constitute rungs on a corporate ladder. All callings are important. Change of callings is part of the natural cycle of the Church, and release is not a personal affront. It is also necessary to ensure that leaders are not overburdened, are meeting personal and family needs, and are maintaining habits of daily personal scripture study. Scriptural references to priesthood and leadership offices, such as minister, pastor, deacon (Greek "diakonos" = servant), teacher, and apostle ("one who is sent forth"), all convey connotations of service rather than rank. Christ taught: "But he that is greatest among you shall be your servant. And whosoever shall exalt himself shall be abased; and he that shall humble himself shall be exalted" (Matthew 23:11–12). It may be helpful to discuss with local leaders in advance the challenge that some may face in returning to seemingly less glamorous positions in their local ward or branch. The prospect of postrelease inactivity should be anticipated, and members should be closely supported throughout transition periods.

ACTIVITY AND VITALITY

The struggle to achieve even meager activity rates in accelerated baptism areas has too often led to complacency when members attend church at all. In most congregations, a minority of active members are responsible for the majority of the growth and progress. Most units have many active but noncontributing or minimally contributing members who participate in the social activities of the Church but fail to press forward along the iron rod and partake of the fruits of the Spirit. It is believed that only about half of active adults pay tithing, while only a small minority of active members read scriptures daily or share the gospel regularly.

It is not so important what stage an individual is at as long as he is making continued progress. There will always be some individuals who rely upon the testimony of others until they can stand on their own. Even outwardly highly active individuals have considerable opportunities for improvement. Members and nonmembers of all walks of life are welcome to attend meetings and benefit from blessings of teaching, fellowshipping, and the Holy Spirit (D&C 46:3–5).

Church attendance, while essential, is not our final goal. Daily scripture reading and adherence to other gospel laws present keys to continued spiritual progress. Missionaries and members must maintain a constant focus on the consistent implementation of basic gospel laws that bring spiritual blessings into the lives of investigators, members, and less-actives alike.

SECTION III.

Introduction to Leadership

M**ANY ADMINISTRATIVE FACTORS CAN** enhance or inhibit church growth. Some of the key factors include strategic planning, church planting, use of mass media, and missionary allocation. Jim Montgomery, founder of Discipling A Whole Nation (DAWN), a group that has helped double and triple evangelical growth rates in many countries, observed that churches which adopt appropriate strategic planning measures on average see their growth rates double.* Most of these factors cannot be readily influenced by individual members or missionaries and are discussed in detail in the principles of leadership section.

Leaders who diligently seek to enhance their outreach effectiveness often find few sources from which to gain information and insight. The *Preach My Gospel* manual, while excellent, is brief. Leadership materials often focus on policies and procedures but offer few principles and even less information. Other faiths have produced a rich missiologic literature addressing considerations such as how to conduct effective media outreach efforts or when it is appropriate to build local chapels, while scarcely any mention of these topics can be found in LDS sources. Missionaries of other faiths can access extensive data and analyses regarding the needs and opportunities of the

---

*   Montgomery, James, "13 Steps to a Successful Growth Program," Dawn Ministries, Undated article, http://www.dawnministries.org/documents/files/books/13%20Steps.PDF.

areas where they serve, while many LDS missionaries serve their entire missions without even a firm grasp of local member activity or convert retention rates. Resources evaluating cultural aspects and local conditions that impact the sharing of the gospel rarely delve deeper than three- to four-page Brigham Young University "culturgrams" written for business travelers. The few books that have attempted to provide insight into effective missionary work rather than merely retelling inspirational stories focus almost exclusively on the role of individual missionaries.

In conjunction with the official *Preach My Gospel* manual, this book covers the basics that are necessary to effectively find, teach, baptize, and retain converts, inspire member-missionaries, and build strong church units. This leadership section provides additional information and principles of church growth that cannot be practically implemented by individual members or missionaries but reflect important considerations for leaders. The material in this section comes primarily from analysis of existing data and from observations of both effective and ineffective leaders.

I do not claim to have all of the answers. I am not a leader and have no aspirations and can provide candid observations without political or administrative constraints. My purpose is not to "inform the Brethren," nor do I deign to "steady the Ark." The following material is offered solely as my personal observations, research, and conclusions. I know that many individuals in leadership positions are aware of opportunities and challenges related to the topics covered here. I recognize that leaders at times have reasons for policies that transcend intellectual understanding and that in some cases there may be critical evidence not available to me. I do however hope that individuals will study and ponder the data so that whatever conclusions they come to will be informed and carefully considered ones. I do not expect that the reader will necessarily agree with every point, but I am confident that a greater awareness of these topics can enhance effectiveness.

Principles of Leadership

LDS PASTORING QUALITY IS EXCELLENT

BY BOTH COMPARATIVE AND absolute standards, the sensitivity, insight, and quality of counsel given by LDS bishops, stake presidents, and other leaders is outstanding. There are occasional exceptions as in any large organization, although the rarity of such exceptions is remarkable. Several factors contribute to the high quality of pastoral LDS leadership at all levels. The LDS Church has a lay clergy without remuneration, except for a modest living allowance given to authorities at the highest levels. Unremunerated service requires dedication and personal sacrifice and eliminates the inherent economic incentives of a paid clergy of other faiths. LDS leaders can focus on feeding the flock rather than themselves (Ezekiel 34:2) and are rewarded with the abundant grace of God (Mosiah 27:5). Personal worthiness is a requirement for LDS leaders at all levels, and most LDS leaders have extensive personal experience in the life application topics on which they counsel local members. Sustaining of LDS leaders by divine calling, rather than by vote, eliminates much of the disunity that exists in other denominations.

PASTORAL VERSUS OUTREACH LEADERSHIP

Over the course of a three-year term, the average LDS mission president is responsible for the baptism of some 2,600 new converts taught and baptized by missionaries under his supervision. Some missions achieve large numbers of baptisms but retain only a fraction of converts. Others achieve higher retention but make relatively few converts in areas of considerable opportunity. Still others suffer from both low retention and few baptisms. Relatively few missions succeed at both baptizing large numbers of converts per missionary and retaining even a bare majority. To a great extent, these differences reflect mission and area leadership.

Although Church doctrine has always taught that the prophet is the only man who will never lead the Church astray, a widespread misconception exists that lesser leaders are virtually infallible. Poor convert retention rates in many areas of the world, slow Church growth in receptive areas, and serious challenges that have remained unaddressed for prolonged periods emphatically demonstrate that this is not the case. A sincere and righteous person can be an excellent pastoral leader, but a poor mission leader. One can study the gospel, strive diligently to live the gospel, teach the gospel, write about the gospel, and serve faithfully in numerous church callings without understanding elementary principles of missionary work. Leaders have varying levels of understanding and experience a learning process.

Outreach leadership poses special challenges for even the most faithful and capable members. Pastoral leaders have considerable accumulated experience in the programs of their local wards, while most outreach leaders have had only remote or infrequent experience with finding, teaching, and retaining converts. Successful outreach leadership requires several attributes beyond those required for pastoral care.

Mission leaders often face the task of organizing new congregations from the ground up with fresh converts and are given broad authority to devise and implement their own policies and programs. In contrast, most congregations are in maintenance rather than growth mode, and programs remain fairly static even with the variable personalities of pastoral leaders. The calling of a new bishop or stake president does little to alter the church experience for the average member, while a change of mission presidents can dramatically impact missionaries, converts, and nonmembers. Outreach leadership demands a much greater ability to collect, analyze, respond, and appropriately act upon information from a wide variety of sources than that necessary for pastoral leadership. Outreach leaders must understand the values, interests, and desires of local nonmembers and develop and coordinate programs to effectively reach them. An understanding of language and culture, people skills, teaching skills, organization, time management skills, the media, and missionary dynamics are essential. While pastoral leaders can successfully act in largely the same way in Utah, the Philippines, or Russia, conducting missionary work in the same fashion in all areas would be a disaster. Most mission presidents who have previously served as pastoral leaders quickly find that the circumstances of the mission field require intense and comprehensive reeducation.

The historical isolation of the LDS Church in the Utah Zion presents unique outreach leadership challenges not faced by groups such as the Seventh-Day Adventists and Jehovah's Witnesses that have always existed as minorities in secular societies. A disproportionately high percentage of mission presidents come from areas of Utah and the Mountain West with some of the lowest member-missionary participation rates in the world. Many individuals who have had little or no ongoing involvement in missionary work since their missions in young adulthood suddenly find themselves in the position of administering international missions with only cursory training. While some elements of Utah church service are applicable to international missionary work, many others are not. The lack of adequate life preparation of leaders as well as of individual missionaries has had profound implications on international LDS growth and retention.

LEADERS VERSUS MANAGERS

Peter Drucker noted: "Effective leaders are not those who are loved or admired. They are those whose followers do the right things. Popularity is not leadership. Results are." A good leader knows what needs to be done, knows how to do it, and is actively involved in implementation, facilitation, and teaching. All effective leaders lead by example. Early mission presidents such as Dan Jones were first and foremost missionaries. Through their own efforts, they brought thousands of converts into the Church. Perhaps the greatest deficiency of LDS outreach leadership today is that most mission leaders lack regular involvement in frontline proselyting activities. Many mission presidents finish their entire mission without ever tracting door to door, without engaging in dedicated street contacting, and without ever teaching a first or second discussion to a nonmember. When direct involvement of leaders in the finding and teaching process occurs at all, it is infrequent. It is rare for modern outreach leaders to bring anyone into the Church through their own efforts.

Finding, teaching, and retention work are not menial tasks, but the very essence of the missionary effort. Tal Bevan stated: "Never hire someone who is more than one step removed from the customer."[*]

---

*   Tal Bevan, Internet Day, September 14, 2000.

Dr. Kevin Evoy noted: "The supervisor should have previously had direct customer experience, and should continue to have some.... If you lose track of your customer's experience at any point where s/he contacts your business, you sow the seeds for a growing, unchecked problem." While the large size of missions today precludes many mission presidents from spending the majority of their time in these activities, the need for all individuals in leadership positions to have personal daily involvement in proselyting has not changed. Even the brightest and most talented leaders are rarely able to develop adequate insight into what is effective or even appropriate in missionary work without regular involvement in all stages of the finding, teaching, and retention processes. Few things are more detrimental to the missionary effort than instructions and policies announced to missionaries and members by superiors who have never tried them themselves. Involvement of leaders in frontline action can have a tremendous moderating effect on mission policies, making them more practical and harmonious with real-world feedback. Those who do not regularly devote time to find and teach nonmembers and retain converts are merely managers, not leaders. No amount of prayer and meditation can bring the Spirit in full measure in the absence of ongoing personal involvement. If the insight and inspiration of a leader are not enough to make him an effective missionary, how can it possibly be adequate for the missionaries and members he supervises?

THE HOLY SPIRIT AND INFORMATION

The Spirit speaks to both mind and heart (D&C 8:2) and not our heart alone, so enhancing our understanding can also increase our receptivity to the Spirit. We are commanded to "study and learn, and become acquainted with all good books, and with languages, tongues, and people" (D&C 90:15) and to "hasten ... to obtain a knowledge of history, and of countries, and of kingdoms, of laws of God and man, and all this for the salvation of Zion" (D&C 93:53). The Holy Spirit cannot draw water from an empty well, nor does inspiration occur in a vacuum. The Lord declared that "it is impossible for a man to be saved in ignorance" (D&C 131:6) and that "the glory of God is intelligence, or in other words, light and truth" (D&C 93:36). We might also ponder whether we can effectively minister salvation to others if we do not understand scriptural outreach principles. The Lord declared: "My people are destroyed for lack of knowledge" (Hosea 4:6), and one wonders whether any fulfillment of this prophecy can be more tragic than the catastrophic convert losses that have occurred in areas where accelerated baptism programs have been implemented by those unaware of their consequences. Effective missionary work does not happen by accident, and the results of zeal without knowledge consistently fall far short of the potential achieved by those who are both dedicated and informed. Gathering the information necessary to become fruitful servants is an essential responsibility of disciples of Christ.

COLLECTING QUALITY INFORMATION

There are few fields where productivity and effectiveness have not been revolutionized by the information age. U.S. Major Matthew Holt stated, "In war, you live and die by information.... This conflict clearly demonstrates that ... technologies offer an advantage for the collaborative exchange of information to assist the unit or to assist command and control. From '95 to today, it's day and night."* U.S. Army Major Bryan Hilferty stated: "That information, I used to get it by people shooting at me. This has changed the pattern of war." Similarly, faiths

---

* Christie, Michael, "Internet as Warfare Tool Comes of Age in Afghan Conflict," Reuters, April 28, 2002.

that have embraced the value of information for planning and implementation of outreach efforts in a time of exponentially increasing
knowledge have experienced an explosion of growth.

Church growth researcher Dr. James Montgomery stated: "Develop,
maintain and use a solid base of data. The Living Bible translates
Proverbs 18:13 thus: 'What a shame—yes, how stupid—to decide
before knowing the facts' (Proverbs 18: 13). The second common
denominator in successful growth programs is that denominations
not only have their heads in the clouds but their feet on the ground.
They see that the way to accomplish their dreams is not through senti-
mental, emotional fantasizing but through a concrete understanding
of their situation. These denominations study their context to see
who is responsive to the gospel and how to best reach them. They
study their own resources to see how big they are, how fast they are
growing, what their effective and ineffective methods are and so on.
They study other growing churches and denominations to find good
ideas for their own programs."*

When missionaries are fully aware of local needs, beliefs, concerns,
and opportunities, they are able to direct their time and energies most
effectively. Jim Rohn noted: "Nothing is more powerful for your future
than being a gatherer of good ideas and information. That's called
doing your homework." He further instructed: "Take time to gather
up the past so that you will be able to draw from your experiences and
invest them in the future. Don't let the learning from your own experiences take too long. If you have been doing it wrong for the last ten
years, I would suggest that's long enough!" New information sometimes dictates that we must change our paradigms and approaches.
Hugh B. Brown taught: "God desires that we learn and continue to

---

*   Montgomery, James, "13 Steps to a Successful Growth Program," Dawn Minis-
     tries, Undated article, http://www.dawnministries.org.

learn, but this involves some unlearning. As Uncle Zeke said, 'It ain't my ignorance that done me up but what I know'd that wasn't so.'"*

There has been an understandable official reluctance to provide large amounts of material on missionary work in the fear that over-regimentation would stifle local creativity and inspiration, yet the deficiency has not been one of overregimentation (the old ward mission handbook had only ten pages), but of failing to convey essential principles at the same time that programs such as missionary dinner programs and "set a date" programs conveyed serious misconceptions. It is no more reasonable to expect each mission president, missionary, and member-missionary to receive the inspiration necessary to effectively build the Church to its potential without adequate education on outreach principles, than to withhold the Doctrine and Covenants and expect each bishop to receive the principles of local church governance by personal revelation.

Research, data gathering and analysis, and ongoing quality improvement processes are necessary for any successful mission. The most relevant data is local, since much institutional research has traditionally been conducted in areas not representative of world outreach. Research conducted in U.S. areas with a large member base and other favorable conditions often has limited applicability to new areas: An African proverb notes that "smooth seas do not make skillful sailors." The little Missionary Department research that is made public is often done so only in a piecemeal fashion, impairing the reader's ability to assess the validity and applicability of research findings. Quality improvement processes have several components: systematic and validated research conducted in both new and existing areas, consistent communication of current and past findings to missionaries, members, and leaders, implementation of appropriate policy and

---

*   Hugh B. Brown, Baccalaureate address, Utah State University, June 4, 1965

program changes based on empiric data, and continuing feedback mechanisms to identify challenges and problems early.

TRANSLATING INFORMATION INTO ACTION

Christian researcher George Barna expressed his disappointment at the failure of his ten-year informational campaign to improve outreach and reverse concerning trends in many Protestant and evangelical churches, stating: "Most of the information users in ministries don't know how to use information. We kill ourselves to give them good information, good research, and they nod their heads approvingly and then they don't do anything with it. Disney, we give them the information and the next day they've got a policy; they've got a program; they've got something to convert that into practical action.'"* He continues: "The strategy was flawed because it had an assumption. The assumption was that the people in leadership are actually leaders. [I thought] all I need to do is give them the right information and they can draw the right conclusions.... Most people who are in positions of leadership in local churches aren't leaders. They're great people, but they're not really leaders."

I believe that many of today's LDS leaders have a much higher capacity for genuine leadership than their average Protestant or evangelical counterparts. However, even the most compelling research findings are often not translated into viable plans for practical action, and when such action occurs at all, it is often very late. In 1996, Wilfried Decoo noted: "Presumably the church has been doing some research on the process of new member integration in recent years, but it is difficult to see how the results of that research have made a

---

*   Stafford, Tim, "The Third Coming of George Barna," *Christianity Today*, August 5, 2002, http://www.christianitytoday.com/ct/2002/009/1.32.html.

difference."* While Seventh-Day Adventists quickly recognized and comprehensively remedied concerning retention trends in the Philippines and Latin America in the 1960s, Latter-day Saints have only recently taken steps toward educating missionaries on convert retention issues after more than forty years of official accelerated baptism programs with fractional retention.

C. Peter Wagner stated: "I knew very little about [church planting] when I started, but one thing I thought I knew was that the best church planters would probably be experienced pastors who had served several parishes and who had accumulated the wisdom and maturity to do it well. Wrong! Not that some fitting this description wouldn't make good church planters because they do. However, experienced pastors do not turn out to be the most likely talent pool. Younger people who still have more options and more flexibility are considerably more likely to do well."† While I have no evidence that younger people are categorically more successful in missionary work, individuals with longtime experience with less effective programs are often unable to adapt to more effective models. Even worthwhile lessons learned during prior service may not always be relevant and applicable within a different culture or within the same culture many years later. James Moss wrote: "Renewal will seldom occur if the pastor has been at the church needing renewal for a long time. I simply don't know of a single instance where renewal occurred after one pastor had three significant loss years in a row. Renewal will best occur at the beginning of a new pastorate."‡ The Savior himself taught that "new wine must

---

* Decoo, Wilfried, "Feeding the Fleeing Flock: Reflections on the Struggle to Retain Church Members in Europe," *Dialogue*, 29/1 (Spring 1996): 97–118.

† Wagner, C. Peter, *Church Planting for a Greater Harvest*, Ventura, CA: Regal Books, 1990.

‡ Moss, James W., Sr., "Contrasting Church Renewal and Church Planting," *People Spots*, 4/1 (January 2001):12.

be put into new bottles" (Mark 2:22).

There is almost always a gap between theory and practice. The average person contains in his library vast amounts of wisdom which are never implemented. The task of leadership is to distill practical insight and to provide a framework that facilitates its implementation. Effective leaders understand that missionaries and members must be mentored with effective example and hands-on teaching. The leader or teacher who believes that he has met his responsibilities simply by giving instructions will inevitably face unpleasant surprises. As a ward mission leader, I have found that regular involvement with missionaries and members in finding and teaching activities is essential to ensure that they are able to implement principles that they have been taught.

COMMUNICATION AND COLLABORATION

Communication between mission leaders has traditionally not been encouraged, and the arrival of a new mission president has typically been marked by wholesale policy changes with little or no transfer of information. Even when communication occurs, it is almost always limited to direct file leaders or others within an administrative area. The fact that so few missions have achieved both quality and quantity in growth suggests that there are few ideal role models or mentors for new leaders. Brian Tracy noted: "No one lives long enough to learn everything they need to learn starting from scratch. To be successful, we absolutely, positively have to find people who have already paid the price to learn the things that we need to learn to achieve our goals." Policies limiting communication between mission presidents are intended to promote renewal and fresh perspectives, but the more common outcome is a system without corporate memory that is often unable to learn from mistakes, where each new leader must perpetually reinvent the wheel to succeed and where improvements that required great insight to implement are swept away with the changing of the guard. Decelerating church growth at a time of great opportunity and decades of crisis-level convert loss suggest that such approaches have failed to accomplish their desired ends.

Although the LDS Church has nearly as many full-time missionaries as all other U.S.-based denominations combined, there is no forum for communication or discussion of missionary matters beyond district meetings, mission conferences, and ward member-missionary correlation meetings. Both on my mission and since, I have learned far more about effective missionary work from peers than from leaders. Most missionaries I have interviewed also suggest that this is the case. The mentoring of a companion and the insight of peers are frequently more relevant and helpful than the decrees of leaders, who often have little direct involvement in finding, teaching investigators, and other core missionary activities. Communication among individuals of the same level in wider circles has sometimes been discouraged with the disparaging misnomer of "lateral revelation." The insight and information of peers, while not to be taken as authoritative, can often stimulate thought and lead to valuable improvements in ways that the counsel of leaders cannot. Communication and sharing of ideas in wider circles does not supersede hierarchal authority, but seeking outside information and experiences is often a necessary element of fulfilling our divine mandate to do all that is within our power to further the purposes of missionary work.

STATISTICS AND REPORTING

While no statistics will ever be able to completely capture the complex realities of an international church, statistics have optimal value only when indicators are chosen that closely reflect the true purposes of building the Church and achieving a vibrant, participating membership that can experience the full blessings of the gospel. I believe that all too often we have been using the wrong indicators. Mission reporting has traditionally focused on immediate and short-term statistics such as baptisms and discussions that often do not accurately reflect these aims. Short-term outcome measures discon-nected from indicators of real growth are easily subverted and produce a selection bias for methodologies that produce flashy immediate baptismal numbers but fail to strengthen the Church correspond-ingly. A ten-minute "doorstep discussion" with a hurried or impatient listener has little in common with a well-taught ninety-minute discus-sion. The baptism of an individual who has attended church only once or twice before and is quickly lost to inactivity bears only the most superficial resemblance to the baptism of a committed and well-prepared convert. If evaluation is the key to excellence, quality statistics with intrinsic meaning can aid in the recognition and resolu-tion of challenges. Active membership and retained converts statistics are far more revealing of true progress than raw membership and total baptism numbers. Similarly, the number of individuals approached with the gospel message in one day is a much more telling indicator of what missionaries are actually doing than reported proselyting hours that include nonproselyting activities and fail to convey how time is being used.

LOCAL REALITY CHECKS

Compared to pastoral leaders who have personal contact with the individuals and programs they direct each week, outreach leaders are insulated from the effects of their policies and have little direct accountability. While pastoral leaders typically live in a ward or branch long term, including after their release, outreach leaders may not see the results of inactivity beyond their brief stay. In combination with the use of short-term baptismal statistics, the lack of accountability for long-term results eliminates any incentive for quality by outreach leaders. It is therefore easy for outreach leaders to advocate ineffective or even harmful policies while remaining out of touch with the ultimate results. Local leaders who live in an area long-term and face local reality checks are often able to make more realistic decisions about convert preparation than transient missionaries.

RECOGNIZING SENTINEL EVENTS

Confucius taught: "A man who does not think and plan long ahead will find trouble right at his door." Difficulties, whether a particular discussion point that multiple investigators do not seem to understand, challenges in finding people to teach, problems in the ward, or poor retention of baptized members, are not necessary phases of church growth any more than illness is necessary for good health. The prudent shepherd watches for sentinel events that can help him to identify potential problems early and correct them before they become entrenched. One mission president in a newly opened area identified problems of inactivity fairly early in that mission and quickly intervened to improve missionary teaching and minimize convert loss. While there were still some challenges, they were of a much smaller scale than in neighboring missions, where numerous branches had to be recombined due to unchecked inactivity.

IDENTIFYING AND REMOVING PATHOLOGIES TO CHURCH GROWTH

In 1990, Elder Boyd K. Packer remarked: "In recent years I have felt, and I think I am not alone, that we were losing the ability to correct the course of the Church."[*] Less effective unofficial programs such as missionary dinner appointments have gained a life of their own while becoming virtually institutionalized in LDS culture, while many core mandates such as President Benson's instruction to flood the earth with the Book of Mormon or President McKay's "every member a missionary" challenge have seen only scant implementation. Other mandates, such as President Kimball's vision of worldwide gospel radio, have never been implemented at all. Tares grow quickly, but wheat is choked out without constant cultivation.

Church growth expert Rick Warren wrote: "The wrong question: What will make our church grow? The right question: What is keeping our church from growing?... All living things grow—you don't have to make them grow. It's the natural thing for living organisms to do if they are healthy.... Since the church is a living organism, it is natural for it to grow if it is healthy. The Church is a body, not a business. It is alive. If a church is not growing, it is dying.... The task of church leadership is to discover and remove growth-restricting diseases and barriers so that natural, normal growth can occur."[†] Warren noted: "If it works, I like the way that you are doing it."

THE CURE OR THE DISEASE?

Every program has a cost in time, effort, and resources. Failure to appreciate the cost of new programs brings unanticipated and undesired consequences. One area presidency concerned at low member activity instructed missionaries in one mission to "spend half of their time with members." Predictably, the number of baptisms fell to

---

[*]   Packer, Boyd K., "Let Them Govern Themselves," Regional Representatives' Seminar, March 30, 1990.

[†]   Warren, Rick, *The Purpose Driven Church*, Grand Rapids, MI: Zondervan, 1995, 16–17.

approximately half its prior level as missionaries diverted time away from contacting and teaching nonmembers to comply with the new directive. Activity rates experienced only a slight transient increase as it became apparent that member activity was not primarily a function of missionaries spending time on social member visits with a smattering of gospel teachings, but of quality prebaptismal preparation and consistency in establishing firm gospel habits. One mission president, concerned at the shortage of active priesthood holders in his area, instructed missionaries to boost male baptisms and "stop teaching women" unless their husband was also interested. This mission achieved its goal of increasing the percentage of adult male converts not through any significant increase in male baptisms, but through a precipitous decline in baptisms of women and youth. In another case, a mission president concerned at the lack of member referrals instituted a ban on tracting and street contacting to encourage missionaries to find through members. When members were not available for visits, many companionships spent vast amounts of time idly that otherwise could have been used to find productively through their own efforts.

These leaders were bright professionals, but had little understanding of core principles of missionary work, and likely had little opportunity to develop an understanding outside of their own trial and error. In each case, the problematic policies demonstrate concern over existing problems but convey a lack of understanding of their true causes and solutions. The failure of these policies and many others was predictable from their inception, yet considerable time and resources were allocated to less effective initiatives at the cost of many souls who could have been found, baptized, and retained with effective, scriptural initiatives. The quotas and bans of managers are almost always counterproductive and stand in contrast to the education, empowerment, and example provided by true leaders.

"PLAYING THE GAME"

A strong social acceptability reporting bias in missionary work filters out much potentially unpleasant information. There is a widespread unwritten belief that all information reported must be positive and that to report negative information implies a lack of faith or personal disobedience. In letters to the mission president, many missionaries who have not had a baptism in months describe in flowery terms how well "the work is going." While one would never wish to deflate enthusiasm, there is also a need for candidness and insight. Many missionaries are apprehensive that mentioning difficulties or concerns, no matter how well-founded, can have negative repercussions for the missionaries, from being labeled as faithless or disobedient to being demoted. In some cases, this is true. One of my brothers was demoted from the position of zone leader in his mission in Germany after he tried to share with the mission president some challenges with the proselyting program that the president had mandated. There is a real danger in surrounding oneself with "yes-men" who simply "play the game" by telling leaders whatever they want to hear. Many leaders are perceptive enough to see through such behavior, yet vital information on challenges is often not conveyed in a timely fashion. Information on challenges and problems is often the most valuable kind, because it provides the greatest opportunity for growth and improvement. Proactive mission leaders are aware of the barriers that many missionaries feel to sharing information on challenges as well as successes and actively solicit feedback in a candid and nonpunitive fashion.

THE TRUE MASTER: THE SAVIOR

Missionaries are occasionally given instruction by mission leaders or visiting authorities that conflict with scripture. The counsel of all lesser authorities should be evaluated in light of teaching of the living prophet and scripture. Some mission leaders expect missionaries to demonstrate a level of obedience to their instructions that the leaders themselves are not willing to render to the living prophet, the apostles, or to scripture. Our primary obedience belongs to the Savior. The fact that mission leaders are called by church authorities does not provide a carte blanche, and the scriptural warning that "many are called but few are chosen" applies as much to leaders as to missionaries. Leaders have a responsibility to adhere to scriptural mandates and can expect the loyalty of their missionaries only to the extent that their own programs and agendas are consistent with scriptural and prophetic teachings. A Chinese proverb declares: "He who sacrifices conscience to ambition burns a picture to obtain ashes."

COST-EFFECTIVE MISSIONARY WORK: DOLLARS AND SENSE

While the number of individuals without the gospel is virtually limitless, church funds and resources are limited. There is a responsibility to use funds as efficiently as possible to result in the greatest good for the most people. Growth has relatively little to do with the amount of money spent in an area but correlates strongly with the work ethic of individual missionaries and members and the way that money is spent. Denominations such as the Seventh-Day Adventists and Jehovah's Witnesses with a fraction of the funds of the LDS Church have achieved rapid and extensive world growth through ambitious outreach projects. The LDS Church has spent far more money per convert than any other major denomination in Eastern Europe, including those with comparable membership requirements and better retention.

One of my mission companions from Ukraine was baptized when he came to church after reading an announcement in the newspaper with only the church name, meeting time, and location. Based on his experience, I discussed with my mission president in Russia the possibility of running advertisements in local newspapers inviting people to church. At the time, these advertisements could be placed for ten dollars or less. He was interested in the idea and checked with regional authorities, who informed him that the Church allocated no funds for mission-level media outreach. Yet the area office allocated to the mission hundreds of thousands of dollars in building and legal fees for a single chapel, and thousands of dollars for youth conferences, travel expenses, and other items with little if any correlation to church growth, while missionaries were allocated only a few copies of the Book of Mormon each week. Rick Warren stated: "When finances get tight in a church, often the first thing cut is the evangelism and advertising budget. That is the last thing you should cut. It is the source of new blood and life for your church."*

PROGRAMS VERSUS PURPOSES: THE POWER OF FOCUS

The past three decades have been remarkable for the proliferation of simple, mission-focused house churches across the world. Within Cambodia alone, the number of Christian believers increased from about 200 to over 100,000 in a ten-year period, with the number of churches doubling almost yearly. How can such no-frills organizations succeed without all of the programs of larger churches? Without organized choirs, enrichment nights, or potluck dinners? While there is some evidence that well-run and purposeful church activities can

---

*   Warren, Rick, *The Purpose Driven Church.*, Grand Rapids, MI: Zondervan, 1995, 202.

play a useful role, many point out that smaller house churches have experienced such explosive growth because of reducing the role of the church to its core missions. The real growth occurred when evangelism became a broad-based, grassroots effort integrated into the daily life of local members who had caught the vision of their potential. Those involved cite the power of consistent focus on a few important objectives: scripture study, faithful living, church attendance, and member evangelism.

One sacrament speaker claimed that for a ward or branch to function fully, 212 individuals would be needed to fill callings. Many Latter-day Saints cite heavy time commitments to church-related activities. Church activities can spread across most of the week for a family with children of several different ages. Wards with the most peripheral programming typically have some of the lowest rates of member-missionary participation. Utah, with thousands of large wards with extensive church programming, averages only 1.5 convert baptisms per year per ward, a convert growth rate of less than 0.5 percent per year. Actual harm is done when member time and resources are consumed by peripheral programs while core tasks such as member-missionary outreach go undone. Evangelist Larry Stockstill observed that any child can take all of the toys out of the closet and clutter the room—it takes wisdom to know which ones not to take out.[*]

Expectations to fulfill callings and attend activities are accompanied by home and visiting assignments, with monthly visitation lists that can be quite long, especially in areas where activity rates are low. In many international areas, active members may hold two or even three callings. Yet many members who would never voluntarily missed a mutual activity or homemaking meeting cannot remember the last time they started a gospel conversation with a nonmember. If the

---

[*]   Stockstill, Larry, *The Cell Church*, Ventura, CA: Regal Books, 1998.

average active member spends numerous hours per week in church activities but fails to accomplish essential tasks, is it any wonder that so many feel burned out rather than edified? At the judgment, will the Savior ask us how many times we attended weeknight church activities, or will he ask us whether we took every opportunity to share the gospel with our neighbor?

At times, we must step back and examine our purpose and mission. Wards and branches do not need to juggle dozens of different programs to receive the full blessings of the gospel: they only need to do the few basic and important things well. The Spirit is gained by consistent obedience to basic gospel laws, not by a plethora of programming.

Scriptures teach that "where there is no vision, the people perish" (Proverbs 29:18). Vision dictates that our ultimate purposes must determine what form the programs will take. Too often this process is reversed, and well-intentioned but poorly conceived programs such as the missionary dinner program and the accelerated baptism program become ends in themselves that can eclipse or subvert the more important processes of teaching members to witness of the gospel regularly and making active, committed proselytes who have undergone a genuine and lasting conversion. We must transcend the small-minded thinking of ineffective programs such as "who is going to feed the missionaries on Tuesday" and focus on the bigger picture of "how are we going to reach our ward area, mission area, or world with the gospel."

In his book *Real Teens,* George Barna warned that the "high level of current religious involvement among teens in misleading."[*] He wrote: "Millions of teenagers are involved in church-related activities each week, but their motivation is relational rather than spiritual. Once their

---

[*]   Barna, George, *Real Teens: A Contemporary Snapshot of Youth Culture,* Ventura, CA : Regal Books, 2001.

relational networks change upon graduation from high school and college, we expect a continued decline in church attendance among the emerging generation unless churches revamp their ministries to reflect the unique cultural customs and expectations of the new breed of young people." While scripture-oriented activities such as seminary and Church Education System classes play a well-documented role, LDS studies have failed to bear out an independent effect of peripheral, nonscripture-based weekday activities in increasing either the retention rates of young people or their faithfulness in scripture reading, Sabbath day observance, church attendance, and personal prayer. Citing the Young Men's Study, LDS sociologist James Duke observed: "The factors that had the greatest influence on the religiosity of young men were: home religious observance (family prayer, family home evening, and family scripture study), agreement with parents' values, having one's own spiritual experiences, having a priesthood advisor or other adult leader who cared, and being integrated into the ward. Programs and activities seemed to have little influence except as they encouraged the other factors listed above."[*],[†]

President Boyd K. Packer stated: "In recent years we might be compared to a team of doctors issuing prescriptions to cure or to immunize out members against spiritual disease. Each time some moral or spiritual ailment was diagnosed, we have rushed to the pharmacy to concoct another remedy, encapsulate it as a program, and send it out with pages of directions for use. While we all seem to agree that over-medication or over-programming are critically serious

---

[*]   Duke, James T., "Latter-day Saints in a Secular World: What We Have Learned about Latter-day Saints from Social Research," Martin B Hickman 1999 Lecture, Brigham Young University College of Family, Home, and Social Sciences, March 4, 1999, http://fhss.byu.edu/adm/hickman_lecture.htm.

[†]   Weed, Stan and Joe Olsen, "Key to Strong Young Men," *Ensign*, December 1984, 66–68.

problems, we have failed to reduce the treatments. It has been virtually impossible to affect any reduction in programs.... We do not seem to be able to solve a problem without designing a program with pages of instruction and sending it out again. The most dangerous side effect of all we have prescribed ... is the over-regimentation of the Church. This ... is a direct result of too many ... instructions.... Local leaders have been effectively conditioned to hold back until programmed as to what to do, how, to whom, when, and for how long. Can you see that when we overemphasize programs ... we are in danger of losing the inspiration and the resourcefulness that should characterize Latter-day Saints? Then the very principle of individual revelation is in jeopardy and we drift from a fundamental gospel principle!"[*]

Dr. Lin Yutang wrote: "Besides the noble art of getting things done, there is the noble art of leaving things undone. The wisdom in life consists in the elimination of non-essentials." Effective missionaries, member-missionaries, and leaders learn to focus and eliminate nonessentials which otherwise become barriers to growth. Rapid growth occurs not through the proliferation of peripheral programming, but by concentrating energies and resources on a few clearly defined, powerful strategies that make the most difference. As we individually and collectively have limited time and resources, we must focus on doing the most important things so that we can bring forth "much fruit" as we abide in the Savior (John 15:5).

HOME TEACHING

Under the vision of home teaching, every family and individual is to be assisted and watched over by a pair of priesthood holders whose role is to friendship, teach, and assist with both temporal

---

[*]   Packer, Boyd K., "Let Them Govern Themselves," Regional Representatives'
       Seminar, March 30, 1990.

and spiritual needs. A story is told of a group of touring musicians from a region of central Russia who desired to join the Church with LDS members in the Midwest for several weeks. The area presidency rejected this request, stating that "you can baptize them if you can guarantee their home teaching." There were no LDS units in their area of Russia, and the musicians returned home unbaptized. This is wise counsel, since the practice of baptizing transients soon to leave an area almost inevitably leads to inactivity, even when congregations exist in their home area. Yet the reality is that even in areas with established congregations, few converts are visited promptly or regularly by home teachers. One North American study found that three months passed before the average convert was even assigned a home teacher, not even considering when or whether they may have been subsequently visited. Outside of North America, monthly home teaching rates run as low as 5 to 15 percent, and there are many wards and branches around the world where no home teaching happens at all. Few international wards ever reach 30 or 40 percent home teaching, and most perform at far lower levels.

There are many reasons why home teaching, although proclaimed as a universal imperative for the world church, has chronically underperformed internationally. A profound imbalance between shepherds and lost sheep has been generated by accelerated baptism programs. In congregations where only 20 percent of members are active, even if qualified priesthood holders represented a full quarter of active membership, the typical companionship of two priesthood holders would be assigned forty members to home teach each month. While some of these individuals are part of families, it is not uncommon for companionships to be assigned eight to twelve households and sometimes more. Even when the monthly visits are completed, there is no reprieve since each subsequent month demands that each household be visited again. It is often difficult for even the most diligent and committed working men with families to coordinate numerous visits each month with their companion and their assigned home teachees. Home teaching presents a major economic and time burden for international members without their own transportation in units that cover large geographic areas. These problems of time, coordination, availability, and expense are compounded by the fact that most individuals on international LDS membership rolls are completely inactive, and many do not wish to be home taught. Being assigned to regularly home teach individuals who do not wish to be visited at all can be highly demoralizing for even the most dedicated members. It is frustrating and unfulfilling for dedicated members to achieve only 25 or 30 percent home teaching, not because of any lack of effort, but because some hostile members refused visits, while others could not find a workable time. The frequent combination of unrealistically long assignment lists with frequent apathetic or hostile receptions leads many members to develop an aversion to home teaching that is not reversed by repeated admonitions from the pulpit.

Monthly home teaching statistics are reported to leaders all the way up to church headquarters, producing considerable pressure on local leaders to report high home teaching percentages. The combination of a paucity of active priesthood holders in relation to official membership and pressure to achieve favorable home teaching numbers sometimes leads local or stake leaders to adopt irregular measures in an attempt to increase home teaching. I have lived in at least two U.S. wards where home teachers were assigned individually without a companion in an attempt to increase the number of assignment lists. A subtler and more widespread but functionally equivalent practice is pairing an active member with an inactive "companion." There is no uniform policy on what constitutes a home teaching visit, and the interpretation varies widely among units and stakes. In several wards, dramatic increases in reported home teaching rates represented not markedly increased home teaching effort, but a liberalization of the definition of a home teaching visit to include any form of contact or even attempt to contact. When standards are not standardized, the statistics are uninterpretable. The relevance of home teaching statistics to the faithfulness of local priesthood holders is confounded by wide variations in reporting practices and the artificial cap placed on maximal home teaching rates by large numbers of inactives who desire no contact. Many chronic zeros on home teaching tallies result from the practice of keeping the names of disengaged and hostile members on the rolls indefinitely unless they request name removal through a largely unpublicized process.

Stories are frequently told of the few individuals who returned to the Church after years of inactivity through the efforts of a faithful home teacher, with the ostensible moral that one should never give up on anyone. The overwhelming majority of such individuals have other roots in the Church, such as upbringing in an LDS home or active family members. Of the large majority of international LDS inactives who were lost shortly after baptism, very few ever return to activity, and there is little evidence that home teaching efforts make a difference. In a Church with over twelve million members, even highly ineffective programs will produce occasional successes if practiced on a sufficiently massive scale, and anecdotal stories of a few successes cannot be considered proof that a program is effective without empiric evaluation and consideration of alternatives.

The Savior's Parable of the Shepherd leaving the ninety and nine to find the one lost sheep seems to bear little resemblance to the modern Church, where nearly two-thirds of the members are completely inactive. The Parable of the Shepherd teaches that efforts must be focused to be effective. I have frequently seen new members who could have been retained with only modest effort fall through the cracks in areas where the efforts of local members and leaders have been spread too thin on home teaching and reactivation programs. Many are so overwhelmed by the responsibility of reclaiming long lists of individuals who have been inactive for years that new converts are rarely contacted or visited promptly when they become just one more name on a long list of primarily unreceptive assignees. My research suggests that for every longtime inactive in the international church who is reactivated through heroic measures, we lose multiple converts and actives out the back door through neglect. The continued emphasis on home teaching and reactivating disaffected and hostile individuals obscures the ability of many congregational and quorum leaders to prioritize crucial interventions for new converts and other receptive individuals for whom these efforts are likely to make a difference. Most leaders are unwilling to accept less than the vision of universal home teaching, leaving local efforts scattered and dissipated. Unwillingness or inability to prioritize and focus interventions on receptive individuals for whom they are most likely to make a difference results not only in ineffective outreach to longtime inactives, but also in failure to retain even receptive new converts and struggling actives.

I believe that no home teacher should be assigned to visit more than four to five households. Longer lists accomplish little except to impose unrealistic demands and discourage the home teacher. Even if four or five visits could be made each month, this would represent a dramatic improvement in the performance of the worldwide home teaching program. Members should be assigned to visit monthly only those who are willing to be visited and taught. Home teaching reports should be standardized to count visits only when individuals receive the maximum contact they allow up to a full visit, representing the home teacher's best effort. A telephone call or doorstep visit should be counted for those who refuse a full visit, but not for active members who can be formally home taught.

Missionary Service

AT YEAR-END 2004, THERE were 51,067 full-time LDS missionaries, down from 61,638 in 2002. The combination of fewer young men in North America arriving at mission age due to shrinking LDS family sizes, poor success in mobilizing international missionaries, and higher standards with the "raising the bar" program resulted in the first major declines in the total number of missionaries serving since missions for young men were briefly shortened to eighteen months from 1982–1984. While the number of missionaries is expected to increase somewhat in coming years, the decrease in LDS family size and fractional rates of mission mobilization present long-term challenges. In the late 1980s, Ezra Taft Benson stated: "The Lord wants every young man to serve a full-time mission. Currently, only a fifth of the eligible young men in the Church are serving full-time missions. This is not pleasing to the Lord. We can do better. We must do better."[*] Sociologist James Duke noted cited the Young Men's Study:[†] "of 100 males born in the church, only 76 were ordained Deacons, 65 were ordained Teachers, 58 were ordained Priests, and only 32% went on missions. My understanding is that these statistics have not improved since 1984 when this study was published. If there is a major challenge in the Church, it is to retain our young people, the

---

[*] Benson, Ezra Taft, *Come, Listen to a Prophet's Voice*, 5.

[†] Weed, Stan and Joe Olsen, "Key to Strong Young Men," *Ensign*, December 1984: 66–68.

rising generation."* This study refers to U.S. membership and only to young men born in the Church, not to converts or those outside of the United States, where percentage rates of mission service are in single digits in most countries. Eighty percent of LDS missionaries come from North America, although nearly 80 percent of convert baptisms occur outside of North America. Even in Latin American nations where the Church has been established for decades, the Church still depends heavily on North American missionaries.

ENCOURAGING NATIVE MISSIONARIES

Native missionaries are essential to optimal Church growth. Joseph Smith taught that missionaries are often most effective in their native lands and cultures: "Take Jacob Zundell and Frederick H. Moeser, and tell them never to drink a drop of ale, wine, or any spirit, only that which flows right out from the presence of God; and send them to Germany; and when you meet with an Arab, send him to Arabia; when you find an Italian, send him to Italy; and a Frenchman, to France; or an Indian, that is suitable, send him among the Indians. Send them to the different places where they belong. Send somebody to Central America and to all Spanish America; and don't let a single corner of the earth go without a mission."† Ezra Taft Benson taught: "When missionaries are called to serve locally, great benefits accrue to the Church in local areas. First, the missionaries can speak the language fluently so that no language training is necessary. Second, the acceptance by local people to the missionaries of their own nation-

---

*   Duke, James T., "Latter-day Saints in a Secular World: What We Have Learned about Latter-day Saints from Social Research," Martin B Hickman 1999 Lecture, Brigham Young University, College of Family, Home, and Social Sciences, March 4, 1999, http://fhss.byu.edu/adm/hickman_lecture.htm.

†   Burton, Alma P., ed., *Discourses of the Prophet Joseph Smith*, Salt Lake City, UT: Deseret Book, 1977, 173.

ality is superior to the reception received by non-nationals. Third, the great benefit which the missionaries themselves receive through their mission experience is not exported from the local area but serves to strengthen and build the kingdom in the homeland. Thus, there must be increased emphasis on the preparation of young men and women to step forward and carry the missionary responsibility in their own lands."[*]

MOBILIZING INTERNATIONAL MISSIONARIES

Foreign missionaries are prohibited or seriously restricted in 119 countries, with over half of the world's population.[†] Native missionaries are allowed in many of these nations. Latter-day Saints must become more effective in inspiring both international missionary service and reliable member-missionary participation if the LDS faith is to become a major world religion. Patrick Johnstone's *Operation World* noted that in 2001 there were approximately 201,260 full-time Protestant missionaries worldwide. [‡] Thirty-six percent of Protestant missionaries come from North America, while 35 percent come from Asia, 11 percent from Europe, 6 percent from Africa, 5 percent from Latin America, and 3 percent from the Pacific. Of these missionaries, 52 percent serve in their own country, while 48 percent serve abroad. Two-thirds of LDS missionaries serve the Western hemisphere with only 12 percent of the world's population, while the major population centers of the Eastern hemisphere remain highly underserved. There are over 12,000 Protestant missionaries from South Korea alone, of

---

[*]   Benson, Ezra Taft, Language Training Mission Groundbreaking, Provo, Utah, July 18, 1974.

[†]   Yohannan, K .P., *Revolution in World Missions*, Carrollton, TX: GFA Books, 2000. See also http://www.gfa.org.

[‡]   Johnstone, Patrick and Jason Mandryk, *Operation World*, Harrisonburg, VA: Paternoster, 2005.

whom 10,646 are serving in 156 other countries.* Over 44,000 Protestant missionaries are serving from India, with 60 percent serving domestically and 40 percent serving abroad. Within the next few years, India is expected to surpass the United States as the leading sender of Protestant and evangelical missionaries. There are only about fifty LDS missionaries serving in all of India, and only a fraction are natives. Gospel For Asia (GFA), a Protestant missionary group started by native Indian K. P. Yohannan in 1980, represents the most remarkable model of international missionary recruitment. GFA now fields over 11,000 native missionaries from India and plans to reach 100,000 missionaries by 2020.† Yohannan's Gospel For Asia group offers from its Web site *Revolution in World Missions,* a free book, which demonstrates sound principles of native missionary recruitment and training and which deserve careful study and consideration by anyone involved in mobilizing international missionaries.†

FOSTERING SELF-SUFFICIENCY OF INTERNATIONAL MISSIONS

Only in relatively few countries outside of North America has the Church consistently experienced self-sustaining rates of native missionary service. The few bright spots deserve closer study for more general implementation. LDS missions in West Africa are overwhelmingly staffed by native missionaries, and it is estimated that there are up to 3,000 returned missionaries in West Africa.§ Mongolia alone

---

*   Johnstone, Patrick and Jason Mandryk, *Operation World.* Harrisonburg, VA: Paternoster, 2005.

†   Yohannan, K. P., "The 10 Major Ministries of Gospel for Asia," http://www.gfa.org/site/about_gfa/brochure/whatdoing.html.

‡   Yohannan, K. P., *Revolution in World Missions,* Carrollton, TX: GFA Books, 2000. See also http://www.gfa.org.

§   Stewart, David, "The Church in Africa," December 15, 2001, http://cumorah.

produces 40 percent of all LDS missionaries coming from the Asia Area, and approximately 10 percent of Mongolia's LDS members have either served or are currently serving missions.* Strides have been made in some areas of Latin America also. In 1999, President Maynes of the South America West Area reported that the number of local full-time missionaries in Peru and Bolivia increased by 70 percent during the prior year, attributing this mainly to "strong priesthood support of missionary preparation classes" and the Church Education System.† It remains to be seen whether this increase will continue or remain sustained. A new vision and new approaches to international missionary service will be necessary to meet the world's needs. Modified elements of the program pioneered by K. P. Yohannan can dramatically increase missionary service rates without compromising standards.

MISSIONARY ALLOCATION

President Spencer W. Kimball described in his vision of world missionary efforts that "the missionaries would be sent where the most good could be accomplished."‡ Barrett and Johnson's *World Christian Trends* reported that "it costs Christians 700 times more money to baptize converts in rich World C countries (Switzerland) than in poor World A countries (Nepal). They noted that the ten least cost-effective countries and territories for Christian outreach with a population over one million are Japan, Switzerland, Bermuda, Denmark, Belgium, Norway, Germany, France, Austria, and Italy,

com.

* Stewart, David, "The Mongolian Miracle," December 16, 2001, http://cumorah. com.

† "Excitement for Missionary Work Surges," *LDS Church News*, June 19, 1999.

‡ Kimball, Spencer W., "When the World Will Be Converted," *Ensign*, October 1974, originally presented at Regional Representatives' Seminar, April 4, 1974.

while the ten most cost-effective countries are Mozambique, Ethiopia, Tanzania, the Democratic Republic of Congo, Sierra Leone, Nepal, Chad, Burundi, Somalia, and Cambodia".* Even after consolidations, twenty-two full-time LDS missions service the ten least cost-effective countries. The ten most cost-effective nations have a combined population of over 225 million. Only Chad, Nepal, and possibly Somalia, with a combined population of 34 million, prohibit foreign missionaries, while the other seven nations allow foreign missionaries wide freedom to proselyte. Although several of these countries are served by small groups of LDS missionaries serving under missions based in neighboring nations, only two—the Democratic Republic of Congo and Cambodia—have their own full-time LDS missions. Barrett and Johnson state that the five megapeoples most responsive to Christianity, per hour of ministry, are the Khandeshi, Awadhi, Magadhi, Bai, and Berar Marathi. Four of these five peoples live in India, where proselytizing is permitted, but no LDS outreach is directed toward any of these groups.

Today, almost one-third of the LDS missionary force is concentrated in the United States, with less than five percent of the world's population. While recent years have seen some progress in consolidating less effective LDS missions in Europe and Japan and the expansion of African missions, less than one-sixth of LDS missions serve the most underserved two-thirds of the world's population. Immigrants from the third world constitute a large percentage of LDS converts in North America, Western Europe and Canada. The proportional overrepresentation of missionary efforts in developed nations and underrepresentation of developing nations is inefficient, since such immigrants can be reached at far less cost in their native lands. Reten-

---

*   Barrett, David and Todd Johnson, *World Christian Trends AD 30–AD 2200*, Pasadena, CA: William Carey Library, 2001.

tion of immigrant converts in most areas is very poor due to the combination of language barriers, frequent lack of member fellow-shippers from the same cultural community, and transient nature of immigrant life. While outreach directed to international immigrant minorities will continue to play an important role in Church growth, especially in Western Europe and other areas where missionary efforts among the local populace are stagnant, similarly robust outreach efforts are needed in the native lands of these peoples. One cannot doubt that heeding President Kimball's call for greater awareness and utilization of missionary opportunities among receptive peoples, coupled with more culturally relevant missionary approaches, would lead to an explosion of growth. Windows for outreach in new areas may be limited, so we must be fully prepared to initiate gospel outreach efforts promptly when opportunities arise.

REACHING THE WORLD

THE DIVINE MANDATE

PRESIDENT SPENCER W. KIMBALL taught repeatedly of the need for powerful strategic planning for reaching every soul with the gospel message: "Could we bring concerted action to a 'lengthening stride' movement that would bring into the missionary activity the good members of the Church the world around. The approach and the attack will need to be planned very carefully. We will need to impress upon stake, ward, and branch leaders around the globe their opportunity and responsibility. There will be need for strong, well-organized stake, ward, and district missions. It cannot be left to a mere suggestion, and a comprehensive score must be kept as a stimulant to the workers. Such a special, organized and developed program could bring many other of the blessings of the Church to more people as we have said."* In the address "When the World Will Be Converted," President Kimball taught:

> The scriptures are replete with commands and promises and calls and rewards for teaching the gospel. I use the word command deliberately for it seems to be an insistent directive from which we, singly and collectively, cannot escape. I ask you, what did He mean when the Lord took his Twelve Apostles to the top of

---

* Kimball, Spencer W., Regional Representatives Seminar, April 3, 1975.

the Mount of Olives and said: "And ye shall be witnesses unto me both in Jerusalem, and in all Judea, and in Samaria, and unto the uttermost part of the earth" (Acts 1:8). These were His last words on earth before He went to His heavenly home. What is the significance of the phrase "uttermost most part of the earth"? He had already covered the area known to the apostles. Was it the people in Judea? Or those in Samaria? Or the few millions in the Near East? Where were the "uttermost parts of the earth"? Did He mean the millions in what is now America? Did He include the hundreds of thousands or even millions, in Greece, Italy, around the Mediterranean, the inhabitants of central Europe? What did he mean? Or did He mean all the living people of all the world and those spirits assigned to this world to come in centuries ahead? Have we underestimated his language or its meaning? How can we be satisfied with 100,000 converts out of nearly four billion people in the world who need the gospel? After His crucifixion the eleven apostles assembled on a mountain in Galilee and the Savior came to them and said: "All power is given unto me in heaven and in earth. Go ye therefore, and teach all nations, baptizing them in the name of the Father, and of the Son, and of the Holy Ghost:" (He said "all nations.") "Teaching them to observe all things whatsoever I have commanded you: and, lo, I am with you always, even unto the end of the world. Amen" (Matt 28:18–20). Again as Mark records the events after the resurrection, he ... then commanded them, "Go ye into all the world, and preach the gospel to every creature" (Mark 16:15). And this was just before the ascension. Do you think he meant Egypt and Palestine and Greece? Do you think he included the world of 33 AD or the world of 1970, 1980, 1990? What was included in his phrase "all the world" and what did he mean by "every creature"? And Luke records the event—"That repentance and remission of sins should be preached ... among all nations, beginning at Jerusalem" (Luke 24:47). Again, his last command. Surely there is significance in these words! There was a universal need and there must be universal coverage.... Remember also that Enoch the prophet beheld the spirits that God had created. (See Moses 6:36). These prophets visualized the numerous spirits and all the creations. It seems to me that the Lord chose his words when he said "every nation," "every land," "uttermost bounds of the earth," "every tongue," "every people," "every soul," "all the world," "many lands." Surely there is a significance to these words! Certainly his sheep were not limited to the thousands about him and with whom he rubbed shoulders each day. A universal family! A universal command! My brethren, I wonder if we are doing all we can. Are we complacent in our approach to teaching all the world? We have been proselyting now 144 years. Are we prepared to lengthen our stride? To enlarge our vision?... Now, how can we do this? We see that there are these elements to be considered: the breaking down of resistance of the nations of the world to receive our missionaries; a greatly increased missionary force (greatly, I emphasize); a better trained missionary army; and better and additional methods and approaches. Now here we will consider each one in its turn. We need to enlarge our field of operation. We will need to make a full, prayerful study of the nations of the world which do not have the gospel at this time, and then bring into play our strongest and most able men to assist the Twelve to move out into the world and to open the doors of every nation as fast as it is ready.*

---

*   Kimball, Spencer W., "When the World Will Be Converted," *Ensign*, October

Brigham Young noted: "We should be a people of profound learning pertaining to the things of the world. We should be familiar with the various languages, for we wish to send missionaries to the different nations and to the islands of the sea. We wish missionaries who may go to France to be able to speak the French language fluently, and those who may go to Germany, Italy, Spain, and so on to all nations, to be familiar with the languages of those nations."[*] Tomorrow's outreach will require large numbers of Latter-day Saints who are fluent in the language and conversant in the customs of the unreached world.

CURRENT PERFORMANCE

Opportunities for sharing the gospel are greater than ever, yet LDS growth rates have decreased. Most missionaries and mission presidents I have asked about how they are going to reach every soul in their area with the gospel message are unable to articulate a viable plan. Replies such as "we're trying to strengthen existing members and reactivate the less active," "we have a new referral program that we're excited about," or "members need to share the gospel more frequently" do not answer the question of how the gospel is to be sounded in every ear within a finite time frame. Rationalizations such as "it's difficult to tract after dark," "working through members is more effective than contacting," or "the culture here is closed to strangers" are not substitutes for well-researched, scriptural, and effective strategies for reaching the world.

While the task of reaching all or even most people with the gospel message may seem daunting, we are unlikely to succeed at some-

---

1974, originally presented at Regional Representatives Seminar, April 4, 1974.

[*]   Young, Brigham, *Discourses of Brigham Young*, Salt Lake City, UT: Bookcraft, 1988, 254.

thing which we do not think about, talk about, or make plans to do. Without specific plans or goals for fulfilling the scriptural admonition to reach large numbers of individuals, church growth falls far short of potential even in highly receptive areas. Receptivity is often high in the early years of religious freedom in a country, but often wanes in subsequent years due to encroaching materialism and saturation of the religious market with competing groups.* Low contacting rates in newly opened nations have serious consequences. Numerous potentially receptive individuals have often already been discipled into other denominations or have succumbed to growing secularism by the time Latter-day Saints finally get around to making even the first contact many years later, if at all.

No efforts are made to track the number of people being reached by contacting or referrals in the vast majority of LDS missions. When measured, the actual number of contacts made by missionaries is often surprisingly low. How can we accurately evaluate progress in reaching the world with little idea of how many people are being reached? A mission with one hundred missionaries who average ten gospel contacts per day per companionship in an area with ten million people will take fifty-five years to provide each person with an average of just one contact with the gospel. If this rate is increased to 100 gospel contacts per day per companionship, the same task could be done in only five years. Since many individuals require multiple exposures to the gospel before they join the Church, the rate at which new contacts are made must be increased. Unless we enlarge our vision and establish powerful strategic plans on a mission, ward, and branch level, how will we ever reach the world with the gospel? Do we have

---

*   Duke, James T., "Latter-day Saints in a Secular World: What We Have Learned about Latter-day Saints from Social Research," Martin B Hickman 1999 Lecture, Brigham Young University, College of Family, Home, and Social Sciences, March 4, 1999, http://fhss.byu.edu/adm/hickman_lecture.htm.

decades or even centuries to reach everyone in our own area once, when much of the world's population still lives in areas without any missionaries at all? Effective and comprehensive outreach never occurs by accident.

THE FORGOTTEN HARVEST: UNREACHED PEOPLES

By focusing resources on unreached and underreached areas, many groups have experienced rapid growth, while among Latter-day Saints strategic plans for reaching these people-groups are almost completely lacking. Only 5 percent of all LDS members live in the continental Afro-Eurasian land mass that is home to over 80 percent of the world's population. There are countless unused opportunities for Latter-day Saints among unreached culture groups where proselyting is permitted by law. In most countries with LDS congregations, the vast majority of the population lives in areas with no gospel witness.

Over one billion people live in the more than 500,000 villages, towns, and cities of India. Although LDS missionaries first arrived in India in 1850, in 2003, there were only 4,000 LDS members in all of India and twenty branches clustered in fewer than fifteen cities, with no plans to open additional cities. The Seventh-Day Adventists baptized over 100,000 new members in India within the first six months of 2000 alone.[*] One might hope that in a few more decades, there will be LDS branches in most of the 300 Indian cities with contemporary populations of 100,000 or more. Yet even this will barely scratch the surface of fulfilling the Great Commission, since only 11.7 percent of Indians live the 300 most populous cities.

Indonesia, the world's fourth most populous nation, has more than

---

[*]   *Maranatha Matters Newsletter*, November 9, 2000, http://www.maranatha.org/ mvimatters/Matters110900.htm.

220 million inhabitants living in over 100,000 villages, towns, and cities, yet only 50 cities have 100,000 inhabitants or more. After more than thirty years of LDS presence in the country, there are twenty-two LDS branches in Indonesia, all but three of which are on the lone island of Java. Latter-day Saints still publish materials and teach in only one of more than one dozen languages with over one million speakers. There are over 35 million Indonesian Christians, and many denominations report spectacular growth. The Seventh-Day Adventists report over 180,000 active members in Indonesia and an impressive 4 percent annual growth. LDS growth has been painfully stagnant with 5,300 members, of whom only 20 to 25 percent are active, after more than thirty years of proselyting, and the Church has lost ground in recent years by growing more slowly (1.32 percent per year) than the Indonesian population (1.63 percent per year). Other Christian denominations have noted rapid growth among the Dayak peoples of Kalimantan and many other people-groups among which there is no witness for the restored gospel of Jesus Christ, in spite of abundant opportunity and wide religious freedoms. Even in the unlikely event that the next few decades lead to the establishment of LDS branches in all major cities of Indonesia with at least 100,000 people, this will still provide the possibility of reaching 14 percent of Indonesians with the gospel message. The other 86 percent numbering nearly 200 million live in smaller towns and villages scattered across 6,000 islands.

Other unreached nations demonstrate similar trends. Of the 1.2 billion Chinese, 28.5 percent live in 370 cities of 100,000 or more. Pakistan's forty-three major cities are home to only 21 percent of the population. Yet China and Pakistan appear to be strongholds of the urban metropolis compared to most of the rest of South Asia. The major cities of Bangladesh and Burma hold 6 percent and 8 percent of the populace, respectively. In Cambodia, it is 3.4 percent. Of

Nepal's 18 million, only 1 percent lives in Katmandu, the country's only large city. The years of 1998–2001 saw the baptism of approximately 3,000 new Latter-day Saints among the 130 million people of Kenya, Uganda, Tanzania, and Ethiopia. The Seventh-Day Adventist Church now has over 4 million active members in Africa and baptized 10,000 converts in Tanzania on a single day, virtually all of whom had already completed prebaptismal Bible study courses.[*] Numerous African nations allow wide religious freedom and are home to thriving Pentecostal and evangelical communities, but have never had any LDS missionaries. Africa is even more rural than Asia: Nigeria is home to one out of four Africans, but only 6.25 percent of Nigerians live in medium or large cities. The urban population of Ethiopia weighs in at 5.8 percent of the national total of 68 million. The list goes on and on.

Most countries with missionaries remain highly underreached. In 2003, there were an estimated 40,000 small towns and villages in Ukraine, but just 60 LDS church units in 28 cities. If the entire full-time missionary force of the Church were concentrated in Ukraine, it could not supply even a single companionship to each town or village. To establish an LDS missionary-to-population ratio in India equivalent to the current ratio in the United States, the number of full-time missions in India would have to be increased from one to four hundred. Even a hundredfold increase would still be vastly inadequate under current paradigms. Yet there remains a need for the gospel to be preached to all people. The Savior made no exclusion for those living in small villages and towns when He commissioned His disciples to preach the gospel to every creature. How can we effectively fulfill our divine commission to reach the unreached, given limited resources

---

[*]   "Mass Baptisms Held in Tanzania," *Adventist News Network*, June 26, 2001, http://news.adventist.org.

and seemingly unlimited needs? We can find answers to questions of outreach by turning to the words of scripture and modern-day outreach, our missionary predecessors, and effective examples of other denominations.

PLANNING FOR THE WORLD'S NEEDS

At current rates, how long will it take for Latter-day Saints to sound the gospel trump in every ear? While both scriptures and modern prophets speak of the need for strategic outreach, we can find relatively few working models in the LDS mission community that we can look to for experience and insight. Other groups and denominations with effective strategic plans provide at least a glimpse of the unrealized potential.

DAWN stands for Discipling a Whole Nation. Judging by their performance, they seem to be serious about that goal. In the mid-1970s, evangelical DAWN leaders established the goal of increasing the number of evangelical churches in the Philippines from 200 to 50,000. Due largely to DAWN's efforts, there are over 60,000 evangelical churches in the Philippines today—more than twice the number of LDS congregations in the entire world.[*] The adoption of DAWN strategies has resulted in an explosion of evangelical growth in Africa, Asia, Eastern Europe, and Latin America. Denominations which have practiced the principles of strategic missionary work advocated by DAWN have seen growth double, triple, and more. DAWN founder Dr. Jim Montgomery observed that churches which adopt appropriate strategic planning measures on average see their growth rates double.[†]

---

[*]   Dawn Ministries, http://www.dawnministries.org.

[†]   Montgomery, James, "13 Steps to a Successful Growth Program," Dawn Ministries, (undated article), http://www.dawnministries.org.

The Seventh-Day Adventist church trained one million lay members for church planting and adopted an initiative to reach one billion homes around the world (and up to two-thirds of the world's population) with Bible study invitations by the end of 2003.* Citing a 2 percent response rate from a pilot study in Minnesota, Pastor Paulsen noted that even a 0.5 percent response rate would generate over five million new Bible study participants. Although their reported annual budget is only about one-fourth of the estimated LDS budget, the Seventh-Day Adventists are doing that which many LDS believe impossible due to limited resources. The Seventh-Day Adventists' vast, concrete, and well-implemented strategic plans provide insight into some of the reasons why the Seventh-Day Adventist Church is growing at three times the rate of the LDS Church, while achieving excellent retention and maintaining high member standards.

Strategic outreach initiatives to unreached peoples by many Protestant and evangelical groups have revolutionized cultural outreach and accelerated church growth. Johnstone and Mandryk's *Operation World* provides a wealth of information for mission planners and detailed country by country breakdown of evangelical mission needs, opportunities, and challenges.† The Joshua Project,‡ Joshua Project II, and Caleb Project§ have cataloged over 17,000 people-groups worldwide and help church congregations and individuals to "adopt" unreached or underreached people groups. Bethany World Prayer Center has created carefully researched profiles on over 1,500 unreached and underreached people-groups worldwide. Global Mapping Interna-

---

*   Rogers, Wendy, "Sow 1 Billion Launched: Bold Plan to Reach the World," *Adventist News Network*, October 15, 2002, http://news.adventist.org.

†   Johnstone, Patrick and Jason Mandryk, *Operation World*, Harrisonburg, VA: Paternoster Publishers, 2005.

‡   Joshua Project, http://www.joshuaproject.net.

§   Caleb Project, http://www.calebproject.org.

tional generates detailed maps of spoken languages, ethnic groups, church growth, and more for mission agencies.[*] Among Latter-day Saints, there are no concerted attempts to educate members about unreached people-groups and no proactive efforts to prepare outreach resources in their languages.

A focus on people-groups is vital in order to successfully reach every nation, kindred, tongue, and people with the gospel. Baptist mission organizer Don Kammerdiener stated: "Looking at the world as a collection of individual nations is not the best approach because it assumes that all people in a nation are the same. Yugoslavia is a classic example. We thought it was one nation, but now we know that there are Serbs, Croats, Bosnians, Muslims—and they are all different."[†] Political boundaries in much of Asia and Africa often reflect arbitrary administrative boundaries of the colonial era that have limited relevance to language or ethnicity. Members of the same people-group may be found in multiple distinct nations (i.e., Kashmir is divided between India, Pakistan, and China), while widely different languages and cultures may be found within the same nation (i.e., the Indo-European languages of North India than Northern Indian languages are much more closely related to English than to the Dravidian languages of Southern India). Consideration of the world in terms of nations inevitably leaves major people-groups unreached or underreached. Protestant church planting has also been enhanced by concerted efforts to evangelize the "10/40 Window"—an imaginary rectangle that stretches from northern Africa and the Middle East to Asia. The 10/40 Window is home to 60 percent of the world's population, but

---

[*]   Global Missions International, http://www.gmi.org.

[†]   "Missionaries Doing Whatever It Takes," *Religion Today*, April 24, 2000, http://news.crosswalk.com.

only 1 percent of the world's Christians.*

THE CHURCH AND THE VILLAGE

As the Church enters the twenty-first century, LDS missionaries stand at the frontiers of the unreached world. No degree of multiplication in the number of full-time LDS missionaries will allow for full proselytization of unreached towns and villages under current policies. New methods and approaches will be needed to successfully reach the remaining billions of inhabitants of millions of towns and villages where there has never been a gospel witness. The Lord stated that when Israel is gathered, He will take "one of a city, and two of a family, and bring [them] to Zion" (Jeremiah 3:14). Not every village, town, and city will be able to sustain an LDS congregation. Nephi prophesied of a day when the Church of Jesus Christ would be "upon all the face of the earth" but foresaw that its dominions would be small (1 Nephi 14:12). Methods of offering the gospel in towns and villages without having full-time missionaries permanently stationed there are needed. Analysis of the counsel of Latter-day Saint prophets, the words of scripture, and the effective example of other denominations can help us to understand the steps of strategic planning and implementation necessary to successfully reach unreached billions with the gospel message. Our challenge and opportunity is to adopt and implement measures to reach the unreached reliably, effectively, and within a reasonable time. The barrier to reaching the unreached is not in them, but in us.

Small towns and villages present unique opportunities and challenges. Throughout history, village dwellers have frequently been considered to be somewhat more religious (and sometimes more

---

*   "Dramatic Church Growth in Equatorial Guinea," *Adventist News Network*,
     April 30, 2002, http://news.adventist.org.

superstitious) than the inhabitants of large cities. Villages often have more cohesive families and lower crime rates than large cities. Villages often face challenges with poverty, education, communications, and infrastructure. The inhabitants of small towns are sometimes more easily swayed by community opinion than inhabitants of large cities.

Dan Jones was the first mission president of the modern dispensation and one of the most effective missionaries of all time. In two missions to the small towns and villages of rural Wales in the 1840s, Dan Jones baptized 6,000 converts and achieved excellent retention. This was done without the benefit of radio, television, or the resources and technology of the modern Church. Dan Jones visited hamlets and small villages itinerantly to give as many people as possible the opportunity to hear the gospel. He used the media to reach people effectively and consistently. Dan Jones used newspaper articles to inform people of upcoming church meetings in their area. He started the first international LDS publication in Welsh and wrote and edited over thirty-two editions, using it as an outreach tool. He would telegraph ahead to cities and villages, informing the mayor that he was coming to "convert the whole town." He taught with a sense of urgency. When receptivity waned in one area, Dan Jones moved on. He obeyed the Lord's word: "If they receive not your testimony in one area, flee to another: for verily I say unto you, Ye shall not have gone over the cities of Israel, till the Son of man be come" (Matthew 10:23). In contrast, many missionaries today have a difficult time understanding when it is time to move on until being asked not to come back by people they teach. Dan Jones recognized that his missionary efforts could not have been nearly as successful if he had spent all his time preaching in one or two major cities without venturing into the villages and hamlets to share the gospel. Dan Jones contacted hundreds of thousands of people by various means. He constantly contacted people everywhere he went and made the gospel message as widely available as possible within a short period.

Modern groups that have adopted approaches similar to those of Dan Jones have also experienced dramatic missionary success. Gospel For Asia (GFA), an evangelical group run by Indian-born pastor K. P. Yohannan, fields over 10,000 full-time local missionaries in India and South Asia.* In a predominantly Hindu nation traditionally resistant to Christian proselytism, GFA's missionaries are organizing an average of six new congregations per day, or two and a half times as many new congregations as the LDS church organizes across the entire world. Why are GFA missionaries, who live on a shoestring budget of $90 to $150 per month, so successful? Instead of seeking to find contacts by repeatedly visiting the few existing members several times per month to ask for referrals, with an hour or two of tracting or street contacting thrown in once in awhile, Gospel For Asia missionaries are constantly breaking new ground. Each GFA van staffed by two missionaries travels to an average of twelve to fifteen remote interior villages each day to share the Christian message. Equipped with bullhorns, VCR equipment, and the "Jesus" video, GFA missionaries reach hundreds or thousands of people each day. Those who are not allocated vans travel on bicycles with bullhorns and lanterns for evening evangelistic meetings. GFA missionaries are also well-stocked with tracts and Bibles and conduct vigorous literature distribution campaigns. Even with only fractional response rates, GFA missionaries experience tremendous success. Gospel For Asia and the Seventh-Day Adventist Church each organize more new congregations in India every four days than Latter-day Saints have organized in the country over the past 150 years.

---

*   Gospel For Asia, http://www.gfa.org. See also Yohannan, K. P., *Revolution in World Missions*, Carrollton, TX: GFA Books, 2000.

An ingenious strategy for reaching remote unreached villages was pioneered by Phillip and Karen Brown, Baptist missionaries in Senegal, to reach the rural Sereer people.* The "Bread of Life" project involved the printing of one million bread wrappers which were distributed freely to vendors at local markets. The bread wrappers, in turn, were passed on to bread customers, who came into town to buy bread from remote villages all over Senegal. The wrappers could be redeemed for gospel literature from Sereer pastors and evangelists in each market. While the wrappers are distributed in ten markets, the bread wrappers found their way into almost all of the 160 Sereer markets, because many vendors attend different markets each day. The pastors keep track of how many gospel stories each person has read. When all fourteen were completed, the person earned the privilege of having an evangelistic team come to his or her village to show the Jesus film. In this way, large numbers of individuals in remote regions were reached, and Baptist churches in Senegal reported a surge in growth.

TRANSLATION OF SCRIPTURES AND OUTREACH MATERIAL

The Book of Mormon is available in part or full in just over 100 languages. Ethnologue catalogs over 6,700 living languages.[†] Fifty-two percent of the 6,700 languages are spoken by less than 10,000 people, and 28 percent are spoken by less than 1,000 people. Eighty-three percent of them are limited to single countries. There are over 273 languages spoken by over one million people each, totaling 5.4 billion speakers. Correlation of language speaker data with a list of Book of

---

* Sprenkle, Sue, "Sereers Crave the Bread of Life," *Religion Today News*, http://www.crosswalk.com/news/religiontoday/525772.html, also reported in *Baptist Press*, May 16, 2001.

† Ethnologue, http://www.ethnologue.com.

Mormon translations demonstrates that the Book of Mormon is available in full in languages spoken by approximately 64 percent of the world's population and in part in languages spoken by 14 percent of the world's population. Based on Ethnologue language speaker data, part or all of the Book of Mormon is available in languages spoken by approximately 78 percent of the world's population, compared to 87 percent claimed in the July 2001 *Ensign*.* The *Ensign* figure may have been calculated by summating the number of speakers of each language with a translation and dividing the total by the world's population, resulting in an overcount because bilingual individuals are counted twice. The Book of Mormon is not available in 204 of the 273 languages spoken by over one million people each, and over one billion people collectively (16 percent of world population). Another 6 percent speak languages with fewer than one million speakers in which the Book of Mormon is not available. The Book of Mormon is printed in 28 languages spoken by less than one million people, with many spoken by less than 100,000 people.

With barely half of the world's 100 most spoken languages and only 25 percent of languages spoken by over one million people having a Book of Mormon translation after more than 175 years, new approaches to speed the translation of scripture are needed. Latter-day Saint scripture translations are initiated when approval is given by the area presidency, usually after missionaries have started teaching large numbers of people who speak a given language. A translation typically takes eight to twelve years to be completed. This policy has resulted in the Church repeatedly being unprepared to enter new nations and cultures. After the fall of the Berlin Wall, missionaries had a Russian translation of the Book of Mormon not because of any foresight of the Missionary Department, but through the donation of a private

---

* "Taking the Scriptures to the World," *Ensign*, July 2001, 24.

member. Major languages such as Ukrainian had no LDS scripture, even though there had been a sizeable LDS Ukrainian community in Canada for decades. Other denominations, such as the Jehovah's Witnesses and Seventh-Day Adventists, swept across Western Ukraine and achieved rapid growth. LDS missionaries entered Ukrainian-speaking regions of Ukraine only six years later after an expedited translation of the Book of Mormon had been completed. Modest growth was still achieved, but the window of high spontaneous religious interest of earlier years had been lost. Several of my mission companions in Russia were transferred to the Baltic States, where they were assigned to learn Latvian and Lithuanian, which had no LDS scriptures until eight to ten years later. Finding, teaching, and baptizing converts without the Book of Mormon and without any official LDS literature presented special difficulties. Recognizing that the Book of Mormon is the key to missionary work, that the gospel message must go to every nation, kindred, tongue, and people, and that the first few years in every newly opened nation represent a time of exceptional receptivity, it would seem that the need for Book of Mormon translations in major world languages could be proactively anticipated. We know from population and linguistic data how many individuals speak each language without having to wait for prolonged missionary contact and field research. Harnessing the translation and outreach expertise of expatriate and immigrant members through global planning and coordination would be central to such a strategy.

With vision and good planning, quality translation of both scriptural and nonscriptural materials into many languages can be completed in only modest periods. Wycliffe Bible Translators has translated the entire New Testament into 611 languages and has translations in progress in another 1,682 languages, starting projects in 84

new languages in 2004 alone.[*] *Operation World* reported that Wycliffe
Bible Translators adopted a strategically oriented plan to translate the
Bible into every language which is anticipated to need one by the year
2025.[†] Through research, visionary planning, and careful coordination, Wycliffe Bible Translators expects to complete a task in 25 years
which would have taken 150 years at the prior rate. By February 2006,
the Campus Crusade for Christ's Jesus Film had been translated into
over 925 languages and had received more than 6 billion individual
viewings, resulting in over 200 million referrals to local churches.[‡]
The Jehovah's Witnesses translated their main proselyting manual
into 126 languages between 1995 and 2001. They also simultaneously
translate and release the *Watchtower* every two weeks in 141 languages
and translate material less regularly into a total of 262 languages.[§]

BOOK OF MORMON AND RELIGIOUS LITERATURE DISTRIBUTION

Although the LDS Church has the largest full-time missionary
force of any Christian denomination, many other groups outpace
Latter-day Saints in the distribution of religious literature by orders
of magnitude. While the Book of Mormon is the "keystone of our
religion" and the "key to conversion," the average LDS missionary
distributes just one copy of the Book of Mormon every five days. Less
than one dollar per LDS member per year is spent on printing copies
of the Book of Mormon, and an average of over seventy dollars of

---

[*]   Wycliffe Bible Translators 2004 Annual Report, http://www.wycliffe.org/wbt-usa/report/Annual%20Report%2004.pdf.

[†]   Johnstone, Patrick and Jason Mandryk, *Operation World.* Harrisonburg, VA: Paternoster, 2005.

[‡]   Jesus Films Web site, http://www.jesusfilm.org/aboutus/index.html.

[§]   Jehovah's Witnesses: Membership and Publishing Statistics, 2001–2005, http://www.jw-media.org/people/statistics.htm.

missionary support fund money is spent on missionary housing, food, and personal expenses for every copy of the Book of Mormon that is distributed. In the 170-year period from 1829 to February 2000, a total of 100 million copies of the Book of Mormon were printed. Approximately 5.0 to 5.6 million copies of the Book of Mormon are printed each year,* or one copy for every 1,200 people. In an era when Latter-day prophets have spoken of the imperative need to "flood the earth with the Book of Mormon," we must ask if we are really doing our all. The total number of copies of the Book of Mormon printed in the history of the Church would more than double in a single year if every LDS member would share a copy with a nonmember once per month, or over the course of a two-year mission, if each missionary would share just three copies per day with nonmembers.

A sense of the possibilities for Book of Mormon utilization can be gleaned from the examples of other groups. On November 11, 2001, the Protestant World Bible Translation Center distributed 370,000 copies of the Bible in an outreach in Ibadan, Nigeria, that drew over 1.3 million visitors, while acknowledging that this effort was grossly inadequate to local needs.† One small Protestant mission group based in Florida with modest resources distributed over 100 million copies of a summary of the four gospels worldwide in less than one decade. In fiscal year 2001, Lands' End distributed over 269 million product catalogs.‡ Gospel For Asia missionaries distribute Christian tracts in bulk, which are printed locally at a rate of $1 per 250 tracts. The Jehovah's Witnesses printed more than 31 million copies of their introductory

---

*   "Taking the Scriptures to the World," *Ensign*, July 2001: 24.

†   "Largest Single-Day Bible Distribution in History Takes Place in Ibadan, Nigeria," World Bible Translation Center Press Release, November 15, 2001, http://www.wbtc.com/articles/news/011115ibadan_distrib.html.

‡   Lands' End 2001 Annual Report, Lands' End Inc., http://199.230.26.96/le/pdfs/2001AR.pdf.

text "What Does the Bible Really Teach?" in 2005 alone. They print 45 million copies of the *Watchtower* and *Awake!* every two weeks, or over one billion copies per year.[20] Over 5,000 tons of Jehovah's Witness literature are distributed in Russia alone each year. While distributing thirty-two-page *Watchtower* magazine is very different from sharing a copy of the Book of Mormon, one might wonder if there is not something that can be learned from these other groups about the feasibility of producing and distributing vast volumes of religious literature. The cost of such outreach is surprisingly small, and common estimates suggest that the budget of the Jehovah's Witnesses organization is only about one-quarter that of the LDS Church.

Many missionaries and leaders have claimed that widespread distribution of the Book of Mormon is ineffective. I challenge such claims, which demonstrate light-minded attitudes toward the Book of Mormon for which the Church is under condemnation.[*] With fewer than five baptisms per LDS missionary per year and world convert retention rates near 25 percent, making a single retained convert requires on average nearly eleven months of full-time missionary labor and nearly $5,000 in missionary support fund money, in addition to other mission overhead. If we are to assume very conservatively that missionary time is worth just $5 per hour, which is below U.S. minimum wage and far below the immeasurable spiritual value of missionary time, the total value of the time and money to find a single retained convert exceeds $16,000. At approximately $2 per Book of Mormon copy, over 8,000 copies of the Book of Mormon would have to be printed for the cost of baptizing a single retained convert under current outreach paradigms. In reality, only about twenty copies of the Book of Mormon are printed per baptized convert today. Our actual

---

[*]   Benson, Ezra Taft, "The Book of Mormon—Keystone of Our Religion," *Ensign*, November 1986.

use of the Book of Mormon is more than two orders of magnitude below the level that would be required for anyone to validly conclude that utilizing large numbers of copies of the Book of Mormon is ineffective. The tiny sum of one dollar per year per member spent on the Book of Mormon is dwarfed by tremendous expenditures for budget, ward social activities, meetinghouse construction, and other high-cost, low-impact items.

Many missions continue to practice restrictive policies about Book of Mormon use. The concept of "flooding the earth" of necessity implies abundance or excess. Many missionaries have no second thoughts about spending a couple hours to travel across town for an appointment with a new contact who has read nothing in the scriptures at all, but most will not loan a copy of the Book of Mormon to the most interested street or tracting contact. This approach requires that the investigator makes a significant commitment to receive the strangers into their home before they have the opportunity to do any thoughtful reading or data-gathering. Do we imagine that our own words are any more convincing or more important than the inspired words of the Lord himself in the scriptures? I have frequently heard the phrase "everyone deserves a chance" used to justify considerable time spent in repeated nonproductive discussions with individuals who have put forth little or no personal effort to plant the seed of faith. Everyone does deserve a chance, so why not provide a real chance to accept the gospel through the Book of Mormon rather than a false chance based on personality or charisma?

Using the Book of Mormon as an initial sieve in the contacting stage can make missionary time vastly more efficient by helping to self-select nonmembers who are receptive to the Lord's word and the gospel rather than to American culture or missionary personalities. Self-selection based on each individual's opinion of the Book of Mormon is much more reliable than arbitrary selection of investigators based on missionary judgment. Additional copies of the Book of Mormon can always be printed to accommodate needs, while missionary time is finite, especially in areas where relatively small missionary complements serve a large population base. The opportunity cost of time is far greater than the economic cost of materials. It is not necessary to distribute a copy of the Book of Mormon to every living person, since only a fraction of people are willing to read it, but it is vital that we make it far more widely available than at present.

While I believe that there are more effective ways to utilize copies of the Book of Mormon than simply distributing them in mass (see The Book of Mormon Loan Program in the Witnesses of Christ section), there is no question that dramatically increasing Book of Mormon publication and utilization rates is one of the greatest needs of the modern missionary program. Our missionary programs will never achieve their potential until we "remember the new covenant, even the Book of Mormon" (D&C 84:57).

OUTREACH BROADCASTING

In 1974, Spencer W. Kimball declared:

King Benjamin, that humble but mighty servant of the Lord, called together all the people in the land of Zarahemla, and the multitude was so great that King Benjamin "... caused a tower to be erected, that thereby his people might hear the words which he should speak unto them" (Mosiah 2:7). Our Father in heaven has now provided us mighty towers—radio and television towers with possibilities beyond comprehension—to help fulfill the words of the Lord that "the sound must go forth from this place unto all the world." Even though there are millions of people throughout the world who cannot read or write, there is a chance to reach them through radio and television. The modern transistor radio can be mass produced by the thousands in a size that is small and inexpensive. We can preach the gospel to eager ears and hearts. These should be carried by people in the marketplaces of South America, on the steppes of Russia, the vast mountains and plains of China, the subcontinent of India, and the desert sands of Arabia and Egypt. Some authorities claim that this tiny miracle will be recorded by future historians as an event even greater than the invention of the printing press. The transistor is an eloquent answer to the illiteracy and ignorance which reign supremely over the earth. The spoken voice will reach millions of hearers who can listen through a $3 or $4 transistor but could not read even an elementary treatise. There are over 7,000 AM and FM radio stations in the United States, with thousands more in other parts of the world. There are innumerable opportunities for us to use these stations overseas, if we only prepare the message in the native languages. Also, missionaries could be supplied with small portable cassette tape players and go into the homes with prepared messages to humble family groups all around the globe. Millions of people are anxious and willing to learn, if only they can hear the "sound" in their own language and in a manner that they can grasp and understand. Just think what can be accomplished when we broadcast our message in many languages over numerous radio stations, large and small, around the world, and millions of good people listening on their transistors are being indoctrinated with the truth. The Lord has blessed the world with many Early Bird satellites. They are stationed high in the heavens, relaying broadcast signals back to almost every corner of the earth's surface. Today there are 67 earth receiving stations operating in 50 countries of the world. Certainly these satellites are only the genesis of what is in store for the future of world-wide broadcasting. With the Lord providing these miracles of communication, and with the increased efforts and devotion of our missionaries and all of us, and all others who are "sent," surely the divine injunction will come to pass: "For verily, the sound must go forth from this place into all the world, and unto the uttermost parts of the earth—the gospel must be preached unto every creature ..." (D&C 58:64).*

Many Latter-day Saints believe that one of the main reasons for the technological explosion of the past two centuries has been to provide new and superior means for sharing the gospel, yet little has been done to utilize new technologies for outreach. Now, over thirty years after President Kimball's inspired mandate, LDS radio outreach remains virtually nonexistent. There is still not a single full-time outreach-oriented LDS radio station anywhere in the world, and the few stations that carry LDS messages are directed almost exclusively toward enrichment of existing members. Characteristic LDS public service television messages are almost entirely restricted to the Americas. There is little organized LDS media outreach in the developing world, where 75 to 80 percent of convert baptisms occur.

Many Protestant and evangelical groups have effectively incorporated broadcasting technologies into their outreach strategies. *World Christian Trends* reported: "Regular listeners to Christian programs over secular or religious radio or TV stations rose from 22% of the world in 1980 to 30% in 2000,"† while George Barna noted that Christian mass

---

*   Kimball, Spencer W., "When the World Will Be Converted," *Ensign*, October 1974, originally presented at Regional Representatives Seminar, April 4, 1974.

†   Barrett, David and Todd Johnson, *World Christian Trends AD 30–AD 2200* Pasadena, CA: William Carey Library, 2001.

media reaches more people than the churches themselves.* Although 119 countries with over half of the world's population prohibit or seriously restrict foreign missionaries,† only four nations (Afghanistan, Iran, Saudi Arabia, and the United Kingdom) with just 2.5 percent of the world's population prohibit independent religious radio.‡ These are important findings that should not be ignored. To reach successfully the remainder of the world with the gospel message, Latter-day Saints will need to learn to work in new ways.

Full-time Protestant outreach radio stations have been broadcasting internationally for over eighty years. Today, there are tens of thousands of Christian radio stations worldwide. Adventist World Radio broadcasts over 1,200 hours of outreach radio and television programs in over 50 languages each week.§ These programs can be heard by 85 percent of the world's population.¶ The Seventh-Day Adventist Church now owns its own satellite system for the satellite broadcasts which have been central to massively successful evangelization efforts, drawing nightly crowds of up to 100,000 and promoting remarkable church growth in Papua New Guinea** and Africa.[14] DVD presentations have been screened to crowds exceeding 50,000 in India. Yet the Seventh-Day Adventists, who are growing at three times the rate

---

* "Christian Mass Media Reach More Adults with the Christian Message Than Do Churches," Barna Research Update, July 2, 2002, http://www.barna.org/cgi-bin/PagePressRelease.asp?PressReleaseID=116&Reference=F.

† Yohannan, K. P., *Revolution in World Missions*, Carrollton, TX: GFA Books, 2000. See also http://www.gfa.org.

‡ "British Ban Independent Religious Broadcasts," *Religion Today*, May 1, 2001, http://news.crosswalk.com.

§ "United Arab Emirates: New Adventist Radio Superstation Begins Broadcasts," *Adventist News Network*, August 7, 2001, http://news.adventist.org.

¶ Adventist World Radio, http://www.awr.org.

** "Papua New Guinea Adventist Evangelistic Series Holds National Attention," *Adventist News Network*, July 17, 2001, http://news.adventist.org.

of the LDS Church, are not satisfied and continue to explore aggressively the potential of new technologies to supplement conventional evangelism.[*]

The Far Eastern Broadcasting Company, which broadcasts Christian messages in over 50 languages, reported receiving over 600 letters per month from listeners in Thailand alone, of which 100 are referred to local churches.[†] Gospel radio stations in India report receiving thousands of letters per month from listeners. Christian radio networks across Central and South America, Eastern Europe, Africa, and Asia maintained by Transworld Radio,[‡] Assemblies of God, and other groups report dramatic responses to gospel radio. One well-known and effective evangelical church growth strategy on the Indian subcontinent is to have local listeners organize Bible studies and then send missionaries to the village to organize a congregation when the group consists of 100 or more believers! While many LDS missionaries have difficulty finding interested people to teach, other denominations which make effective use of media ministries are often faced with the opposite problem of large numbers of interested believers with few missionaries or pastors to teach and disciple them.

Finnish Christian broadcaster Hannu Haukka observed: "Radio and television waves cannot be taken hostage, captive, or be chained. They do not respect boundaries. They are free to visit every home and tell every occupant about the love of God."[§] Religious radio can carry messages continuously, in contrast to the brief periods of exposure churches receive in the secular media. Religious broadcasting has

---

[*]   Munoz, Julio, "Evangelism Think-Tank Explores Potential of New Technology," *Adventist News Network*, October 9, 2002, http://news.adventist.org.

[†]   Far Eastern Broadcasting Company, http://www.febc.org.

[‡]   Trans World Radio, http://www.twr.org.

[§]   *Religion Today* News Summary, April 13, 2000, http://news.crosswalk.com.

become remarkably inexpensive. Seventh-Day Adventists, Assemblies of God, and many other groups that conduct regular radio, television, and satellite outreach broadcasts throughout the world have only a fraction of the income of the LDS Church, primarily because most of their members live in developing nations. Groups unable to hire full-time staff for religious broadcasting have achieved success with short programs looped to play continuously or with on-demand audio.

While the Bible is available online in over 100 languages, the Book of Mormon is officially available online only in English, even though less than 50 percent of LDS members and less than 40 percent of Internet users speak English. While English-speaking members benefit from abundant enrichment resources, online LDS materials in other languages consist mainly of conference talks and curriculum materials for existing LDS members. Official LDS outreach sites such as mormon.org contain only a superficial overview of beliefs, and virtually none of the standardized outreach resources—not even the Testimony of the Prophet Joseph Smith or the Book of Mormon—are available online in major languages other than English and Spanish. While Latter-day Saints have made some technological strides in recent years, such as the online broadcast of the LDS General Conference in over fifty languages, this technology is overwhelmingly directed toward existing members rather than outreach. Greater utilization of the resources and opportunities the Lord has already provided for sharing the gospel would result in an explosion of growth.

FOSTERING RELATIONSHIPS IN THE UNREACHED WORLD

When a referral is submitted by an individual who lives in a city without an LDS congregation, the referral information is placed in a folder at the respective mission office and remains there until full-time missionaries begin proselyting in that city, often years or decades later, if at all. In the interim, no attempt is made to contact the individual or even to acknowledge receipt of the request. In an age when missionaries in some areas work for days without teaching a discussion, the handling of referrals in areas without Church units provides great opportunity for improvement.

Referrals are time-sensitive. Individuals may feel exploited when they respond to a message promising Church information or a missionary visit but never receive any acknowledgment. Few customer service departments would feel that they could simply ignore out of area requests. At a minimum, such individuals would benefit from a letter informing them regarding the absence of local congregations and providing contact information of the nearest mission office and LDS congregations. Interested individuals living in cities without missionaries can be sent copies of the Book of Mormon or other church literature by mail, rather than having to wait for the missionaries to hand-deliver them years later, if at all, when interest may have waned and contact information may no longer be valid.

An editorial in *The Economist* observed: "Western governments would do better to give a helping hand to those courageous individuals who are working to keep the flame of independent thought flickering. Often the best deliverers of such help are not embassies or visiting politicians, but non-governmental agencies. Tiny amounts of money—a printing press here, an internet-linked computer there—can make the difference between survival or extinction for a local party or lobby group."* The same is true of church outreach in new areas. Many international LDS congregations have begun with a core of individuals in unreached areas who maintained contact with the Church until missionaries were sent, yet such responsiveness on the part of the

---

*   "Stopping the Rot," *The Economist*, May 4, 2002.

Church has been the exception rather than the rule. Increased attention to prompt follow-up of referrals in cities and branches without missionaries, even if by correspondence or telephone, could pay rich dividends. A little effort to cultivate strategically oriented relationships with individuals in unreached cities and with members of under-reached people-groups can make a decisive difference for entering a city or country on the right foot for rapid and sustained church growth.

Church Planting

THE DIVINE MANDATE

CHRIST COMMANDED HIS DISCIPLES: "Go ye into all the world, and preach the gospel to every creature" (Mark 16:15). Christ expressed the urgency of giving everyone an opportunity to hear the gospel and noted that even with good planning, hard work, fervent prayer, and our best efforts that we will ultimately fall short of the gospel mandate of reaching everyone. Christ taught: "But when they persecute you in this city, flee ye into another: for verily I say unto you, Ye shall not have gone over the cities of Israel, till the Son of man be come" (Matthew 10:23). The need to enter new areas of opportunity promptly is linked to the need to leave stagnant, unreceptive areas to free up manpower and resources, because "the harvest is truly great, but the laborers are few" (Luke 10:2). In modern revelation, the Lord commanded: "Enlarge the place of thy tent, and let them stretch forth the curtains of thine habitations: spare not, lengthen thy cords, and strengthen thy stakes" (Isaiah 54:2, 3 Nephi 22:2). He further declared: "Go ye forth unto the land of Zion, that the borders of my people may be enlarged, and that her stakes may be strengthened, and that Zion may go forth unto the regions round about" (D&C 133:9). President Spencer W. Kimball taught that we must prepare to "open the doors of every nation as fast as it is ready" and to reach every creature with the gospel trump.* The limiting factors in establishing the Church must be the receptivity of local people and the opportunity to preach to them, not our lack of preparation or effort. New converts must be gathered into congregations to ensure that they are not lost (Alma 26:5).

The divine mandate for reaching everyone with the gospel message and gathering converts into congregations can be accomplished in two ways, and both are necessary. One is gathering the "pure in heart" out from small towns and villages to central locations with itinerant proselytizing, as was done by Brigham Young, Wilford Woodruff, Dan Jones, and other early LDS missionaries. The second method is to create accessible local congregations.

CHURCH PLANTING ACCELERATES MEMBERSHIP GROWTH

Church planting refers to the process of strategically organizing congregations in new areas to make the Church accessible to as many people as possible. Saturation church planting involves planting as many congregations as the receptivity of local people will support. Church planting is a key element of successful church growth strategies. Dr. C. Peter Wagner stated:

> New churches grow better than old churches. Built into new churches is a potential for growth that older churches no longer have. This does not mean that older churches cannot grow. They often do. Nor does it mean that all new churches grow. Frequently they do not. But across the board, growth is more likely with less effort in newer churches. Phil Jones, a researcher for the Southern Baptist Home Mission Board, reported: "If

---

* Kimball, Spencer W., "When the World Will Be Converted," *Ensign*, October 1974.

baptism rates per 100 members are used as a measure of efficiency for a church, then young churches are more efficient
than old churches. The older a church gets, the less efficient it
is in baptizing new converts." The late Keith Lusk did a similar
study of churches of all denominations in the Santa Clarita
Valley of California and found that in 1986 older churches were
baptizing at the rate of four baptisms per 100 members per year,
while newer churches were baptizing at the rate of 16 baptisms
per 100 members. It is not surprising, then, that overall growth
increases as new churches are started…. I am one of the strongest supporters of church renewal, and I believe that if renewal
comes to our existing churches, much subsequent evangelism
will be done. But good as this is, it is not enough. Old wineskins need to be patched, but new wineskins are even more
desperately needed. Remember this simple fact: It's easier to
have babies than to raise the dead! Not that all existing churches
are dead, or even that most of them are. Most can and should
be brought to life by the power of the Holy Spirit. Still the most
exciting part of the hospital is the maternity ward.[*]

Young LDS wards and branches generally have much higher convert
baptism rates per capita than older wards and branches. Careful case
studies of LDS missions in many countries demonstrate with few
exceptions a strong trend for a disproportionately large amount of
convert growth occurs in relatively newly opened wards and branches.
The more rapid growth rate of small, new congregations has been
repeatedly validated across many denominations. Seventh-Day Adventist Euro-Asia field secretary Jeff Scoggins reported that "the building
of smaller congregations results in the same net number of baptisms

---

[*]   Wagner, C. Peter, *Church Planting for a Greater Harvest*, Ventura, CA: Regal
    Books, 1990.

that larger congregations gained in a given year."* This results in much higher growth rates per member in small, newly organized units than in large, long-established ones. Scoggins also noted that establishing small churches "doesn't concentrate members in one spot," facilitating outreach across broader areas. In an era when the LDS Church is growing at less than 3 percent per year in spite of the opening of many new nations to LDS missionaries, Southern Baptists have achieved annual growth rates of 100 percent in many areas of the developing world by applying principles of church planting. An excellent and freely available manual entitled Church Planting Movements by David Garrison of the International Mission Board of the Southern Baptist Convention concisely captures the vital principles of years of field church planting research collected from the most rapidly growing areas.[†] While not everything in this booklet is applicable to Latter-day Saints, it articulates principles of rapid yet sustainable growth that corroborate many of my observations in the LDS mission field. Church planting approaches can help us to go through open doors instead of banging our heads against closed ones.

CHURCH PLANTING IS TIME-SENSITIVE

The book of Acts records: "A vision appeared to Paul in the night; there stood a man of Macedonia, and prayed him, saying, Come over into Macedonia, and help us. And after he had seen the vision, immediately we endeavoured to go into Macedonia, assuredly gathering that the Lord had called us for to preach the gospel unto them' (Acts 16:9–10). Many miraculous conversions occurred in Macedonia as a

---

*   Kellner, Mark, "Russia: Church Planters Near Goals in Former Soviet Union," *Adventist News Network*, June 17, 2003, http://news.adventist.org.

†   Garrison, David, Church Planting Movements, Southern Baptist International Mission Board, October 1999, http://www.imb.org/CPM/default.htm.

result of Paul heeding the Spirit's call and traveling to Macedonia to preach the gospel without delay.

Dan Jones, a successful LDS missionary to Wales in the early days of the Church, would telegraph ahead to cities and villages, informing the mayor that he was coming to "convert the whole town." He used newspaper articles to inform people of upcoming church meetings in their area. Prospective converts heard the message and self-selected themselves based on interest and desire. Dan Jones made the gospel message as widely available as possible within a short period and contacted hundreds of thousands of people by various means. When receptivity waned in one area, he moved on. He obeyed the Lord's word: "If they receive not your testimony in one area, flee to another." He taught with a sense of urgency. Dan Jones did not go back to visit repeatedly investigators who were not keeping commitments. He relied on the Spirit to convert, rather than attempting to win noncommittal souls through prolonged socialization. In contrast, many missionaries today have a difficult time understanding when it is time to move on until being asked not to come back by people they teach. As a result of these practices, over 6,000 people came into the Church during Dan Jones' two missions to the British Isles.

Many studies document that receptivity is time-sensitive and often declines over time, especially when many competing religious groups are present.* The best period for missionary work is the period of spontaneous religious interest, when large groups of individuals will turn out to investigate denominations, often with nothing more than a simple invitation. However, there is often a period—sometimes brief, and sometimes lasting decades—between the establishment

---

*   Duke, James T., "Latter-day Saints in a Secular World: What We Have Learned about Latter-day Saints from Social Research," Martin B Hickman 1999 Lecture, Brigham Young University, College of Family, Home, and Social Sciences, March 4, 1999, http://fhss.byu.edu/adm/hickman_lecture.htm.

of basic religious freedom and unrestricted opportunities for foreign missionaries in a nation. A high dependence on intensive efforts of full-time foreign missionaries therefore results in a loss of some of the best opportunities. Even in areas where full-time missionaries are permitted, successful establishment of self-sufficient and self-perpetuating branches leads to vastly improved growth.

ACCELERATED BAPTISM PROGRAMS CRIPPLE CONGREGATIONAL GROWTH

Some claim that the collapse of hundreds of LDS wards and branches in Latin America from 2000 to 2004 demonstrates that church planting does not work. The failure of many new units has led to a retreat from congregational expansion into new areas. Church planting has largely been discounted in the LDS mission community because of the belief that the problems of struggling small units arise primarily from deficiencies of size or socialization.

In fact, the lack of durability of many new LDS congregations is most frequently caused by accelerated baptism practices that generate large numbers of poorly committed members who are lost to inactivity soon after baptism, dissipating the time and enthusiasm of active members with fruitless reactivation tasks. I have traced the collapse of many new congregations to patterns of indiscriminate and rushed baptism of individuals poorly prepared to sustain their own spiritual needs, let alone serve in the Church.

Accelerated baptism programs have survived in North America for many years, since congregations with a strong base of lifelong members are able to retain function and achieve some growth through births, even if convert retention is poor. However, such programs are particularly devastating in international areas, where congregations depend upon the participation of new converts for both maintenance and growth. Accelerated baptism programs lead to a proliferation of inactives and actives with serious problems that the few committed, active members are often unable to absorb. Under such circumstances, vast numbers of nominal members are necessary to achieve the modest core of actives needed to sustain congregational functions.

In spite of relatively few new cities being opened for missionary work in recent years, the newly opened smaller cities continue to account for a disproportionately large segment of convert growth. Adequate prebaptismal teaching and preparation is the most significant missing ingredient preventing Latter-day Saint church planting approaches from reaching their potential. For church planting to be successful, deliberate and methodical steps must be taken starting in the planning phase even before the congregation is established to minimize the loss of future converts to inactivity. All missionaries must be dedicated to the careful teaching, thorough preparation, and rigorous prebaptismal qualification of potential converts, since even short periods of unprincipled quick-baptize programs can cause irreparable damage to nascent congregations. These principles are prerequisites to the success of church planting efforts and to the ultimate health of every congregation, since inactivity saps the resources and vitality of any congregation and hampers community outreach.

CHURCH PLANTING VERSUS UNIT SPLITTING

The dynamics of unit splitting are less favorable than those obtained by the fresh planting of new churches, especially in areas where member activity rates are low. Split units are not truly church plants but inherit many of the problems of the parent unit. Existing members bring established personalities, attitudes, and behaviors that are not always conducive to growth. Split units typically face preexisting activity problems from their inception, so that large amounts of missionary and member time are already diverted from community outreach to ongoing attempts to home teach and reactivate lost members. Nonetheless, even split units often achieve higher growth rates than their parent units, as long as the units retain an adequate core of active members to fulfill essential tasks.

CONGREGATIONAL SIZE, FELLOWSHIPPING, AND GROWTH

Many assume that the better staffing of peripheral programs in larger units results in better fellowshipping of newcomers than in smaller units. However, it is likely that the reverse may be true. C. Peter Wagner cited research that forty active adult members is the ideal size for members of a congregation to maintain personal relationships with everyone else.[*] He noted that this can expand to as many as eighty while still retaining most interpersonal and fellowshipping qualities. He continued: "When it goes past 80 toward 200 the relationships are increasingly strained. By the time it gets to 150 most groups are so stressed out that they can no longer handle the thought of strangers entering the group and thereby increasing the stress. Without knowing they are doing it or without even wanting to, they relate to strangers like two identical poles of magnets." Although unit size is only one of many factors influencing fellowshipping, many visitors have anecdotally reported being warmly welcomed by members in mission branches and small wards while being virtually ignored in some large wards.

---

[*]   Wagner, C. Peter, *Church Planting for a Greater Harvest*, Ventura, CA: Regal Books, 1990.

"BUILDING FROM CENTERS OF STRENGTH"

Since approximately 1993, the "building from centers of strength" policy has governed international LDS expansion. This policy focuses on building congregations in selected "centers of strength" and often directs missionaries to spend large amounts of time working with members and attempting to reclaim inactives. It relies on the assumptions that "critical mass" of members is necessary for church growth and that congregations become more effective and mature over time. The "centers of strength" program demonstrates awareness that prior methods of expansion often failed to build healthy and sustainable congregations and represents a response to very real concerns about poor convert retention and inadequate unit strength.

While its intentions are noble, the way in which the "centers of strength" policy has often been implemented has created new difficulties. The diversion of vast amounts of missionary time away from finding and teaching receptive people to less productive reactivation efforts has contributed to the sharp decline in LDS growth rates from 5 percent annually in the late 1980s to less than 3 percent at present. Directives to "strengthen members" and to "spend more time with less-actives" are often presented as nebulous vagaries that offer little practical insight, and reactivation successes have been meager. The "centers of strength" policy has drastically reduced the rate at which new, faster-growing congregations are organized in receptive areas. Expansion into new areas is based primarily on logistical and administrative considerations, while making little allowance for local conditions, needs, and opportunities. It is common for congregations to be established in several small cities surrounding a mission headquarters, while much larger cities in the mission area remain without any gospel witness for years or decades.

From both scriptural and practical standpoints, the "centers of strength" policy faces substantial difficulties. Neither Paul's missionary journeys nor Dan Jones' methods would be permissible under the modern "building from centers of strength" policy. Unique modern opportunities like that presented by the man from Macedonia in Paul's vision have been routinely declined. In Mongolia, the request of a local group with over one hundred families, who expressed a desire to join the LDS church, to send missionaries to their city located midway between two cities with existing congregations was declined without further investigation. One Latter-day Saint who traveled to Kenya noted: "I was told that even if a whole village was ready to be baptized, they could and would not oblige them. They were to stay in the large cities or areas where they already had large populations of Church members and build up a 'Center of Strength.'" The number of Protestants in Kyrgyzstan has grown from virtually zero to over 60,000 since 1993,* although no LDS missionaries had been assigned to the country through 2005. The Kostroma region has been a rare island of exceptional religious freedom in Russia since 1989 and is located in close proximity to the two Moscow missions, yet there have been no LDS efforts to proselyte anywhere in the entire region. Hundreds of other examples could be cited of remarkable opportunities that have been passed up while vast numbers of missionaries assigned to less productive areas experience little success.

It is difficult to see how policies that drastically restrict outreach can be construed to be consistent with repeated scriptural mandates to spread the gospel tent over the whole earth and "spare not." While the need for the Church to be established "in wisdom and in order" is undeniable, one wonders if there is wisdom in unresponsiveness and

---

* Johnstone, Patrick and Jason Mandryk, *Operation World*, Harrisonburg, VA: Paternoster, 2005.

inflexibility that do not allow the utilization of even the most remarkable opportunities. The "centers of strength" paradigm lacks the vision
of sounding the gospel in every ear embodied in saturation church
planting approaches, which maintain that local congregations should
be available to all people based on their receptivity and that outreach
to new areas should not be held hostage to the problems of stagnant
existing units and carnal members in other areas. LDS missionaries
belatedly arriving in new areas often find that many of the seekers
of earlier years have already been disciplined into other churches,
making outreach more difficult. The limiting factor in church growth
should be the receptivity and willingness of local people to accept the
gospel message, not our failure to provide them any opportunities.

If the concept of an obligatory "critical mass" of members represented the key to building successful congregations and if maturity
were an inevitable result of time or of missionary visit quotas, we
would expect to see great strength in nations where the Church has
been established for many years. Such areas—Japan, Mexico, Chile,
Brazil, and so forth—should represent model successes for the Church
in new areas. Yet in these nations, we find crises of rampant inactivity,
low home teaching, and declining growth rates far more frequently
than we find positive examples. If we are to believe that the "centers
of strength" in nations where the Church has long been established
represent successful worked models, then the future of "Mormonism"
looks bleak indeed. Fortunately, saturation church planting offers
more productive and exciting possibilities.

The real difficulties of the "building from centers of strength" policy
arise from misidentification of the root causes of congregational insta-
bility, slow growth, and low convert retention. Small international
congregations are not unstable because they lack a "critical mass" of
members, but because continued quick-baptism tactics generate vast

numbers of inactives while producing few committed converts who join the Church prepared to serve. Low retention is not primarily a problem of socialization that is solved by conglomerating larger and larger congregations but is improved by rigorous prebaptismal preparation of prospective converts to ensure lasting commitment. Members gain strength not by quotas of missionary social visits but by a consistent focus on daily scripture reading, personal prayer, tithing, church attendance, and adherence to other gospel laws. Properly organized new congregations can more quickly and consistently achieve rapid growth and spiritual self-sufficiency than older and larger ones with less flexible members and entrenched problems. When the true pathologies are understood, they can be remedied in more effective and scriptural ways that do not compromise our core mission to make the gospel message available to all people.

THE NEEDS-RESOURCE ALLOCATION MISMATCH

The average LDS missionary in North America spends only nine hours each week teaching investigators.[*] Having "no one to teach" or only a few investigators who are not progressing are the greatest frustrations of most LDS missionaries today. In contrast, teaching opportunities far exceed the ability of the small missionary contingent to meet with all receptive listeners in many developing nations. Interested prospective converts in areas of the world where proselyting is legal but where church units do not exist are told that they cannot be taught and that perhaps, if they are fortunate, some representatives may be assigned to their area years or decades from now. The needs-resource allocation mismatch is that the large majority of world missionary resources are directed toward a small fragment of

---

[*] Oaks, Dallin A., "The Role of Members in Conversion," *Ensign*, March 2003.

the world's population. Nearly two-thirds of LDS missions serve the 12 percent of the world's population that lives in North and South America, and less than one-sixth of the missionary force serves the least reached 80 percent of the world. Even in areas of the eastern hemisphere where LDS missionaries serve, outreach tends to be heavily skewed toward large urban centers and a few smaller satellite towns. "Centers of strength" perpetuates and exacerbates this needs-resource allocation mismatch by focusing a disproportionate amount of resources to established areas, while devoting little or no resources to larger areas with no gospel witness. If there is not time to "go over all Israel" and reach everyone in the world once, how can there be time to give a few fortunate peoples dozens or hundreds of opportunities at the neglect of others?

BUILDING SELF-SUFFICIENT AND SELF-PERPETUATING BRANCHES

Every missionary and mission leader should understand how new congregations can become self-sufficient and self-perpetuating from their inception, because local self-sufficiency leads to substantial increases in both long-term growth and retention. The volatile political situation in many nations permits local missionaries while limiting foreign ones, so the prompt and successful training of local members and missionaries is vital to reaching growth potential. Denominations that are able to rapidly and reliably organize many vibrant, growing, self-sufficient congregations with only a few full-time missionaries or expatriate member-missionaries have a tremendous advantage over faiths that require vast amounts of time and missionary manpower to organize a few struggling units.

The initial phase of laying the foundation of new congregations is often the most critical. The Apostle Paul wrote: "According to the grace of God which was given to me, as a wise master builder I have laid the foundation, and another builds on it. But let each one take heed how he builds on it" (1 Corinthians 3:10). Some new branches quickly become self-sustaining and self-perpetuating, while others grow stagnant in spite of the continued inflow of foreign missionary manpower and resources. Some converts join the Church better converted and more dedicated to service than many longtime members who lack essential gospel habits. What makes the difference? By consistently ensuring the presence of growth-generating gospel habits in new converts before baptism, effective missionaries can reproducibly and relatively rapidly establish branches of members who are spiritually self-sufficient. When the principles of proper teaching and preparation are not followed, newly created branches inevitably face rampant inactivity and serious member problems that no amount of time or "critical mass" of members is able to reverse fully.

Unless the active members are fully living the gospel and are avid fellowshippers, an existing member base is not necessarily an asset to church growth. Alma describes a situation where "the wickedness of the church was a great stumbling-block to those who did not belong to the church, and thus the church began to fail in its progress" (Alma 4:10). In contrast, Ammon and his brethren organized anew vibrant congregations consisting of the entire population of several cities. These units were created in areas without existing members who could provide mentorship and fellowshipping. Yet full retention was achieved "as many as were converted unto the Lord, never did fall away" (Alma 23:6). In the context of a weaker Nephite church plagued by frequent apostasy, exposure of the Anti-Nephi-Lehite investigators to Nephite congregations would not have been a positive event. The paradigm of the Anti-Nephi-Lehites, whose righteousness exceeded that of the Nephites, may provide a more suitable model for the

Church in new areas than the centers of strength "Church of Zara-hemla" or "Church in Utah" model. Church units do not have to be stagnant to be solid.

The Church can often be built up for real and sustained growth more successfully in new areas, where prospective members can be taught correctly from the beginning, than in established areas, where many existing members hindered missionary efforts through inconsistent examples, casual attitudes toward gospel laws, and cliquish behavior. By 1993, one of the first two branches formed in my mission city had been split into five branches, while the other branch had barely grown at all and could not be divided. In part, this was due to the disruptive behavior of a few active members in the second branch who managed to offend or embarrass most investigators. I spent the first seven months of my mission in another branch which was experiencing similar problems. While we experienced some success finding through our own efforts, a copy of the Book of Mormon was returned to me on several occasions by investigators who stated that they liked its message and enjoyed our discussions but did not want to return to the local congregation since they did not feel any spirituality or friendship from the members. It was often impossible to inspire such investigators to join the Church when member conduct was visibly inconsistent with gospel principles. In contrast, I later had the opportunity to serve in one exceptionally well-functioning branch, where similar missionary efforts produced tremendous results, because investigators were positively impressed not only by the Book of Mormon and the missionary discussions, but also by the quality of church services and the examples of church members. Vibrant, missionary-oriented congregations can be a great asset to missionary work, but relatively few LDS congregations fit this description.

At the time a companion and I opened a city in Russia for missionary work, there were three part-active members in the city who had previously been baptized elsewhere and a larger number of inactives. The core of our active membership came almost exclusively from investigators whom we taught and baptized. Instead of serving as a core for the "center of strength," the old semiactive members were inconsistent in attendance and in the fulfillment of other church responsibilities. The newly baptized members who were taught with more rigorous standards and better preparation than the older members achieved greater consistency in the fulfillment of daily scripture reading, weekly church attendance, and other basic gospel habits than some individuals who had been members for several years. Later, another companion and I worked to revitalize a group in a major city with approximately thirty nominal members of whom approximately five were active or part-active. Missionary work in the area had been very slow previously, and missionaries had struggled to build a functioning congregation. Although we worked intensively with existing members, by the time we left three months later, seven of the ten who attended weekly were individuals whom we had taught and baptized. Once again, we found that new converts who were properly taught were better able to live up to basic gospel standards and strengthen the Church than long-time members who had been taught and baptized by missionaries employing accelerated baptism approaches.

SUBSIDIZATION AND DEPENDENCY

LDS leaders have long cited the need for local missions to become self-sufficient, both for manpower and for funds. Most international LDS missions are still heavily reliant on both U.S. missionaries and U.S. funds for the work of the Church. In many cases, it is difficult to determine how years of missionary effort have built genuine "centers of strength." In Germany, LDS membership actually declined between 1996 and 2004 in spite of the efforts of four to six full-time missions. The greatest church growth experienced in Germany within the past fifty years was in East Germany before the fall of the Berlin Wall, when local member-missionaries successfully found, taught, and baptized new members without the help of North American elders and sisters. When North American missionaries were introduced, growth and retention rates declined sharply. Prolonged subsidization of stagnant areas with North American missionaries may foster complacency, reduce member participation, and take the feeling of ownership and responsibility for local growth away from native members. Even in areas where relatively greater church growth is occurring (although with fractional retention), such as Latin America and the Philippines, U.S. missionaries and U.S. money continue to serve as the major drivers of both expansion and maintenance efforts. Longtime wards and stakes in these areas have not achieved sufficient health or vitality to provide for their own needs, let alone those of their communities.

When a new congregation is organized, it is generally expected that missionaries will be permanently assigned with no exit strategy. In the early Church, itinerant missionaries built up healthy congregations and then left, with leaders visiting from time to time to provide supervision. Rapidly growing denominations today send full-time missionaries to get new units standing on their own feet as quickly as possible before moving on to new areas. The goal of self-sufficiency must be established from the outset. The best time to set the church in order is at the beginning.

OUTREACH: COMMUNITY OR CORE-BASED?

Effective missionary approaches all make the gospel message widely available while allowing investigators to select themselves out based on their level of interest and commitment. As a result of focusing on core-based approaches and neglecting community approaches, the Church experienced slow growth in Eastern Europe, falling far short of expectations at times when other faiths were experiencing unprecedented growth. By the time a solid core of LDS members had been trained and the missions were ready to contemplate earnest member-missionary outreach, the prior high level of spontaneous religious interest in the community was gone. The seekers of prior years had either been absorbed into other denominations, or they had succumbed to growing materialism. Getting even trained core members to reach out and share the gospel became a continuing struggle.

Rick Warren wrote:

I suggest you grow the church from the outside in, rather than from the inside out. Start with your community, not your core! This is opposite the advice given by most books on church planting. The traditional approach to beginning a new church is to build a committed core of mature believers first, and then start reaching out to the community. The problem I have found with an 'inside-out' approach is that by the time the church planter has 'disciplined' his core, they have often lost contact with the community and are actually afraid of interacting with the unchurched. It's easy to ... [develop] such a close knit fellowship that newcomers are afraid or unable to break into it. Too often, a core group planning a new church spends so long in the small group stage that they become comfortable with it and lose their sense of mission. The fire of evangelism dies out. The problem with most small churches is that they are all core and nothing else. The same fifty people come to everything the church does. They've all been Christians for so long they have few … unbelieving friends to witness to.*

The best time to firmly establish member habits of daily scripture reading, Sabbath Day observance, and consistently sharing the gospel with nonmembers is before baptism, not at some future date when members have reached an arbitrarily defined state of maturity. Attempts to instill such basic gospel habits in "mature" members who have reached a comfort zone and began to stagnate are far less successful than efforts starting well before baptism to ensure that prospective members are consistently implementing core gospel laws from the beginning.

LDS MEMBER-MISSIONARY CHURCH PLANTERS

Church planters are typically full-time missionaries, although LDS expatriate members serving as church planters without official assignment in the Russian Far East, Armenia, Georgia, Kazakhstan, and other areas have been some of the most fruitful member-missionaries of the modern age. Even today, many of the active LDS members in Magadan, Vladivostok, and Yerevan are acquaintances of the early member-missionary church planters. Similarly, senior couple missionaries with little grasp of the local language and limited work schedules achieved an initial degree of success in Mongolia that has rarely been approached by larger numbers of linguistically proficient young missionaries. The increased strength of units started in this way relates to the greater strength of investigators and members who are not subsidized during the teaching process or after baptism, helping them to achieve a degree of self-sufficiency from the outset. The lack of pressure on investigators for rapid baptism from member-missionary church planters with professional and family responsibilities is also

---

*   Warren, Rick, *The Purpose Driven Church*, Grand Rapids, MI: Zondervan, 1995, 138–39.

helpful in attracting a higher quality of converts than is achieved by full-time missionaries who employ accelerated baptism tactics.

While LDS member-missionary church planters have achieved significant success working in isolation, better training, coordination, and strategic planning could expand the benefits of member-missionary church planting to many other areas. The Seventh-Day Adventists have institutionalized the organization and coordination of member-missionary tentmaker programs in the Global Mission Pioneer program, contributing to rapid, consistent, and widespread growth in receptive areas.

THE ECONOMICS OF CHURCH PLANTING

Church planter C. Peter Wagner wrote:

A pragmatic objection you will hear is that we can't plant new churches because the start-up cost is too high. The truth of the matter is that in terms of dollars spent by the sponsoring church or agency, new church planting can be the most cost-effective method of evangelization. I like Lyle Schaller's reply to some Methodist leaders who told him that if they started 500 new churches they would need $100 million, and that there was no way they could find the money. Schaller says, "That is the wrong question based on questionable assumptions.... A better beginning point is the Great Commission (Matthew 28:18–20). "... Back in 1980 I was invited to do a pastors' seminar for a presbytery in Texas. They were rather pleased to tell me that they had started two new churches in the past decade and that they were planning another for the 1980s. I asked them why only one. "That's all we can afford right now," they replied. On impulse I asked them how much each one cost and they told me it was $500,000 per church. I made a mental note. One month later I did a similar seminar for the pastors of an Assemblies of God district in North Carolina.... As I was having lunch with the district superintendent, Charles Cookman, I asked him how many new churches they had started in the 1970s. "Oh," he said, "I'm glad you asked. We set a goal of 70 new churches for the seventies, but we actually planted 85." Again on impulse I asked him how much they cost. He did some calculations on his paper place mat and said, "Each one cost about $2,500." No wonder the growth rate of the Assemblies of God is several times that of the Presbyterian Church (U.S.A.). It costs Presbyterians 200 times as much to start a new church! Of course, the Presbyterians operate on a set of assumptions that the Assemblies of God do not. They assume that the founding pastor needs a college and seminary education ... and that land and a building are necessary up front. Those assumptions require a substantial budget. In the long run the Assemblies of God church is also worth $500,000, but their assumption is that the money to pay for staff, land, and buildings should come from the people subsequently won into the new church rather than up front.[*]

By focusing on church planting and minimizing assumptions of what is needed to start a new congregation, the Assemblies of God have achieved high growth rates even in areas that have traditionally been considered recalcitrant to evangelism. At present, 10,000 people per day are joining the Assemblies of God, while Methodists are actually losing ground. Dr. Wagner further noted: "My friend, Carl F. George ... was called in for consultation with the leaders of a regional body of one of the mainline denominations. They wanted

---

[*]   Wagner, C. Peter, *Church Planting for a Greater Harvest*, Ventura, CA: Regal Books, 1990.

him to identify barriers to growth. He discovered a budget item of $250,000 per year for the support of a number of 'missions' that in 30 years had not been able to become viable enough to support themselves. He also discovered that they said they couldn't afford to plant new churches. George wisely persuaded them to close the missions and divert the $250,000 per year into new church development. It made all the difference in the world."*

Even without a paid clergy, Latter-day Saint church planting operates under assumptions that more rapidly growing faiths do not. Contemporary LDS mission paradigms insist that every newly opened city or congregation requires the permanent assignment of at least one full-time missionary companionship and a freestanding Western-style meetinghouse to be built within a few years, almost always with funds from the U.S. church. While the intention of such policies is to ensure that new converts are well-cared for, such practices are more restricting than empowering. They ultimately hamper growth by making outreach in new areas prohibitively expensive, while stifling local self-sufficiency and condemning nascent congregations to patterns of dependency from their inception. Under such paradigms, opening new cities for missionary work is a losing proposition: members are viewed as resource-consuming liabilities rather than as productive assets. This is not because church planting is ineffective but because of nonscriptural assumptions that make the cost of expansion into new areas prohibitive. The greatest asset of the Church is not its fixed real estate, but the testimony and conviction of its members.

The cost of a single LDS chapel in Ufa, Russia, is estimated at $2.5 million by one media source.† Other LDS meetinghouses in Eastern

---

* Wagner, C. Peter, *Church Planting for a Greater Harvest*, Ventura, CA: Regal Books, 1990.

† "Mormonsky Khram Otrkylsya v Ufe," [Mormon Church Opens in Ufa—

Europe have cost several hundred thousand dollars each—many times that which local tithes can ever be reasonably expected to collect. Faster-growing denominations have found inexpensive but reliable ways to provide international church facilities. Some faiths build churches from appropriate materials that are available locally, whether wood or bricks, bamboo in Southeast Asia, or even mud and straw in Sub-Saharan Africa. Others meet in members' homes. Still others purchase and remodel apartments as houses of worship. Meetinghouse policies help one to understand why the Seventh-Day Adventists start more new congregations in Russia, Ukraine, and many other areas of the world in a single year than Latter-day Saints are able to start in a decade. In Russia and Ukraine, the Seventh-Day Adventists purchased 291 church meeting places, including apartments, cottages, and other sites, for a total of $3.5 million.*

THE CHURCH AND THE CHAPEL

As a missionary in Russia in the early 1990s, I found that many members and missionaries spoke of anticipated chapels as a panacea to growth problems. Low growth and activity? Poor convert retention? Lack of respect in the community? A chapel would change everything, many claimed. In 2000, Dr. Thomas F. Rogers, my former second mission president, conducted a survey of seventeen current and prior mission presidents in the former Soviet Union to assess perceptions of the challenges of church growth. One of his most startling findings was that respondents cited the lack of permanent church buildings as one of the major causes of low convert retention and member activity rates. President Rogers rightly challenged this assumption,

---

Russian], *Mir Religii*, May 30, 2001.

*   Kellner, Mark, "Russia: Church Planters Near Goals in Former Soviet Union," *Adventist News Network*, June 17, 2003, http://news.crosswalk.com.

noting: "During my first mission in North Germany and Berlin ten years after World War II, we observed how at least five beautiful new chapels—donated by a former president of our mission and millionaire—were rarely half full, and the spirit in them correspondingly tepid, by contrast with the Begeisterung with which our East German members crowded into the dilapidated near ruins they had managed to rent near Berlin Alexanderplatz and elsewhere in the East Zone."[*]

Over the past decade, dozens of meetinghouses have been constructed or remodeled from existing structures throughout Eastern Europe, even in cities with relatively few active members—Klaipeda, Vilnius, Engels, Solnichny, Sochi, Tallinn, Cherkassi, Ploesti, Ufa, Vyborg, Gorlovka, Donetsk, Debrecen, Gyor, Dunaujvaros, Szekesfehervar, three in Budapest, and many more. Now that an increasing number of chapels have been built in the Former Soviet Union, many are still underfilled and underutilized.

My research has found no evidence that the construction of chapels has had any measurable, independent, positive impact upon growth, convert retention, or member activity. In the most cases, the growth rate of local units actually slowed after chapels were built. As missionaries in St. Petersburg, my companions and I had ten or twenty investigators attending branches in rented schoolhouses or music halls on many Sundays. Members who have visited the chapels that have since been erected have commented both on the beautiful atmosphere and on the paucity of investigators. This slowing can often be attributed to other factors, but there are some instances where chapels have actually harmed local growth. Two branches in one city in Hungary were consolidated due to severe member contention over

---

[*]   Rogers, Thomas F., "Mormonism's First Decade in the Former USSR: Patterns of Growth and Retention," Presentation at Mormon History Association Meeting, Copenhagen, Denmark, June 2000.

meetinghouse-related issues that resulted in mass inactivity. In many other cities, member activity and church growth have declined due to much longer travel distances to remote freestanding chapels than to prior, more central rental accommodations.

The fact that the absence of chapels was the most common "cause" of low retention cited by many mission presidents reveals little about church growth but provides a fascinating window into our own assumptions and difficulty in dissociating the blessings of "the Church" from fixed religious real estate. As President Rogers correctly noted in his insightful analysis, church growth does not depend on buildings. It depends on faith and the consistent application of scriptural outreach principles.

CHURCHES WITHOUT WALLS

In contrast to widespread modern assumptions about the indispensability of freestanding chapels, both the scriptures and LDS history suggest that buildings are of little relevance to Church growth. The early Christian church was primarily a house church with few real estate holdings. Paul wrote: "Salute the brethren which are in Laodicea, and Nymphas, and the church which is in his house" (Colossians 4:15). When sent to Rome, Paul preached the gospel for two years from a hired house (Acts 28:30). Numerous other passages refer to apostles living and teaching in the houses of local members in their travels, allowing the gospel to be widely preached while minimizing expenses.

Christ taught that it is the gathering and not the building that gives life to our worship: "For where two or three are gathered together in my name, there am I in the midst of them" (Matthew 18:20). Paul noted: "Every house is builded by some man; but he that built all things is God" (Hebrews 3:4). Alma's efforts to dispel the notion that worship can occur only in designated meetinghouses is as relevant to modern mission planners as to the ancient Zoramites: "Behold thy brother hath said, What shall we do? For we are cast out of our synagogues, that we cannot worship our God. Behold I say unto you, do ye suppose that ye cannot worship God save it be in your synagogues only? And moreover, I would ask, do ye suppose that ye must not worship God only once in a week? I say unto you, it is well that ye are cast out of your synagogues, that ye may be humble, and that ye may learn wisdom" (Alma 32:9–12).

The most spectacular LDS growth has historically occurred in areas without meetinghouses, and the same is true today. Many years elapsed between the restoration of the Church in 1830 and the construction of the first LDS meetinghouse. The Church of Jesus Christ of Latter-day Saints was initially a "house church" meeting in homes, stores, and even in the open air. Resources were directed to the printing of the Book of Mormon, missionary travel, and other projects far more important than the construction of meetinghouses. The most successful modern missionaries, including Dan Jones, Brigham Young, Wilford Woodruff, and others, rarely had the benefit of an LDS chapel in which to preach. While buildings provide amenities, they do not build testimony. The lack of a freestanding meetinghouse cannot hinder growth, although the misplaced belief that buildings are essential can become an impediment.

The fastest growing churches worldwide are churches without meetinghouses. In recent years, cell churches or house churches—organized religious groups meeting in the homes of members—have achieved sustained, dramatic growth rates in many areas.* Such groups generally also experience warm fellowshipping and high retention.

---

*   "Missionaries Doing Whatever It Takes," ReligionToday.com feature story, April 24, 2000, http://news.crosswalk.com.

In China alone, conservative estimates suggest that the house church movement has attracted 30 to 40 million adherents. David Garrison and many other church planting experts have pointed out that chapels funded on foreign money can breed dependency and stunt growth.[*] Church planter C. Peter Wagner stated: "Mark Platt ... says, 'There is great wisdom in delaying the purchase and development of property so that the new church can put its best efforts ministering to people.' I agree.... I do not think I am wrong in saying that the most common conscious decision that church planters have made through the years to lock their church under the 200 barrier is to buy and build too soon. I recommend that you postpone buying land, and especially building as long as you possibly can. In most cases when you first begin thinking, 'Maybe it's time to build now,' it's probably too soon. Postpone building at least until you are past the 200 barrier with 350 active adults, or better yet 500."[†] Rick Warren, pastor of the fastest-growing Baptist church in the history of the United States, wrote: "To accommodate our continuous growth we used seventy-nine different facilities in the first fifteen years of Saddleback's history.... I'm often asked, 'How big can a church grow without a building?' The answer is, 'I don't know!' Saddleback met for fifteen years and grew to 10,000 attenders without our own building, so I know it's possible to grow to at least 10,000! A building, or lack of a building, should never be allowed to become a barrier to a wave of growth. People are far more important than property."[‡] My Protestant acquaintances who have served as successful church-planting pastors or missionaries consis-

---

[*]   Garrison, David, *Church Planting Movements*, Southern Baptist International Mission Board, October 1999, http://www.imb.org/CPM/default.htm.

[†]   Wagner, C. Peter, *Church Planting for a Greater Harvest*, Ventura, CA: Regal Books, 1990.

[‡]   Warren, Rick, *The Purpose Driven Church*, Grand Rapids, MI: Zondervan, 1995, 46

tently give one piece of counsel: "Don't construct a church building too early." The LDS policy of building meetinghouses in new areas based on raw membership alone without regard to member activity or tithing faithfulness was reversed only in 2001, leaving hundreds of expensive but underutilized church buildings throughout the world. The construction of a chapel can slow growth momentum. The church without walls is not a relic of the past but the wave of the future for exponential growth in frontier areas.

LOCATION, LOCATION, LOCATION

Accessibility and visibility are the first and second most important factors, respectively, in selecting meeting place locations. While many denominations position their churches strategically on main roads to attract walk-in visitors, North American LDS meetinghouses are frequently tucked away deep in residential neighborhoods where few nonlocals are aware of their existence. Well-chosen locations offer many benefits. In Kyiv, Ukraine, the mission rented a central cultural palace on a main street as one of its meeting places. In Ulaan Baatar, Mongolia, a central, well known historic children's theater was remodeled into a chapel. The prominent and centrally accessible locations contributed significantly to attracting more investigators without regard to whether the location was owned or rented.

The Polish Warsaw chapel was first chapel built in Eastern Europe. It is a beautiful and expansive edifice built on donated funds not long after missionaries first entered the country. Yet after its construction, the church in Warsaw collapsed from six branches down to one and has remained at just one native branch through the time of this writing in spite of having over four hundred members on the rolls. Warsaw has also had the lowest activity rate of any major city in Poland, although it was the only Polish city with an LDS chapel for many years. While space does not allow comprehensive discussion of all challenges here, I believe that poor location is one of several major factors that have harmed growth. In a city with over 1.6 million residents, the Warsaw chapel is located on the far western periphery. When I visited in 1999, a taxi ride from the city center to the chapel cost $9 U.S., a prohibitive sum for local members. A one-way trip to the chapel on public transportation typically took between one and two hours from other regions of the city. Members and investigators who lived in central areas of the city found that the location was inconvenient; for those the other side of town, inconvenience bordered on inaccessibility. Many programs were considered over the years to identify and address the low activity and retention rates, but none seemed to consider the remote location of the meetinghouse as a factor. Neither the beauty of the chapel nor its fine facilities compensated for its inaccessibility and inconvenience of both time and money for members and investigators. In the rush to build a freestanding chapel, mission and area leaders failed to consider the needs of local people.

In Riga, Latvia, local congregations met in a humble yet capacious remodeled apartment in the city center. The location was convenient and could be easily reached from anywhere in the city. A visiting authority noted that the facilities were among the best in Eastern Europe. A year later, the construction of a freestanding chapel on the periphery of the city was announced to replace the prior accommodations. Whatever the facilities, the new location could only disadvantage members and investigators.

An LDS member who travels extensively internationally wrote:

I do informal surveys of Church members in developing countries of the cost of transportation to get to church. In many cases, it is simply astounding the costs to reach church. Many times, I have found that members are spending 20 to 30 percent

of their monthly income to pay for transportation costs to get
to church. What member in the United States would be willing
to pay 20 to 30 percent of their income, on top of tithing and
fast offerings to be part of church? I was a branch president in
Portugal of a large, geographically dispersed branch, with about
100 active and about 400 in the branch. I laid out where all
the members lived and plotted the bus routes they had to take
to get to church. We found that some had to make three bus
connections and that their bus fares added up to a significant
portion of their monthly income. We convinced the mission
president to split the branch and rented a store front next to a
major bus terminal, that any place in the city could get to in
one trip, and within two weeks of splitting, we had doubled
our attendance and now had two branches with both 100 in
attendance. In Kenya, when you attend church, you find congregations of almost entirely male members. I asked where the
wives and children were, and I was told that they could not
afford to have the rest of the family come, so the fathers would
come and hear the teachings and then go home and share what
they learned with their families. For those in priesthood positions, who have to come to church multiple times during the
week, the cost of transportation becomes an enormous financial
burden. I think little consideration is given to the actual cost to
the local members in regard to transportation. I would much
rather see a dozen small storefronts that are filled each Sunday
throughout a city rather than two large beautiful chapels that
are mostly empty.

FINDING THE CHURCH

Missionaries work hard to find investigators. Can interested investigators find the Church? The LDS Internet meetinghouse locator has been extremely helpful in recent years, although many international contacts do not have Internet access and meeting times are not listed for many international units. A senior missionary serving in a large Central European capital told of an LDS member who moved to the city. She looked for the Church for two or three months but was unable to establish contact. The only LDS number listed in the local telephone directory was for a family history office which was open only two evenings per week for two hours, so the telephone rang unanswered when she called at various times. After several months of searching, she encountered LDS missionaries on the street and was able to get church meeting information. Many investigators and members have reported having difficulty connecting up with the Church in their area before making the connection under fortuitous circumstances. One wonders how many others were not so fortunate. A chapel telephone number is of little value unless it is listed in the telephone book and there is either a person there to answer it regularly or there is a message with useful information. Many newspapers allow religious groups to announce meeting times and locations at minimal cost, and other community opportunities for publicizing the local congregation may be available. The "visitors welcome" sign on almost all LDS meetinghouses is enigmatic, since I have never seen any accompanying sign that would inform prospective visitors of the time or day that meetings are held. Expecting nonmembers to receive personal revelation about meeting times is a less effective finding method.

MEN, WOMEN, AND THE GOSPEL

TOO MANY WOMEN?

MANY CONGREGATIONS OF THE international Church struggle with the lack of adequate local priesthood leadership and small numbers of active Melchizedek priesthood holders. A predominance of female attendees is frequently noted. "There are too many women in the [local] Church," stated one mission president. The problem of "too many women" is a frequent theme of discussion by missionaries and mission leaders and has been the target of numerous local initiatives over the years in the form of restrictions on the teaching of women in order to remedy the lack of local priesthood and "fix" the imbalance. Yet official LDS membership statistics today show that 49 percent of LDS members are male, while 51 percent are female. An examination of the membership rolls of most units where the problem of "too many women" is noted typically reveals the presence of a large number of adult male members, the vast majority of whom are inactive. Even in nations where mission leaders have long decried the paucity of local priesthood leadership, national census data show only marginally more female than male members. The 2002 Chilean census demonstrated relative parity between self-identified female and male LDS members, especially among young adults—20,985 versus 20,780 in the fifteen to twenty-nine range and 18,700 versus 14,617 in the thirty to forty-four range. The real pathology is not that too many sisters are living their covenants, but that international male activity and retention rates are low.

RETENTION OF MALE AND FEMALE MEMBERS

While North American data suggest that that the retention rate of female converts is only slightly higher than of male converts, the discrepancy in some international areas is much greater. Lowell C. "Ben" Bennion and Lawrence Young report: "For the U.S. as a whole, only 59% of baptized males ever receive the Melchizedek Priesthood. In the South Pacific, the figure drops to 35%; in Great Britain, 29%. In Mexico (with almost 850,000 members) the figure is 19%; and in Japan, only 17% of the male members ever make it past the Aaronic Priesthood."[*] A review of ordination statistics from the 1983 LDS Church Almanac reveals that the rate was 70 percent in Utah, 52 percent in Canada, 39 percent in Africa, 38 percent in Scandinavia, 34 percent in Europe, 25 percent in South America and the West Indies, 23 percent in Central America, and 21 percent in Asia. While by far not all members who have received the Melchizedek Priesthood remain active, it would be extremely unusual for an adult male who remains active to not be advanced beyond the Aaronic Priesthood. Armand Mauss noted: "In order to form new stakes you have to have a certain number of active priesthood holders. If we cannot hold our new male converts around long enough to get the Melchizedek priesthood, we cannot create new stakes."[†]

Bennion noted that "one couple who returned from Quezon

---

[*]   Bennion, Lowell C. and Lawrence Young, "The Uncertain Dynamics of LDS Expansion, 1950–2020," *Dialogue*, 29/1 (Spring 1996): 19.

[†]   Stack, Peggy Fletcher, "Growing LDS Church Goes Global," *Salt Lake Tribune*, February 10, 1996.

City in the Philippines in 1993 reported that only 30 percent of their mission's members were active, and 90 percent of the active members were female."* Although many males were baptized, few became participating members. Peggy Fletcher Stack reported that in Brazil "the wards and branches sometimes are like dysfunctional families, with overwhelming social needs and too few capable male volunteers to staff the all-male administration. Men make up less than one quarter of the converts and only a small percentage stay active long enough to fill administrative positions."† International LDS units where the number of active adult men approaches the number of active adult women are rare.

The gender discrepancy among active members is not new, nor is it restricted only to international areas. Goodman and Heaton wrote in a 1986 article that "for every 100 LDS women in the prime marriage ages (20–29 years) there [were] 89 LDS men."‡ They further noted that the gender disparity among active LDS single adults in North America was even more out of balance: "For all singles over 30 there are 19 active men [who attend church weekly] for every 100 active women." They write that single LDS men and women are "mismatched on vital demographic characteristics. Single women over thirty have higher levels of education, occupation, and Church activity than single men. Marriage to an active male is demographically impossible for many active single females over thirty. And even when there are available males, they may possess other characteristics that rule them out as potential mates. Obviously, marriage is not a universal solution to

*   Stack, Peggy Fletcher, "Growing LDS Church Goes Global," *Salt Lake Tribune*, February 10, 1996.

†   Stack, Peggy Fletcher, "Brazil Leaves Impression on LDS Church," *Salt Lake Tribune*, April 5, 2003.

‡   Goodman, Kristen L. and Tim B. Heaton, "LDS Church Members in the U.S. and Canada: A Demographic Profile," *AMCAP Journal*, 12/1 (1986): 88–107.

singleness if the only acceptable marital option is marriage to an active LDS partner."[*]

THE GENDER DISPARITY AND RELIGIOSITY

The higher religiosity of women in almost all religious faiths has been noted from time immemorial. William Alexander, Earl of Sterling, observed in 1637 that women were "to piety more prone." Almost all faiths that report participation by gender report a preponderance of women. A casual observer attending a Catholic mass, a Protestant sermon, or an Orthodox liturgy in almost any country will typically find that women attendees outnumber men, often significantly. George Barna found that women make up 60 percent of participating Christians and that women are more likely than men to read the Bible, pray, share the belief in Christ with friends and acquaintances over the course of a year (27 percent versus 21 percent), serve as a spiritual mentor (19 percent versus 13 percent), set personal spiritual goals (41 percent versus 29 percent), and participate in discipleship programs.[†]

Studies of Latter-day Saints have demonstrated similar findings. James Duke noted: "Barry Johnson and I did a study a few years ago of LDS families. We included 31 different items or measures of religiosity. Of these items, women were more religious on 26 items, one item was essentially even, and men were more religious on only four items.... Women are more likely to feel they are strong members, to attend church weekly, to pray daily, to feel their prayers are answered,

---

[*]   Goodman, Kristen L. and Tim B. Heaton, "LDS Church Members in the U.S. and Canada: A Demographic Profile," *AMCAP Journal*, 12/1 (1986): 88–107.

[†]   Wingfield, Mark, "Women Carrying Big Load at Church," *The Baptist Standard*, April 3, 2000.

and to have spiritual experiences."*

The spiritual devotion of women has been observed even in non-Christian cultures. Mahatma Gandhi stated: "To call women the weaker sex is a libel: it is man's injustice to woman. If by strength is meant brute strength, then indeed, is woman less brute than man. If by strength is meant moral power, then woman is immeasurably man's superior. Has she not greater intuition, is she not more self-sacrificing, has she not greater powers of endurance, has she not greater courage?"† Rates of alcoholism, tobacco use, drug abuse, and violent crimes are lower among women than men worldwide. In virtually every nation, the vast majority of the prison population consists of men, while most regular church attendees are women. One wonders if we should not accept that a somewhat higher rate of religious participation among women is a normal state and not a pathology to be stamped out. Trying to "fix" the situation generally proves to be frustrating and unproductive, like swimming against the tide or trying to defy gravity.

STUNTED GROWTH

In one family member's mission, the mission president mandated that women had to attend church at least three times to even receive a copy of the Book of Mormon or to receive the missionary discussions. One wonders if such an arbitrary criterion represents a valid indicator of spirituality when interested visitors are denied the teaching that provides them the impetus to return. On several occasions, I have seen missionaries following their mission policies turn away interested

---

* Duke, James T., "Latter-day Saints in a Secular World: What We Have Learned about Latter-day Saints from Social Research," Martin B Hickman 1999 Lecture, Brigham Young University, College of Family, Home, and Social Sciences, March 4, 1999, http://fhss.byu.edu/adm/hickman_lecture.htm.

† Mahatma Gandhi, as quoted in *Young India*, April 10, 1930.

female investigators who attended church without so much as offering a copy of the Book of Mormon or a missionary discussion. Yet the same missionaries would often make multiple visits to male investigators who had never taken the effort to attend church even once. I know of several other missions with similar policies designed to increase the proportion of male baptisms by restricting the teaching of women rather than through better outreach to men. It is difficult to imagine that this is what Christ had in mind when he sent forth His disciples to teach the gospel to every creature. In almost every case, such policies have predictably led to significant declines in the overall conversion rate and have slowed increase in active membership. Although few missions enforce such restrictive policies, the fact that they exist at all suggests that better education of leaders is necessary.

Some programs have fostered selective sharing of the gospel based on gender. A 1998 *Ensign* article referred to a new program in Central America advocated by the area presidency: "The goal is to have what we refer to as the 'shepherding ratio' be 10 members per active priesthood holder. Missionaries are concentrating on baptizing potential Melchizedek Priesthood holders, with the goal of adult men representing at least 25 percent of total baptisms."* While the "shepherding ratio" concept of 10 members per active Melchizedek priesthood holder might sound reasonable to someone with no familiarity with the international Church, the reality that member activity rates in Latin America typically run at 20 to 25 percent or below would mandate that Melchizedek priesthood holders constitute 40 to 50 percent of active membership in order to achieve just one active Melchizedek priesthood holder for every ten total members. Such a rate is incompatible with a family church seeking to involve men, women, and

---

*   "News of the Church. Conversation: The Church in Central America," *Ensign*, August 1998, 79.

children. The percent of active membership this would represent is not even achieved in Utah and would be unachievable in most Latin American missions due to fractional activity rates.

The goal of building congregations of faithful active members is far more important than achieving contrived demographic ratios in inactivity-ridden areas. Initiatives based on the misdiagnosis of "too many women" predictably generate their own pathologies. If the right leg is injured, is it appropriate to cripple the left leg to make the two similar? What would turning away an interested investigator of one gender possibly have to do with gaining an investigator of the other? There can never be too many women, men, or any kind of people in the Church. The gospel is for all people willing to obey God's commands. God is not a respecter of persons, and one soul is as precious as another.

The solution to the problem of few active international priesthood holders must involve improving male convert retention rather than discouraging prospective female converts. Programs of adequate prebaptismal preparation can triple or quadruple local convert retention rates in low-retaining areas and are far more effective at building a strong local priesthood leadership base than artificial attempts to increase the proportion of men by restricting the teaching of women. It is possible to focus outreach efforts on men and families without discouraging receptive seekers of either gender.

WOMEN AND GROWTH

The immense contribution of women to the growth of the Church has often been underappreciated. While I focused my finding efforts as a missionary primarily on men and families (and, I believe, appropriately so), I have come to appreciate that many young women baptized in their teens by other missionaries have gone on to serve as the core of the native missionary force in nations such as Russia, Ukraine, and Mongolia. Mongolia, which has the highest rate of convert missionary service in the world, sent out a number of native elders approaching the number of native sister missionaries for the first time only in 2003. On my mission in Russia, several of the strongest branch presidents and local leaders were men who had been former atheists but were been baptized several years after their wives or daughters after seeing the fruits of the gospel in their lives. Most of them expressed no interest at all in the gospel when their wives joined. Had their female family members been turned away from the Church because of policies to teach only men and families, these priesthood leaders would have been lost to the Church. Many young men and women raised in the Church by convert mothers have gone on to serve missions and strengthen local units. I have often wondered how many thousands of such more have been lost to the Church forever because of policies restricting outreach to their wives and mothers. Every woman has male family members and acquaintances, and women often have an influence on men that other men do not. Faithful women who are living and sharing the gospel inevitably bring faithful men into the Church as well, yet the souls of women are of equal value in their own right.

Female LDS members account for the majority of member-missionary referrals. Similar trends exist in other denominations. The average Jehovah's Witness puts in over sixteen hours each month witnessing to others, and 56 to 75 percent of Jehovah's Witnesses are women.[*] George Barna reported in a 1994 study that most U.S. Christian evangelizers are women. David Yonggi Cho, pastor of the world's largest church, the 750,000-member Yoido Full Gospel Church in

---

[*]   Stark, Rodney and Laurence R. Iannaccone, "Why the Jehovah's Witnesses Grow So Rapidly: A Theoretical Application," *Journal of Contemporary Religion*, May 1997, p. 140.

Seoul, South Korea, stated: "Women are underused in the church. We use them on telephone—they talk constantly—they love to talk on the phone. Put Jesus in their mouth to talk! So women are a tremendous strength in church because of culture—but in Western culture—you are afraid of using women. But once women were given the freedom to work [as member-missionaries] ... there was an explosion of [church growth]."* One woman brought 365 families into Yonggi Cho's church within a single year.

Missionary work continues to be seen as primarily a priesthood responsibility, yet the role of women as investigators, member-missionaries, and missionaries is at least as significant as the role of men. A focus on fully involving both men and women to build the Kingdom of God is necessary to achieve optimal church growth.

---

* "Breakfast with David Yonggi Cho and Rick Warren: A Conversation between Two Innovative Pastors," July 23, 2001, http://www.pastors.com/articles/ChoInterview.asp.

Convert Retention for Leaders

THE MAIN ELEMENTS OF effective retention programs are discussed in the earlier Convert Retention chapter. This section can help mission leaders to identify causes of continued poor convert retention beyond the purview of individual missionaries that have unwittingly been perpetuated in modern programs. An awareness of history can help us to understand what can be done to stem the losses and dramatically improve convert retention in harmony with standards set by scriptures and modern prophets.

ACTUAL PERFORMANCE VERSUS THE DIVINE MANDATE

It is striking to compare the scriptural teachings and results of the Book of Mormon and early LDS missionaries to the British Isles to the fractional retention rates of the modern LDS missionary program. From 1840 to 1890, over 97 percent of LDS converts baptized in the British Isles left relatives and property and crossed land and sea to join the saints.* President Hinckley counseled that "it is not necessary that we should lose [any of] those who are baptized,"† yet only one-

---

*   Stark, Rodney, "The Basis of Mormon Success: A Theoretical Application," in James T. Duke, ed., *Latter-day Saint Social Life: Social Research on the LDS Church and Its Members*, Provo, UT: Religious Studies Center, Brigham Young University, 1998, 29–67.

†   Hinckley, Gordon B., *LDS Church News*, July 4, 1998.

quarter to one-fifth of converts remain active in most international missions. In some areas of Latin America, 30 to 40 percent of LDS converts today never return to church after baptism.* In these same nations, other faiths such as the Jehovah's Witnesses and Seventh-Day Adventists consistently retain at least 70 to 80 percent of their converts long-term. In 2001, the sole convert-based area of the Church with a member activity rate above 50 percent was the Africa West area, where proselyting was performed primarily by native African missionaries with no formal MTC training.† In no administrative area of the world Church today have MTC-taught missionaries achieved even the 50 percent convert retention rate routinely surpassed by their predecessors who taught discussions over longer periods or even by modern missionaries with no MTC training at all.

The discrepancy between the results mandated by ancient and modern prophets and those achieved in actual practice reflects a similar discrepancy between the instructions given by ancient and modern prophets and actual programs and policies widely implemented in the mission field today. The legacy of the 100 percent convert retention of Ammon and his brethren and the heritage of nineteenth century retention well over 90 percent in the British Isles have been supplanted by an ongoing retention crisis.

THE STANDARDIZED MISSIONARY PROGRAM

During the first half of the twentieth century, many missions developed their own lessons and teaching protocols. Some missions had no formal program for teaching the gospel. Missionaries would prayerfully determine what they felt each investigator needed to be taught.

---

*   Hancock, Wayne, Russia Moscow Mission Conference, December 2000, as quoted by Ivan Makarov.

†   LeBaron, Dale E., Devotional, Ricks College News Release, April 5, 2001.

The teaching process was generally protracted over many months, and many investigators studied with the missionaries and attended church for six months to a year prior to baptism. The decision to baptize an investigator was generally not made until the investigator had demonstrated consistent effort to put his or her life in harmony with the gospel and had become well integrated into the local congregation. However, the lack of a systematic program for teaching the gospel in many areas had significant drawbacks. It was difficult to know what investigators and new converts were being taught and whether the spontaneous teachings of missionaries were doctrinally sound. Some felt that missionaries were taking too long to baptize converts who might be ready for baptism at an earlier date.

The period of 1948–1957 saw strides being taken toward standardized teaching protocols as the independent efforts of Richard Lloyd Anderson, Willard Aston, and several others attracted attention. In the early years following World War II, many missions began to adopt the fifteen-lesson plan developed by Richard Lloyd Anderson. In these missions, investigators continued to study with the missionaries for several months prior to baptism. The Anderson discussions were viewed as a great step forward, because they offered a clear and standardized approach to teaching the gospel without compromising the prebaptismal preparation of investigators. Even though this plan was not adopted in all missions, it tripled the number of conversions in many missions that adopted it and nearly doubled missionary productivity worldwide, while maintaining convert retention rates above 50 percent.[*] The Anderson program offered the benefits of standardization and higher baptism rates without compromising

---

[*]   Cowan, Richard O., "Worldwide Church Growth," in Ricks, Stephen D., Donald W. Perry, and Andrew H. Hedges, eds., *The Disciple as Witness: Essays on Latter-day Saint History and Doctrine in Honor of Richard Lloyd Anderson*, Provo, UT: FARMS, 2000, p. 111.

convert retention. These benefits can be attributed to a purposeful and appealing style of teaching basic doctrines of the gospel with a focus on key topics relevant to the conversion process, a commitment-based focus on basic gospel laws, and a reduction in the number of investigators who monopolized missionary time without keeping commitments.

In 1952–1953, the first official missionary manual was published by the LDS Missionary Department. The manual, entitled *A Systematic Program for Teaching the Gospel*, contained seven brief lessons and selected "reasoning principles" and teaching points. It drew heavily on Willard Aston's work and also incorporated significant contributions from Richard Lloyd Anderson, Glenn Pearson, and Reid E. Bankhead, who had helped to pioneer the implementation of standardized discussions and teaching methods in different areas. Quality prebaptismal preparation was strongly emphasized. The 1952–1953 manual taught: "Whatever you do, don't minimize any expressed feeling of unworthiness until you have found out what prompts it. Do not encourage anyone into the waters of baptism if there is reasonable doubt that he has failed the principles of repentance. Make sure he understands its importance, and complies with it." Although the manual was published by the Church, its implementation was optional, and many missions continued to employ their own plans.

A remarkable book by Willard Ashton entitled *Teaching the Gospel with Prayer and Testimony*, published in 1956, gave further impetus to standardization. This book further delineated a systematic approach to teaching doctrines of the gospel and offered much helpful insight. The use of an adapted six-discussion program resulted in a sharp increase in convert baptisms even in non-Christian nations such as Japan.[*]

---

[*] Britsch, R. Lanier, *From the East: The History of the Latter-day Saints in Asia, 1851–1996*, Salt Lake City, UT: Deseret Book, 1998, 103–104.

The trend toward shorter teaching protocols with six or seven lessons continued to spread.

THE ACCELERATED BAPTISM PROGRAM

As standardized programs based on the sound scriptural teaching principles of Richard Lloyd Anderson and others gained acceptance, growth rates increased in LDS missions worldwide, while convert retention rates remained relatively high. Some believed that opportunities for even greater growth could be found by incorporating elements of corporate structure, marketing psychology, and well-known salesmanship techniques into the standardized missionary program. Nonscriptural elements were added to the missionary program that promoted rapid baptisms, while unwittingly undermining the conversion process. It is beyond the scope of this work to provide a comprehensive historical overview of the events resulting in the development of the accelerated baptism program. These events are described in detail in other sources.[*]

In brief, Elder Henry D. Moyle was given charge of the Church missionary program in 1959. He introduced a rapid standardization in which missionaries were instructed to teach and baptize investigators over very brief periods, and goals, high-pressure deadlines, and marketing tactics came to replace scriptural standards and personal conscience as guidelines for when investigators should be baptized. Missionaries were instructed to challenge investigators, still unaware of the most basic expectations of church membership, to accept a baptismal date not more than two to three weeks in the future on the first or second visit. The prior focus on investigator needs and concerns gave way to focus on baptismal numbers. Minimized periods

---

[*]   Quinn, D. Michael, "I–Thou vs. I–It Conversions: The Mormon 'Baseball Baptism' Era," *Sunstone*, 16:7/30 (December 1993).

of teaching, a lack of meaningful baptismal standards, and pressure from leaders to achieve baptismal quotas combined to result in a tragic period of rushed baptisms, rampant inactivity, and later mass excommunications. Official LDS news organs lauded "astronomic growth," while failing to report dismal convert retention rates that had fallen below 10 percent in some missions. Baptism had become uncoupled from the conversion process, becoming an end of its own.

Quinn observed that many senior Church leaders objected to Elder Moyle's tactics. Elder Harold B. Lee cautioned missionaries in France: "Conversions are not merely the result of a system, not merely the result of a machine operation.... We are not concerned primarily with how many baptisms you get."[*] Elder Moyle confided that Apostles Joseph Fielding Smith and Harold B. Lee were in "real opposition" to his "accelerated missionary program."[†] By "May 1961, 'nearly all' of the apostles were 'gravely concerned about the pressures being put on missionaries to baptize to fill a quota of baptisms.'"[‡,§] In July 1963, Joseph Fielding Smith, then President of the Quorum of the Twelve, challenged "the unorthodox way with which young-sters had been baptized in the Church."[¶] Elder Moyle was relieved of his responsibilities for Church finance and the missionary program. President McKay instructed missionaries "to discontinue such things and bring the missions back to a normal proselyting program."[**]

---

[*]   "Excerpts from a Discourse by Elder Harold B. Lee," March 29, 1960, French Mission Diary, 1., as cited by Quinn.

[†]   Ernest L. Wilkinson diary, September 6, 1960, as cited by Quinn.

[‡]   Quinn, D. Michael, "I–Thou vs. I–It Conversions: The Mormon 'Baseball Baptism' Era," *Sunstone*, 16:7/30 (December 1993).

[§]   Ernest L. Wilkinson diary, May 25, 1961 and September 6, 1960, as cited by Quinn.

[¶]   Ernest L. Wilkinson diary, July 9, 1963, as cited by Quinn.

[**]   Barton, Peggy Peterson, *Mark E. Peterson: A Biography*, Salt Lake City, UT: Deseret Book, 1985, 122.

During this period, D. Michael Quinn estimates that approximately 90 percent of all British baseball baptism youth and 100,000 or more "converts" churchwide were excommunicated.* David O. McKay, Mark E. Peterson, Harold B. Lee, Gordon B. Hinckley, Marion D. Hanks, Joseph Fielding Smith, and others who opposed the abuses of the accelerated baptism program were able to expunge at least some of the excesses. One general authority who served on the missionary committee stated of Elder Moyle: "We spend a lot of time cleaning up after him." The cleanup was at best incomplete. Many who had promulgated rush baptisms during the "baseball baptism" era were elevated to important Church offices where they continued to exert their influence, and the missionary program continued to draw many key elements from the accelerated baptism program. International convert retention rates have remained at or below 25 percent for over forty years, never approaching the much higher rates routinely achieved before the accelerated baptism program was introduced.

THE SECOND CLEANUP

Ongoing accelerated baptism programs fueled poor convert retention rates and caused real growth to stagnate. The second major period of institutional cleanup came as many apostles spoke out strongly to condemn quick-baptize schemes and tried to educate mission and area leaders. President Thomas S. Monson taught new mission presidents: "Chaos results when we baptize without teaching. We have baptisms, but we don't have converts, and every president of the Church has extended the plea: 'Teach, that people may be converted, and then baptized and confirmed members of the Church.' I thought it significant, too, that the Lord added, even after the word baptize, 'teaching

---

*   Quinn, D. Michael, "I–Thou vs. I–It Conversions: The Mormon 'Baseball Baptism' Era," *Sunstone*, 16:7/30 (December 1993).

them to observe all things' whatsoever the Lord hath commanded you."* In 2002, the First Presidency issued a directive that all converts must have attended several sacrament meetings prior to baptism and be consistently keeping all commitments.† Apostles serving in Chile and the Philippines worked to educate local leaders and reverse quick-baptize programs.

The new missionary manual, *Preach My Gospel*, was published in September 2004, superseding the old missionary guide. The *Preach My Gospel* manual educates missionaries on factors important to convert retention for the first time in the history of the standardized missionary program. Missionaries were instructed to baptize converts only when they were consistently keeping commitments. The convert preparation checklists, which previously had listed only mechanical activities such as receiving a discussion that did not reflect an investigator's true preparation or worthiness, were revised to include consistency in keeping core commandments, including scripture reading and church attendance. These changes provide hope for the future and attest to rising awareness and insight into the causes of and solutions to the problem of low convert retention in both the missionary department and among Church membership as a whole.

While the few missions that applied scriptural principles of teaching and prebaptismal preparation quickly achieved very high convert retention rates, convert retention remained extremely low in the many missions that continued to practice accelerated baptism programs, while other missions made only slight adaptations and experienced marginal improvement. Official directives on ensuring regular church attendance and consistent observance of divine commandments before baptism were ignored by many mission and

---

* Monson, Thomas S., *LDS Church News*, June 24, 2003.

† First Presidency letter, December 11, 2002.

area leaders and individual missionaries. While the dictionary defines "several" as "three or more," the First Presidency directive that converts must attend church several times before baptism and be consistently keeping all commitments before baptism has been reduced by many mission and area leaders to policies that investigators should attend church once or twice before baptism, with no mention of consistent observance of commitments at all. Many leaders who had been raised under the banner of the accelerated baptism program did not agree with these changes and continued to focus on rapidly achieving large numbers of baptisms with little, if any, regard for true conversion or convert retention. Programs rushing converts to baptism within arbitrary periods from ten to twenty-one days, "doorstep discussions," and many other tactics of the quick baptism era continued to be advocated by some mission presidents.

ACCELERATED BAPTISM ELEMENTS TODAY

Official teaching materials, while much improved, continue to incorporate many subtler elements of the accelerated baptism program. It is important for those who desire to achieve quality results and promote full convert retention to recognize residual elements of the accelerated baptism program in official instructional materials that can undermine the conversion process and harm investigators. These elements conflict with prophetic directives and send ambiguous messages that can subvert the conversion process through inadequate pre-baptismal preparation. The entire teaching protocol has been shortened to just four discussions, down from six prior discussions, and the recommended discussion teaching time has been cut to just thirty to forty-five minutes, leaving the average convert with less recommended instructional time than a single LDS Sunday block meeting schedule.

THE MISSIONARY HANDBOOK

The *Missionary Handbook* or "white bible," the pocket handbook carried and read daily by all missionaries, continues to instruct: "Commit investigators to baptism during the first or second discussion, and renew the commitment at each subsequent discussion.... Help each investigator meet all qualifications for baptism." It also notes: "a. Teach two or three discussions per week to each investigator or investigator family. b. Ensure that investigators are contacted daily by members or missionaries." No exceptions are mentioned for individuals who may not be ready to accept the baptismal commitment on the first or second visit or for those who may find daily contact too intrusive. To absorb and incorporate the critical information and commitments in the discussions, most investigators cannot handle more than about one formal discussion per week and contacts two to three times a week. Individuals with jobs, families, and other commitments need the time and opportunity to read, ponder, and contemplate for themselves without pressure. Instructions calling for daily contact with each investigator are intrusive and fuel the "quick-baptism" mentality, because this intensive practice is unsustainable for meaningful periods. Frequency of contact should be based on individual investigator needs and availability, not on such sweeping directives. Investigators taught to provide spiritual self-nourishment through daily scripture reading do not require daily contact to remain receptive.

BAPTISMAL GOALS

Official materials continue to instruct missionaries to establish and report monthly baptismal goals, even when they have no serious investigators. The implication is that missionaries with faith are able to successfully find, teach, and baptize converts within the course of one month, virtually regardless of investigator challenges or concerns, and that those who do not meet their goals are not faithful or obedient. The mission president will also be able to compare the missionaries' reported goals with their subsequent baptismal figures. This practice exerts both strong internal and external pressure on missionaries to meet arbitrary monthly baptismal goals. Many missionaries feel discouraged or unworthy if they do not meet their monthly goal. This further drives away the Spirit and impairs the missionary's judgment, making him or her only hunger more for what he or she perceives as an opportunity for redemption through future rush baptisms. Missed arbitrary monthly baptismal goals were a source of great frustration and discouragement early in my mission. When I abandoned monthly baptismal goals and turned my focus wholly toward achieving many fresh contacts daily and meeting investigator needs, the number of baptisms rose to levels considerably higher than that of earlier goals, and the quality of converts improved dramatically.

Baptismal goals ignore the moral agency of others. Missionaries should set goals for their personal effort, such as the number of individuals to be contacted, but never for results that depend upon the response of others. The focus on setting monthly baptismal goals and deadlines undermines convert retention, is manipulative of both the missionary and the investigator, and demonstrates misunderstanding of gospel principles of moral agency and prebaptismal preparation. D. Michael Quinn observed that "even self-imposed 'baptism goals' can cause missionaries to engage in exploitation of potential converts."* Investigator needs must never be sacrificed to meet arbitrary baptismal goals.

---

*   Quinn, D. Michael, "I–Thou vs. I–It Conversions: The Mormon 'Baseball Baptism' Era," *Sunstone*, 16:7 (December 1993), 41.

The affliction of chronically low retention in missions where baptismal "covenants" have been employed demonstrates that God neither recognizes nor respects the promises some make for arbitrary baptismal numbers. God grants according to His will; ours is only to obey and pray that His will be done. Great missionaries such as Ammon, Wilford Woodruff, and Dan Jones never established numerical baptismal goals or deadlines but put forth their best efforts and worked according to the Holy Spirit. Mahatma Gandhi noted: "A man of faith does not bargain or stipulate with God." Those who bargain with God for immediate baptisms are afflicted with a deep lack or misunderstanding of faith.

Monthly baptismal goals and their accompanying push to reach month-end deadlines conflict with scriptural requirements for adequate convert preparation. My brother, who served a mission in Canada, noted in one of his first letters home that his first mission president asked him in front of a mid-month zone conference, "Elder Stewart, are you going to have a baptism this month?" Even though he and his companion had no serious investigators at that time, his answer, "I'll try," was deemed unacceptable. The mission president instructed him that the proper answer was "yes." The message was clear that finding, teaching, and baptizing converts within abbreviated periods of only a few days is both appropriate and expected and that missionaries who worked hard and were obedient to mission rules could consistently achieve monthly baptisms even with no one to teach at mid-month. The mission president lacked regard for the moral agency of investigators and other factors outside of the missionaries' control. The pressure exerted to encourage missionaries to baptize quickly to meet goals fostered a deep retention crisis. Elder Stewart shared the agony of quick-baptize tactics in one of his subsequent letters home: "My senior companion ... did everything within his power to make sure that [an investigator] was baptized by the end of the month so that it can show in our numbers that we had a baptism for the month of June. Yesterday our investigator was baptized. I felt that it was rushed for the sake of numbers. If I had any say, I would have waited until next month.... I have learned since that the bishop also felt the baptism was horribly rushed. There is nothing I can do about it. My companion wants to baptize, so he will baptize, regardless of whether or not the person is ready, just as soon as they say they will. There are many people here who have been baptized for the sake of numbers, but then have been excommunicated or have become inactive." Subsequent letters reported that the "convert" became inactive almost immediately following baptism.

Elder Hartman Rector Jr., a proponent of monthly baptismal goals, had an influential role in the Missionary Department for many years. Countless mission presidents and missionaries were taught the "Rector system." Elder Rector's book *Already to Harvest*, * one of the most widely distributed missionary books of the past two decades, contains a "positive" example of missionaries who covenant with the Lord to be obedient and to eat, sleep, and breathe the goal of achieving twenty-five baptisms for the month. He details how the missionaries worked hard to find individuals willing to accept the baptismal challenge. Some prospective "converts" were taught and baptized within a single day. As the end of the month approached, the missionaries even made font calls for baptism and baptized untaught visitors after only a cursory interview, ultimately achieving their statistical goal. Conspicuously missing from Rector's "miraculous" story of the missionaries achieving twenty-five baptisms in one month by such methods is follow-up of how many of these "converts" were still active one year or even one month later. One can be assured that baptism

---

*   Rector, Hartman, Jr., *Already to Harvest*, Salt Lake City, UT: Randall Book, 1985.

is not the end of the story, although it is likely that it may have been very close to the end of the "converts'" activity in the Church.

A chapter in Elder Rector's book is entitled "Baptize Now!" He stated that investigators are ready to be baptized when they have "repented of their sins and are willing to live in obedience to the Ten Commandments." For Rector, prebaptismal repentance consists of promising to live the Ten Commandments and refrain from further wrongdoing, regardless of past conduct. Prospective converts can be living in violation of the Word of Wisdom, the Law of Chastity, or other fundamental gospel directives until literally the day before baptism and still be considered ready to be baptized as long as they express willingness to live by these commandments in the future. Elder Rector wrote: "When these conditions of faith and repentance are met, then the candidate should be baptized immediately—which means that baptismal fonts should be made available whenever they are needed." Nowhere in this definition is there a place for the scriptural mandate of bringing forth the fruits of repentance by righteous living. Rector wrote that while baptismal services should be conducted by the ward mission leader after invitations have been extended to the investigator's friends and family, "there are times when this is not possible. Then the baptismal service should be held as soon as possible. Many times it is necessary to help people know what they should do." There is no mention of helping investigators to "count the cost" to determine whether they are prepared, and involvement of the ward family in the teaching and fellowshipping process prior to baptism is viewed as expendable. For proponents of the accelerated baptism program, it would seem that prebaptismal fellowshipping, church attendance, and other commandments are mere niceties that must often be sacrificed to achieve the momentary expediencies of rushed baptisms. The fact that such programs and methods have been widely taught and accepted as effective examples rather than being condemned as improper demonstrates how far the pendulum has swung toward low-commitment, quick-baptize programs. Catastrophic rates of convert retention worldwide document the spiritual devastation left in the wake of all-important monthly baptismal goals. One can believe that the intentions of the proponents of accelerated baptism plans were good and that the dismal retention rates which resulted from their programs were not anticipated or desired, yet one can also appreciate the grave danger of violating scriptural principles to accomplish an agenda.

BAPTISMAL COMMITMENT
AND BAPTISMAL DATES

Official materials make no mention of church attendance as a consideration in determining whether the investigators may be ready to commit to baptism. The baptismal commitment is placed in the second discussion before most investigators have even attended church, as a holdover from the early accelerated baptism program era. The difficulty with routinely asking investigators to make an immediate and lifelong commitment to Church membership when they have not put forth the effort to attend church even once should be obvious, yet this practice continues to be the rule rather than the exception. Most can appreciate the impropriety of proposing marriage on a first or second date. Baptism is an eternal commitment that is no less significant than marriage: scriptural imagery refers to the Church as the bride of Christ (Matthew 25:1–14, Ephesians 5:22–32). Thoughtful individuals are put off by the pressure to accept baptism quickly, recognizing that hasty, pressured decisions are inconsistent with their efforts to find and accept eternal truths. Most investigators reject the second discussion baptismal commitment. The practice of premature solicitation of baptismal commitments has driven away large numbers of sincere investigators, even as those who reach baptism are rarely adequately prepared. It is almost never appropriate to ask investigators to who have not yet attended church to accept the baptismal commitment.

The current discussions instruct missionaries to help investigators "progress toward a specific day and time when they can enter into the covenant of baptism and receive the ordinance of confirmation." Missionaries are instructed to extend the baptismal challenge only with a specific date and time. This unscriptural practice creates serious and unnecessary difficulties. The missionaries are generally imposing a completely arbitrary, often very proximate, date, without basic information on the investigator's performance in regard to essential commandments. The Word of Wisdom, the Law of Chastity, the Ten Commandments, and numerous other gospel laws have generally not even been discussed at all at the point in the discussions when missionaries are instructed to extend the baptismal commitment. How can a missionary without this information possibly have adequate criteria even to assess a reasonable time frame for investigator preparation? How can an investigator rationally commit to baptism at all, let alone in the immediate future, when the missionaries have not yet disclosed basic membership expectations?

The large majority of investigators in most areas miss their initial missionary-imposed baptismal dates, which should provide its proponents with some hint as to the problematic nature of this practice. The challenge of dealing with investigators who were not baptized on their scheduled day is acknowledged in the *Preach My Gospel* manual (p. 148). This problem is a serious one, since prospective converts who miss baptismal dates because of personal concerns while the missionaries are trying to pressure them forward become less likely to respond to future invitations. An achieved goal strengthens and encourages, while a missed one has the opposite effect. A missed baptismal date frequently implies to investigators that they are unworthy, when in fact the only error is often one made by the missionaries in establishing arbitrary premature dates without accounting for the investigator's needs, pace of progress, and input. Some Missionary Department research suggests that only one-fifth of those who accept a baptismal commitment ever go on to be baptized, so it is remarkable that such practices of premature solicitation of the baptismal commitment and unilateral imposition of short-term baptismal deadlines have remained institutionalized in the LDS missionary program ever since the era of Henry Moyle.

THE INTERVIEW

Most LDS baptismal interviews focus on nominal belief and professed future intentions with little regard for the investigator's record at fulfilling basic commitments reliably. In the section on conducting baptismal interviews, the *Preach My Gospel* manual provides nineteen questions for the interviewer to ask prospective converts (p. 206). There are four questions of belief, two questions on repentance, four questions on major past transgressions that would require a mission president interview, four questions to assess understanding of gospel laws and principles, and five questions asking if the prospective convert is willing to adhere to specific gospel laws. Not a single question asks whether the prospective converts are currently living gospel standards, regularly attending church, reading scriptures daily, and obeying other commandments. While the guide suggests that a baptismal interview should not be scheduled "until the investigator is keeping the commitments and meets the standards" (p. 207), this assessment is not part of the interview at all.

The lack of specific standards on any meaningful period of obedience to gospel laws before baptism often makes lifestyle requirements more nominal than real. While everyone would agree that it is necessary for new converts to give up alcohol and tobacco prior to baptism, investigators who say that they have quit smoking or quit drinking alcohol can be baptized within one week or less of this event in most missions, leading to catastrophic relapse rates.

Local leaders are not permitted to evaluate the prospective convert's preparation, which is assessed exclusively by transient missionaries who bear no responsibility for looking after the converts after baptism and have no vested interest in quality. This is one of the key reasons why LDS convert retention rates have fallen far below the rates of many other outreach-oriented denominations. There is an inherent conflict of interest when convert preparation for baptism is assessed exclusively by missionaries, since the desire to reach arbitrary mission and companionship baptismal goals often supersedes objective considerations of the prospective convert's comprehension, commitment, and record. When missionaries believe that "God wants everyone to be baptized" and that God also wants them to meet their arbitrary monthly baptismal goals, baptismal interviews become a rubber stamp formality rather than a meaningful safeguard for both the investigator and the Church. While it is possible for young elders to develop insight consistently into the conversion process and conduct quality interviews, this requires considerable discipline and training.

One can appreciate how interviews focusing on nominal belief and future promises alone have generally failed to provide insight into the need for additional preparation of even the most poorly prepared converts in high-turnover, quick-baptize areas. In contrast, Moroni instructed: "And they were not baptized save they brought forth fruit meet that they were worthy of it" (Moroni 6:1). Moroni taught that preparation for baptism must be assessed by a present conduct demonstrating that essential gospel habits have been firmly established and that the investigator has the obligatory determination to "serve [Christ] to the end" (Moroni 6:3).

Evaluation of the convert's consistency in attending church, studying scriptures daily, and obeying other commandments is the most important element of a proper baptismal interview. Properly conducted interviews offer an essential check to ensure the requisite convert preparation that will lead to full activity and provide a powerful tool to facilitate additional prebaptismal preparation and subsequent long-term activity of those who would be lost to the Church if baptized prematurely. Just as a premature birth can endanger an infant's health or cause permanent damage, premature baptisms lead to the loss of many of converts who could have been fortified and retained with better preparation. Many converts held back at their initial baptismal interview to allow better preparation have later noted that this was "the best thing anyone ever did for them" since it reinforced the serious nature of gospel covenants and helped them to become strong members with firm gospel habits.

BAPTIZE, BAPTIZE, BAPTIZE

Prophetic messages of the necessity to ensure adequate prebaptismal preparation are undermined by an ongoing emphasis of many lower authorities on raw baptismal numbers virtually without regard to retention. One mission president serving in Latin America reported in 2003: "I have been told clearly by members of our area presidency that my success is measured only in terms of the number of baptisms." A mission newsletter message from one North American mission president provides a glimpse into the type of instruction many missionaries receive:* "In the month of August we had 59 baptisms and in the month of September, which had five full weekends we had only 65 baptisms. But for the extra weekend in September we would have had 54 baptisms. Our question to each of you missionaries is: What ever happened to our goal of having 100 baptisms in a month and 1,000 baptisms this year? As the year has progressed we have been sliding down rather than moving up toward this goal. Lest any of us forget, we are here to do two things—teach and baptize.... Before we came to Missouri, we met with our then Area President.... He told us there were only five things to remember about being a mission president. They were BAPTIZE, BAPTIZE, BAPTIZE, BAPTIZE, and BAPTIZE! We hope we have not lost sight of that goal.... You must do all in your power to reach our goal to baptize weekly.... We testify that with faith we can baptize 100 souls in a month and we can baptize 1,000 souls this year." One LDS bishop in an area enfeebled by ongoing quick-baptize practices observed: "In this message there is no mention of quality, only quantity.... How are young men going to respond to such a message? Should we really set dates of baptism for investigators and have goals for baptismal numbers? Surely we should invite people to be baptized only when they are ready as the scriptures indicate. The methods described above resemble more high-powered business sales techniques than training and motivation for the Lord's missionaries."

Many individuals have promoted quick-baptize techniques to ingratiate themselves to higher-ups, meet mission goals, or produce glowing statistical reports. Such motives are neither pure nor "single to the glory of God" (D&C 4:5). The Kingdom of God can only be built up by the principles of the celestial world (D&C 105:5) and is harmed greatly by impure quick-baptize practices. A Chinese proverb

---

* *Zion's Harvester: Missouri Independence Mission Newsletter*, October 2001.

states: "He who sacrifices his conscience to ambition burns a picture to obtain the ashes."

WHY ARE STANDARDS NECESSARY?

Specific and consistently applied standards generate more predictably successful outcomes. Some object to clear and powerful prebaptismal standards, noting that some exceptional individuals taught without these standards become active, while a few go inactive in spite of appropriate teaching. It is not clear that any valid principles or lessons can be distilled from the stories of those few individuals who manage to remain active in spite of cursory prebaptismal teaching. Some individuals have survived speeding across town while ignoring traffic lights, while others have been involved in automobile accidents in spite of obeying the rules of the road. It is possible that one may escape without infection after a surgery performed by a surgeon who did not wash his hands or use antibiotics. Some individuals never brush their teeth and never develop a cavity. What should one deduce from such stories? Do a few survivors make such behaviors safe and appropriate? No one would consider these behaviors desirable for himself or for a loved one. Few drivers would dare to guess which red lights they can race through without stopping, yet many missionaries feel that they can successfully rush converts to baptism at the neglect of basic principles if they feel "prompted." Low worldwide LDS convert retention rates suggest that missionaries and leaders do not have the ability to discern accurately which converts can forgo adequate preparation. Instead of looking at the minority who survived reckless experiences without major harm, we might be better served to examine the casualties of these practices and their cost to society. While few measures have an all-or-none impact on outcome, empirical standards have been widely adopted by informed societies because of their tremendous success at minimizing problems and fostering predictable positive outcomes on a large scale. Only by applying specific standards to all are consistent positive outcomes achieved. The fact that we cannot avoid every problem does not mitigate our responsibility to put forth our very best effort to ensure that problems do not occur.

When daily scripture reading, consistent church attendance, and adherence to other basic gospel laws are optional for baptism, we cannot be surprised that convert retention remains the exception rather than the rule. Nothing that is essential to the conversion process and to the investigator's prospects for long-term activity should be optional.

Gospel-based prebaptismal standards may seem formulaic, just like a physician washing his hands and giving a dose of antibiotics before surgery. Divine commandments such as daily scripture reading, tithing, and temple marriage may also seem rigid and formulaic to those do not understand the gospel, yet consistent obedience to divine laws brings power. Scriptural standards are empowering rather than restricting, just as God' commandments make us free. Appropriate standards provide room to individualize to meet specific needs. However, the individualization typically comes in the form of additional effort for those who demonstrate concerning trends, rather than as an exemption from essential standards deeply rooted in gospel teachings. There is virtually never any valid role for quick-baptize approaches. The few converts who remain active in spite of such approaches would almost always be retained with improved preparation and teaching, while most of those needlessly lost because of quick-baptize approaches could be retained with longer and more thorough preparation.

WORKING TOGETHER VERSUS WORKING APART

Recognizing inadequate member involvement in the missionary program, church leaders dissolved stake missions in 2002 and designated the bishop and stake president as the "head of local missionary efforts." "The missionaries are your helpers," explained one apostle in remarks directed to LDS bishops. Yet bishops have no direct jurisdiction over full-time missionaries, nor are they given any authority to assess the preparation of new converts for baptism or adjust baptismal dates to reflect worthiness and preparation. These issues are decided by the full-time missionaries alone. Official policies require the introduction of prospective converts to a member of the bishopric or branch presidency before baptism, but do not require their agreement or consent. Wilfried Decoo, an experienced Belgian church leader who became the president of a branch of 200 members with only 10 percent activity at the age of 22, noted that "branch presidents and bishops are not allowed to evaluate the readiness for baptism of even seriously troubled and eccentric converts if missionaries and mission leaders are determined to baptize them."[*] I am aware of dozens of incidents where a local bishop or branch president disagreed with missionaries who wanted to rush poorly prepared converts to baptism, and in virtually every case, the missionaries were instructed by their mission or area president to proceed with the baptisms. Recognizing the crucial role of member involvement in the retention process and the dismal retention rates of accelerated baptism programs, it seems that little could be more foolish than proceeding with rush baptisms over the objections of mature local leaders. In such circumstances, the missionaries can hardly be considered helpers to the local leaders who

---

[*]   Decoo, Wilfried, "Feeding the Fleeing Flock: Reflections on the Struggle to Retain Church Members in Europe," *Dialogue*, 29/1 (Spring 1996): 97–113.

will bear the responsibility for ensuring that every effort is made to home and visit teach the uncommitted and often hostile "converts" monthly for the rest of their lives, long after the missionaries have left. Instructions naming LDS bishops and branch presidents as the titular "heads of local missionary efforts" while failing to grant them any authority to regulate or supervise the baptism of converts in their congregations present local leaders with the unenviable dilemma of responsibility without authority. They have no voice in determining the preparation of converts for baptism, yet even crisis-level inactivity almost immediately following baptism is almost inevitably attributed by local missions to "poor fellowshipping" of the new converts rather than poor teaching or inadequate preparation. It is difficult for bishops to establish relevant leadership or feel true ownership of a missionary system that simultaneously disenfranchises them. Cooperation in ward missions should never be a one-way street in which members are expected to jump on the bandwagon of the latest missionary initiative while missionaries continue to act unilaterally in rushing unprepared converts to baptism. Both member responsiveness to missionary requests and missionary responsiveness to the wisdom and maturity of local leaders are essential for any missionary program to reach its potential.

WHAT IS THE HURRY?

Over the past decade, I have visited with many new converts and investigators in many nations about their experiences with the teaching process. While most individuals express respect and appreciation for the missionaries, by far the most common criticism of the teaching process is that many felt pressured or rushed to baptism. Pressure to accept baptism rapidly drives away many honest and sincere people, while leaving most of those who are baptized with serious unresolved

issues. The devastation that has been left by accelerated baptism protocols leads one to wonder: what is the hurry? Are we rushing converts
to baptism so that they can go inactive faster? Rampant inactivity
following accelerated baptism programs is not an anomaly; it is the
natural and expected outcome of such approaches. Some speak as
if delaying baptism a few weeks to allow better preparation represents a tremendous spiritual tragedy and denial of blessings, while the
catastrophically poor retention rates incurred by accelerated baptism
practices and the subsequent years of poorly productive reactivation
work are regarded as inconsequential or inevitable. After extensive
research, I have been unable to ascertain what alleged benefits experienced by the fraction of converts who remain active in spite of
accelerated baptism policies can possibly compensate for the nearly
immediate loss of the large majority of converts. Time is not a threat
to true and life-changing conversion.

Accelerated baptism programs violate the prime rule of therapeutic
intervention: "first do no harm." The few individuals who would
perhaps remain active and faithful in spite of brief teaching periods
certainly suffer no harm from longer preparation periods and, in most
cases, experience considerable benefits. In contrast, many converts
who could have been retained with more thorough preparation are
lost after being rushed to baptism unprepared. While longer teaching
in itself does not guarantee weekly church attendance, daily scripture
reading, or good fellowshipping without additional effort, performance in all of these areas is almost uniformly poor when converts
are taught and baptized over abbreviated periods. Investigators must
never be denied the opportunity to complete the repentance process
prior to baptism in order to meet a goal or arbitrary date. Spirituality
is not acquired suddenly. Joseph Smith taught "the things of God are
of deep import: and time, and experience, and careful and ponderous

and solemn thoughts can only find them out."[*]

A HISTORICAL PERSPECTIVE

President Heber J. Grant's account of the high standards of prebaptismal preparation he adhered to while preaching the gospel in Japan provides some perspective on how far modern accelerated baptism programs have drifted from the moorings of scripture and the teachings of inspired church leaders.

Gaburo Kikuchi, the second convert [in Japan], for a number of years has separated himself from the Christian sect to which he belonged, because, he said, they did not teach the Bible, and he has been teaching the people the truths of the Bible in the parks in the city of Tokyo, having audiences of from five hundred to one thousand five hundred people. He seems to be a very sincere, determined man, and I have enjoyed my conversations with him. The day I baptized him, before attending to that ordinance, I told Brother Kelsch to try to discourage him from becoming a member of the Church and that I would do the same, because I told him I desired him to study more and to comprehend more before he was baptized. He came to the hotel before I was out of bed in the morning and insisted upon baptism. When I told him that he had better study more and get a better comprehension of the gospel, he said, "It is true. I believe it. I want to be baptized. And I can understand it better after I have been baptized and confirmed a member of the Church." I knew this was true; so I told him he would be persecuted and he quoted the scripture, "Blessed are ye, when men shall revile you, and persecute you, and shall say all manner

---
[*]   Smith, Joseph Fielding, ed., *Teachings of the Prophet Joseph Smith*, Salt Lake City, UT: Deseret Book, 1976, 137.

of evil against you falsely, for my sake." Brother Kelsch and I went on in this line, trying to discourage this man. I referred to the drivings of our people, to the killing of the Prophet Joseph Smith and his brother Hyrum, and to the fact that many men had to give up their lives for the truth; and I wanted him to be thoroughly converted. He said, "It is true; and if I die and am the first martyr in Japan, it would be the best thing that could happen to Japan." "That's enough," I said, "I'll baptize you."[*]

Speaking from abundant experience in an area where quick-baptize approaches had spoiled most of an already difficult harvest, Wilfried Decoo suggested "a longer period of preparation before an investigator is baptized." He wrote:

On the one hand, I understand and appreciate the sense of urgency that accompanies our proselyting system at present: We have long been taught that these are the last days, that the harvest time is short. If people have truly repented and accepted the gospel, they should not have to jump through a lot of hoops to get to the baptismal font. Also, the missionaries themselves understandably look to the number of baptisms as measures of their own success. Yet, on the other hand, in our preoccupation with sheer numbers we have often baptized people prematurely in the expectation that some spiritual form of "natural selection" would eventually separate the weak from the strong. For many new members, and for the church units which they have joined, our experience in Europe and elsewhere has shown us the drawbacks of this proselyting philosophy. It has produced the opposite of the desired result. Instead of saving souls, it

---

[*]   Grant, Heber J., LDS General Conference, April 1902, as cited in *Gospel Standards*, Salt Lake City, UT: Improvement Era, 1943, 206.

has placed in spiritual jeopardy at least half of those baptized by persuading them to make sacred covenants which they were not ready or able to fulfill. Why could we not ask prospective converts to attend church meetings and keep the commandments [regularly] before baptism? We might lose some who are not stable or fully converted, or whose early enthusiasm cools somewhat in the process; but those who endure for that year will be far more likely to endure for a lifetime. Furthermore, local leaders could become more involved than they are now both in the decision to accept new members for baptism and in the process of their integration into the church unit, which would enhance their sense of responsibility for new members. All of this might mean that missionaries who first introduce a given investigator to the gospel will not be in town for the baptism, but that consideration should not take precedence over adequate convert preparation. A longer preparation might also help avoid or lessen tragic clashes with family, friends, and the larger community. Candidates will have more time to work out tensions, to brace themselves for a new and overwhelming change in life, and even to invite family members and friends to join in the investigation process, which will be less threatening given the longer time frame. Some people will probably attempt to dissuade the potential convert from baptism, but others might be intrigued enough to become investigators themselves. In any case, if the potential convert cannot stand up to the social consequences of joining the church, it is better to learn that before baptism than afterward.[*]

---

[*] Decoo, Wilfried, "Feeding the Fleeing Flock: Reflections on the Struggle to Retain Church Members in Europe," *Dialogue*, 29/1 (Spring 1996): 97–113.

LDS MEDIA

INDIGENOUS LITERATURE
AND CHURCH IDENTITY

PUBLISHERS SUCH AS DESERET Book have been major contributors in defining contemporary U.S. Mormon culture. The vast array of resources, from "historical fiction" to capture the interest of teens who have difficulty with archaic scriptural vocabulary, to self-help books on parenting, adds an immersive element to Mormon life. Whether official or unofficial, indigenous church literature plays an important role in developing a sense of community within the Church and in fostering the perception of the LDS faith as an acceptable local religion rather than a foreign one. There are two Seventh-Day Adventist publishing houses printing indigenous literature in the United Kingdom alone, yet no nation outside of the Americas has a single publishing house dedicated to printing locally written LDS literature.

U.S. members often fail to fully appreciate the challenges faced by non-English speaking saints. Former Belgian bishop Wilfried Decoo observed: "I well remember a leadership meeting at which a local leader asked a visiting general authority if it would be possible for the church distribution center in Frankfurt to make available books from the Deseret and Bookcraft companies, even in English for local

English-speaking members, with permission perhaps to translate some of the more popular books into other languages. The visiting authority responded categorically that the scriptures should be enough for any of the Saints. Yet in the foyer I observed his wife reading a book by Hugh Nibley and his daughter a novel by Jack Weyland."* Although most non-English speaking members are appreciative of the resources they have, most also acknowledge a desire for more.

The desire of U.S. leaders to maintain central control of international units has often hindered the autonomy necessary for local members to develop a strong indigenous Mormon identity. Faithful non-English publications by local members have often been officially discouraged,†‡ or at best, not encouraged. Even in the LDS international magazine, the overwhelming majority of articles are written by U.S. authors, perpetuating the perception of an American church looking out at the world rather than a truly integrated world faith. Decoo points out that the result is an informational and cultural religious void in societies that place a high value on information and culture. Japanese Mormon Jiro Numano wrote: "If Japanese members were given the editorial responsibility for the international church magazine in Japan, *Seito no Michi*, members might read the entire magazine with the enthusiasm now reserved for the few pages devoted to local news."§ The Church's English-speaking leadership has been concerned that it would not be able to ensure orthodoxy in indigenous non-English literature, and non-English LDS-speaking populations are

---

*   Decoo, Wilfried, "Feeding the Fleeing Flock: Reflections on the Struggle to Retain Church Members in Europe," *Dialogue*, 29/1 (Spring 1996): 118.

†   Decoo, Wilfried, "Issues in Writing European History and in Building the Church in Europe," *Journal of Mormon History*, Spring 1997.

‡   Numano, Jiro, "Mormonism in Modern Japan," *Dialogue*, 29/1 (Spring 1996).

§   Numano, Jiro, "Mormonism in Modern Japan," *Dialogue*, 29/1 (Spring 1996), 224–225.

typically too small or of too modest means to make local resource development attractive for the commercial entities that specialize in English-language LDS products. However, suitable solutions could be found for such concerns if the need for indigenous international literature were recognized.

REPORTING PERFORMANCE

Although I had read hundreds of articles and dozens of books on the international Church, nothing prepared me for the finding in my travels that only a small minority of international LDS members attend church at all. The *LDS Church News* and other official publications speak in glowing terms about "explosive," "astronomic," "dynamic," or "miraculous" growth in Latin America, the Philippines, Japan, and other areas, while carefully avoiding mention of the fact that only a fraction of nominal members are active. Official media continue to laud "rapid growth" in superlative terms, giving no intimation of the sharply declining growth rates and crisis-level inactivity. The LDS media are generally silent on quality independent research and census data that fail to validate adequately the desired image of rapid growth and high activity. In every case, there is a vast unacknowledged discrepancy between official church membership figures and the number of individuals identifying themselves as Latter-day Saints. Even reports in the secular media touting "rapid LDS growth" are typically based upon raw membership figures provided by church public relations personnel without any disclosure of activity rates or correlation of church data with self-identified affiliation figures. An official church press release ahead of the April 2005 LDS General Conference was entitled: "Over 12 Million Worldwide United in a Single Purpose."[*]

---

[*]   "Over 12 Million Worldwide United in a Single Purpose," LDS.org press
       release, April 1, 2005, http://www.lds.org.

Managing Public Affairs Director Bruce Olsen noted: "The numbers don't tell the real story." While it is true that the human and spiritual elements transcend that which can be fully described by statistics, it is equally apparent that statistics are being misused when reports imply that raw membership figures represent believing, active, and participating members. The sacrifice, belief, and devotion of many faithful members are indeed great, but the experience of the fraction of faithful, active members cannot be indiscriminately extrapolated to membership as a whole.

With few exceptions, LDS media convey the message that: "All is well in Zion; yea, Zion prospereth, all is well" (2 Nephi 28:21). One need only read further in the verse to learn what the Lord feels about those who teach or believe this. Proponents of selective reporting claim that their mission is to publicize only faith-promoting material. Which style of reporting better builds and conveys faith: the systematic exclusion of data that one does not find favorable or candid acknowledgement of challenges and harmonization of faith and facts? Jim Rohn observed: "Affirmation without discipline is the beginning of delusion." Do we, like the ancient Israelites, have ears that will only hear "smooth things" rather than "right things"? (Isaiah 30:10).

I do not mean to imply that LDS media should be preoccupied with the unworthy or the problematic. Yet we must not misrepresent the international Church by presenting only selective positive data, while avoiding reference to serious but unfavorable findings. Quality journalism would demand at least a brief discussion of challenges and a line or two of objective data on activity rates amid the flow of flowery blandishments to provide context and perspective. Most members have some awareness of challenges but may turn to sources that are not as reliable if they are unable to find quality information in official sources. Members are not looking for sore spots but want to be respected as intelligent human beings who need enough information to determine what is really happening and to draw their own conclusions regarding causes and effects. No intelligent person likes being told what to think.

The way in which we report our growth and the extent to which we are willing to be candid about challenges defines the potential for improvement. Selective reporting fuels complacency and is anathema to any attempts at constructive learning. Jon Madonna wrote: "Nothing stops an organization faster than people who believe that the way that they worked yesterday is the best way to work tomorrow. To succeed, not only do your people have to change the way they act, they've got to change the way they think about the past." The great pianist and composer Frederic Chopin observed of striving for mastery: "Every difficulty slurred over will be a ghost to disturb your repose later on." We must be able to report graciously and respond appropriately to negative trends as well as positive ones.

Christian researcher George Barna observed: "In all of the evaluation research we have conducted during the past two decades, I have seen firsthand that *you get what you measure*."[*] If we do not measure and transparently report meaningful indicators of member participation, we cannot be surprised when our rolls swell with nominal members who do not participate. Attempts to "promote faith" by selective reporting inevitably backfire. In the 1960s, the Seventh-Day Adventist Church candidly acknowledged its problems with member inactivity in the Philippines and instituted sweeping measures to improve retention. Today, there are over one million active Seventh-Day Adventists in the Philippines, and the Seventh-Day Adventist Church is growing rapidly. Latter-day Saints experienced similar retention issues in the

---

[*]   Barna, George, *Transforming Children into Spiritual Champions*, Ventura, CA: Regal Books, 2003, 126.

Philippines, but due largely to selective "all is well in Zion" reporting, destructive quick-baptize practices continued unchecked for over forty years. Only a fraction of today's half-million nominal Filipino Latter-day Saints ever attend church at all.

The lives and spiritual welfare of the millions affected by quick-baptize policies and other organizational snafus must take precedence over "all is well in Zion" messages. We cannot attempt to build up something that is true by any means other than truth itself. Albert Schweitzer declared: "Truth has no special time of its own. Its hour is now—always." Zion must be built up upon the laws of the Celestial Kingdom, or it cannot be built up at all (D&C 105:5). Achieving grassroots awareness of the prevalence and the causes of retention and growth problems is a mandatory step toward creating lasting solutions. Acknowledgment of our own inadequacies and failures may stretch us beyond our comfort zones, but it offers the only way to grow beyond past backslidings toward future victory.

ABOUT THE AUTHOR

David Grant Stewart, Jr., MD, is a pediatric orthopedic surgeon in private practice in Las Vegas, Nevada. At his high school graduation, his principal announced that "It has been a long time since we have seen a student like David, and it will be a long time before we see another one like him." He was one of thirteen national advanced placement scholars in the United States in 1991, and was the first to attend Brigham Young University. He was a presidential scholar at Brigham Young University, being graduated with summa cum laude honors in molecular biology in just two years. Dr. Stewart received his medical degree from the University of Colorado School of Medicine. He completed a surgical internship and an orthopedic surgery residency at the University of Texas Medical Branch and completed fellowship training in pediatric orthopedic and scoliosis surgery at Children's Hospital Los Angeles. Dr. Stewart is a member of the Alpha Omega Alpha medical honor society and has received numerous awards for excellence in clinical practice and medical research and for his contributions to international health.

Dr. Stewart served a full-time LDS mission in St. Petersburg, Russia, from 1992 to 1994. He has had a lifelong interest in missionary work. He has dedicated thousands of hours to the study of missionary work from 1991 to the present and has conducted missionary research in over twenty countries. He has written on LDS topics, including church growth, missionary work, and DNA and the Book of Mormon, and has been interviewed on Church growth issues by the Associated Press, *Salt Lake Tribune, Newsweek,* PBS, and other major media outlets. Dr. Stewart is fluent in several Eastern European languages and is active in international medical charity and education work in Asia and Eastern Europe. He lives in Henderson, Nevada, with his wife and young children.